D0916915

STUDIES IN
SOCIAL POLICY
AND PLANNING

Alfred J. Kahn is Professor of Social Work (Social Policy and Social Welfare Planning) at the Columbia University School of Social Work, where he has been a member of the faculty since 1947. Since 1948, he has served as consultant to the Citizens' Committee for Children of New York, a spokesman of authority in the recent public debate over proposed children's allowances. In 1966 he completed a study of the feasibility and desirability of adapting the British Citizens' Advice Bureau to the American scene, which was published as *Neighborhood Information Centers, A Study and Some Proposals.* The author has served as consultant to federal, state, and local agencies and departments concerned with the planning of social services, delinquency and child welfare, and with patterns of administration and staffing. Recently appointed to New York's Housing and Development Administration Advisory Committee, Professor Kahn has also undertaken overseas assignments for the Department of Health, Education, and Welfare, the State Department, the United Nations, and foreign governments as a consultant.

Professor Kahn is the author of a series of major studies and reports dealing with delinquency and community planning for children. As an internationally recognized authority, he has written and spoken on social planning, social welfare research, the development of social work knowledge, and community mental health. His earlier works include *Planning Community Services for Children in Trouble, A Court for Children,* and *Issues in American Social Work* (editor), numerous monographs and articles. Various studies of his are being translated for study in Europe and South America.

STUDIES IN
SOCIAL POLICY
AND PLANNING

Companion Volume to THEORY AND PRACTICE OF
SOCIAL PLANNING

ALFRED J. KAHN

Columbia University
School of Social Work

RUSSELL SAGE FOUNDATION

NEW YORK   1969

© 1969
RUSSELL SAGE FOUNDATION

Printed in the United States of America
Library of Congress Catalog Card Number: 70–83536

for NANCY VALERIE KAHN

PREFACE

THE PRESENT work and a simultaneously published companion volume, *Theory and Practice of Social Planning*, share an overall goal. They would conceptualize and illustrate both specialized planning for social programs or fields and the social aspects of more general planning endeavors. Of particular concern here is the demonstration through use of a number of critical planning concepts often discussed only in the abstract.

Author and reader, of course, are concerned with *specific* policies and with programs in *specific* fields. The studies presented—they are short monographs rather than true chapters—introduce issues and problems in a variety of high-priority areas. The specific rationale for selection and the manner in which each study is employed are discussed in the first chapter.

The author's many debts and inevitable disclaimers are listed in the Preface to the companion volume. He also envisages future obligations to those who will render these primitive attempts obsolete as social planning develops and is systematically studied.

ALFRED J. KAHN

Columbia University
New York, 1969

CONTENTS

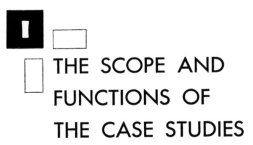

THE SCOPE AND
FUNCTIONS OF
THE CASE STUDIES

Social planning is still in its infancy. Nonetheless, by drawing upon the accumulated experience of several disciplines in a diversity of fields of practice, it is possible to identify the elements of an intellectual framework for such planning. Even more tentatively, it is possible to locate such framework with reference to the political environment in which planning is inevitably embedded.

In brief, a total planning process involves:

- a variety of *preliminary explorations*, including efforts to clarify the right to plan, to create a planning unit or coalition, to define leverage and scope, etc.;
- *definition of the planning task*, both following upon and leading to reality assessments and inventories, value analysis and choosing;
- *policy ("standing plan") formulation* on the basis of empirical exploration; further value probing and choice; definition of the system; consideration of relevant functions; choice of boundaries; assessment of potential opportunity costs and social costs; consideration of some of the major policy options available in the light of historical experience, goal hierarchies, and the foregoing considerations;
- *programming*, as growing out of policy formulation and resource assessment and as including a wide range of issues from administrative structuring and manpower assignment to budgeting and time-phasing, and including feedback for policy review in the light of programming realities;
- a system of *reporting, evaluation, and formal feedback*.[1]

Experience also supports an effort: to go beyond the relatively brief illus-

---

[1] See Chapter XII, "The Framework in Perspective," in the companion volume, THEORY AND PRACTICE OF SOCIAL PLANNING.

trations employed in outlining the framework and to offer more complete delineation of some aspects of a planning framework in action; to deepen the formal definition of some of the concepts and to suggest the relevance of a host of additional and only partially conceptualized variables; to look somewhat more specifically at problems of planning in several of the key facets of the social "sector" or social welfare, as well as at major problems in meshing social concerns with economic and physical considerations.

It is to these matters that the present volume is dedicated. Obviously, whatever the length of the work, no claim of complete coverage can be made for each of so many fields. Sanction, total context, and community preferences may be by-passed for purposes of illustrating ways of thinking about planning, but not in "real life" policy planning and programming. Thus, we introduce some of the fields (poverty and delinquency) as vehicles for looking at many aspects of the planning process, while others are more narrowly employed to elaborate one concept, such as task definition (the "income security" discussion) or local-level programming (family and child welfare). Context and political impact are considered in some detail where we are relatively all-inclusive (poverty), but not where only the intellectual aspects of the strategy are highlighted (delinquency). A central concern, intergovernmental relations, is introduced here only selectively (community mental health).

Our stance in the presentation also shifts from chapter to chapter, from that of uninvolved analyst (the city), to critic (the war against poverty), to advocate (family and child welfare), thus demonstrating both the variety of possible planner stances and our own degree of involvement.

Each of these fields would merit many volumes, so that one collection of case studies must be limited in the elaboration of each "case," selecting varying degrees of completeness and focus in the light of the planning framework being advanced. What is more, one work cannot attempt to include all possible topics within the social domain. Thus, attention is directed only to fields of considerable concern to the United States in the late nineteen-sixties: poverty, the city, income security, delinquency, community mental health, social services at the local level, the problems of developing countries. Nonetheless, an even larger number of fields and problems is not specifically addressed: race relations, manpower, area redevelopment, urban community development, tax policy, the aged, union welfare programs, health planning, education, recreation.

THE PLANNER'S POINT OF ENTRY AND SCOPE

In a world of diverse and complex programs, one seldom begins with a clean slate. The planner is often programmer, sometimes policy planner;

the task definition is frequently a given and sometimes inflexible. System boundaries are often not challengeable. Occasionally, the nation, a state, a city, or a voluntary organization experiences that kind of crisis, shock, resolve, transfer of power, challenge, or charismatic leadership—often in some combination—which permits a relatively comprehensive undertaking. Political reality, resources, and intellectual flexibility join in encouraging a fresh look. Then, no holds should be barred. One examines task, system conceptualization, boundaries, all policy parameters—or at least one could. The Great Society's anti-poverty war presented such an opportunity, and was therefore "monitored" over a three-year period, providing the most extensive "case" in this volume.

It would, of course, represent considerable progress in the development of planning theory if one could identify the key issues relevant to a decision as to whether to "pitch" a planning effort on a comprehensive or a partial plane, whether to accept task or system as givens or to challenge them, whether to accept, as offering great potential, or to reject, as too restrictive, a proposal which emphasizes only programming. Clearly the dimensions which are relevant include political and resource feasibility, intellectual mastery, the intensity of dissatisfaction with what is, organizational stability or imbalance, the qualities of available leadership—and similar concerns— all in some pattern of interaction with the given facet or field. However, available knowledge does not permit one to be more specific. There have been too few recorded planning process evaluations or case studies and virtually no experiments at all in this field. Even practice reports are rare, yet they would be the basis for practice "wisdom" and more inclusive theory. Thus, one notes that the planner looks at his mandate, tests the limits, assesses political leverage, decides whether the basic questions have been asked recently, and does what his instincts tell him is right. The official, in turn, in choosing his planning staff, selects that level of creativity and potential for boat-rocking that his own assessments call for. One would hope for more than these guidelines as planning experience accumulates.

Although it is difficult to formulate "rules" for degrees of comprehensiveness, one can recognize situations where relatively ambitious plans were made. The United States anti-poverty war of the 'sixties was one such effort. Yet, while the effort sought to be basic and significant, and although this is the most broadly-conceived "case" in the volume, it is by no means complete.

For one thing, limitations of space dictate some choice as between a policy and a program emphasis in the presentation, and the former is selected for this particular illustration. More fundamentally, however, a national-level, problem-oriented planning approach inevitably confronts questions of system boundaries and task definition. These issues were resolved with reference to the anti-poverty war, because of both political and organizational considerations, in a way which precluded truly comprehensive domestic-sector planning. Indeed, the political configuration on the national scene, in which this particular undertaking was launched and implemented, permitted only modest innovation in policy and program initially, despite apparent staff aspirations, but with increasing thrusts towards comprehensiveness as the program itself generated both relevant experience and some "consumer" support.

To suggest the nature of that local-level planning which seeks to be comprehensive, we have chosen the field of juvenile delinquency. Here it is easier than it is in the poverty field to agree that prevailing task definitions may be counterproductive. We argue that the delinquency-specific system for which one plans should be confined largely to the case-service arena, since primary prevention and provision are more advantageously conceived in broader social context. To keep the illustration within bounds, we do not cope with conflicting public preference-patterns or the claims of competing professional bureaucracies as these impinge on the planner in the field of corrections.

TASK

At times, the planner's contribution may be to suggest that a vital step has been missed. As scholars, officials, staffs, and clients debate the reform of income-transfer programs, one may point to the fact that the definition of the task is yet to be resolved. Each of the major proposals suggests its own definition. The income-security chapter thus illustrates competing task definitions in a specific field and considers the consequence of attempting to reconceptualize the components from competing elements into subsections of a more comprehensive whole. The stance would appear appropriate, since a Presidential Commission is charged with precisely such assignment. Because the resulting hypothesis is only partially developed and the complexities are many, the chapter forgoes the programming implications which follow.

Task definition is an art as much as it is an assessment of reality. It is an expression of value, as it is an assessment of feasibility. The problem of planning for the humanization of the urban environment is introduced as the second illustration of task definition. Like the poverty question, it requires that one confront the issue of the level of system to be addressed. Here a historical perspective is employed to examine alternative solutions and to note that broadened scope, the position which we advocate to strengthen the anti-poverty effort, is not necessarily always the answer. The city planners must also—as must all planners—attend to questions of their expertise and leverage.

BOUNDARIES

The setting of boundaries for an intervention or service system, we have argued, is a question of policy as well as a technical matter.[2] Implicit boundary decisions are made in all planning efforts. Major redefinitions of the planning task always carry profound implications for field boundaries. At times, even when the effort is more modest, attention to boundaries may have major consequences.

Two chapters deal specifically with boundary questions. In relation to community mental health, it is argued that boundaries that are vague and all inclusive interfere with adequate development of a specialized network. Family and child welfare are presented as an illustration of separate fields which need to be amalgamated. In the latter instance, the author becomes the planner-advocate, and we take the position that a boundary redefinition is the critical point of departure in sound programming.

Because the focus here is quite limited and the purpose is to sharpen the boundaries issue (and federal-state relationship questions), the community mental health chapter, in particular, will appear truncated to the informed. We have dealt with the outcome of a process and not with the internal debate, thus not fully acknowledging that many of those involved may have considered some of the questions raised, even if the policies and programs eventually enacted suggest otherwise. Similarly, because the focus is on the boundaries issue, not on substantive fullness, here, as in other chapters, experts may disagree about some of the evidence.

PROGRAMMING

Programming in social welfare includes everything that is relevant to administration. Its concerns range from a preoccupation with coordination and cost effectiveness to questions of staffing, control, pace, timing, capital investment, centralization-decentralization, project location, record systems, and so on. Each of the fields mentioned in these chapters would lend itself to an illustration of a host of programming problems. However, to keep the presentation within manageable proportions, we illustrate programming with reference to objectives delineated in the earlier volume.[3] The focus is

---

[2] See the companion volume, Chapter V.

[3] Chapter X in the companion volume.

on that type of programming which may assure maximum service access, effective channeling, case integration, and agency accountability. The bias is toward a universal social service system. And, to assure maximum advantage from a single illustrative chapter, the point of departure is the relevant family and child welfare material, which is also presented to illustrate the boundaries problem.

HORIZONS

For a variety of reasons, it is poor and developing countries that have sometimes confronted the question of how to conceptualize the relationships between the economic and the social. Review of the solutions posed in theory and practice suggests a formulation that is perhaps relevant to a country in any stage of development. Clearly, there can be no separate economic, physical, and social sectors *if planning would become relatively comprehensive*. Comprehensive planning, however, may be viewed from, or may emphasize physical, economic, or social aspects. But in the West, particularly in the United States, we do not now choose fully comprehensive planning in the sense of addressing a complete economic and social system. Thus, most of our planning efforts are likely to be formulated as physical, economic, and social. Nor have we successfully conceptualized the "social system" or social sector per se. Nonetheless, there is reason to feel, as is argued in the final chapter, that social planning need not limit itself to the traditional social fields and their interrelationships, despite their major importance. The social planner may have considerable impact as well if he introduces his concerns and goals into such diverse realms as tax policy, transportation, and housing programs.

OTHER CONCEPTS

Chosen to highlight the major planning topics listed (topics judged to require special attention at this time as strategic in enhancing planning), these illustrative chapters, ranging from the relatively complete to the deliberately selective, also touch on a variety of other aspects of the full planning process.

Several social service programming innovations, based in both decentralization and in employment of so-called indigenous personnel, are described in the anti-poverty "case" chapter. As does the chapter on delinquency, this chapter also provides an opportunity to look in some depth at the components of universalism and particularism, or selectivity, as a social service strategy. Humanitarian ideals in the West have leaned toward universalism since the French Revolution, but problems of access, cost, and intervention theory constantly offer counterpressures.

The centralization-decentralization issue has implications for planning structures, policy, and programming. It partakes of value elements, technical considerations, and financial realities. Several of these are illustrated: the interplay between program chosen, financing decisions, and level of government that carries out the program (income security); the rationale for and limitations of decentralized planning (poverty, Model Cities, and community mental health); the values of decentralization from a service-delivery perspective (social services at the local level); the dilemma in seeking to combine true decentralization, as opposed to empty ritualistic forms, with the reality of federal funding (community mental health).

In the policy realm, several of the chapters illustrate consensus types of strategy for planning (delinquency, mental health, social service, and income security), but the poverty and city-planning chapters note the alternative modes which often prevail: "planning" in a conflict or at least conflicting-interest context. One also comes to recognize that, just as constituencies may differ, so do professional interest groups; and their preferences, organizational rigidities, and powers may shape the ultimate disposition of boundaries (family and child welfare, mental health and general medicine, medical and non-medical psychiatric models).

CLASSIFICATION

Were there available any standard system of classification of planning issues, modes, concepts, or priorities, it would be appropriate to expect that our case illustrations would follow such a system. It appears quite clear, however, that in the present stage of development of theory and practice in social planning, any typology would be premature. We have thus adopted the practice, already described, of selecting illustrations of various degrees of completeness and diverse in scope and giving attention to concepts and elements deemed in particular need of attention or emphasis.

Nonetheless, the reader will note a variety of possibilities and some rudiments of several schemes. As suggested in Chart A, one might, for example, adopt a scheme that contrasts problem-centered with field-centered planning. In general, it is the former which tends towards the comprehensive, the redefinition of planning task, the reconceptualization of system. Such basic re-examination occurs only on occasion in specific social and political context.

An alternative plan would list all stages in a planning process and would

Chart A APPROACHES TO CLASSIFYING LEVELS AND TYPES OF PLANNING "CASES"

	"Case" Presentation						
	Anti-Poverty War	Delinquency	Income Security	The City	Community Psychiatry	Social Services at Local Level	Developing Countries
A. Scheme Employed in This Volume							
Comprehensive Approaches	X	X					
Concept-Focused Cases			X	X	X	X	
Perspectives							X
B. Planning by Problem or Field (Sector)							
Problem-Centered Planning	X	X					
Field (Sectorial) Planning			X	(?)	X	X	X
C. Classification by Process or Planning Concepts							
Task and System	X		X	X	X		
Policy	X	X		X			
Programming		X			X	X	
Evaluation and Feedback							
D. Classification by Sector and Governmental Level							
Sectorial-National				X		X	
Sectorial-Local		X				X	
Cross-Sectorial-National	X						X
Cross-Sectorial-Local				X			

place each case within one category. While artificial, since we are describing a dynamic process in which phases are interlooped, such an approach facilitates illustration and communication of concepts and is of obvious didactic value. Our more modest "concept-oriented" system is merely an incomplete version of such an approach.

To classify by sector and level of government is to follow a relatively traditional, but still very useful, approach. Highlighted are both boundary issues and questions of intergovernmental relationships.

Chart A suggests where the several subjects would be located under the possible classification systems. Clearly, each has some utility, as would (a) more politically-minded schemes: consensus, bargaining, conflict contexts for planning; (*b*) classification by discipline: city planners, economists, social workers, etc. as planners; (*c*) differentiation between the synopticist or comprehensivist and the "disjointed incrementalist" (a classification we find difficult, since one discovers a continuum rather than a dichotomy);[4] or (*d*) distinction between public as contrasted with voluntary efforts. It is reasonable to expect that, in the coming years, case studies and demonstration efforts will create increasing awareness of the dimensions along which planning in the United States may be most fruitfully classified for purposes of research, theory development, teaching, and actual operational requirements. For the moment, it may be that our attempt to avoid closure will contribute to our purpose: to communicate specific concepts and to suggest the back-and-forth, recursive, spiraling process which is becoming identifiable as social planning.

---

[4] See the companion volume, Chapter XII.

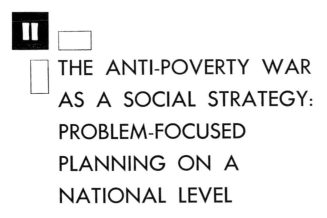

THE ANTI-POVERTY WAR AS A SOCIAL STRATEGY: PROBLEM-FOCUSED PLANNING ON A NATIONAL LEVEL

THE UNITED STATES "war on poverty," examined from the time of the initial program discussions late in 1963 through the debate preceding the substantial 1967 Amendments to the Economic Opportunity Act, offers an enlightening case history of

- ☐ problem-focused social planning
- ☐ particularistic (selective) as opposed to universalistic policy strategies
- ☐ efforts to encompass institutional change as well as case service approaches within one effort
- ☐ a basically "disjointed incrementalist" orientation, masked by political rhetoric as a comprehensive planning effort
- ☐ the tension which develops under incrementalism as its limitations become clear
- ☐ the interplay between politics and planning.

While one case "proves" nothing, analysis of the Great Society's anti-poverty effort thus does shed further light on several planning and policy issues discussed in the companion volume. From the perspective of the author, it also argues for a broad view of social planning in its relationship to economic and physical plans and programs.[1]

---

[1] A portion of this chapter relies upon an earlier and somewhat differently focused effort of the author, "Poverty and Public Policy," in Frederick T. C. Yu, Editor, *Behavioral Sciences and the Mass Media* (New York: Russell Sage Foundation, 1968), 93–123.

By way of background, it is necessary, first, to comment on poverty as a concept, to examine its prevalence, and to review efforts to define it in monetary, cultural, and social-psychological terms.

HOW MUCH POVERTY

The anti-poverty planning effort began with very loose definitions of the concept, the fixing of a very imprecise poverty line,[2] and only rough approximations of prevalence. More systematic work refined the analysis and provided for routine reporting of relevant data thereafter. Most heavily relied upon by the Council of Economic Advisors and the Office of Economic Opportunity, after the first round of discussion, was the analysis developed by the Research Department of the Social Security Administration.[3]

By the standards under which President Franklin D. Roosevelt referred to "one-third of a nation" in 1933, one-eighth was poor in 1964. By 1947 standards, poverty totals had declined from one-third to less than one-fifth. The 1964 standards would have defined one-half the nation as poor—if applied in 1933. A fixed $3,000-standard, applied in 1929, would have placed

---

[2] Three-thousand-dollars a household was the commonly-used, early yardstick, originally making no allowance for region, size of city, agriculture or industrial labor force membership, presence of young children, etc.

[3] Many of the early documents in the anti-poverty effort and much of the thinking during the first year are assembled in books of "readings" of which the following two are representative: Margaret S. Gordon, Editor, *Poverty in America* (San Francisco: Chandler Publishing Company, 1965); Louis A. Ferman, Joyce L. Kornbluh, and Alan Haber, Editors, *Poverty in America* (Ann Arbor: University of Michigan Press, 1965).

A major "pre-poverty war" source is James N. Morgan *et al.*, *Income and Welfare in the United States* (New York: McGraw-Hill Book Company, 1962). An earlier pioneering contribution by Robert J. Lampman appears in Joint Economic Commission, *Low-Income Population and Economic Growth* (Washington, D.C.: Government Printing Office, 1959, paperback).

Considerable discussion was aroused by the Conference on Economic Progress, "Poverty and Deprivation in the United States" (Washington, D.C.: Conference on Economic Progress, 1962, pamphlet). See also, Oscar Ornati, *Poverty Amid Affluence* (New York: The Twentieth Century Fund, 1966, paperback); and Robert Lampman, "Income Distribution and Poverty," in Gordon, *op. cit.*, 102–114. The Social Security analyses are reported in the following articles by Mollie Orshansky, all of which appear in the *Social Security Bulletin*: "Counting the Poor: Another Look at the Poverty Profile," 28, No. 1 (January, 1965), 3–29; "Who's Who Among the Poor: A Demographic View of Poverty," 28, No. 7 (July, 1965), 3–32; "Recounting the Poor—A Five Year Review," 29, No. 4 (April, 1966), 20–37; "The Poor in City and Suburb, 1964," 29, No. 12 (December, 1966), 22–37; "The Shape of Poverty in 1966," 31, No. 3 (March, 1968), 3–32. *The Economic Report of the President* and the *Annual Report of the Council of Economic Advisors* for the years 1964, 1965, 1966, and 1967 contain relevant material (Washington, D.C.: Government Printing Office, 1964, 1965, 1966, 1967).

two-thirds of the nation in poverty.[4] In terms of 1964 constant dollars, the following were the percentages of families with incomes under $3,000.

Table 1   FAMILY INCOME UNDER $3,000[a]

Year	Percentage	Year	Percentage
1947	31	1956	22
1948	32	1957	22
1949	33	1958	22
1950	30	1959	21
1951	28	1960	20
1952	27	1961	20
1953	25	1962	19
1954	27	1963	18
1955	24	1964	18

[a] In terms of 1964 constant dollars.
Source: Department of Commerce, Office of Business Economics, as published in House of Representatives, *Report on Economic Opportunity Amendments of 1966*, Report No. 1568 (Washington, D.C.: June, 1966).

Poverty, clearly, is a relative concept, containing within it elements of social definition that are somehow reflective of both a society's potential and its requirements. Indeed, these two factors seem interrelated.

The Social Security Administration's poverty line now generally used in the United States is "set at pre-tax income levels at which most families of a given size do in fact purchase a nutritious diet." However, both standards of nutrition and patterns of income disposal are highly variable over time and among places. A Japanese observer comments that, in pre-industrial traditional society, the poor are surrounded by other poor and lack a yardstick. Their poverty is, in a sense, invisible even to themselves, just as it is taken as part of a normal life by others.[5] Poverty, in fact, becomes an issue of public policy only as the stage of socio-economic development begins to

---

[4] The sources, in the order given, are: Fritz Machlup, "Strategies in the War on Poverty," in Gordon, *op. cit.*, 447. Oscar Ornati, "United States," in Organisation for Economic Co-Operation and Development, *Low Income Groups and Methods of Dealing with Their Problems, Supplement to the Report* (Paris: Organisation for Economic Co-Operation and Development, 1965), 96. Robert Lampman, "Ends and Means in the War Against Poverty," in Leo Fishman, Editor, *Poverty Amid Affluence* (New Haven: Yale University Press, 1966), 212–213. Victor Fuchs, "Toward A Theory of Poverty," in Task Force on Economic Growth and Opportunity, *The Concept of Poverty* (Washington, D.C.: The Chamber of Commerce of the United States, 1965), 73.

[5] Koji Taira, "Japan," *Low Income Groups and Methods of Dealing with their Problems*, 135–150. S. M. Miller argues, however, that international communication now creates visibility for poverty even in the most underdeveloped countries. S. M. Miller, "Poverty," *Transactions of the Sixth World Congress of Sociology* (London: International Sociological Association, 1967), 173–185.

make it manageable. It is no coincidence that the society which launched an effort to "wipe out" poverty in the United States was being widely described as "affluent."[6] The anti-poverty effort is the product of an "age of mass consumption," to use W. W. Rostow's term.

The following relationships may be hypothesized: The adequate functioning of a society at a given stage of development demands assurance of social institutional arrangements to solve problems of production, distribution, socialization, motivation, internal and external defense, and so on (the sociologist's and anthropologist's "functional prerequisites"). Such arrangements, in turn, are dependent on assurance of adequate physical development and stamina of its members (to pilot a jet plane or serve as a foot soldier, for example), adequate education and training (to work in a modern hospital or to understand a wiring diagram for television repair), and related standards of housing, transportation, clothing, etc. The series of social mechanisms, which translates the demands from institutions into expectations of individual modal performance, eventually leads through a diverse series of paths to conceptions of need and of what a society might offer its members—indeed, to what it must offer its members and what their rights are. Definitions of the poverty line, by-products of the process, thus must be expected to change—and they do change—as technological, political, and resource variables influence basic institutional change.

Orshansky and her collaborators have reported on the United States poverty picture today in this spirit.[7] The poverty line used, computed at a "stringent level of living" and assuming both relatively sophisticated shopping practices and enough mobility to permit some choice, is "drawn separately for each of 124 different types of families described by the sex of the head, the total number of other adults, the number of children under 18, and whether or not they live on a farm." The anchor point in the index is "the amount of income remaining after allowance for buying an adequate diet at minimum cost. . . ." By this standard, the non-farm poverty line (1963) for a family of four was placed at $3,190, at $1,540 for a single person, and $4,135 for a family of six.[8] Some of the findings obviously relevant to an anti-poverty strategy may be summarized briefly:

---

[6] John Kenneth Galbraith, *The Affluent Society* (Boston: Houghton Mifflin Company, 1958), 329. "An affluent society, that is both compassionate and rational, would no doubt secure to all who needed it the minimum income essential for decency and comfort."

[7] Orshansky, in the articles listed in footnote 3 on page 11.

[8] We here report 1963, 1964, and 1965 data, even where there has been some updating, since the intent is to reconstruct the 1964–1965 policy reviews and debates. Statistics refer to 1964 except as specified.

- ☐ The 1964 poverty population stood at 34.1 million people, 18 percent of the non-institutionalized population (down 1.2 million from 1963). By 1965 the total was down to 31.9 million.[9]
- ☐ Fourteen and eight-tenths million of the poor were children and of these 4.4 million were in families with no male head of household.
- ☐ Of all youngsters in poverty, nearly half were in homes with at least five children. Households judged poor included nearly one-fourth of the nation's children. Income in the large, poor families was so low that many would have been poor even if they had had only two children.
- ☐ Thirty percent of the non-institutionalized aged (over 5 million individuals) were in poor households (1963).
- ☐ The almost-fifteen-million poor children and their 7.5 million poor parents (or adult relatives caring for them) accounted for three-fourths of the persons in poor families. Of the aged poor, 2.7 million were living in families.
- ☐ Adding the following totals among the poor accounted for two-thirds of the entire category: 15 million children under eighteen, 5.5 million over sixty-five, 1.5 million women who were family heads and homemakers.
- ☐ Among families with male heads, employed as of March, 1964, 7 percent of the white families and 31 percent of the Negro families were in poverty.
- ☐ Half of all United States poverty was in the South, a geographic area with double the national poverty rate.
- ☐ Poverty in farm areas affected 23 percent of families, contrasting with 14.1 percent of families with non-farm residences, yet most poverty was concentrated among non-farm people, since most of the work force is not in agriculture.
- ☐ Three out of ten poor people were non-white (1963), a rate three and a half times that of whites. In fact, one of every two non-whites was in the poverty group (three out of five children). Non-white children accounted for 5.75 million of the 15 million children in poverty. (The Negro-white gap is widening.)[10]
- ☐ Families headed by women accounted for one in three of the nation's poor, but only one in ten of all families (1963).
- ☐ Heads of almost 30 percent of all families called poor worked full time for the entire year.
- ☐ Nearly 40 percent of the children in poverty were in the family of a worker with a full-time job all through 1963.
- ☐ Poor families experienced an unemployment rate three times the rate in

[9] The total was 25.9 million in 1967, one in eight persons. While the anti-poverty program claimed some or all of the credit, most of the shifts may be attributable to more basic trends in the economy.

[10] Daniel Patrick Moynihan, "Employment, Income and the Ordeal of the Negro Family," in *The Negro American, Daedalus*, 94, No. 4 (Fall, 1965), 755. By Orshansky's 1966 calculations, one in three non-white families was poor, as was one in ten white families. Non-whites made up one-third of the nation's poor.

non-poor families, a higher rate of complete withdrawal from the labor force, and more long-term and disabling illness.

☐ The 1963 gap between the incomes of the poor and the poverty-line was $11.5 billion.

Major studies tend to converge in their findings about poverty-linked characteristics and the high-risk groups for poverty: farm workers, female-headed households, Negroes, the aged, those with less than eight years of education, the large family with young children (even if the father is present). Oscar Ornati has calculated the greater likelihood of poverty for these and related types of families and shown that the factors are highly predictive. When several of the factors combine, the likelihood of extreme poverty is very great. Most of these elements operate even when the economy does well.[11]

The relativity of the poverty line is dramatized by a series of preliminary reports defining poverty levels in other countries. Selecting cut-off points well below the Orshansky income standards, these analyses yield widely varied rates.[12] An Italian report talks of one-quarter of the population in poverty or distress, while a "rough" Norwegian hypothesis places the poor at 6 percent of the population. A British report places 18 percent of all households in poverty (the comparable United States ratio being 20 percent).[13]

Of some relevance to the analysis of the contents of the initial anti-poverty legislation is the fact that the poverty totals for 1964 included almost all of the more than 8 million recipients of public assistance in the United States. Grant levels were below even the most modest of poverty lines; a large proportion of states were not meeting minimal needs even as they computed and budgeted them. Furthermore, as reported by Ida Merriam, of the Old Age, Survivors and Disability Insurance ("social security") recipients for 1962, two-thirds of the couples had a total retirement income below $2,500 and four-fifths of the others had a total retirement income below $1,800.[14] Sar Levitan concludes that of 11 million retired OASDI beneficiaries in 1962, age sixty-five and over, 41 percent were living in poverty in the sense then used.[15]

---

[11] Ornati, *Poverty Amid Affluence.*

[12] Organisation for Economic Co-Operation and Development, *Low Income Groups and Methods of Dealing with Their Problems.* Also, Brian Abel-Smith and Peter Townsend, *The Poor and the Poorest* (London: G. Bell and Sons, Ltd., 1965, paperback).

[13] Orshansky, "Recounting the Poor."

[14] Ida Merriam, "Overlap of Benefits Under OASDI and Other Programs," *Social Security Bulletin,* 28, No. 4 (April, 1965), 24.

[15] Sar A. Levitan, *Programs in Aid of the Poor* (Washington, D.C.: The W. E. Upjohn Institute for Employment Research, 1965), 3–4.

With nearly 10 million United States workers earning under $1.50 an hour as the anti-poverty effort began and with much enforced idleness among several employee groups, one could understand a finding that two-thirds of impoverished family heads were nevertheless work-force members, often with full-time jobs. Salary levels could not meet the needs of large families, and mothers with many children at home needing care could not go to work.[16]

There is extensive documentation of the consequences of poverty status for health, longevity, education, productivity, and perspectives on life—but this material will not be summarized here.[17] Most Americans apparently now accept the general notion that extreme poverty should be coped with through public policy; but the question is, what policy? The poverty brought into focus by statistical analyses and case reports is not "one lump," to use Tennyson's phrase. That the several different subgroups subsumed require different and independent help and services was propounded as far back as the British Royal Commission on the Poor Laws and Relief of Distress, which met from 1905 to 1909.

Before reviewing the options available and the choices actually made, another dimension must be introduced: the discussion of the "culture of poverty" and of low-income "life styles"—and the related efforts to extrapolate policy from social science findings.

"THE CULTURE OF POVERTY"

Oscar Lewis' *Children of Sanchez* popularized the concept of a "culture of poverty" and gave some insight into the social-psychological concomi-

---

[16] Sar A. Levitan, "The Poor in the Work Force," in Chamber of Commerce of the United States, Task Force on Economic Growth and Opportunity, *The Disadvantaged Poor: Education and Employment* (Washington, D.C.: The Chamber of Commerce of the U.S., 1966), 297–322. Charles E. Silberman, "The Mixed-Up War on Poverty," *Fortune*, LXXII, No. 2 (August, 1965), 156.

[17] For example: Lola M. Irelan, "Health Practices of the Poor," *Welfare in Review*, 3, No. 10 (October, 1965), 1–9. Catherine S. Chilman, *Growing Up Poor*, United States Department of Health, Education, and Welfare, Welfare Administration, Division of Research (Washington, D.C.: Government Printing Office, 1966). Oliver C. Moles, Jr., "Training Children in Low-Income Families for School," *Welfare in Review*, 3, No. 6 (June, 1965), 1–11.

Martin Rein concludes that the evidence about the direction of causation among poverty-health-housing, etc. is confused, and that several intervening variables may operate. This does not preclude the view that the conventional wisdom is obviously correct: the poverty status carries negative consequences for most people and is not a desirable one. See Martin Rein, "Social Science and the Elimination of Poverty," *Journal of the American Institute of Planners*, XXXIII, No. 3 (May, 1967), 146–163.

tants of a life in poverty which extends from generation to generation in a Mexican slum. His more recent work provides similar insight into Puerto Rican experiences.[18]

Lewis' use of the term is quite restricted and is meant to refer only to a few members of the poverty group included in the Orshansky statistics. As summarized by Dr. Robert Coles, a psychiatrist:

> The term . . . refers to people who are not only poor, but who have given up all hope, or have never had any hope of doing anything about their poverty, and who live in that sense totally isolated, socially and psychologically, from the rest of the Nation in which they live.[19]

Social scientists have found that the poverty-culture idea, used somewhat loosely, may serve a variety of purposes, some of them mutually contradictory.

Novels, social surveys, field studies, autobiographies, and agency case studies over the years have documented the fact that poor people sometimes (but by no means always) differ from others in their value systems and perspectives on life, in their attitudes on social and political issues, in their sexual behavior and child-rearing patterns, in the content of the aspirations they hold for their children, in the roles of husband-wife-teenager, in the priority accorded various house furnishings and amenities, in relationships with aged parents and other relatives, as well as in other ways. Also, data have shown the persistence of poverty from generation to generation in certain sections, or regions, or parts of the city, in certain ethnic groups, in certain occupational strata, in certain families.

The question naturally has arisen as to whether a group's style of life does not contribute to its poverty or, indeed, actually cause it. (In fact, this assumption was part of conventional wisdom until recently.) From this stance, transition has been made to the theory that, in a period of general prosperity, one should attribute to intergenerational cultural transmission both (using Galbraith's phrases) *case poverty*, that related to the afflicted

---

[18] By Oscar Lewis: *The Children of Sanchez* (New York: Random House, 1961); *Five Families* (New York: Basic Books, 1959); *Pedro Martinez* (New York: Random House, 1964); *La Vida* (New York: Random House, 1966); and "The Culture of Poverty," *Scientific American*, 215, No. 4 (October, 1966), 19–25.

[19] Hearings before the Subcommittee on Executive Reorganization of the Committee on Government Operations, United States Senate, *Federal Role in Urban Affairs* (Washington, D.C.: Government Printing Office, 1967), Part 7, November 30, 1966, 1594.

For a sophisticated research review of what is known of the poor as a social category, with characteristics both of achievement and ascription, see Edwin J. Thomas and Robert D. Carter, "Social Psychological Factors in Poverty," in Meyer N. Zald, Editor, *Organizing for Community Welfare* (Chicago: Quadrangle Books, 1967), 195–261.

individuals, and perhaps much of *insular poverty*, the poverty derived from the failure or depletion of an area's economy.[20] Such a view tends to generate either a pessimistic or somewhat punitive perspective ("they were born that way and are destined to be that way"), or a completely socio-therapeutic and individually-rehabilitative anti-poverty policy ("education, retraining, and the like are the way to end the cycle").

A related issue has also developed. Some of the investigators of the lives of poor people have concluded that in some senses the value-systems, relationships, and behavior patterns uncovered represent "reality" adjustments, are functional for the group, have much to commend them, and should be protected. While this has appeared as a refreshing antidote to the assumption that upward social mobility and economic improvement must always point toward the middle-class suburban "ideal," it, too, has developed some potentially unsatisfactory consequences.

Attention to what poor people are and how they live tells one a good deal about why and how they are closed out of the cultural mainstream and why services, facilities, and governmental mechanisms are unavailable to them. Such insight, therefore, tells public officials, planners, and administrators that one must restructure education, health, and social service techniques and delivery modes if these are to become equally available to the most disadvantaged poor. In fact, it is unlikely that many people who are fully capable of grasping economic and social opportunities will be able to take the crucial first steps unless there is restructuring.

On the other hand, the need and desire thus to take account of preference and modes of coping, in assuring needed adaptability at the point of a potential user's initial contact and entry into a service system, may lead to the reshaping of certain systems to serve the disadvantaged (those in "cultural poverty") and consequently to offer something less than what everybody else gets. One might cite the "unequal" character of "separate but equal" education or the frequently unsatisfactory state of "clinic" medicine or slum schools. Thus a sentimental, if sincere, over-enthusiasm for "life styles of the poor" may defeat the long-term objectives of the reformer. Particularism, or selectivity, whether based on an individual means test or an assessment of the needs of disadvantaged groups, does seem to carry negative consequences.

Confronting some of these dilemmas and dangers, one must also note that they are compounded by loose use of the term "the poor." "The poor," of course, may be all of those who at a given moment fall beneath the Social

---

[20] Galbraith, *op. cit.*, 325–326.

Security Administration's poverty line, but he who uses the phrase must recall that the group is not a fixed caste. In fact, Levitan reminds us that one-fifth of the group left the category in 1962, and one-fifth entered it in 1963. Other economists document entry into and departure from this status within the course of one year through both changed circumstances and by virtue of minor definitional changes.[21]

The man in the street, the social scientist, and the policy-maker all tend to forget that "the poor" in the sense used by the various analyses are nothing more than a statistical category, an abstraction, a product of analysis. They are not members of one interacting social group. They are not necessarily always the same people as those described in the "culture of poverty" literature. Or, even more likely, the objects of the various cultural case studies probably constitute a small subsection from the overall poverty category and *include some people whose incomes are above any given poverty line*. To generalize from Oscar Lewis' or any other case studies to a group called "the poor" is therefore reckless. Referring to Lewis' work, Coles comments:

> I do not think that in the United States of America today we really have a significant culture of poverty, and I have worked with migrant farm children, with Appalachian children, as well as city children.[22]

A number of authors have shown that there is, in the course of the current poverty discussions, a dangerous tendency "to apply to all those who are poor or who are manual workers . . . " those characteristics "taken as typical of the more unstable bottom group."[23] Those who follow this path thus ignore the remarkable congruence of aspirations and values shared in many economic strata, the continuous social integration that accompanies economic mobility, and the readiness of many disadvantaged citizens to grasp opportunity fully as social obstacles are removed. They also fail to ask whether some of the valued characteristics may not be ethnic, religious, and regional and capable of perpetuation "after poverty."

Recent work has suggested that the "culture of poverty" notion may be helpful, if utilized to a limited degree and carefully specified. Ohlin's review,[24] among others, supports the following generalizations:

---

[21] Sar A. Levitan, "The Poor in the Work Force," *op. cit.*; Silberman, *loc. cit.*

[22] Coles, in Hearings, U.S. Senate, *The Federal Role in Urban Affairs*, Part 7.

[23] S. M. Miller, "The American Lower Class: A Typological Approach," *Social Research*, 31, No. 1 (1964); reprinted in Frank Riessman, Jerome Cohen, and Arthur Pearl, Editors, *Mental Health of the Poor* (New York: The Free Press, 1964), 139–154.

[24] Lloyd Ohlin, "Inherited Poverty," in Organisation for Economic Co-Operation and Development, *Low Income Groups*, 273–285.

- □ Only some poor people participate in "the culture," no matter where the line is drawn.
- □ Much of work published early in the anti-poverty planning period (Michael Harrington's, for example) thus over-extended the concept.
- □ The "culture" may contain advantageous as well as handicapping traits (helplessness and alienation, but also personal trust and mutual aid).
- □ It is useful to distinguish the underpaid working class from the marginally-located underclasses, Miller's "unstable bottom group."
- □ A person who is part of the long-time poor must, in effect, learn certain social skills to survive in his disadvantaged status. However, "once this happens the chance of altering his condition by solving the original problem is no longer enough."[25]
- □ Many social institutions (education, law enforcement, health, employment, etc.) tend to alienate, close out, become unavailable to, reject, or discriminate against a society's most submerged elements. Since such institutions are the doorkeepers to opportunity, the most disadvantaged cannot escape their poverty and may give up. The "hopelessness" thus resides not in their "culture" alone, but in the mutual estrangement between such culture and the large society.[26]

On balance, Ohlin calls for "a careful mixture . . . of financial aid, clearly defined opportunity, and skillfully administered social services to aid individuals and families to escape from the culture of poverty." To those who see in this view a lack of respect for cultural differences and for the positive values in the culture of poverty, he cites recent research to the effect that "values of a culture regarded by the participants as desirable are cherished in this type of cultural change and harmful ones left behind."[27]

OPTIONS IN COPING WITH POVERTY

Poor people did not conceive, request, plan, or launch the "war against poverty." The campaign was defined as urgent by President Johnson and it was he who, through dramatization, won it the backing required for the first forays. There are those who claim that, consciously or not, an effort thus was made to channel the civil rights movement into a socially acceptable mould. In this sense, the anti-poverty war might be seen as a strategy for racial integration.[28]

---

[25] *Ibid.*

[26] Schorr speaks of conditions which cause, affect, or perpetuate poverty as a "syndrome of mutually reinforcing handicaps." Alvin Schorr, *Slums and Social Insecurity* (Washington, D.C.: Government Printing Office, 1963).

[27] Ohlin, *op. cit.*

[28] Elinor Graham, "The Politics of Poverty," in M. E. Gettleman and D. Mermelstein, Editors, *The Great Society Reader* (New York: Vintage Books paper edition, 1967), 225.

Such a view is plausible if not validated.[29] Certainly, the debate over the anti-poverty program took place at a time of civil rights militancy, which made participants aware of deprivation traceable to discrimination and injustice suffered by Negroes. It also took place during a period of fiscal capability: balanced and steady economic growth, relative price stability, a margin available to the federal budgeters for 1964. (From 1964 through 1967, the period under discussion, those with the most expansive proposals could postulate financing through *increased* government income from the *growing* gross national product—without disturbing existing stakes of any groups.) Finally, there was constant concern with the significant and continuous unemployment total—particularly high unemployment among uneducated youth in the urban slums.

Although not designed by a social planning staff, the anti-poverty effort was shaped after an extended study and policy debate, beginning with compilation of data about inequality of income distribution early in the nineteen-fifties, continuing with Congressional highlighting of economic deprivation in specific areas of the country, followed by economic analysis and policy conceptualization (Galbraith, Lampman), and capped by impassioned public reporting, dramatization, and a degree of inevitable oversimplification (Harrington, MacDonald).[30] Economists, other social scientists, welfare experts, administrators, and political leaders were involved at various points and in many ways—and a parallel public discussion was launched in the media. Ultimately, a Presidential proposal emerged in a bill submitted to the Congress in March, 1964—reflecting both the research and analytic processes and the outcome of conflicts and rivalries, different concepts of strategy, interdepartmental competition, and bargaining. Relatively few changes were made in the Congress, and the Economic Opportunity Act (Public Law 88–452) was signed on August 20, 1964.

This is not formal, comprehensive social planning. It is, however, a problem-centered approach, which, perhaps, most closely approximates the "incrementalist" view of a planning process. It may be examined as such. A complete "internal" picture of the decision-making is not available and

---

Also see Ben B. Seligman, *Permanent Poverty* (Chicago: Quadrangle Books, 1968), Chap. 9.

[29] Nor was the strategy, if actually adopted, successful.

[30] Sar A. Levitan, "The Design of Federal Antipoverty Strategy" (Ann Arbor, Michigan: Institute of Labor and Industrial Relations, 1967, pamphlet). The various Levitan poverty reports cited in this chapter are consolidated in his *The Great Society's Poor Law: A New Approach to Poverty* (Baltimore: The Johns Hopkins Press, 1969).

may never be.[31] Present purposes are served, however, by review of the options theoretically available and analysis of what actually emerged.

The economists posed choices as between what they describe as *aggregate demand* and *structural strategies*. Welfare experts considered *residual* versus *institutional* orientations to programming. And the policy-makers faced still other possibilities.

The choices were not necessarily mutually exclusive in theory, but they represented real alternatives in the sense that neither the level of funding available nor any coherent task definition could sustain them all. If there was to be a "mix," then, what would be the balance?[32]

Aggregate demand.   One could seek new ways to improve the economy's performance on the assumption that money, goods, and "opportunities" would "trickle down" or "spill over" to the disadvantaged and thus end poverty.

Structural strategies.   On the assumption that the problem had to do with the discrepancy between the economy's needs and the quality, capacity, motivation, location, or availability of the labor force, one could give special help to individuals and groups unable to enter into the labor force. One also could create special, protected jobs, by way of preparing people to enter the regular job market in the future. These strategies place major focus on changing the capacities of poor people, not on institutions.

Area redevelopment.   Either on the assumption that the problem was a lack of investment capital or labor-force quality, or both, one could give special help to regions, areas, cities, or industries not able to keep up with the general performance of the economy.

Redistribution.   Because many of the poor are too old, too young, or too ill to work and many have been long deprived, one could consider either redistribution of *wealth* (hardly likely to be taken seriously) or *income* redistributional measures, particularly improved grants to OASDHI (social security) beneficiaries and public assistance recipients—two concentrated subcategories of obviously poor people.

Amenities and benefits in kind.   Either targeting on "the poor" or, in the context of a more general effort to improve community resources for everybody, particularly on city dwellers, one might provide more services,

---

[31] *Ibid.*

[32] The options are variously formulated and evaluated by a large number of authors in Gordon, *op. cit.*; Ferman, Kornbluh, and Haber, *op. cit.*; Levitan, "The Poor in the Work Force"; Martin Rein and S. M. Miller, "Poverty, Policy and Purpose: The Dilemmas of Choice," in Leonard H. Goodman, Editor, *Economic Progress and Social Welfare* (New York: Columbia University Press, 1966), 20–64; Rein, *op. cit.*

facilities, and goods, ranging from health to education to housing, thereby raising living standards despite poverty-line income.

Capital funding. On the assumption that some people could "make it" in the economy if given grants or loans to launch them on farms or in businesses, one might facilitate low-interest or interest-free loans or grants. Few expected this strategy to help many poor people since most were not considered to have the required competence—yet all agreed a small group could be reached this way.

Power. Little discussed at the time that the 1964 Act was under consideration, but soon a central theme in the civil rights movement and some local anti-poverty efforts was a newly-phrased option: to concentrate on overcoming the "powerlessness" of the poor. The theme was sounded early in the Harlem Youth Opportunities Unlimited (Haryou) planning report for the President's Committee on Delinquency and Youth Crime. It was phrased in political science terms by others. The premise was that the economies of slum areas were stagnant, their services inferior, and their residents discriminated against because slum populations lacked an economic and political base of power.

Thus, "the possibility that the anti-poverty program can contribute to the growth of low-income power lies in delivering to the poor and their leaders control over the programs and the funds to be funneled into their slums and ghetto communities."[33]

Or, as Warren Haggstrom expressed it:

> . . . since is is more likely that the problem is one of powerlessness [rather than only one of lack of money], joint initiative by the poor on their own behalf should precede and accompany responses from the remainder of society. In practice this initiative is likely to be most effectively exercised by powerful conflict organizations based in neighborhoods of poverty.[34]

---

[33] Richard A. Cloward, "The War on Poverty: Are the Poor Left Out?" *The Nation*, 201 (August 2, 1965), 55–56. Also see, Harlem Youth Opportunities Unlimited, Inc., *Youth in the Ghetto: A Study of the Consequences of Powerlessness and a Blueprint for Change* (New York: 1964, processed): "Even a cursory examination of the power potentials in the Harlem community reveals that there are few, if any, examples of primary and consistent power in the hands of resident individuals and groups. . . . The community can best be described in terms of the analogy of a powerless colony. . .," 79.

[34] Warren C. Haggstrom, "The Power of the Poor," in Frank Riessman, Jerome Cohen, and Arthur Pearl, Editors, *Mental Health of the Poor*, 221. For a legal–political science rationale, see Edgar and Jean C. Cahn, "The War on Poverty: A Civilian Perspective," *Yale Law Journal*, 73, No. 8 (July, 1964), 1317–1352. The position is well summarized by Peter Marris and Martin Rein, *Dilemmas of Social Reform* (New York: Atherton Press, 1967), Chap. II. Haggstrom's subsequent experience, summarized in as yet unpublished writings, left him quite disillusioned about the possibilities for officially-sanctioned community action to seek "power."

Except for the last, these options all assume the possibility of an anti-poverty effort based on *consensus*. One carries on research, debates alternatives, bargains, trades, and makes choices. In contrast, some of those who proposed coping with "powerlessness" as a primary strategy conceived of it as a *conflict* strategy. A shift of power could take place only as an outcome of social struggle among those with competing interests.

Within these options there are, of course, major alternatives with regard to *scale*. Any one of these might be a massive or a relatively minor effort. To give poor people enough money to fill the gap between their incomes and the Social Security Administration poverty line would have cost $11 or $12 billion a year, yet the initial discussion was in terms of less than $1 billion. Even by 1967 the highest totals projected were between $2 and $3 billion. Grants-in-aid to states for all programs were running at about $12 billion annually at the same time. Obviously these "facts" about potential scale would eliminate some options and limit even more. On the other hand, enthusiastic response, great success, or new growth rates and federal revenue might affect the picture and permit escalation—possibilities planners cannot ignore.

Various *time* perspectives were at stake as options were considered: income redistributional measures through public assistance or social security increases would be clearly on target and rapid, at least in delivery. Strategies based on promoting economic growth are inevitably of somewhat longer range. Structural measures tend toward an intermediate time-commitment. Area redevelopment partakes of some elements of the demand and some of the structural options. Some amenities may be developed quickly. The planners, then, needed to balance immediate visible effects against what they considered basic results.

Aggregate demand approaches do not differentiate the poor or the disadvantaged. One launches fiscal, monetary, and related measures to promote growth. All of the other potential approaches encompassed by the repertoire as listed may assume either that one is, in coping with deprived people, dealing with an emergency needing temporary buttressing or with the normal state of the system. Some brief elaboration is in order—since here, too, those planning the anti-poverty effort needed to make choices, implicitly or explicitly.

In considering social policies it has been found useful to distinguish *residual* from *institutional* approaches to modern social welfare.[35] The former

---

[35] Harold L. Wilensky and Charles N. Lebeaux, *Industrial Society and Social Welfare* (New York: Russell Sage Foundation, 1958).

perspective postulates that, generally, the forces of the market place, the family, and other primary institutions (church, neighborhood, etc.) meet basic needs. Where temporary malfunctioning or crisis (depression, flood, or epidemic) leaves individuals in difficulty, welfare measures are developed. These are seen as temporary, and, as interim measures, they are not expected to be really adequate or too comfortable. Systematic coverage is not required. Although residual services may be available as a right and may formally be free of stigma, their being defined as episodic and crisis-meeting seems to transfer to many such services the aura of blame and personal inadequacy which characterized all relief measures from the fourteenth to the early twentieth century.

Institutional approaches, by contrast, find certain new problems and needs inherent in the industrial-urban system even when it works well (unemployment because of technological progress, health problems in the aged with increased longevity, help for mentally-retarded adults who are alive because of advances in medicine, or playground requirements because of increased leisure). Institutional perspectives on intervention thus involve seeking to change or supplement the system to cope with new social realities. Social security, day care, Medicare, new cultural resources, and many other programs associated with the Great Society or the welfare state are seen as realistic responses to social change, as relatively permanent, as needed by the total community and carrying no stigma for their use.

Residual responses tend for the most part to create case services involving relief, treatment, rehabilitation of the deviant and disadvantaged individual. Institutional responses may be in several categories:

☐ efforts to affect the system by fiscal, monetary, or social policy (tax laws, interest rates, retirement options), by regulatory legislation, or by change in institutions (new concepts of the school, for example)
☐ creation of new, universalistic social utilities[36]
☐ creation of case services, which (whether medical, psychiatric, psychological, or social work) are available on a diagnostic basis, see deviance as "illness" broadly defined, and do not introduce moral judgment or social disabilities into the "treatment."

It will be recognized immediately that the federal government had some involvement in programs on all these levels before 1964, and that the involvement has increased since that time, apart from the Economic Opportunity Act.

---

[36] Alfred J. Kahn, "New Policies and Service Models: The Next Phase," *American Journal of Orthopsychiatry*, XXXV, No. 4 (July, 1965), 552–562. Or see Chapter VI in the companion volume.

THE ECONOMIC OPPORTUNITY ACT AS AN
ANTI-POVERTY STRATEGY

It is not necessary for present purposes to distinguish the 1964 Act from 1965 amendments or to review all administrative arrangements and subsequent proposals. The following listing quickly conveys the character of the "war" as defined in the Act. The totals describe the quantitative *targets*.

Administered by Office of Economic Opportunity (O.E.O.)

Job Corps (Title I A). Fiscal 1966 appropriation, $310 million (10,000 young people in 139 centers for 1965; 64,000 young people in 193 centers for 1966)

VISTA (Title IV A). Fiscal 1966 appropriation, $16 million (2,000 in training or work in 1965 and 5,000 in 200 communities in 1966)

Community Action Program (Title II A). Fiscal 1966 appropriation, $663 million ([includes Head Start and Migrant programs]; 500 grants to 350 communities in 1965; 650 grants to 600 communities in 1966)

Administered with the Department of Health, Education, and Welfare

College Work-Study (Title I C). Transferred in 1966 to United States Office of Education budget (45,000 students plus 64,000 for the summer in 800 institutions for 1966)

Adult Basic Education (Title II B). Fiscal 1966 appropriation, $30 million (35,000 trainees in 1965; 70,000 trainees in 1966)

Work Experience (Title J). Fiscal 1966 appropriation, $125 million (88,000 people in 1965; 112,000 people in 1966). This program was *assigned* to HEW, whereas all others not administered by OEO were technically only "delegated" to other agencies.

Administered by the Department of Labor

Neighborhood Youth Corps (Title I B). Fiscal 1966 appropriation, $259 million (150,000 in part-time work at 275 sites and 70,000 more in summer work for 1965; and 215,000 in part-time work at 430 sites, plus 50,000 more in summer work for 1966)

Administered by the Department of Agriculture

Loan programs for rural areas (Title III). Fiscal 1966 appropriation, $35 million (7,000 small loans for 1965; 14,490 small loans for 1966)

Administered by the Small Business Administration

Employment and Investment Incentive Loans (Title IV). Included in Community Action Program budget until fiscal 1967 (1,000 loans in 1965; and 3,000 in 1966)

While the Act and the 1965 amendments had additional facets to be mentioned subsequently, and while additional changes were introduced during 1966, from migrant programs to efforts to incorporate the aged into the effort ("foster grandparents"), the drift was clear: *This was essentially a case service strategy, apparently continuous with a basically-residual tradition in American social welfare.*[37] Rhetoric aside, the emphasis was on changing people's attitudes toward work and school, equipping them with basic skills, giving them an economic toehold through loans (if they were poor risks for the usual loan sources), helping them remain in school—in short, on remedying defects in an individual or his immediate circumstances which stood in the way of his adequate participation in the economy and thus (presumably) his emergence from poverty. The economy's allegedly decreasing need for unskilled workers was taken account of in provision for work training, and it was assumed that, once trained, the no-longer-unskilled would find work. "Dropouts" were to be educated and counseled, and the economy was assumed to have places for them.

Yet, this was a structural approach with a difference. Earlier programs emphasized moral defects and psychological problems. Counseling was considered the core service. Now to a considerable degree, the spotlight was placed on education and on enhancing labor-market skills. In addition, there was special and refreshing emphasis on the youth. The cycle could be broken by offering broader horizons to the very young through preschool programs, and trying to rescue, redirect, and give a part in society to unemployed adolescents, who could be accommodated in several types of job training and guidance counseling programs. Critics, therefore, could not dismiss the effort entirely as "more of the same." The President and lieutenants proclaimed a departure:

"The days of the dole in our country are numbered."

"The purpose . . . is to offer opportunity, not an opiate."

"Handouts are rejected."

The goal is "to break the chains of poverty."

Appropriations and program-focus never matched these extravagant claims, yet those who would take the goal-statements literally—and their numbers did grow over the next several years—could attempt to use the instrumentalities of the Economic Opportunity Act (EOA) to depart from the professions, programs, and orientations previously employed to cope with poor people and to seek what some rather exaggeratedly came to call "basic institutional change"; i.e., new programs and redistribution of "power." They were reinforced in this view by the inclusion in the Act of an ambiguously-phrased Community Action Program (CAP), apparently seen as the "ven-

---

[37] Alfred J. Kahn, "The Societal Context of Social Work Practice," *Social Work*, 10, No. 4 (October, 1965), 145–155.

ture capital" of the undertaking and budgeted for 32 percent of the whole in 1964 and 44 percent in 1965. The concept was never fully spelled out: the Community Action Program was charged with facilitating an attack on the "roots of poverty," through self-help efforts in areas generally the size of a municipality, but to vary in accord with the situation. On the basis of 90 percent federal funding, these efforts of public or nonprofit agencies were to "give promise of progress toward the elimination of poverty or a cause or causes of poverty. . . ." The Office of Economic Opportunity (OEO) announced from the beginning, "the door is always open for new programs and new approaches. Since community needs and resources vary, considerable latitude is allowed in the development and conduct of a CAP."

Undoubtedly, most congressmen, administrators, and citizens saw community action as participation by the poor in a socio-therapeutic self-help sense—and thus part of a selective or particularistic case service approach to poverty.[38] However, there were also those who perceived in the EOA, particularly in the CAP, a domestic prescription for a political and social revolution, legislatively inaugurated, taxpayer funded, and implemented by application to Washington.

In brief, *the country had enacted an essentially structural–case service– residual program—with some ambiguous "change" ingredients.* In our terms, while the overall thrust was clear, there were some conflicting concepts of the planning task and some "hidden agendas."

THE ANTI-POVERTY PROGRAM IN CONTEXT

The available choices from the anti-poverty repertoire, we have said, are not all mutually exclusive. Moreover, the data presented about the poverty "group" make it abundantly clear that one approach could not possibly touch all: the children, the aged, the employed fathers of large families, the discriminated-against, the unskilled, the alienated, the husbandless, the farmers. Yet in the search for the new, the "planners" had initially at least ignored the stimulation of aggregate demand, giving money to poor people, scheduling any new area development approaches, or expanding general social amenities. Their potentially innovative, case services approach emphasized job placement and training more than was common in social services. There also was stress on local service coordination and some provision for it. Furthermore the Act offered a broader invitation to self-help than ever before proclaimed nationally. Its rhetoric and its CAP structure also

---

[38] See *New York Times* report of interviews with Adam Yarmolinsky and Richard Boone, October 29, 1967. Also see Daniel P. Moynihan, "What is Community Action?" *The Public Interest*, No. 5 (Fall, 1966).

opened the possibility of a fight for "power," of a departure from the traditional consensus approach to social policy. By placing funds in the locality and calling for participation of residents another chain of developments of unknown significance was set off. Thus, a problem-focused effort served to highlight needs of a deprived group, assemble new resources (almost a billion dollars the first year), and to launch new administrative vehicles. In a sense, problem-focused planning was here seen under relatively advantageous conditions. Of course, there were inherent limitations in the level of funding, apparently fixed from the time of initial discussions and never much increased. A little over 1.25 percent of the federal budget or .25 percent of the country's gross national product could not buy many things. Once an overall pattern was set, alternatives were forgone. This would be a foray, perhaps, not an all-out "war."

But this could occur only in a governmental milieu, which was not ignoring some of the other options, and was sufficiently uncoordinated in its total social welfare policy so that the innovations did not end the old commitments or, indeed, interfere with additional commitments through other programs.

Both before and after the writing of the 1964 act, economists favoring aggregate demand or selective economic measures debated the structuralists. Neither completely dismisses the other, the issue being the degree of optimism or skepticism about the extent to which a booming economy can count on poverty to solve itself.[39] The evidence for a combined strategy seems clear. Economic growth is a "necessary condition" for adequate social policy, but such growth helps only some poor families—not all. Lampman, Levitan, Titmuss,[40] and many others have documented this point well. It was clarified by Joseph A. Kershaw, Director of the Office of Research, Plans, Programs and Evaluation, and Robert A. Levine, Chief of the Research and Plans Division of the Office of Economic Opportunity, in the early years.[41] These authors note that "labor flexibility [through structural approaches] will allow a given demand increase to create more employment

---

[39] Conference on Economic Progress, *op. cit.*; *1964 and 1965 Annual Report of the Council of Economic Advisors*; Ferman, Kornbluh, and Haber, *op. cit.*; Gordon, *op. cit.*; L. E. Gallaway, "The Foundations of the 'War on Poverty,' " *American Economic Review*, 55, No. 1 (1965), 122–131.

[40] Richard A. Titmuss, "Choice and the 'Welfare State,' " Fabian Tract 371 (London: The Fabian Society, 1967). Reprinted in Richard A. Titmuss, *Commitment to Welfare* (New York: Pantheon Books, 1968).

[41] Joseph A. Kershaw and Robert A. Levine, "Poverty, Aggregate Demand, and Economic Structure," *The Journal of Human Resources*, I, No. 1 (Summer, 1966), 67–70.

and less inflation."[42] The planning issue is not one of choice but of *blend* or *mix*—a subject to which we shall return.

The Economic Opportunity Act stressed structural measures, but the country also was already heavily committed to demand management (at least when things slowed down). Guided by the analyses of the Council of Economic Advisors, propelled by the success of the 1965 tax cut, encouraged by an unprecedented period of industrial expansion without recession, supported by a 1965 record in which United States growth excelled that of previously high-performing nations, the country continued a variety of policies which stimulated and supported aggregate demand. The President periodically dramatized the federal government's role, whether it related to influencing the balance of payments, guiding interest rates, or affecting prices. And the argument of success overcame earlier hesitations. It was no longer headline news when President Lyndon Johnson noted in his January, 1966, *Economic Report* that it is a main task of federal economic policy to

> . . . use fiscal and monetary policies to help to match total demand to our growing productive potential, while helping to speed the growth of that potential through education, research and development, manpower policies and enlarged private and public investment. . . .

Similarly, while the 1964 Economic Opportunity Act did not face the fact that available income-transfer programs did not reach at least half of the poor, an Advisory Council on Public Welfare was considering next steps.[43] In fact, the country's overall commitment to amenities (social utilities), case services in at least some realms as a "right"—indeed, to a general strengthening of health, education, and welfare minima—appeared clear.

There was in 1964 and continues to be a commitment to the concept of area redevelopment, although there are contradictory notions about its nature.[44] Thus far, the least controversial steps (highway building) have been taken. We have yet to decide whether we will re-invest in the economies of areas that the market would by-pass or help economically viable spots and permit them to absorb personnel from the less successful hinterlands. Shall we, too, aid large-scale labor migration? At stake is a fundamental question: criteria for economic viability where retraining, credit, and "public goods" will not alone put an area into a competitive stance.

---

[42] *Ibid.*, 69.

[43] Advisory Council on Public Welfare, "*Having the Power, We Have the Duty*" (Washington, D.C.: Government Printing Office, 1966).

[44] Sar A. Levitan, *Federal Aid to Depressed Areas* (Baltimore: The Johns Hopkins Press, 1964).

The subject is too large for adequate coverage here; but, in effect, the unresolved issues about area redevelopment are counterparts of all the strategy alternatives involved in the anti-poverty war. Depressed-area programs do not thus far appear to be an encouraging means to reduce poverty, according to Levitan.[45]

The concept of socially guaranteed minima is not a static one. Automation creates pressure for a more highly-educated labor force. The civil rights revolution demands more equitable access to jobs, housing, education, health services, and opportunities. New technology and knowledge generate their own pressure and demands.

In this context, the country sought to strengthen the provision of basic minima, insure against previously ignored common risks (especially major illness in old age), strengthen public facilities and social utilities, transportation, public recreation areas, child care facilities, and to recapture urban amenity. The services are valuable per se, but they could also be viewed as part of a total investment in human resources expected to do much to break the poverty cycle.[46] One could respond quite differently to the Economic Opportunity Act of 1964 as a strategy if one remembered that other things were also in process. The Congress that passed the Act and rounded it out a year later also enacted:

- ☐ The Elementary and Secondary Education Act of 1965
- ☐ The Appalachian Regional Development Act of 1965
- ☐ The Economic Development Act of 1965
- ☐ The so-called Medicare Amendments to the Social Security Act, 1965
- ☐ The Manpower Act of 1965 (building on manpower legislation launched in 1961)
- ☐ The Heart Disease, Cancer and Stroke Amendments of 1965
- ☐ The Older Americans Act of 1965
- ☐ The 1965 (building on 1962) Social Security Amendments related to work experience and basic adult education
- ☐ The Housing and Urban Development Act of 1965
- ☐ The Community Mental Health Amendments of 1965
- ☐ The Higher Education Act of 1965
- ☐ The Drug Abuse Control Amendments of 1965
- ☐ The Tariff Act of 1964, which provided financial aid in retraining workers affected by the importation of competitive goods.[47]

---

[45] Levitan, *Programs in Aid of the Poor*, 23.

[46] Michael S. March, "Poverty: How Much Will the War Cost?" *The Social Service Review*, XXXIX, No. 2 (June, 1965), 141–156.

[47] Interestingly, it is a report of the United States Conference of Mayors which lists this item among legislative efforts to solve economic and social problems. U.S. Conference

Table 2   ESTIMATED FEDERAL FUNDS FOR PROGRAMS ASSISTING
THE POOR

Fiscal Years 1960–1968

(Administrative Budget and Trust Funds in Billions of Dollars)

Category	1960 (Actual)	1963 (Actual)	1966 (Actual)	1967 (Est'd)	1968 (Est'd)
Education and Training					
HEW—Elem. & Sec. Ed. Act of 1965	—	—	1.0	1.1	1.3
Other	.1	.2	.5	.7	.7
OEO-NYC, Job Corps, CAP, etc.	—	—	.7	.9	1.3
Labor—MDTA, etc.	—	—[a]	.1	.2	.3
Interior	.1	.1	.1	.1	.1
VA	.1	—[a]	—[a]	.1	.1
Subtotal	.3	.3	2.5[b]	3.1	3.8
Health					
HEW—Health Insurance for the Aged and					
Disabled (HI & SMI)	—	—	—[a]	1.4	1.7
Public Assistance Medical Care	.2	.4	.7	1.0	1.2
Other	.2	.3	.6	.7	.8
VA—Hospital and Domiciliary Care	.3	.4	.4	.4	.4
OEO—CAP, etc.	—	—	.1	.1	.1
Subtotal	.7	1.0	1.8	3.6	4.2
Cash Benefit Payments					
HEW—OASDI	4.0	5.3	6.8	6.8	8.5
Public Assistance	1.8	2.3	2.8	2.9	3.0
Railroad Retirement	.3	.3	.3	.3	.4
Labor—Unemployment Benefits	.5	.6	.4	.4	.4
VA—Compensation and Pensions	1.6	2.0	2.3	2.4	2.4
Subtotal	8.3	10.4	12.7	12.8	14.6

[a] Less than $50 million.
[b] Figures may not add because of rounding.
Source: Executive Office of the President, Bureau of the Budget, January 19, 1967.

The combination of programs in the field of basic education, manpower development, elementary and secondary education, preschool education, counseling, retraining, placement, and work experience begins to address a large category of additional needs and problems shared by many Americans but also vitally affecting the poverty group.

In fact, the executive branch itself emphasized that OEO programs were only part of the anti-poverty effort when, from 1964, it issued somewhat forced budget estimates of total costs of programs for "the poor" (*Table 2*).

of Mayors, *Economic Opportunity in Cities* (Washington, D.C.: U.S. Conference of Mayors, 1966), 5.

Table 2   ESTIMATED FEDERAL FUNDS FOR PROGRAMS ASSISTING
THE POOR (cont.)

Fiscal Years 1960–1968

(Administrative Budget and Trust Funds in Billions of Dollars)

Category	1960 (Actual)	1963 (Actual)	1966 (Actual)	1967 (Est'd)	1968 (Est'd)
Services, Economic and Community Development, etc.					
Agriculture—Food Programs	.2	.3	.4	.4	.5
Other	.2	.3	.5	.3	.2
Commerce—EDA and Appalachia	—	.1	.2	.3	.2
OEO—CAP and other	—	—	.6	.6	.6
HEW—VRA, WA, etc.	—ᵃ	.1	.1	.1	.1
HUD—Public Housing & Rent Supplements	.1	.1	.1	.2	.2
Urban Renewal and other	.1	—ᵃ	.3	.3	.8
Interior—Services to Indians, etc.	.1	.2	.2	.2	.3
Labor—Employment, Youth, and other services	—ᵃ	.1	.1	.2	.1
SBA (Econ. Opp. Loans)	—	—	—	—	—
Subtotal	.7	1.2	2.6	2.5	3.1
Totals: Administrative budget	5.1	6.8	11.8	13.0	14.6
Trust funds	4.9	6.2	7.7	9.1	11.1
GRAND TOTAL	9.9	13.0	19.6	22.0	25.6

ᵃ Less than $50 million.
ᵇ Figures may not add because of rounding.
Source: Executive Office of the President, Bureau of the Budget, January 19, 1967.

As the Economic Opportunity Act programs were implemented in 1965, 1966, and 1967, particularly those in manpower, early childhood education, and health, it became apparent that, despite a rationale—and perhaps even a justification—in terms of the need to reach citizens previously ignored or by-passed by inaccessible or inappropriate service, EOA programs overlapped and were potentially or actually competitive with other Great Society efforts. Because of significant problems of coverage and quality, the issue might be deferred for a while. Competition might stimulate some of the older efforts to new levels of service. Nonetheless, the need for planning and coordination of the anti-poverty efforts with the others would have to be faced seriously. The EOA made what proved to be a feeble beginning. It provided for an Economic Opportunity Council of top federal officials and for a National Advisory Council of citizens. Two types of "preference" were specified to assure coordination: The OEO director would favor projects which were components of an approved community-action program; heads of other federal agencies granting assistance under poverty-related programs not covered by EOA would also give priority to such projects. Yet, as experience proved, these were all permissive provisions and did not resolve questions of prerogative, scope, leadership. Nor did they overcome the fact that local community-action agencies had no comprehensive planning mandate.[48]

ANTI-POVERTY PROGRAMS IN ACTION

The programs began with a burst of enthusiasm and ambiguity. If there were to be expanded social services—and this, after all, was the clearest mandate—it was necessary either to use existing organizations and agencies or to create administrative structures, hire space, and recruit staff. Or one could contract to have these steps taken. Federally operated components, particularly the Job Corps and VISTA, proceeded to create operating vehicles and to contract for service. The majority of the effort, however, was to be locally designed and based: here OEO invented the concept of a local community-action agency (CAA) as the means for planning and implementing anti-poverty programs, "community action," at the local level (CAP). Approximately three-quarters of these agencies were sponsored by private, nonprofit groups (almost all of them newly established for the purpose), and one-quarter were governmental in the first year. As the anti-poverty program evolved, these new organizational devices, bearing some relationship to the "special districts" tradition in American government, were to prove as important to the anti-poverty effort as the substantive social service programs per se.[49]

The early months were particularly difficult. The OEO was to operate, to plan, to fund, and to coordinate. It was to deal with local governments and states, with neighborhood groups, and with projects. And it operated under an annual appropriation system requiring rapid allocation and quick claims of success. For present purposes, the "blow-by-blow" description of how a program was eventually "fielded" is not relevant except to note the inherent

[48] These provisions and their limitations are carefully reviewed in Advisory Commission on Intergovernmental Relations, *Intergovernmental Relations in the Poverty Program* (Washington, D.C.: Government Printing Office, 1966), especially Chap. III.

[49] R. Sargent Shriver, before the House Committee on Education and Labor, April 12, 1965, as reported in Committee on Education and Welfare, House of Representatives, *Examination of the War on Poverty*, Report of Hearings, April 12, 13, 14, 15, 29, 30, 1965 (Washington, D.C., 1965), 600. Along similar lines, see Office of Economic Opportunity, *The First Step on a Long Journey*, Congressional Presentation, April, 1965 (Washington, D.C.: Government Printing Office, 1965), 2 volumes. Also, *Intergovernmental Relations in the Poverty Program*, Chap. III and 163.

obstacles to programming when a problem-focused effort is assigned, at least in part, outside the normal departmental structures and to a new office of uncertain future. Excitement and attention win enthusiastic adherence, competent new staff, and creativity; ambiguity, rivalry, and lack of lead time wipe out some of the advantages.

Testifying before a Senate subcommittee, Sargent Shriver gave the following quantitative summary of OEO claims:

This up-to-date summary reveals that in our first 21 months, OEO has:

—created nearly a thousand community action agencies in urban and rural areas where 70 percent of the nation's poor live.

—involved 8 million poor through their direct participation in our programs.

—provided work and training opportunities for over 600,000 poor in 1966, with 365,000 in Neighborhood Youth Corps alone.

—established 160 legal services projects in cities and villages, on Indian reservations, and in migrant camps. These legal service programs are now available to 700,000 poor families. 37 of the 50 largest cities have received OEO Legal Services grants.

—established Head Start, the first national child development program, reaching over half-a-million poor children and their families in each of the past two summers, and another 200,000 during the regular school year.

—recruited the largest army of part- and full-time volunteer Americans in peacetime history. In Head Start alone, more than 100,000 people have donated time and talent.

—recruited, trained and put to work more than 3,000 VISTA Volunteers.

—created 600 neighborhood social service centers, of which 360 are urban multi-purpose centers where a range of services is available and readily accessible to meet the total needs of the poor.

—opened 107 Job Corps Centers in which more than 27,000 young men and women are receiving training for productive careers.

—put college within the reach of more than 20,000 disadvantaged teenagers through Upward Bound programs in 244 colleges, universities and secondary schools.

—established neighborhood health service centers in Denver, Boston, New York, Chicago and Los Angeles, and received requests for 75 more.

—helped 4 million older Americans avail themselves of Medicare benefits through Operation Medicare Alert.

—brought adult literacy courses to 300,000 adults.

—created new careers for over 50,000 of the poor who are now working as health aides, legal aides, neighborhood block workers, teachers' aides, recreation assistants, and others.[50]

---

[50] Hearings, United States Senate, *Federal Role in Urban Affairs*, Part 2, 401. Participa-

It will be some time before the OEO as a whole is evaluated comprehensively—if it ever is.[51] None of the components could achieve its optimum effects in a few years. Nobody knew, by 1967, whether it had conquered any poverty at all. The most optimistic claimed that from 5 to 15 percent of "the poor" were "reached," a very vague term. There is reason to doubt that any rigorous evaluation will ever be possible: one could not control the influences of other components of governmental intervention, ranging from monetary and fiscal policy to Title I of the Education Act of 1965; the early years were so characterized by lack of program standardization between places and by the need for trial and error and for training that it would be difficult to know what was being measured; from the very beginning, people of conflicting value stances held out diverse goals for the program (from decreasing the numbers in poverty at a given moment to breaking the "cycle," to getting "power" to the poor, to weakening the alleged monopoly of the voluntary social welfare sector, to promoting social conflict, to "cooling" the urban ghettos); the financial investment was so small in relation to the problems addressed that the specific impact of the EOA stimulus would be difficult to isolate; from the beginning, the partisan nature of the appraisals and efforts at reform made it difficult to separate the claim from the reality or to expect complete candor from any source.

Yet, a reading of Congressional hearings and reports, including those of the minority party, analysis of subsequent amendments and of OEO policy and program changes and innovations, review of reports by the Chamber of Commerce, the Conference of Mayors, and independent scholars, and analysis of press reports will permit a general overview of what occurred up to the time of the 1967 legislation—of programs conducted, processes launched, and responses generated.[52]

---

tion totals increased substantially in several programs late in 1967. Details are reported in *Report of the Committee on Labor and Public Welfare, United States Senate, on S2388, Economic Opportunity Amendments of 1967* (Washington, D.C.: Government Printing Office, 1967).

[51] The most comprehensive effort at the time of the preparation of this chapter was reported in the many-volume *Examination of the War on Poverty*, Hearings Before the Subcommittee on Employment, Manpower and Poverty, Committee on Labor and Public Welfare, United States Senate (Washington, D.C.: Government Printing Office, 1967). Chaired by Senator Joseph S. Clark of Pennsylvania, the Committee commissioned and published a large number of studies and consultant reports which are included in this 22-volume series.

[52] Hearings, United States Senate, *Federal Role in Urban Affairs*, Parts 1–7; *Examination of the War on Poverty* (House of Representatives); Levitan, "The Design of Federal Antipoverty Strategy"; Marris and Rein, *op. cit.*; United States Conference of Mayors, *Economic Opportunity in Cities* (Washington, D.C., 1966); United States Chamber of

Program components

Job Corps. The residential job training program for boys and girls from sixteen to twenty-one years of age was serving over 38,000 late in 1967 and had a cumulative total of 125,000 by that time. There were over 120 urban and conservation centers.[53] The Job Corps started slowly, was plagued by difficulties arising from misconduct of some trainees in areas near the centers, and by per capita costs so high as to create a Congressional revolt and cuts. Some of the specific programs were excellent, others failures. Few seemed able to hold trainees long enough for them to be trained. Some of the training was useless or meaningless. There were complaints that private enterprise, which contracted to operate many of the programs, profitted excessively. It was difficult to get data on which to balance appraisal of outcomes, particularly since participants were in a high-risk category. The approximately one-third of participants who remained long enough did seem to be aided. The most comprehensive reviews suggested that, for all the rhetoric, OEO had not clarified the relative emphases among counseling, job orientation, skill training, and placement in all the job programs. In the long run, to be effective, Job Corps and Neighborhood Youth Corps would need to be interrelated with a variety of Department of Labor manpower programs.[54]

Neighborhood Youth Corps. By late 1967, the Neighborhood Youth Corps had 139,000 youths enrolled in in-school programs and 80,000 out-of-school youngsters among its participants. The summer total was 300,000. This, too, was a training program for the sixteen-to-twenty-one-year-olds but

---

Commerce, *The Concept of Poverty* and *Poverty: The Sick, Disabled and Aged* (Washington, D.C., 1966); *Congressional Record*, 1964, 1965, 1966, 1967 sessions; *Examination of the War on Poverty* (Senate); *Economic Opportunity Act Amendments of 1967*, Hearings Before the Committee on Education and Labor, House of Representatives (Washington, D.C.: Government Printing Office, 1967), 2 parts. Published since this appraisal are Levitan, *The Great Society's Poor Law*, and Daniel P. Moynihan, *Maximum Feasible Misunderstanding* (New York: The Free Press, 1969).

[53] Given the variety of ways of counting and inconsistency among reports, all statistics in this section are only approximations.

[54] See Sar A. Levitan, "Work and Training for Economic Independence," *Poverty and Human Resources Abstracts*, July–August, 1967.

Considerable data and study reports are summarized in *Economic Opportunity Act Amendments of 1967*, Part 1.

Consultant reports on the Job Corps, Neighborhood Youth Corps, and the anti-poverty work-experience programs, as submitted to the Senate's Subcommittee on Employment, Manpower, and Poverty by Sar A. Levitan and Harold L. Sheppard appear in *Examination of the War on Poverty*, Staff and Consultants Reports, I. Also see, *Youth and the War on Poverty* (Washington, D.C.: The Chamber of Commerce of the United States, 1967).

it was nonresident, combining some education and public employment. Where possible, trainees were to remain in school or return to school. Particularly at the beginning, there was apparently excessive nepotism, and ineligible (non-poverty) enrollees took up summer program space; but the general response was positive.

It was alleged by some observers that proportionately few Youth Corps enrollees were given meaningful work and training. Others cited "case" successes. One evaluator suggested that part of the enthusiasm for the Corps derived from the belief that the money prevented riots in urban ghettos. Clearly, the program was a way to give young people money, while they remained in an "aging vat." Of course, OEO goals and claims were more expansive.[55] While there were many positive case stories, one could not evaluate this in terms of long-term employment effects; research reports were in conflict. Perhaps the most useful actual outcome of the program, a basis for government to serve as "employer of last resort" on a limited scale, could not be claimed publicly.[56] In 1966, the effort was transferred to the Department of Labor in the expectation that the move would improve training aspects.

Adult basic education.   Expected to develop through assistance to state and local educational authorities via the United States Office of Education, this program began very slowly and achieved little volume. It was repealed in 1966, but a similar program was added to the Elementary and Secondary Education Act, and some local community-action agencies received OEO funding for adult basic education under general authorization. Increasingly the view prevailed that such programs should be in the context of general manpower efforts.

Work training programs.   In the 1964 Act, a Work Experience and Training Program was the only anti-poverty program element actually assigned to another agency (Health, Education, and Welfare) by OEO for administration, as contrasted to delegation. Building on earlier community work and training efforts in public welfare, the new program enrolled over 53,700 people in mid-1967, over 77,000 having previously gone through the courses. Participants were welfare recipients or those close to dependency. The 1966 EOA amendments introduced the Labor Department into the administration of the efforts, but there had been little more than token action in this direction by the time of the 1967 Congressional reviews. For the

---

[55] Levitan, in *Examination of the War on Poverty.* Also, his "The Neighborhood Youth Corps: Help or Handout?" *American Child,* 49, No. 2 (Spring, 1967), entire issue.

[56] Levitan, "The Neighborhood Youth Corps."

most part the programs were welfare department–conducted, unrelated to other local manpower programs, and thus did not constitute a significant contribution to employability, despite sound recruitment and the mounting of some good individual programs.

The Community Employment and Training Program was added in 1965 to offer employment and training to chronically unemployed poor and to undertake community improvements. About 8,000 jobs were authorized in fiscal 1967, OEO having delegated responsibility for operations to the Labor Department after the early months. There was evidence of both effectiveness and a need for expansion.

A third component, the New Careers program, enacted in 1966, focused on offering entry-level employment opportunities in subprofessional positions (health aides, teachers' aides, public safety assistants, etc.). Over 9,000 positions were authorized for 1967.

Parallel to all of the above, the Labor Department began, in 1967, a Concerted Employment Program to concentrate on problems in inner-city slums and centers of rural poverty. Utilizing pooled funds from other programs, the CEP attempted a many-faceted, comprehensive effort. It had, by mid-1967, been launched in 19 cities and two rural areas.

Noting, in addition, the several employment programs under local community-action programs, the constantly-developing efforts under Labor as authorized by the Manpower Development and Training Act of 1962, and the activities of the United States Employment Service, a Senate subcommittee stressed the fragmentation of federal manpower programs. The subcommittee found a need to see the next phase of anti-poverty manpower efforts in the context of an overall federal effort especially focused on coordination at the local community level. The subcommittee recommended interim steps, but its conclusion is especially relevant to our analysis: "To achieve this objective completely goes beyond the scope of the Economic Opportunity Act. . . ."[57]

Head Start.   By far the most popular of the service programs, Head Start was designed to help deprived youngsters make up the deficiencies, which handicap them as they enter school and are never subsequently overcome. Conceived in child development terms, it was to unite early childhood education with health services, social service help to families, parent involvement, and local community organization. Few programs even *approximated* the model; the difficulties of staffing and finding space were enormous; program quality was often suspect; formal research evaluations were mixed.

---

[57] *Report . . . on S2388,* 28.

Nonetheless, many children were eventually enrolled. There were 200,000 year-round slots and a larger summer effort (over 400,000). Some of the children seemed to carry over the results into kindergarten and first grade; medical-dental-developmental defects were uncovered in the screenings. Many parents became involved. The program was specific, reasonable, and popular. After two years, it was clear that some form of preschool program backed by federal funds would be expected in the future on the American scene. Some small "ripple effects" in the "regular" schools became visible. In many cities without publicly-supported kindergartens, it became necessary to face the consequences of a preschool program that led nowhere. Everywhere, the problem of the relationship between Head Start, day care, kindergarten, and programs funded under Title I of the 1965 Education Act became urgent. A federal Follow-Through program was projected in 1967. Clearly, Head Start was a "change agent."

Rural and small business loans. Reports were few, but the approach was familiar and acceptable. Particularly in several urban ghettos, good use seemed to be made of these modest "venture capital" funds, when commercial sources were not available. There was perhaps some lack of clarity as to whether, and to what degree, social service, rather than business, criteria were to govern—both in the selection of the eligible and in the terms of the loans. By 1967, the annual rate was over 16,000 agricultural loans.

Local social service programs and contracts. Local community-action agencies housed Head Start, Neighborhood Youth Corps, and a variety of job counseling and referral programs, particularly for adolescents. In multi-service centers, which they operated, or through contract arrangements with both voluntary and public agencies, they offered casework, child welfare services, special programs for the aged; but job training and counseling were central. There was a community organization component and a new pattern for employing the "uncredentialed" (*see below*). By 1967, there were multi-service centers or referral units at over 700 locations in 300 communities, yet surprisingly little was known about programs, staffing, service rendered, or standards. Clearly, some more services were being made available and decentralization had become possible; but data about effectiveness, efficiency, innovation, and user satisfaction were mixed. To a considerable extent, center limitations were traceable to a conflict as to whether the centers housing local programs were to be judged in terms of service output, development of local leadership, or employment of poor people.[58] Some of

---

[58] Kirschner Associates, "A Description and Evaluation of Neighborhood Centers, A Report for the Office of Economic Opportunity" (Albuquerque, N.M., 1966, mime-

the contracts with existing agencies seemed to expand services to the very poor; others served to finance, but not change, the existing network.

Of special interest to social welfare personnel was the manner in which many service centers, in their eagerness to serve as bridges to elements of the population previously ignored, rejected, or not reached by social service programs, began to develop new social service liaison roles. Professionally trained social workers, preprofessional case aides, and locally recruited "indigenous" social work aides implemented the Act's charge to mesh the several types of services that a case might require. Often frustrated by case loss in the referral process and by promised service which was not delivered, these workers became "advocates" of their clients, following through and sometimes pressing other agencies ("case advocates," "urban agents," etc.).

Here several ways branched off. In some places, the frustrations in seeking service were so great that Community Action Agencies began to operate more of their own specialized programs. In others, they brought legal services to bear, helping clients vis-à-vis welfare, school, or housing agencies. In still others, it seemed most urgent to develop community pressure to change an unresponsive agency or to organize community groups. Groups of neighborhood people who shared common interests as welfare recipients or as parents of children in a given school were helped to come together and to make representation to those in charge.[59]

Inevitably, each approach created some opposition and fresh problems, too. If CAA's developed services, they were in competition with public and private agencies, which had experience, some power, standing, and often greater competence. Their legal activities threatened officials and staff, who preferred a consensus approach and were shocked at the charge that some clients were unfairly treated and that legal rights had been undermined. Where social action was launched, there were complaints that public monies were being used to "fight City Hall" and to create political opposition. It was also alleged that poor people's needs for service were being ignored or frustrated so that they might be recruited for social action.

In retrospect, while all these complaints were true in some places, the most valid general charge would appear to be that *the investment purchased*

---

ographed). Other major sources are Robert Perlman and David Jones, *Neighborhood Service Centers* (Washington, D.C.: Government Printing Office, 1967); and Bertram M. Beck *et al.*, "Neighborhood Service Centers: A Study and Recommendations," in *Examination of the War on Poverty* (Senate), Staff and Consultant Reports, III, 733–786.

[59] For some of the patterns, see Frances Piven, "Participation of Residents in Neighborhood Community Action Programs," *Social Work*, 11, No. 1 (January, 1966), 73–80.

relatively little direct personal service or even accountability. Local agencies were constantly planning, recruiting, or training; yet the sum total of information, diagnostic service, counseling, placement, day care, recreation, or homemaking produced was quite modest. Some attributed this to the limited technical skills and experience of the new local leadership, others to the effort to combine service and social action.[60] Perhaps the most significant results were achieved in the service-starved small towns and rural areas where Office of Economic Opportunity social services, in many ways quite traditional, undertook what private philanthropy and public funds had long before given to the cities.

This experience confirmed the need to coordinate social services at the local level, to decentralize, and to provide for the advocacy and accountability functions. It did not clarify who could do what. Choices were yet to be faced locally on the interrelationships of OEO-funded social services, welfare-funded social services, the expanding community mental health and retardation programs, the opportunities for social service opened up by the neighborhood facilities plans in the urban renewal and Model Cities programs of the Department of Housing and Urban Development, the possible social service projects arising out of the Department of Commerce's Economic Development Act, as well as several new remedial employment and placement programs.

The issue of whether a social action–committed, community-action agency or center was actually a good locus for social service delivery was gradually "discovered," but scarcely resolved. It was well into 1967 before one heard public proposals that the two functions, service and community action, might perhaps have quite separate local outlets. A group of outside consultants concluded that, in fact, the objective of legitimating the power of the poor would be subverted either by overall preoccupation with organizing services per se or by efforts to attain extraneously-defined political goals.[61]

Employing "indigenous personnel." No program was spelled out in these terms in the original Act; yet, as indicated above, several relevant projects were launched in 1965 and 1966. Within the Office of Economic Opportunity, there was early adoption of the idea of "new careers" in the social services as a consequence of efforts to involve the poor, to make programs locally relevant, to increase communication with the deprived, and to face

---

[60] "The evidence indicates that it is extremely rare to find both aggressive community action and well-executed service programs within the same center." Kirschner Associates, *op. cit.,* 22.

[61] Kirschner Associates, *op. cit.,* 55.

staffing problems arising from shortage of professional personnel. Related to this concept was the view that the development of the economy permitted and required new emphasis on employment in the personal service sector—and that openings for the poorly educated would be considerable if tasks were analyzed and subdivided. Qualitatively, results were mixed, yet most observers agreed that an important movement had been given necessary support.[62]

VISTA. The Volunteers in Service to America, a domestic version of the Peace Corps, needed time to clarify its mission and to develop procedures for selection, training, placement, and administrative control. There were troublesome incidents and obvious blunders. Nonetheless, the program was soon stabilized, at about 4,000 volunteers, and accepted as useful.

Health centers and other special demonstrations. By the second year, the flexibility allowed by the community-action titles of the Act also permitted either direct funding—or funding through local community-action agencies—of a variety of service innovations. There were special "prep" schools in ghettos, unusual job programs, family planning, many special projects— some of questionable value and others likely to affect existing structures or to create new service models. Several were standardized and given OEO names. By 1966, following direct OEO initiative, a program of neighborhood health centers for the poor was setting the pace and having obvious catalytic impact where traditional public health had not yet entered and Medicaid had had little impact. Yet the coordination of health programs had become an issue—especially after the passage by Congress of legislation in 1966 (P.L. 89–749) facilitating and mandating state level planning and integration of the vast array of federally-funded health efforts.

Neighborhood legal services. To all except the die-hard opponents of anti-poverty efforts and some conservative bar groups, this was one of the great "successes" from the beginning—even though initial coverage was extremely limited. Local community-action groups followed the leads of two or three pioneering programs[63] in using the institutions of the law to protect and affirm the rights of poor people, particularly in their dealing with administrative agencies and service departments. Whereas legal aid for the poor usually was limited to defense in criminal cases, the new services could be employed to win for the poor privileges once available only to the more affluent (to sue for divorce, for example). Once problems relating to the

---

[62] See page 276.

[63] Department of Health, Education, and Welfare, *Proceedings of Conference on Extension of Legal Services to the Poor* (Washington, D.C.: Government Printing Office, 1964).

legalities of "group practice" and alleged "advertising" were solved, the programs were able to attract competent legal talent and law school volunteers. The service was popular in the neighborhoods. By mid-1967, over 155 local projects, working out of 700 locations and spending $30 million, employed 100 full-time attorneys and had reached 200,000 cases in a nine-month period. All but felony trial work and the kinds of cases that private attorneys take for a fixed share of potential monetary awards were included in the loads. A privately-funded National Office for the Rights of the Indigent became an informal center of coordination and leadership, loosely related to the civil rights Legal Defense and Education Fund. Research and consultation were also provided by centers at two universities.

Migrant program. This small, OEO-operated effort reached fewer than 2 percent of the migrant farm group as it achieved its peak in 1967. Housing, adult education, and day care efforts were included, and reports from observers were positive. By 1967, noting that much of United States poverty was rural, efforts were under way to launch a substantial rural anti-poverty effort, well beyond the original Economic Opportunity Act conception.

Scale. The length of the listing and obvious creativity of some of the program components tend to blur any appraisal. The reality remained: the OEO budget was well below the poverty "gap"; the total number of people served was a small percentage of the statistically-counted poor. Two observers reported the following after the Detroit riots during the summer of 1967:

> Despite record employment, the Michigan State Employment Service estimated 56,000 seeking jobs, 11,000 of them long-term unemployed, and 70,00 out of the labor force entirely—the "hidden unemployed." Unemployment among Negroes in the slum areas was twelve per cent. Yet at the same time, only 1,400 persons, white and nonwhite, were enrolled in MDTS [Manpower Development Training System] projects in the entire metropolitan area. The Neighborhood Youth Corps had a total of 3,500 enrolled. The Work Experience and Training program had enrolled 1,700 persons. Only 340 Detroit boys were recruited for the Job Corps in fiscal 1967.[64]

Community action

By an Office of Economic Opportunity decision, local planning and program administration were assigned to a new entity called a Community Action Agency. It had a free hand to invent ways to abolish poverty. This vehicle, influenced by community development experience abroad, the

---

[64] Sar A. Levitan and Garth L. Mangum, "Programs and Priorities," *The Reporter,* September 7, 1967, 21.

Ford Foundation "grey area" programs in education, and the projects funded by the President's Committee on Delinquency and Youth Crime, was the major innovation of the anti-poverty effort and, as such, requires more detailed discussion than accorded other elements.

No one could predict exactly what would occur. Goals were broadly stated, the rhetoric was considerable, and much initiative seemed possible. However, governmental and bureaucratic realities being what they are, the sums allocated had to be spent rapidly while the hard questions of implementation were faced. Although there may be debate about how to abolish poverty, the effects of local expenditure are readily visible. Small wonder, then, that during the first two years most communities took their cues from OEO about community-action projects.

> They are designed to coordinate the fight against illiteracy, unemployment, poor health and poor housing. They aid the migrant farm workers and Indians on reservations. . . . are focusing on early childhood development, remedial education, literacy courses, job development and training, day care, homemaker services, community organization, legal aid to the poor and health services.[65]

In short, with significant exceptions, Community Action Programs would do more of what was done under other titles of the Act, but with freedom to design service-delivery modes, priorities, and program focus in accord with local preference. Many of the service programs already described constituted the major CAA vehicles: Head Start, Neighborhood Youth Corps, multi-service centers, etc. This was essentially a social service effort—in the broad sense of the term.

In fact, despite high-sounding phrases about the "roots" of poverty and its "elimination," the community of the Community Action Program was seldom of a character, size, or potency appropriate or adequate, in the era of industrialized megalopolis, to eradicate poverty. Few community-action programs could affect industrial development or consumer demand sufficiently to assure jobs for their people, and none could offer transfer payments or other funds in sufficient sums over long enough periods of time for those unable to work.

The CAP was controversial, even in its service role, from the start. The Act permitted funding of separate demonstration projects, but seemed to accord priority to coordinated efforts developed through city-wide Community Action Agencies (CAA)—which might, in a large city, have neighborhood boards in poverty areas. Coordination made sense to the drafters, since one of their goals was to end fragmentation and lack of service in-

---

[65] Office of Economic Opportunity, *The First Step on a Long Journey*, I, 48.

tegration. Preference was to be given to applicants who combined many "components" in a program, according to the director's early statements.

Since there were often struggles for control of the local Community Action Programs, there was no unanimity in this view. In effect, a closed-out project, professional group, voluntary sector, ethnic bloc, or political faction could raise the slogan of "avoiding monolithic local CAP's" to assure innovation and creativity. Office of Economic Opportunity directives and Congressional sentiment did not follow a consistent line either, each year's "climate" affecting specific amendments. Some flexibility was sought by making it possible for a neighborhood to qualify as a "community" for community-action purposes, whereas the original legislation had specified a state, metropolitan area, county, city, town—or several such units in combination. Most early CAP's were coterminous with city (19 percent), county (58 percent), or multi-county (21 percent) boundaries.[66] Nonetheless, the long-term processes of bureaucratization, central control, and uniformity were evident quite early. A problem-oriented strategy has a limited amount of innovative venture capital and scant mandate for creativity. Then the issue arises as to whether one wishes to preserve the separatism, and how this may be protected so as to prolong a change process —or whether the time has not come to coordinate and reassign the program elements. For Office of Economic Opportunity programs, the debate was well under way early in 1967. Local Community Action Agencies seldom were effective instruments for local coordination and were often seen as "one more piece of local structure" to be coordinated.[67]

The issue of local freedom or "coordinating" control had another dimension: the balance between federal and local decision-making. In some ways the program was liberating for cities. At the beginning particularly they dealt directly with Washington, with only token state intervention. Later, after protests, a state and regional structure was implemented, but the contrast with more traditional structures was considerable. This did not resolve many issues, however, chief among them the question of whether Community Action Agencies should have relatively broad block grants, in the context of which they would make specific project decisions, or whether Washington should review detailed program elements. Who, in short, was really to do the planning and programming?

Washington had most of the new money, but local matching was required. As a practical matter, it would have required a far larger bureaucracy than Office of Economic Opportunity had to process many detailed projects

---

[66] Advisory Commission on Intergovernmental Relations, *op. cit.*, 43.

[67] For example, *ibid.*, 161.

quickly. For a period, tight controls were attempted with disastrous consequences: everywhere agencies waited too long for decisions, staffs resigned,
momentum was lost. The outcome was a compromise. Increasingly large
portions of the funding were for federally operated or specified elements
assigned out of OEO ("national emphasis" programs). Head Start was the
prime example. At the same time, those block funds that went to local
Community Action Agencies had fewer federal strings attached (although
the local bindings seemed often to grow simultaneously). The Office of
Economic Opportunity effort did not resolve the tensions in American
federalism, but it did dramatize that the issues of central and local prerogative are unavoidable as each new social policy thrust is launched.

The full measure of the experience becomes apparent only as we turn
next to the "community organization" or social action aspects of community
action. What, then, of the much-quoted phrases indicating that, to be approved, a Community Action Program must be "developed, conducted
and administered with the maximum feasible participation of residents of
the areas and members of the groups served. . . ?"

Much energy was invested in disputes about membership on local anti-
poverty boards and criticism of the actions of such boards. For a period,
Office of Economic Opportunity guidelines were vague and inconsistent.
Publicity and an OEO stance for "one-third public, one-third private, and
one-third poor" gradually had impact. While great variation persisted, big
cities achieved an average of one-third from target areas on their boards,
but a debate about an economic means test as a qualification persisted. The
1966 amendments required that one-third of boards be "poor," selected by
"the poor." Of the poor on boards, they were variously elected and selected
in a two-to-one ratio by early 1966. For the most part, too, Negroes formed
a larger proportion of board membership, either as public members or as
"the poor," than they constituted a proportion of poverty populations.
They also constituted considerably higher proportions of CAP staffs than
they did of the population in most of the areas served.[68] The justification
for this resides in the very high poverty rate among non-whites. The facts
do hint at a problem nonetheless: in a significant number of sections of the
country, especially in the South, the anti-poverty effort was seen as a program for Negroes. Negro community members faced the dilemma of recognizing the advantage of universalism and yet not wanting to deprive their
fellows of needed service. In some places, civil rights militants saw Community Action Agencies in their social action roles as legitimate and effec-

---

[68] "Summary Report of the Investigative Task Force of the Ad Hoc Subcommittee on
the War on Poverty Program," *Federal Role in Urban Affairs*, Part 6, 1312–1315.

tive outlets to combat Negro "powerlessness"—thus reinforcing the notion that it was largely a program for them. By 1967, widespread interest in locally controlled "black institutions" and "black power" had redefined the development as a positive one for many participants and observers.

The organization, pressure, local conflicts, and activity surrounding selection of boards for local community-action agencies dramatized the several conflicting interpretations of "community action" and launched a debate as to whether this was what the Congress had intended.

A search of the record certainly justifies the conclusion that the legislative purpose was far from clear. Most of the evidence suggests a democratic and socio-therapeutic intent, much like that in traditional community organization and community development: if people help design services, their needs will have increased attention, and the very act of participation will increase their competence as members of the community. Under such circumstances, programs which are developed are more likely to be utilized and to be effective.

As indicated, to a small minority, from the very beginning, and to a somewhat larger group subsequently, there was in the notion of "maximum feasible participation" an additional concept. Richard Cloward commented,

> The antipoverty program, precisely because of its mandate to "involve the poor," can help to bring about the political preconditions for major economic changes: but this can happen only if the forms of involvement lead to new bases of organized power for low-income people. Economic deprivation is fundamentally a political problem and power will be required to solve it. . . .
>
> The possibility that the antipoverty program can contribute to the growth of low-income power lies in delivering to the poor and their leaders control over the programs and funds to be funneled into their slums and ghetto communities.[69]

Favoring "evolutionary development of social reforms," a settlement leader argued for "consensus" rather than "class warfare." Two social-policy analysts observed that a "political action" rather than a "socio-therapeutic" concept of a CAP required sacrifice of the broad coalition upon which the anti-poverty effort was founded locally and nationally. Rational planning cannot proceed without such consensus.[70]

In a significant number—*but a minority*—of situations locally organized community-action groups developed considerable political consciousness,

---

[69] Cloward, *op. cit.*

[70] Margaret Berry, Letter to the Editor, *Social Work*, 10, No. 1, (January, 1965), 106; Marris and Rein. *ob. cit.*

wrested control of the local apparatus for themselves, and used their new-found power politically. Yet, despite publicity and debate, these remained obvious exceptions. The long-term trend was for the bureaucratization and absorption of the Community Action Programs into the governmental system. As summarized by Cloward and a colleague subsequently:

> . . . we see no evidence that involvement of the poor by government will generate a force for social change by nurturing the political capabilities of the poor. Rather governmental programs for the poor are likely to diminish whatever political vitality the poor still exhibit. . . . Further prospects for so-cial change will be increasingly shaped not by low income influence but by the expansionist forces of public bureaucracies. . . . If the emerging . . . programs successfully impart competitive skills, the bureaucracies pursuing their own enhancement may thereby succeed in raising low income people into the middle class. In this way the clients of the bureaucracies can, one by one, join the middle class political majority, and government involve-ment can indeed be said to have increased their political influence. . . .[71]

To which one must comment with Seymour Martin Lipset, that a coun-try which does not have rigid status groups, has never nurtured a working-class party, and in which the impoverished continue to build their personal perspectives on premises of social mobility cannot expect an anti-poverty war to have other consequences, even if some early enthusiasts based them-selves on the premise that the poor were a homogeneous, unified, rigid caste —and knew it.[72]

Nonetheless, Community Action Programs generated more than thera-peutic and educational results and did start processes of sufficient potency to be labeled as "institutional change." Local action and protest launched in Community Action Agencies did revise departmental and governmental administrative procedures and policies and affected state legislation. The Neighborhood Legal Services were almost as potent, as long-ignored con-stitutional rights of the disadvantaged were asserted and created spiraling effects on governmental agencies, particularly influencing welfare investiga-tion and the processing of public housing applications. Similarly, Operation Head Start seemed to generate a wave-effect, which would alter public

---

[71] Richard A. Cloward and Frances Fox Piven, "The Professional Bureaucracies: Benefit Systems as Influence Systems," in Murray Silberman, Editor, The Role of Government in Promoting Social Change (New York: Columbia University School of Social Work, 1965).

[72] Seymour Martin Lipset, The First New Nation (New York: Basic Books, 1963), 290. The Poor Peoples' Campaign of mid-1968 was of course an activity of the civil rights movement. The welfare mothers who joined had narrow goals. The support from across the political spectrum saw the enterprise as a way to help the poor individually, not to unify or solidify the status.

school programs, both in its substantive impact and in legitimating parent involvement in schools.

Participants in protest and social action activities were clearly a small minority of "the poor" and the most advantaged of the group, at that.[73] When they became truly militant, it was under the leadership of leaders trained before or outside of the poverty program. Mass protestors and demonstrators were unified, not by identification with poverty status, but by shared interests in housing, welfare, or civil rights. Lessons were learned in the experience by some of the deprived, however, particularly in large cities: Community Action Programs in several places achieved a scale of indigenous organization and a degree of militancy not predictable a decade earlier. Clearly, one could not ignore the institutional innovation and change impacts of some of Community Action Programs, while noting that these gains were modest, limited in area, and that the major thrust was toward treatment-remotivation-socialization-education-relocation of the individual poor person.

To some people, the limited institutional-change potential of the Community Action Program is no defect at all. They ask whether the very premises involved in assigning special prerogatives to "the poor" in the control of neighborhood programs are not questionable, since this is a device allegedly seeking "democratic control" by removing a program from the normal political process. They inquire: could the many devices for electing or designating representatives of the poor actually succeed? Should not one have expected the less-than-token turnouts for elections of "representatives" of "the poor?" Furthermore, is a reverse economic "means test" (i.e., only the poor may vote) desirable for local community participation? Is it not a bit of neo-Marxist romanticism that would create a variation of Greek democracy applying only to the poor of the nineteen-sixties and expect special wisdom to emerge? Should elected officials actually be excluded, while people of questionable constituencies vote? Should one deliberately exclude technical competence? In this view, planning for local involvement in Community Action Programs calls for neighborhood-based groups, not chosen by means test, plus parallel organization of independent interest groups, whatever their incomes (minority groups, civil rights, tenants, etc.). People who do not join organizations of the poor do participate in considerable interest-group activity. (Indeed, in some places the local anti-poverty program became a battleground for ethnic-group control of jobs and related patronage, as in the case of Negroes and Puerto Ricans in New York.) Our pattern of democracy by consent of the governed through

---

[73] Kirschner Associates, *op. cit.*

our general political machinery will continue and should not be expected to be changed by the anti-poverty war.

Arguments such as these were heard with increasing frequency, as the anti-poverty effort entered its second and third years. Governors demanded that their veto rights be protected (but seldom exercised them). Mayors would relinquish neither their formal rights nor the informal power which local funding requirements gave them. Congressmen, too, felt closed out. By mid-1967 it was clear that the balance of pressure had shifted: from a search for ways to bring "the poor" into policy-making, programming, and activity to the search for vehicles to protect prerogatives of legislators, mayors, and the non-poor of the cities. In effect, then, the anti-poverty effort was going to become part of ongoing government whereas, for a while, it had been a thing apart.

Similarly, while the socio-therapeutic value of local initiatives was appreciated and the validity of locally designed service-delivery modes and priority rankings was perceived, increasing value was to be placed on "national emphasis" items—program components in community action deemed promising by national technical experts and legislators. As such programs increased, the parameters of local decision-making and planning were narrowed.

Had participation of the poor led to decreased "powerlessness"? Not basically, of course, in the sense that the poor individually lack skills, competence, access, and resources. Yet, while expectation of general political impact is probably excessive and any other generalizations are premature, it is possible that what has occurred as a result of the participation of the poor on boards and committees, even where such participation does not approximate control, may be a very significant, more general democratization of voluntary social agency boards and public advisory committees in the welfare fields. Already, where local anti-poverty units contract with local or city-wide programs for service, some of the groups have insisted upon dealing only with agencies which in themselves are governed by reasonably representative community boards. (The 1967 amendments even provided a mandate for such practice in use of what became known as "delegate agencies.") Thus the social welfare network will feel the impact of the Community Action Program more than the general political system. It may be expected that some services now available largely to the middle class may become accessible and suitable to the needs of the more disadvantaged citizen as a consequence of this process.

More may occur to confirm the expectations of the most expansive proponents of the effort. In one low-income community of Columbus, Ohio, residents were "given" a settlement house and its properties and, through a neighborhood "foundation," hired staff and began to run programs and contract for services. Several cities created community corporations with similar prerogatives as their local community-action outlets. Here "maximum feasible involvement . . ." does mean providing local people with a stake in community property and services as a way of coping with the more general urban problem of alienation of individuals—particularly disadvantaged individuals—from the political process. There is no expectation that poverty can be *conquered* by the success of such efforts, even if many neighborhoods in many cities should copy the device, but what might eventually develop would be a significant increase in participation in decision-making (which does not mean control) by members of deprived communities. In some ways, the structure recalls the Yugoslav worker communes with their self-government and control over some resources, an analogy likely to confirm the worst fears of conservative opponents of the anti-poverty effort.[74]

On balance, one tends to agree with an Office of Economic Opportunity official's personal assessment:

> . . . observers have assessed these local programs against the intoxicating concepts contained in such terms as "innovation," "comprehensive," "coordination," "ability to deal with the causes of poverty," "social change," "grass roots development"—all of which have become part of the armamentarium of every antipoverty warrior. Measured against any one of these concepts, the record of the CAP to date is largely one of failure.
>
> Few of the programs developed and funded have represented really new ideas. It can also be said that to date the programs could be better described as piecemeal rather than comprehensive! Coordination has been onesided—sometimes the community action agency modifies certain of its programs to achieve better coordination, but similar modification almost never happens in existing agencies. As for the causes of poverty, the programs hardly seem to be oriented in that direction; in truth, few community action agencies have any notions about causality about which they could do anything on a local level.[75]

Yet, granting all this, one is left with evidence from many cities that poor people can contribute significantly to policy development and programming and that they can help staff social service programs. One knows that

---

[74] The Columbus, Ohio, experiment and rationale, including constitution and by-laws, are reproduced in *Federal Role in Urban Affairs*, Part 9, 2048–2104. Also, Milton Kotler, "Two Essays on the Neighborhood Corporation," in Subcommittee on Urban Affairs, Joint Economic Committee, *Urban America: Goals and Programs* (Washington, D.C.: Government Printing Office, 1967), 170.

[75] Melvin B. Mogulof, "A Developmental Approach to the Community Action Program Idea," *Social Work*, 12, No. 2 (April, 1967), 13. A Senate study confirmed that CAP was largely service—with little concern for "power," and that "the number of innovative programs is exceedingly small." See Howard W. Hallman, "Community Action Program:

the process is more meaningful if "the poor" can actually dispose of re-sources, control or affect hiring, and evaluate programs. One also knows that the redistribution of power creates many ripples in the community—to the point that, as of mid-1967, there was no consensus as to the balance of in-fluence and the relative emphasis on getting the poor's "advice" or assuring them policy control. These matters could be resolved only in broader con-text. Visibly, the Community Action Agency had become the vehicle for political involvement and "take off" of significant numbers of previously closed-out minority group members, most of them Negro. Here was a semi-protected, semi-monopoly political arena, in a significant number of localities (albeit a relatively small part of the whole). This, too has long-run significance for the local political scene. In fact the closing-in on the Office of Economic Opportunity and local Community Action Agencies late in 1967 was in part at least a consequence of the fear that this effect would produce even more ripples.

Other aspects of the experience

If only briefly, several other elements of the anti-poverty experience should be brought into the inventory.

For one thing, the entire problem of public-voluntary relationships in the social sector attained new urgency.[76] The framers of the Act, OEO leaders, and some local-level workers, talked expansively at the onset about by-pass-ing the "welfare establishment" and its "professionalism." Local community council, social agency, and social work professional leadership were ignored. And, indeed, there were departures of great significance. Each of the fol-lowing occurred in only a limited number of places, and often with quali-tative limitations, too, yet there were these innovations: more emphasis on job counseling and work training; flexible use of indigenous non-creden-tialed personnel; the evolution of a "case advocacy" role, which increased case accountability and follow-through; the beginnings of service decentral-ization; the organization of agency clients to exert pressures in relation to programs and policy; the representation of "the poor" and other minority-group members on boards allocating funds to and contracting with social agencies. Whatever the partial nature of some of these developments, and despite the many issues raised and not solved by the anti-poverty effort, several of which have already been suggested, the voluntary sector could not but take notice—and be swayed.

An Interpretative Analysis of 35 Communities," in *Examination of the War on Poverty* (Senate), Staff and Consultant Reports, IV, 899–902.

[76] See Whitney Young's comment, in *Federal Role in Urban Affairs*, Part 14, 2942.

Voluntary agencies gradually did begin to reflect some innovation in staffing and professional practice. In fact, some of the new approaches had been pioneered in or noted by such agencies even before the creation of the Office of Economic Opportunity. Perhaps more slowly than sought, changes began to appear in professional practice, designed to increase the "relevance" of social services to the poor. The social work profession was a strong support of the anti-poverty effort from its inception.

But the voluntary sector was more than a change-object; it was also a resource. To the extent that anti-poverty programs were not operated directly by the federal government or local anti-poverty agencies, they needed to be mounted in existing or new public agencies or in existing or new voluntary agencies. If in the latter, a system of funding and accountability was needed.

The relationship of anti-poverty services to the remainder of the elements in the public social service network has already been mentioned. Obviously, the question is more complex: planning requires a stance in regard to the voluntary sector as well—and, within the voluntary, a point of view about the funding of sectarian programs, the creation of new voluntary (or are they semi-public) community corporations with public funds and related possibilities. The anti-poverty-drive experience has produced a variety of experiments, no modal operational patterns, and little philosophic or legal precedent. The anti-poverty program projects the issue; it does not solve it.

Secondly, although there were those who were eager to win elections to local or city-wide community boards, and although civil rights and welfare rights groups achieved an unprecedented amount of client organization based on self-identification as relief recipient or "poor," a program structure with an economic means test and a requirement of such self-identification obviously also has some limitations. Particularly in the first year, there was evidence of mothers who would not take their children to Head Start because it was for "the poor." Some community-action agencies had similar experience with certain of their service programs. As already mentioned, there were areas of the country in which "poor whites" abandoned the programs to "poor Negroes." Once again, then, the issue is joined: that of the relative advantages and disadvantages of a program for those below a given income level as contrasted with universal provision. Clearly uneasy about some of the experience, Office of Economic Opportunity directives moved gradually to define projects as serving poverty-areas and demanded that representatives of the area be area residents—thus decreasing application of an individual means test. Such a test was not eliminated for Job Corps or Youth Corps applicants, but in most programs there was a partial shift to *priority* for the very poor, rather than exclusivity. This might both decrease stigma and counter the tendency of programs exclusively assigned to the poor to be of low quality. On the other hand, the process raises questions about the desirability of going the whole way toward universal service —a subject to which we shall return shortly.

THE INTERDEPENDENCE OF POLICY INSTRUMENTS

From the beginning of the anti-poverty discussion, social scientists had warned of the need to recognize and provide for "interdependence of policy instruments" for coping with the multi-faceted phenomenon of poverty amidst affluence in a welfare state committed to sustaining economic growth, avoiding excessive governmental control-regulation-operation, and protecting the purchasing power of the consumer.[77] In fact, some of the prototype operations on which OEO's local-action pattern was based, such as New Haven's Community Progress, Inc., or the Ford-supported North Carolina Fund, were considerably more comprehensive than what emerged in most places in the anti-poverty effort.[78]

The Office of Economic Opportunity's champions and friendly critics, somewhat captured by their own rhetoric, were slow to face the consequences of the limited options which had been enacted in Economic Opportunity Act and the level of funding which had become the pattern. It also took time before the Community Action "score" could be tallied and —despite the obvious impact—the overall outcome found lacking. One of the designers of the strategy and a strong friend of the anti-poverty effort joined the analysts of 1964:

> Education, economic development, and physical development are basic to any serious attack on poverty. Yet the Office of Economic Opportunity has only limited and peripheral responsibilities in these areas. The programs are under the control of other departments of the federal government. Without effective power to coordinate, OEO cannot support coordination of resources at the local level through Community Action Programs. Local programs currently mirror that weakness.[79]

---

[77] For example, Gordon, *op. cit.*, the source of this section title; Ferman, Kornbluh, and Haber, *op. cit.*, etc.

[78] Community Progress, Inc., *The Human Story* (New Haven, Conn., 1966).

[79] Richard W. Boone, Executive Director of the Citizens' Crusade Against Poverty, before the Subcommittee on Employment, Manpower, and Poverty of the Senate Committee on Labor and Public Welfare, March 16, 1967. *Examination of the War on Poverty*, Part I (1967), 231. Or, Richard W. Boone, "Do We Need an OEO?" *New Generation*, 49, No. 3 (Summer, 1967) 2–6.

The original Act was premised on the potential of increased impact through coordination. Limited in its own scope, OEO was charged with coordination of government-wide activity against poverty. Several vehicles were provided: the Economic Opportunity Council, chaired by the OEO director; provision for the director to request reports and to direct cooperation by other agencies; authority to operate information services about all government programs available to states and communities; provision for preference by all governmental agencies to projects that are components of local community action. But OEO, of course, also had direct operational responsibilities and was to delegate or contract for certain other services. The result, according to one consultant—whose conclusions are generally confirmed—was to bring into operation "the Gresham's Law of Administration that operations tend to drive out staff work." The operating responsibilities absorbed "virtually all the energies of . . . leadership." Although there were some significant exceptions, work on the negative income tax and some long-range program projections, it was obvious that the Act did not provide a sufficiently large umbrella to cover all that was necessary.[80] Nor was the OEO director armed with the necessary power and sanctions.

A serious attack on poverty could not long ignore major options not assigned to OEO. Indeed, this point had been made publicly, from time to time, from the beginning. By mid-1965, the OEO director himself was talking of the need to go beyond the Act to cut unemployment as an anti-poverty measure.[81] A year later the chairman of the House subcommittee concerned had urged the poverty fighters to place new emphasis on employment. Legislation in 1966 expanded work counseling and training components of the anti-poverty effort and adopted very modest programs to implement a principle which had been urged for several years: that the government should become "employer of last resort." Tax incentives to business to employ the poor were proposed in the Senate. Investments in urban ghettos, preferably under indigenous control, were discussed increasingly.

Meanwhile, other by-passed options were receiving renewed attention and study, after a period of eclipse during the early excitement over the Economic Opportunity Act. A variety of interests converged to urge putting more money into the hands of people whose resources will not command an adequate living standard no matter how low the unemployment rates. The Commissioner of Social Security had estimated that one-quarter to

<hr />

[80] James L. Sundquist, "Issues of Organization and Coordination," in *Examination of the War on Poverty* (Senate), Staff and Consultants Reports, III, 788.

[81] Speech by R. Sargent Shriver, as reported in the *New York Times*, July 30, 1965.

one-third of all United States poverty could be alleviated by improvement of social insurance, including unemployment insurance.[82] Late in 1966, both political parties endorsed the notion of a substantial boost in social security benefits designed to counter some of the increases in the cost of living. The Congress was considering substantial proposals by early 1967 and enacted them at the end of the year. It also considered and rejected other proposals[83] to require that the states meet their own estimates of budgetary needs for relief recipients.

Paralleling all this, there was the discussion of a "guaranteed annual income," a phrase variously interpreted and applied by some only to the unemployable, and by others to all below the poverty-line. Here the OEO planning staff took the lead. The device which had most attention, the negative income tax, began as an esoteric idea, but, by late 1966, had become familiar to readers of scholarly economics journals, general circulation magazines, and Sunday supplements. President Johnson announced that a special commission would undertake a two-year study of proposals and report early in 1969. In the meantime, other groups focused on children's allowances as a possible alternative or additional measure.[84]

Other elements on the social sector agenda were also addressed in Congressional committees with new vigor: the pattern for continuing federal aid to education, efforts to improve urban amenity and safety, health needs, housing, and the overall manpower problem.

The country's mayors dramatized the notion that the parameters of an anti-poverty effort could not be defined by the program of the Office of Economic Opportunity when they, as the United States Conference of Mayors, issued a report on *Economic Opportunity in Cities*[85] early in 1966. They discussed housing, slum clearance, and urban renewal *before* Community Action. Area economic-development tools, ranging from public works and loans to tax policy and land availability, were deemed to require attention equal to that accorded employment programs. Education, income transfers, and welfare services were addressed in broadest context. The community-action principle and involvement of the poor were endorsed, but a flexible design was urged.

Concern with the "interdependence of instruments," the relationship of

---

[82] Robert H. Ball, "Policy Issues in Social Security," *Social Security Bulletin*, 29, No. 6 (June, 1966), 7.

[83] Advisory Council on Public Welfare, "*Having the Power. . . .*"

[84] See Chapter IV.

[85] *Op. cit.*

new initiatives to old programs, and with personal prerogatives engendered more basic coordination questions than OEO could confront. An official advisory body, friendly to the OEO, positive about community action, yet dedicated to rationality in intergovernmental relations, asked whether the CAA should not become part of local government. How, the group asked, can local government be adequately coordinated and accountable otherwise? An escape clause could be left for private CAA's, where there was no local governmental will or capacity to carry the responsibility.[86]

Reports from associations of public officials and testimony at health, labor, welfare, and urban problem hearings conveyed from American mayors what became a familiar and urgent theme: the proliferation of federal bureaus, agencies, administrations and programs had confounded the city when it sought to deal seriously with its problems and to take advantage of federal legislation. Cities tried to reorganize themselves so as to coordinate their own planning and operations; a few of the largest assigned resident liaison personnel to Washington.

This, however, was not enough: the urgency of improved coordination of the federal domestic program became a major theme. The advent of the Economic Opportunity Act had, if anything, complicated matters. Its own titles scattered anti-poverty efforts among a host of departments and its unfulfilled coordination mandate related only to anti-poverty programs, not to the entire domestic effort. In continuing the Office of Economic Opportunity in 1965 and 1966, the Congress had delegated some program components to other agencies (especially the Department of Labor and the United States Office of Education), the better to interrelate or to consolidate efforts; but these were small moves. Careful analysis of manpower programs showed the waste and inefficiency that reigned as a result of failure to concert the diversity of federal programs, which had grown in fragmented fashion, experimentally, so as to meet new needs. OEO only complicated things further. Unless the Washington programs could achieve administrative realignment and fiscal consolidation, there would be little hope for effectiveness at the local level, where manpower programs meet people.[87]

As already noted, experience with the anti-poverty effort raised similar questions about diverse programs for local social service centers: local preschool, day care, and Head Start programs; neighborhood health centers—

---

[86] Advisory Commission on Intergovernmental Relations, *op. cit.*, 163.

[87] Sar A. Levitan and Garth L. Mangum, "Making Sense of Federal Manpower Policy" (Ann Arbor, Mich. Institute of Labor and Industrial Relations, 1967, pamphlet).

and so on. Model Cities legislation provided financial incentives for coordinated planning, but responsibility was upon the locality, which could not eradicate rivalry and piracy among federal agencies. Besides, only a limited number of cities and—within these—only certain sections of large cities were eligible for Model Cities planning funds.

Recognizing these problems, the Executive Branch had issued directives to federal departments as to which was to take the lead in some of the program planning: Economic Opportunity, Housing and Urban Development, Health, Education, and Welfare, or Labor. The problem was that there was no overall pattern of responsibility. Departmental planning and problem-oriented planning could go quite far, but the possibility of creating a more comprehensive instrument had to be faced. The decision was not easy in a context in which departments had their own constituencies, bureaucracies, and bargaining traditions. And there were those who would transfer the issue to the states with unrestricted block grants of federal income tax funds. However, the arguments were strong for strengthening of the executive branch and the creation of some kind of social planning instrument or "presence"—so that the domestic economic, social, and physical policies and programs might maximize their accomplishments. Even those who had argued, early in the anti-poverty effort, that an over-emphasis on coordination would decrease the pressure for institutional change began to recognize that both localities and federally-operated programs cannot achieve even minimal efficiency unless coordination is accorded its place.

CHOICES

Both friends and foes of the Office of Economic Opportunity were agreed by early 1967 that a change was needed. Of those who focused seriously on social strategy rather than on political advantage alone, some wanted to strengthen administration and accountability. Others sought to clarify and support the relative mandates for operation and coordination: the OEO should continue "focusing attention on the problem of poverty, . . . serving as an advocate for the poor within the Federal Government, . . . conducting and overseeing a number of useful programs."[88] Some wanted to "spin off" programs and to build up federal-state-local coordination and planning capacity in OEO (the motives ranging from the desire to kill OEO to convictions about how best to deliver services). Others merely proposed reassigning what they considered good and curtailing or dismantling the rest of the enterprise. Many sought to decrease ambiguity about community

---

[88] *Report on . . . S2388*, 2.

action, trying generally to reassert the prerogatives of local elected political authorities. And, in the context of public maneuvering, there were those who espoused specific measures, which were inconsistent with their basic intent. Thus, advocacy of control by "the poor," rather than by local authority, was often a partisan effort to limit city mayors of the other party rather than an attempt to implement a theory of government.

The President's 1967 "War on Poverty" message to the Congress had gone well beyond OEO, grouping proposals in health, Model Cities, housing, and transportation with suggested amendments to the Economic Opportunity Act, but not locating responsibility for interrelating planning or policy on the federal level. OEO was called upon to strengthen both its anti-poverty coordination role in Washington and its guidance to local Community Action Program agencies, which were to do as much in their neighborhoods. In general, the community-action mission was now specified in a form less likely to get out of control and to create political problems:

> Its basic purpose is to stimulate a better focusing of all available local, state, private and federal resources upon the goal of enabling low-income families, and low-income individuals of all ages, in rural and urban areas, to attain the skills, knowledge, and motivations and secure the opportunities needed for them to become self-sufficient. . . .

Implementation in the administration view would involve focus on (1) "community capabilities for planning and coordinating," (2) "better organization of a range of services," (3) more "innovative approaches," (4) "maximum feasible participation of residents of the areas and members of the groups served, so as to best stimulate and take full advantage of capabilities for self-advancement and assure that those programs and projects are otherwise meaningful to and widely utilized by their intended beneficiaries. . . ."[89]

Illegal "direct action" and picketing, as well as partisan political activity, were to be clearly outlawed.

Here, then, was a case service–structural strategy with little ambiguity. Nor would it be seriously attacked in the Congress. The debate centered around the level of funding, extent of administrative reform, degree of future reliance on OEO or other agencies, and the roles of elected officials. Doubts about community action as social protest were henceforth to be resolved: "The focus of such problems shall be upon opportunity and self-help. . . . In short, the community action program should move poor people

[89] "Economic Opportunity Admendments of 1967, Conference Report," Title II, Section 201 (Ninetieth Congress, First Session), House of Representatives Report 1012.

through their own efforts into the mainstream of American life." The emphasis was to be placed on resident participation in program planning, administration, staffing, and evaluation, including the programs of local agencies which were to receive contracts. Neighborhood organizations could be given technical help and facilities, but should focus on "specific problems and programs rather than on abstract objectives such as 'power.' "[90]

The administration's initial proposals added up to what students of bureaucracy have called "routinization of charisma."[91] An anti-poverty "movement" was to become a "normal" function of governmental organization, more accountable, and less exposed to attack (and therefore less innovative):

> Cumulatively, the adjustments suggested . . . add up to a law which will in some respects be less useful than the present Act for the processes of trying, testing and learning. But it will be a law, which, while still retaining flexibility for needed innovation, is better suited to the complexities of effective and efficient administration.[92]

But among the staunch friends of the anti-poverty effort there were those who insisted on returning to two fundamental questions: through what structure and procedures might a special problem-oriented effort offer major pressure for reform of ongoing service systems; should not the recognition of the interdependence of policy instruments result in more emphasis on coordination?

Thus:

> . . . all OEO operational responsibilities could be delegated to other federal agencies allowing it to concentrate on improving the effectiveness of community action programs, and develop planning, development and monitoring and evaluation functions consistent with its role as planner and catalyst.
>
> . . . It would attempt to answer such questions as: What national economic and fiscal [sic] policies are best calculated to address poverty?[93]

Or, as Paul Ylvisaker testified:

> Is now the time to integrate the poverty program into the more traditional structure of government and community action? The answer, I think, depends on whether one is ready to say "yes" to two other questions: First,

---

[90] Report on . . . S2388, 45–46.

[91] H. H. Gerth and C. Wright Mills, From Max Weber: Essays in Sociology (New York: Oxford University Press, 1946), 53–54, 297.

[92] Economic Opportunity Act of 1967, Proposed amendments, Summary, Congressional Record, April 14, 1967, S5163.

[93] Boone, Examination of the War on Poverty, 233.

is the purpose of integration to expand rather than contract the motivation and influence of the poverty program? Second does the alternative structure have the same (or improved) capacity to fulfill the essential purposes of the poverty program? We in New Jersey have answered "yes" to these two questions.[94]

The proponents of OEO had no difficulty in writing a bill which would give the director more responsibility for coordination and planning (but the problem of *general* domestic policy coordination was not faced, so the solution remained partial). They designed improved state and local instruments as well. Efforts would be made, in particular, to increase the planning and coordination capacity of the local community-action agency—to the point where it might turn to outside groups for most of the service operations.

However, this much done, it was not possible to discuss in rational terms what had become known as the "spin off" issue. For, as the debate became bitter and partisan, the dismantling and transfer of programs was seen—as it, indeed, was, for conservatives in Congress—only as an attack upon and a vote of no confidence in the anti-poverty effort as such—not as a possibly valid strategy for long-term strengthening of service and as a way to free OEO to serve as planner, coordinator, and advocate of the poor.

When a group in the Senate attempted to utilize the EOA amendments as the vehicle for a very large public employment program (as a response to the 1967 summer riots), the members were rebuffed, both on grounds of economy and for expanding OEO's operational role. Yet job training was increased to a point where it exceeded all CAP appropriations.

The advocates of OEO as planner launched an interesting issue and did carry its implications at least one step further. There was a long and difficult debate whether local community-action agencies should receive large "general" grants for their own programming (a necessity, one would assume, if a local planning capacity was to develop), or whether the stress was to be on "national emphasis" budgeting, which allows little local flexibility. The national emphasis meant specific allocations for Head Start, Neighborhood Legal Services, Foster Grandparents, Upward Bound, etc. Associated in the public discussion with the issue of local political and protest activity (did one want to risk more local "power"), this debate never touched on the planning problem of the balance between centralization and decentralization and its resolution. What would the premises be of each resolution? OEO proponents urged that one-half of CAA funds be assigned each way. The

---

[94] Paul N. Ylvisaker, before the Subcommittee on Employment, Manpower and Poverty, March 15, 1967.

Congress made a larger shift to "national emphasis." No one noted the *implicit issue* between an anti-poverty strategy based on use of specified services to increase opportunity and individual capacities (Washington experts selecting and designing the services) and one focused either on community competence or power. Nor did many of the champions of earmarking deal with Detroit Mayor J. P. Cavanagh's conclusion that, "earmarking completely negates citizen participation."[95]

Similarly, a debate about whether the poor were to have up to or *at least* one-third of local anti-poverty board membership and whether the mayors and local officials could or should be potent in such programs, was defined in terms of support of or opposition to OEO. There was little serious talk about the relative advantages and disadvantages of informal and self-selective participation in choice of local leadership as opposed to the formal and presumably more democratic official machinery—or of the program consequences of creating new and parallel coordination and operational instruments rather than reforming the statutory machinery. The eventual "compromise" was a delayed decision on behalf of "City Hall" or the "general community," rather than control by "the poor" alone (depending on one's interpretation)—but only on limited partisan political grounds. Local government was authorized, but not required, to take over control of local community-action agencies, to that time 80 percent non-governmental in their sponsorship. One-third of the members of anti-poverty boards were to be elected or appointed officials and at least one-third "representatives of the poor." The remainder would represent agency-community interests.

The terms voted were sufficiently ambiguous to support the status quo where the local mayor did not want to increase his control of anti-poverty corporations, but they could be used to affirm City Hall's role wherever the local government considered itself left out. (Indeed, political strategy may have exaggerated the change so as to help pass the 1967 bill.)[96] At the end, the Office of Economic Opportunity's life was extended for two years, relatively little of the predicted dismantling took place, and funds were uncut for 1968 despite expectations. The politics of urban crisis and the civil rights revolution had defeated some of the anti-OEO strategists and the "routinization" and "bureaucratization" had been somewhat reassuring; but some potentially valid reforms were not even considered in the context of a

---

[95] *Examination of the War on Poverty* (Senate), Part 1, 389.

[96] One notes, for example, that as of late 1968 about 96 percent of existing community-action agencies had been redesignated as their communities' official anti-poverty instruments! *Community Development*, February, 1969, 7.

debate in which the public issue became one of loyalty to OEO. The question of the future of OEO was to be deferred until a later date.

A debate as to whether the matching requirements for local Community Action Program funding were to revert to the original 10 percent, remain at 20 percent as voted in 1966 (the eventual decision), or increase significantly tended to divide friends and foes of OEO, as did the question of whether localities could continue to contribute their shares "in kind." There was no occasion to consider the more basic question of federal-local fiscal relationships (would block grants generate freedom or waste?) or to ask whether, given *other* federal funding patterns, one arrangement or another was best to create the desired local response.

While the debate went on, authorization and appropriations were delayed. Almost six months of fiscal 1967 had passed before the decisions were made, and many programs had to be closed or curtailed because of the uncertainty. The situation was a more extreme form of what had occurred the previous year. Administrators could not plan, "scarce" staff left—and "the poor" wondered whom to believe. A problem-oriented crusade does generate initiative, but it sacrifices stability. Americans do not yet know how to mix these elements for utmost impact.

LESSONS FOR PLANNERS

This segment of the anti-poverty case story does illustrate a type of "incrementalism," if the term is not necessarily assumed to imply constant improvement: policies and programs do grow, respond to needs, and find their way in the political market place. They are not without their components of rationality. Formal and informal feedback occasionally are extremely potent.

In another perspective, however, one sees here the limitations of bargaining, political strategy, and disjointed interventions. There is a case to be made for a more comprehensive overall social planning thrust. An anti-poverty effort should be related to fiscal and monetary policy, to manpower policy, to trade policy, to patterns of intergovernmental relationships, to city rebuilding and other efforts to humanize the urban environment. Failure to consider such relationships in the early stages of OEO led to conflict and wastage, to local confusion and inefficiency. True, experience led eventually to return of certain programs to the Departments of Labor and Health, Education, and Welfare, and more of this was projected.[97] True, ex-

---

[97] Early in 1969, President Richard M. Nixon moved to transfer the health center and foster grandparents programs to the Department of Health, Education, and Welfare and

perience highlighted the need for operational coordination with Housing and Urban Development and with the Department of Transportation, and some of this was mandated. Yet much of this was obvious and could have been predicted at the start; time and money might thus have been saved.

Even more important, a more thoughtful and comprehensive anti-poverty strategy from the beginning conceivably—but by no means certainly—might have avoided the arbitrary politicization of the increments as time went by. Such comprehensive strategy, if devised and even partially rejected initially, would have placed in the hands of the friends of the anti-poverty effort a rationale and long-range program which, when enriched by feedback and experience, would have guided their responses to the political attacks of 1967. Lacking policy and program, they energetically defended some targets, sacrificed others tactically, and assumed that protection of the OEO status quo was the only way to help the poor.

None of this is to argue that a comprehensive plan in 1964 would have determined actions in 1967. Rather, that the issues unfaced, the policy choices hedged, the problems evaded in 1964 (either to create widespread support or because they were not then understood) came back to plague the policy-makers in subsequent years. And because no comprehensive planning vehicle was developed, the battleground became largely political, with friends of the anti-poverty effort not necessarily in a position to select stances which would advance their goals. They had become only loyal constituents of OEO.

In the real world, planning cannot hope to replace politics. It can hope, however, to guide politicians.

In favor of this particularistic (selective), problem-focused, and only partially elaborated approach, it may be claimed that it generated attention, resources, and excitement. It attracted competent and creative people. It launched, through community-action agencies, some of the change processes described above, processes which a more rational overall plan, oriented to services and therapeutic self-help, might not have given us. The concept of "maximum feasible participation" migrated from anti-poverty to health and welfare services, from Model Cities to the universities. Yet these developments, too, might have come; first, from the civil rights movement—which provided much of the anti-poverty program's local community-action perspective; second, from a planning process which would have led inevitably to problems of decentralization and local power.

---

to delegate operation of Head Start and the Job Corps to HEW and the Department of Labor, respectively.

The American welfare state is, in a basic sense, at a crossroads. The anti-poverty experience makes it a bit easier to talk about issues and policies and to stress that planning does not necessarily mean monolithic central control. We perhaps have learned that there is less threat in—but less is achieved through—truncated programs, which are patched up annually until they take some shape. Partial, problem-focused efforts that ignore basic policy dilemmas are easier to take, but they do not generate many of the options. Concern with city and state coordination that ignores the uncertainty in Washington is bound to lead to frustration. True, the ethic is not outraged by a program "for the poor"—unless the poor become politically active—yet eventually the issue of relating the particularistic to universal health, education, housing, and manpower provision must be faced. Whether or not the country wishes to formalize a process to be called social planning or comprehensive planning, it can hardly avoid a more focused policy dialogue and some effort to make the federal policies and programs more *coherent*. (This word often covers "indicative" planning in the French sense.)

The spine of the modern-day supporter of laissez faire may chill at the talk of new forms of income transfer, of job creation or guarantee through governmental programs and incentives, or of area development and of new social resources. Yet it is all relatively tame talk in the context of current precedents for fiscal and monetary policy, wage and price intervention, further plans to use tax programs to maintain economic growth and to control inflation. Nor is it intrinsically more "radical" than a publicly financed highway program that supports an expanding automobile industry; atomic energy, power, and mineral policies that sustain private enterprise; federal distribution of television and radio rights to benefit private corporations; or a federal pattern of aircraft research-and-development support and purchase via private enterprise.

The society's agenda requires attention, whether piecemeal or comprehensively—or in some combination of the rational-comprehensive and the political. How shall we seek to

- □ humanize the urban environment
- □ assure social justice for racial and ethnic minorities
- □ strengthen the family in its new roles
- □ cope with the relationship of the individual and the primary group to a myriad of bureaucracies
- □ assure a constantly-redefined income, health, education, social service minimum to all
- □ reform delivery of human service to maximize effectiveness and utilize scarce manpower resources efficiently
- □ bring government close to people?

The inevitable planning process could be enhanced if, with specific reference to the most deprived members of the society, the United States could clarify whether it is actually dedicated to a higher degree of income redistribution or not, whether its commitment is to equality of opportunity or to a greater degree of equality in actual consumption rights, whether it requires the leverage of policy control at the center or is prepared to give states and cities command over enough resources to allow them real options. Are institutional approaches to be premised on the relative fixity of the poverty-status or on mobility?

Similarly, with reference to intergovernmental relations, if the thrust is toward decentralization and coordination in relation to service delivery, on the neighborhood level, should we not reform city and county government, building towards "maximum feasible participation" of citizens? Once inspired by Community Action Programs, is the participation process not hampered by the assumption of continued separatism, participation through private bodies or new public agencies in relation to this one goal?

These are but a few of the issues relevant to a policy debate and study of preferences in planning. They suggest that one cannot, with the incrementalists, rest with a situation in which programs are always passed by bargaining, and the policy issues are avoided because they are sensitive. For eternal opportunism leads to stalemates, ambiguities, and checkmates. Not always, but occasionally and increasingly, the society has a right to know in what direction its welfare state is facing and to assent or create new direction.

Has the time not come, for example, after several years of the effort, to know whether the affluent United States needs to reinforce the poverty-status to cope with poverty or whether, with tenBroek, who believed that people labeled poor never overcome discrimination and stigma, we are prepared to build upon premises of mobility and to affirm that, in our quest for true equality, we declare poverty "as a classifying trait . . . inherently discriminatory . . . an irrelevance like race, creed or color."[98]

Would such an affirmation not serve truly to implement the goals of 1964?

---

[98] Jacobus tenBroek, *California's Dual System of Family Law*, reprinted from *Stanford Law Review*, 16, Nos. 2 and 4 (March and July, 1964), and 17, No. 4 (April, 1965), 644.

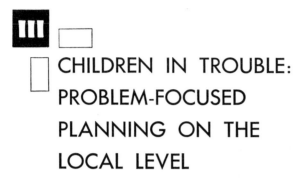

CHILDREN IN TROUBLE:
PROBLEM-FOCUSED
PLANNING ON THE
LOCAL LEVEL

THE PLANNING of services for children in trouble in an urban area poses the challenge of interrelating a problem-oriented approach (toward "delinquency") and an effort to conceptualize and organize a viable local pattern for social services, using that term in its broadest connotations. The pressure to create a *complete* network to deal with delinquents per se is as strong as the logic of experience is convincing that this is unnecessary, inefficient, and probably self-defeating.

In this chapter, a relatively comprehensive planning perspective is taken, in a somewhat different sense from that in Chapter II. Almost all elements of a plan: task, policy, program, are dealt with. An attempt is made to outline all components of a program, deriving them from a policy stance. Considerable specification of program parameters is involved. Here, however, the planner-as-expert offers the results of studies and explorations to those who would make policy. No effort is made to describe what occurs during implementation. The interest-group and political aspects of the totality are not confronted, nor are costs calculated or program details elaborated. The provisions for evaluation and feedback are by-passed.

Even the relatively comprehensive cannot consider—or at least specify—all details. To some extent, the limitations are practical: one chapter does not afford room for everything. More to the point, however, a comprehensive perspective may focus on policy and program parameters, rather than on program details. Particularly in the instance in which the organizations and units involved in planning are autonomous, or partly so, an "indicative" approach is preferable. Policy and program parameters are specified, and maximum programming options left to the network components.

TASK AND POLICY

To consider juvenile delinquency in the United States is to face a phenomenon about which feelings run high. The public feels strongly about assaults, robbery, and defiance of community norms, and it cannot ignore such activities involving a very significant minority of youth in the ten-to-seventeen-year-old age group.[1]

In 1966, it is estimated, 745,000 cases of alleged juvenile delinquency, traffic offenses excluded, came before the courts, or about 642,000 different children. The totals represented an increase of 7 percent in a year in which the child population increased by only 2 percent. The continuing upward trend began in 1949, and was interrupted only briefly in 1961. There is no expectation of cessation.

At about the same time, one may estimate very roughly, well over one million (and perhaps two million) additional youth cases were processed by the police in a less formal fashion. Approximately 55,000 children were in training schools for delinquents, and a small additional number was in diagnostic and reception centers, prisons, reformatories, and local jails. Over 10,000 were in juvenile detention facilities—all these latter statistics overlapping, to a degree, with the court total of 642,000.

Sophisticated estimates compute the prevalence of juvenile delinquency at "nine times the yearly incidence for boys and ten times the yearly incidence for girls." Perhaps even more useful is the notion that a national delinquency rate of 2 percent of the population at risk, when analyzed from the perspective of the likelihood that a given child will appear in court between the ages of ten and seventeen, yields 11 percent; that is, one child in nine (one out of six boys) may be expected to appear in court during the years of officially-defined "childhood." In some neighborhoods of large American cities the rate is many times higher, and the likelihood is that one-third to one-half of all boys will reach court at some time.[2] In fact,

---

[1] The most commonly used age range for delinquency in the United States.

[2] For documentation of the above and for the remainder of this section, for further references, and for more detail, see: Alfred J. Kahn, *Planning Community Services for Children in Trouble* (New York: Columbia University Press, 1963), Chap. I; Alfred J. Kahn, "From Delinquency Treatment to Community Development," in P. F. Lazarsfeld, W. H. Sewell, and H. L. Wilensky, Editors, *The Uses of Sociology* (New York: Basic Books, 1967), 477–505; President's Commission on Law Enforcement and Administration of Justice, *The Challenge of Crime in a Free Society*, and also *Task Force Report:*

studies conducted for the President's Commission on Law Enforcement and the Administration of Justice suggest that about 40 percent of all male children now living in the United States will be arrested for nontraffic offenses at some point during their lives!

Two-thirds of all United States delinquency cases are handled by courts in predominantly urban areas. Boys are referred to courts more than four times as often as girls. Minority group members are considerably "overrepresented" in the court population—but only if one does not take into account their concentration in poverty, poor housing, and undereducated groups.

Of all court-referred juvenile offenses:

□ 42 percent are committed against property (larceny, auto theft, burglary, robbery, vandalism);

□ 8 percent are offenses against a person (homicide, assault, rape, other sex offenses);

□ 12 percent are "offenses against public order and decency" (weapons, drugs, drunkenness, disorderly conduct);

□ 4 percent are serious motor vehicle violations (not routine traffic offenses);

□ 27 percent are conduct unacceptable in children, but not constituting crimes in adults (truancy, ungovernable behavior, running away, curfew violations).[3]

Girls, it might be noted, are referred far more often than boys for offenses which are not crimes in adults (52 percent as compared with 20 percent). A large portion of their cases involves sexual misbehavior.

About half of all alleged juvenile misbehavior, some of it serious and some of it minor, is handled informally by courts. Three of ten cases in the total group for whom the complaint is substantiated are dismissed with a warning or adjustment. Of all other cases processed in the courtroom, half the children involved are placed on probation; one-fifth are institutionalized, and an equal number are placed under "informal supervision."

It is generally understood that these limited statistical approximations, derived for the most part from sample series and from service statistics in-

---

Juvenile Delinquency and Youth Crime (Washington, D.C.: Government Printing Office, 1967); contain extensive footnotes and bibliographies. John Ball *et al.*, "Incidence and Estimated Prevalence of Recorded Delinquency in a Metropolitan Area," *American Sociological Review*, 29, No. 1 (February, 1964), 90–93. Donnell M. Pappenfort *et al.*, "Children in Institutions, 1966: A Research Note," *Social Service Review*, 42, No. 2 (June, 1968), 253.

[3] "Juvenile Court Statistics, 1965," Children's Bureau Statistical Series, No. 85 (Washington, D.C.: Government Printing Office, 1966). "Other" offenses total 7 percent.

dependently compiled by localities and states, do little to differentiate among actual behavior, detected behavior, reported behavior, and behavior evaluation. Complex elements of social stratification, social control, ethnic prejudice, administrative discretion, and cultural differences among regions or between the city and rural areas affect the location and assignment of cases to any or all of these categories.[4]

Inevitably, then, given a group so constituted, no single scientific or commonsense etiological explanation or effort to characterize all delinquents stands unchallenged, despite the apparent certainties propounded by authors, lecturers, and experts from all related professions. Thus,

> many delinquents attend church and apparently believe in religious doctrine; many delinquents have "normal" leisure time habits—in fact, vandalism and gang fights have been known to occur en route from recreation centers and ball games. Some delinquents are psychiatrically disturbed, but many are not; the connection (if any) between the psychiatric disturbance in a child and his delinquency is often not clear. Some delinquents do seem to be "fighting" their schools but their problems become even more acute when they leave school and prove unable to hold employment. TV programs obviously do not affect all children who watch them in the same way—or the "copied" violence would increase several thousandfold. Finally a surprisingly large number of delinquents seem to come from law-abiding families who accept basic social mores, do not dispute traditional "virtues" and do not deliberately teach delinquency as a way of life.[5]

Similarly, to follow a recently popular approach, explaining delinquency as the product of the "normal" youth culture of lower-class boys who feel closed out by the opportunities of the larger society, is to ignore the fact that substantial numbers—perhaps the majority—do not take part in the unlawful activity.

On the one hand, sociological, psychological, psychiatric, anthropological, and religious hypotheses are produced and are impressively tested on some populations, seeming to hold in some places for some groups; and, on the other, no one pattern (even complex multiple causation models) covers the *entire* delinquency phenomenon.

---

[4] For detail, see Kahn, "From Delinquency Treatment to Community Development," or Alfred J. Kahn, "Social Work and the Control of Delinquency," *Social Work*, 10, No. 2 (April, 1965), 3–13. A basic reference is Thomas P. Monahan, "On the Incidence of Delinquency," *Social Forces*, 39, No. 1 (October, 1960), 66–72. Ball, *op. cit.*

[5] Kahn, "From Delinquency Treatment to Community Development," 479–480. Hyman Rodman and Paul Grams review theories of causality, with special attention to the family, in *Task Force Report: Juvenile Delinquency and Youth Crime*, 188–221. Includes extensive bibliography.

Although it has only recently been understood and articulated, the explanation is actually simple and reasonable: *delinquency is not a unitary phenomenon, a single "malady" affecting individuals. It is an administrative category, an artifact of social policy and social provision,* hardly ever yielding exactly the same conduct in the same types of individuals in any two jurisdictions. We would do better to talk of "children in trouble" or of "delinquencies" than of "delinquency." Social scientists might find it more helpful to study the social-definitional process by which all these diverse elements are categorized together than to seek to explain all of the individual participants by one behavioral hypothesis. In short, what are the societal factors that determine how the delinquency label is used, for what social purposes, where, and with what consequences?

At the same time, it would be useful to intensify the research by which some social and behavioral scientists select, from among those qualifying for this administrative label, viable subgroups which may be studied etiologically: the retreatist gang (narcotics-users, etc.), the fighting gang, the firesetter, the sexually promiscuous girl from a given social milieu, and so on.[6]

The social planner or practitioner will draw upon social science findings, selecting from among them in accord with the level of understanding sought and the type of intervention contemplated. For example, he will use all available help to determine which are the delinquents requiring clinical help—and what types of problems they face which need clinical solution. At the same time, he will turn to sociological findings of several kinds, as he seeks to contribute to preventive work on a social institutional level.

More basically, perhaps, as he proceeds with his central role of contributing to improved institutional provision for coping with the delinquencies, the social planner will need to consider what society's creation and utilization of this administrative category and all its attendant machinery mean for his work.

Grouped together are the equivalents of adult crime, when committed by a child, as well as deviant and defiant behavior in children, which society wants to stop. The behaviors of these several types come into focus, however, only if noticed and not "screened out" by a variety of community "doorkeepers" who have a diversity of motives.

---

[6] For example, Irving Spergel, *Racketville, Slumtown, Haulberg: An Exploratory Study of Delinquent Subcultures* (Chicago: University of Chicago Press, 1964). James F. Short, Jr., and Fred L. Strodtbeck, *Group Process and Gang Delinquency* (Chicago: University of Chicago Press, 1965). James F. Short, Jr., "Juvenile Delinquency: The Sociocultural Context," in L. W. Hoffman and M. L. Hoffman, Editors, *Review of Child Development Research*, 2 volumes (New York: Russell Sage Foundation; I, 1964; II, 1966), II, 423–448.

In effect, the system of social stratification, public facilities, and social control appear to come together and to define certain people in specified situations as requiring actual or potential application of potent sanctions. Specific acts or circumstances are seen by the defining social unit as so endangering it or its members as to require the application of severe self-protective measures.

> The cut-off point of definition of delinquency may be determined to be that point at which actions are perceived as undermining social control at sensitive spots. This may account for some of the regional, social class and ethnic differences: society's control mechanisms take a different view of the significance and hazard in deviant behavior depending on where it is socially located. And behavior normal for a social subgroup may be seen as delinquent if it threatens the mores which prevail in the community power structure.[7]

From this point of view, services to juvenile delinquents may be seen to be related to a correctional system, which is characterized by its potential for the deprivation of liberty. A variety of consequences follows from such potential and demands specific modes of protection of rights and provision for help and treatment under potential or actual deprivation of liberty. Where there is potential for deprivation of liberty and for treatment in custody or other form of control, there are also likely to be stigma and rejection. Thus, we would wish to be sure to screen cases adequately before admitting them into a system designed for delinquents and we would wish to organize to assure reintegration into the mainstream as soon as possible and appropriate. Herein lies the planning and social practice challenge.

The undertaking is complicated by an obvious degree of social ambivalence about goals with and for young people handled as delinquents. The result is a pattern of intervention, service, help, neglect, and punishment which seldom follows any single conceptualization of the task very far. It has been taken as a mark of twentieth-century humanitarianism that we have been willing to develop a treatment rationale for our broad control measures; statutes everywhere promise delinquents the help, education, treatment, and care that would be offered by a good and competent parent. Indeed, such rationale has often been used to justify the lack of due process and other protections against infringement of individual rights. While the label "delinquent" now carries a stigma, it was invented as a non-criminal status to facilitate helping children. There is widespread consensus that current practice, at least, does not assure for many young people processed by the anti-delinquency machinery the type of helping measures promised

---

[7] Kahn, "From Delinquency Treatment to Community Development," 487.

by humanitarian slogans or the strivings of the most enlightened practitioners. In fact, there are those who are so disappointed with the reality that they assert children would be far better off in regular criminal courts, with access to all constitutional protections, and thus less likely to be subject to adjudication, probation, or institutionalization.

Yet the difficulties and failures should occasion little surprise. Helping a delinquent child (one who is psychologically disturbed, in social "trouble," reacting to home pathology, or reflecting organic difficulty) is likely to require a most complex series of interventions, involving constant and imaginative integration and coordination of schools, police, courts, detention facilities, many social and medical agencies, clinics, institutions, hostels, and child care agencies. One does not readily undo years of deprivation, conditioning, or pathological interpersonal experience. In this sense, a complete scientific, rehabilitative approach in dealing with this problem is an as-yet "untried weapon."

Ten years of findings in studies of services to delinquents are summed up as follows:

> Facilities are in short supply, poorly staffed, have partially developed programs. All the components of a necessary intervention network are seldom present in one place at one time—or are not adequately coordinated. Whatever the philosophy and objectives of the juvenile court movement or of individual agencies and treatment facilities, for the parent and child brought into the network of delinquency services the impact is largely one of punishment, deprivation and control. What is defined as social control through individual help and therapy emerges as control through threat, separation and surveillance. It is not very effective because these latter mechanisms never block successfully and fully action flowing from very strong motives.[8]

A complex and costly undertaking is unlikely to be fully supported and, if supported, is unlikely to succeed, given only partial commitment from and the conflicting conceptions of the general public. Yet it is obvious that work with delinquents takes its cue from several different publics, which do not share fundamental objectives, or at least have somewhat differing interpretations of phraseology they may endorse. Even where the issues have been carefully debated and statutes carefully worded, values and goals are in

---

[8] Kahn, "From Delinquency Treatment to Community Development," 488.

For detailed documentation, see Kahn, *Planning Community Services for Children in Trouble*; or President's Commission, *The Challenge of Crime in a Free Society*, and *Task Force Report: Juvenile Delinquency and Youth Crime*. Also, National Council on Crime and Delinquency, *Correction in the United States*, constituting *Crime and Delinquency*, 13, No. 1 (January, 1967).

transition, and incumbent staffs may not be working in complete consensus. One overall policy seldom governs an entire state. Somewhat different perceptions govern related professions and disciplines. Significant pressure groups are ever alert and monitor departures from the norm of which they disapprove.

In the face of all this, with recognition of the limitations of knowledge and technology, one also takes account of the projections of even higher totals of delinquency, recidivism, and service failure. One then concludes that knowledge must be assembled, technology assessed, personnel prepared and deployed, service choices made, resource allocation guided, innovations monitored and evaluated—all in the context of continuing efforts to reach goal consensus. In short, there is a strong case for planning—and little alternative.

Although in the real world of federal, state, local, and voluntary anti-delinquency planning, significant analysis of goals and values would precede further discussion, we shall not here elaborate this aspect. The central purpose of the present chapter is to *illustrate* a total approach to urban programming for children in trouble, not to assume that conclusions here will be considered to have universal applicability—where other values may take over or new conceptual anchoring points may be introduced. In this spirit, we shall take for granted the overall value positions accepted by the major standard-setting bodies: the National Council on Crime and Delinquency, the United States Children's Bureau, The National Council of Juvenile Court Judges, The Standard Juvenile Court Act.[9] This by-passing of the value debate and of a search for service standards makes it possible to clarify an approach to planning that is problem-oriented, impinges on several service systems, has reason at some points to permit segregation of clientele, while also seeking integration of systems. Special attention will be addressed to the ties of the delinquency system both with local general social services and with the community psychiatry network.

In short, the goal is control, treatment, and rehabilitation of delinquents and prevention of delinquency where possible—in a context of community protection. Where appropriate, one would wish to deal with delinquents within a system serving all children—but it is necessary to clarify when and where this may not be appropriate or possible. It also is assumed that the

---

[9] United States Children's Bureau, "Standards for Juvenile and Family Courts," Publication No. 437, prepared by William H. Sheridan (Washington, D.C.: Government Printing Office, 1966). Extensive footnoting re standards, legal precedents, and structure appears in President's Commission, *Task Force Report: Juvenile Delinquency and Youth Crime.*

community will not long tolerate any approach that openly undermines the social control system.

The definition of the planning task and the general orientation toward policy—and thus the point of departure for programming—have recently been clearly delineated by the President's Commission on Law Enforcement and Administration of Justice. The Supreme Court's 1967 decision *In re Gault* is very much in evidence:

> The formal sanctioning system and pronouncement of delinquency should be used only as a last resort.
>
> In place of the formal system, dispositional alternatives to adjudication must be developed for dealing with juveniles, including agencies to provide and coordinate services and procedures to achieve necessary control without unnecessary stigma. Alternatives already available, such as those related to court intake, should be more fully exploited.
>
> The range of conduct for which court intervention is authorized should be narrowed, with greater emphasis upon consensual and informal means of meeting the problems of difficult children.
>
> The cases that fall within the narrowed jurisdiction of the court and filter through the screen of prejudicial, informal disposition methods would largely involve offenders for whom more vigorous measures seem necessary. Court adjudication and disposition of those offenders should no longer be viewed solely as a diagnosis and prescription for cure, but should be frankly recognized as an authoritative court judgment expressing society's claim to protection. While rehabilitative efforts should be vigorously pursued in deference to the youth of the offenders and in keeping with a general commitment to individualized treatment of all offenders, the incapacitative, deterrent, and condemnatory aspects of the judgment should not be disguised.
>
> Accordingly, the adjudicatory hearing should be consistent with basic principles of due process. Counsel and evidentiary restrictions are among the essential elements of fundamental fairness in juvenile as well as adult criminal courts.[10]

By way of digression, it also may be noted that, in all service planning involving stigmatized and feared categories of people, the gap between rhetoric and fundamental ethic makes planning especially difficult. Adult corrections, delinquency, mental health, retardation, and addiction are among the categories sharing this problem. Planners need to instigate constantly and contribute to the policy dialogue; then they must exert efforts to assure that the professional groups responsible for consistent follow-through

---

[10] President's Commission, *Task Force Report: Juvenile Delinquency and Youth Crime*, 2.

(here judges, probation officers, social workers, teachers, and institutional personnel are central) are clear about and in harmony with the central hypotheses and values of the overall strategy. The process is a dynamic one, yet gross discrepancies, especially common in these fields, are self-defeating.

PREVENTION THROUGH LAW ENFORCEMENT

The recent work of the President's Commission on Law Enforcement and Administration of Justice has restored to rightful attention the entire problem of firearms control, detection of criminals, rapid apprehension, and swift judicial process.[11] Obviously, yet too often forgotten, more effective police work, the foundation of law enforcement, will decrease some juvenile delinquency or bring it under increased control. Police need special preparation for general patrol and apprehension activity involving children. Special provision (*see below*) is also necessary to process children reported to or apprehended by the police. Much consideration of police-community relations is needed, if law enforcement is to develop the community support on which its effectiveness depends.

But, when workers in delinquency talk of prevention, they generally refer to the elimination of personality developments and social conditions that produce antisocial deviance. Is such primary prevention in the province of an anti-delinquency effort?

THE LIMITATIONS OF DELINQUENCY-SPECIFIC
PRIMARY PREVENTION

There is a large social investment in what is conceived as personality-oriented and social condition–focused, primary delinquency "prevention" in the United States. Through the nineteen-forties and -fifties, while delinquency rates climbed, states and cities created youth boards, committees, and governor's commissions; and they joined with the voluntary sector in heavy expenditures for recreation programs and—to a smaller extent—guidance programs and mental health lectures, on the assumption that this would cut the incidence of delinquency. There is no evidence that any of it had effect on the categories of activity classified as delinquency. Small wonder: the targets were diffuse, the investment often limited, and the motives for deviance powerful.

When the Kennedy Administration launched the President's Committee on Delinquency and Youth Crime, it was decided to concentrate on that

---

[11] See President's Commission, *The Challenge cf Crime in a Free Society,* Chaps. 1, 4, 5, 10, 11, and the supporting, specialized Task Force reports.

large portion of the delinquency problem which is located among the poor, uneducated, deprived youth population of the urban ghettos and slum areas. The ideological keynote had been sounded in the writing of Richard A. Cloward and Lloyd E. Ohlin.[12] The authors are concerned with group rates, not with individual actors. In brief, the "subcultural" delinquency phenomenon, with which they deal, is interpreted as the product of the discrepancy between socially-conditioned motivation to have the goods and comforts of an affluent society and lack of access to such goals. Lower-class youth are seen as closed off from the "opportunity structure," which opens the door to adequate social participation. They lack the education, skills, habits, and attitudes necessary "to make it." Some find illegitimate means to the same goals. Others lack access to either legitimate or illegitimate means. The reactions and responses vary from aggression to extreme withdrawal.

Since the "opportunity structure" concept was soon converted into a popular slogan and thus never made very precise, this general emphasis on environmental deprivation in a field that had, for some years, been dominated by clinicians did have significant effect on delinquency programs.[13] The government-aided projects of the early nineteen-sixties and those voluntary projects they influenced turned toward what they saw as primary prevention. Although clinical treatment, recreation programming, and law enforcement were continued or even stepped up, new preventive ingredients were added. The change was particularly noticeable in the big cities. Remedial education, job counseling and training, and "protected work" projects all became extremely important. They were soon followed by more basic efforts to change urban school systems the better to serve deprived youth and offer them entry into the word of education—the primary doorway to opportunity. Fundamental reforms in state employment services and other counseling programs for poorly-educated youth were proposed and sometimes carried out. Anti-dropout campaigns and "return-to-school" efforts were launched. Where the market economy did not offer employment to the unskilled, jobs were sometimes created in the public or nonprofit sector.

---

[12] Richard A. Cloward and Lloyd E. Ohlin, *Delinquency and Opportunity* (Glencoe, Ill.: The Free Press, 1960). The first relevant statute was the Juvenile Delinquency and Youth Offenses Control Act of 1961. For subsequent thought about these theoretical issues and reference to empirical work, see Paul Lerman, "Individual Values, Peer Values, and Subcultural Delinquency," *American Sociological Review*, 33, No. 2 (April, 1968), 219–235.

[13] Kahn, "From Delinquency Treatment to Community Development."

As the process continued, it became increasingly difficult to focus on youth alone. Enriched day care programs were begun for preschoolers, to overcome the home-engendered handicaps, which they carried to school and from which many never recovered. At the same time, the adults in the community were involved in a community organization process designed to give them competence to cope with their children and to affect their own political and social destinies. The theoretical basis was that youths reared in a community of defeated and impotent adults are unlikely themselves to grasp and utilize opportunity and to become fully participating members of the wider society.

The delinquency-focus had by this time become artificial and handicapping. Employment services were not able to receive with great enthusiasm the clientele of job counseling and training programs called "delinquency preventive," for they realistically perceived that employers would not open many job opportunities to young people presented as being pulled back from the brink of crime by means of these new endeavors. Moreover, once the blinders had been removed by the new programs, all concerned could see that improved urban education, job training, counseling, and placement were needed for all youth, and especially in the deprived areas. Where such programs were successful, their results were expected to go well beyond delinquency prevention. In fact, the anti-delinquency efforts of the President's Committee on Juvenile Delinquency and Youth Crime had, from the very beginning, joined up with the Ford Foundation "grey area" (urban slum and fringe areas) projects to reform urban education as it reached the most deprived population elements.[14] Both of these efforts, in turn, covering only a limited number of cities, were soon encompassed in the even broader and more basic effort to achieve "quality integrated education" in many of the urban systems, which had permitted the schools serving deprived minority groups to become segregated de facto, below standard, and almost irrelevant to the experiences of their users—who, in turn, saw them as custodial institutions.[15]

By 1964, the logic of the process had become everywhere apparent. A larger frame (the anti-poverty war) had been placed around all of these efforts. (We have already asked whether even that frame was of sufficient size.) The "pockets of poverty" and the populations living below the poverty line would be approached in an integrated effort at self-help, remedial services, and opportunity-engendering programs.

---

[14] Peter Marris and Martin Rein, *Dilemmas of Social Reform* (New York: Atherton Press, 1967).

[15] Kenneth B. Clark, *Dark Ghetto* (New York: Harper & Row, 1965).

For present purposes, the account need not be carried any further. Clearly, *law enforcement activities apart, delinquency is hardly the basis for organizing primary prevention.* To the extent that the issues in delinquency "causation" are social deprivation; lack of community "competence" to participate in public decisions; lack of good education or adequate access to socializing experiences; need for job guidance, counseling, and placement; need for decent employment—the population addressed and the social goals involved extend well beyond delinquency. One might say as much for urban renewal, the provision of decent housing, the improvement of neighborhood life, and other environmental reforms.

In these efforts one cannot pinpoint the "delinquency prone"—what could that mean in areas of high prevalence? The larger society has a stake far greater than delinquency prevention: equality of opportunity, equity, economic growth, social stability, strengthening local democracy—and prevention of a whole range of costly antisocial deviance. The skills and sanctions involved in efforts of this sort also go well beyond what is required for expertise in dealing with delinquents.

What, it may be asked, about the clinical dimensions? Is primary prevention of delinquency not here possible? Future research may reveal that certain of the delinquencies are genetically, organically, or developmentally determined in a direct line relationship. Then, in the public health sense, one might seek to destroy the agent, strengthen the host, or break the link between them. This would be true delinquency-specific primary prevention. Given all that has been said about the delinquency category, this is an unlikely development. Primary prevention from the clinical side may involve efforts to decrease experiences producing intrapsychic maladjustment, interpersonal pathology, poor physical growth, unwholesome peer relationships, and so on. Such a goal calls, among other things, for: good prenatal care; assurance of adequate nutrition; parent education; family planning; mental health consultation in pediatrics, public health nursing, and early childhood education; wholesome recreational and group programs. Again, *the outcome is expected to be far more than decreased delinquency.* The planning would be frustrated if it were segmented among those concerned with different, if overlapping, social problems such as delinquency, retardation, and neurosis among others.

While all of this may be obvious, it is often ignored in practice. Public sentiment backs delinquency prevention more readily than "effective support for child development." The planner, however, cannot afford to be confused. Planning with reference to delinquency does have validity—but on other levels.

NON-DELINQUENCY-SPECIFIC SECONDARY PREVENTION

Anti-delinquency planning, we have argued, does not of itself address broad institutional change, income transfers, new social utilities, or basic developmental services. The concern with all these is widely ramified in our society. Obviously, if social planning is needed with reference to delinquency, it is in the realm of case services. Here, too, severe limitations should be imposed, particularly with reference to what the public health field likes to call secondary prevention.

Secondary prevention refers to early case finding and the marshaling of those measures which deter growth of pathology and avert any serious disability. The very nature of the delinquency phenomenon calls for careful consideration of social strategy in this realm. In brief, teachers and others who deal with young children are very efficient at identifying those in need of some kind of special help or program adjustments. Schools, mental health and general medical facilities, and many supporting institutions could use cues available to them for identifying populations to be considered for special services. More detailed evaluation, and sometimes specific personality diagnosis, physical assessment, or other appraisal often should follow the teacher's screening. There is little disagreement in this area, although very little has been done.

At the preliminary screening phase, there is no need to know fully what the ultimate adolescent or adult maladjustment will be if no help is forthcoming. The evaluative categories are usually organic, psychiatric, psychological—or whatever else is needed to choose helping measures. "Delinquency-prone" or "vulnerable" classifications do not tell one what to do—and this is the key to policy.

There is no reason the efforts of teachers in such screening of children for special help should not be buttressed by other general screening devices, to be employed in schools, health centers, or even as part of preregistration developmental assessments. Sound planning in this field has been confused, however, by strong advocacy in some quarters of a delinquency-specific screening tool to be employed in the elementary grades.[16] The issue

---

[16] Eleanor T. Glueck, "Efforts to Identify Delinquents," *Federal Probation,* 24, No. 2 (July, 1960), 49–56; Alfred J. Kahn, "Public Policy and Delinquency Prediction: The Case of the Premature Claims," *Crime and Delinquency,* 11, No. 3 (July, 1965), 217–228; Jackson Toby, "An Evaluation of Early Identification and Intensive Treatment Programs of Delinquents," *Social Problems,* 13, No. 2 (Fall, 1965), 160–175; Stanton Wheeler and Leonard S. Cottrell, Jr., *Juvenile Delinquency: Its Prevention and Control* (New York: Russell Sage Foundation, 1966), 22–27; John R. Thurston *et al., Classroom Behavior: Background Factors and Psycho-Social Correlates,* 2 volumes (Madison: Wisconsin State

of whether such devices have as yet been validated or tested under realistic operational conditions is not here immediately relevant, since it is certainly technically possible to develop screening devices.[17] Not to be questioned here is the employment of prediction studies in the context of comprehensive etiological research relating to coherent subgroups among those labeled as delinquents. The issue, rather, is whether delinquency-prediction instruments should be used in schools or related primary institutions to identify as high delinquency-risks children who have not yet justified such characterization on the basis of their overt behavior. Here Wheeler and Cottrell offer a most coherent summary of the rationale for a negative view:

> The assumption is that the public responds to a person informally and in an unorganized way unless that person has been defined as falling into a clear category. The official labeling of a misbehaving youth as delinquent[18] has the effect of placing him in such a category. This official stamp may help to organize responses different from those that would have arisen without the official action. The result is that the label has an important effect upon how the individual is regarded by others. If official processing results in an individual's being segregated with others so labeled, an additional push toward deviant behavior may result. Their association with others who are similarly defined may make the category "delinquent" or "criminal" much more salient for them as well as for others' views of them. In other words, the individual begins to think of himself as delinquent, and he organizes his behavior accordingly.[19]

There is no evidence that professional competence and ethics will overcome this objection. One should not introduce case finding devices to select "potential delinquents" from a population not yet in serious trouble—or even (as in the case of the Glueck instrument) too young to qualify for delinquency.

This line of analysis, based on recognition of delinquency as a category with negative consequences arising from the decision to apply potent sanctions, carries additional implications for secondary prevention. There is every reason, even where some antisocial behavior, which could qualify a child for a delinquency classification, has already occurred, to seek help through the mechanisms applicable to all children. Indeed, all the research evidence indicates that a combination of special privilege, limited detection

---

Department of Social Welfare; I, 1964; II, 1965, mimeographed). Each of these sources contains extensive bibliography and reference to the considerable literature in this field.

[17] See sources cited in the last note for an appraisal of the state of the art.

[18] Here we would insert: or the labeling as a likely delinquent of a child who is rated in a given way on a prediction instrument, *but has not yet even misbehaved.*

[19] Wheeler and Cottrell, *op. cit.,* 22–23.

resources, alternative interventive possibilities, and social policy already has this effect. Only a small portion of the delinquencies are processed by the specialized anti-delinquency machinery. The argument of the above quotation is again relevant. Where there is misbehavior, response by police and courts "may initiate processes that push the misbehaving juveniles toward further delinquent conduct, and, at least, make it more difficult for them to re-enter the conventional world."[20]

Community practice is actually based on these premises even though it is seldom rationalized in other than sentimental terms. First offenders and minor offenders are given "a second chance." Police "warn" parents but make no formal note of many offenses. One turns to doctors, ministers, counselors, social workers, psychiatrists, private schools, military academies, and settlement house programs for alternatives to police and court action. The age of responsibility is constantly being raised, so that the delinquency procedure is not even applicable to the very young. In 1968, a British White Paper proposed an end to prosecution of children under the age of fourteen: court jurisdiction should involve only "care and protection," even if an offense has been committed. In some instances, the ban would apply up to the age of seventeen.[21]

In our view, striving to avoid the use of specifically anti-delinquency machinery and seeking alternative measures is wise practice. The effort can be strengthened, systematized, objectified. Secondary prevention, even in relation to behavior that might technically qualify as delinquency, is best organized on a more generalized basis. It is part of child health and development services and the field of general social service. *To organize secondary prevention with reference to delinquency per se is self-defeating, since the very labeling creates new conditions and limits the interventive possibilities.* The major exception is obvious but important: policing and general law enforcement. Careful, visible patrol and swift and efficient apprehension of offenders are important and effective. Here one has a form of secondary prevention which merges with general case finding for case services. It is delinquency-specific. Those who require services specific to delinquents are to be sorted out from those who may be helped in the general system.

In short, special delinquency programs belong in the realm of direct case services (*tertiary* prevention in public health) and should be planned spe-

---

[20] *Ibid.*

[21] The Home Office, *The Child, the Family, and the Young Offender* (London: Her Majesty's Stationery Office, 1965) and *Children in Trouble* (London: Her Majesty's Stationery Office, 1968).

cifically for those for whom the alternatives have been exhausted or are not appropriate. Here is the locus of the planning challenge in this field, and much remains to be accomplished.

THE DELINQUENCY-SPECIFIC CASE SERVICE NETWORK

Certain categories of behavior—the specifics varying over time, among places at a given time, and among population groups—are regarded as evidence of so severe a threat to the community or as so accurate in their predictions of future threat, that the anti-delinquency case service network is called into play. Even here a variety of options exists, so that police and courts may refer children for service elsewhere without formal processing, but the likelihood of such outcome decreases with the severity of the offense, in the sense of adult criminal categories. Nonetheless, initially at least, some kind of screening must be performed at the doorway to the network. The task is usually assigned to police juvenile bureaus and to juvenile court intake services.

Planning of the relevant service network therefore begins with attention to the preliminary screening, involving some elements of discretion to refer out to non-delinquency-specific services or to drop the matter. We then turn to the court, the vehicle for formal ajudication of status, and to those helping and rehabilitative instruments which base themselves on the network's unique character: the actual or potential deprivation of liberty. While the discussion of these measures will occupy most of the remainder of this chapter, space will permit only brief reference to major issues and perspectives. Again, the purpose is illustration, not detailed programming. Citations indicate where a line of analysis is developed further.

Police juvenile bureaus

All police officers share in basic protective, deterrent, and enforcement activity and, for the most part, no youth specialization is involved. Some departments find it useful to assign special officers to patrol rounds in recreation areas and "hangouts" frequented by young people and to have other specialists to work with youth gangs. Still others undertake recreational activity with the debatable intent of contributing to "prevention." All police departments are involved in a major way in case finding, detection, and apprehension of young offenders, and the argument for some specialized staff to guide or to carry out these responsibilities is convincing.[22]

---

[22] See Chap. VI, "The Policeman and the Child," in Kahn, *Planning Community Services for Children in Trouble*, 206–229.

Of course all policemen "locate" cases, in the sense that they apprehend young people violating the law, are asked for advice by parents and other members of the public, and receive complaints. All police must therefore receive training in the handling of young people. They need to be knowledgeable about juvenile court law and should operate under clear instructions as to how to process given types of offenses. Although discretion is not avoidable, the experience is that rules should be relatively clear cut in determining who is taken immediately to juvenile court (or, if court is not in session, to a detention facility), who is referred for the consideration of a desk officer or juvenile specialist, and who is "noticed" but not formally processed further. In general, the equivalents in a child of serious adult crime must always be in the first category and very trivial matters in the last.

The bulk of the youth situations which come to the police involve exercise of considerable discretion and therefore require somewhat more expert handling than the policeman on the beat or in a patrol car can undertake. The main function of a police juvenile bureau is to render this service. The size of a city, its overall manpower situation, and its pattern of organization must determine whether police juvenile specialists work out of the courthouse, a central unit, or local precincts. The latter is clearly desirable, since the primary task is to process most of the complaints reported on the beat, to accept complaints about young people or requests for help which come directly to the office, and to monitor the overall youth delinquency problem in the area. Wherever located, a juvenile officer needs special training with reference to the law, court procedures, community resources, criteria for exercise of considerable discretion, and the actual handling of personal contacts with children, parents, complainants, and agency representatives. Some police departments have found it possible to assign interested college graduates to this task, and a few have even arranged for special social work training for some of their juvenile officers. Manpower realities suggest the college-degree standard and an effort to recruit a number of officers or civilian workers trained in social work or psychology as consultants and training specialists. Without this degree of specialization a department is not equipped for the function.

The juvenile specialist reviews the form filled out by the policeman on the beat or considers the complainant's statement, clears the case in police and court files and the Social Service Exchange, as appropriate, carries on telephone contacts with agencies already involved with a family where appropriate, visits the home if necessary (and if the staffing pattern permits), interviews parent and child (with the parent present if the child is seen), occasionally consults community agency records—and then settles the next step. Again, relatively little action is necessary where a court petition is mandated or where the matter is too trivial for attention. Much work may be needed where discretion is involved. The premium, however, is on rapid screening.

The screening task is simply stated but seldom well discharged. Where the case is not in an offense category destined for immediate court processing, the juvenile officer must decide whether

☐ The matter is so trivial that it may be forgotten.

☐ The matter is sufficiently trivial and the evidence that the child has a problem so limited that a letter to the parents is sufficient, relying completely on their discretion as to the next step.

☐ An interview with parent and child is necessary, with the possibility of social agency referral, clinical referral, initiation of other specialized services or court action.

In effect, then, the juvenile officer is a specialized screening instrument who channels a very large proportion of all cases which reach him (probably over 95 percent) to the basic services or helping facilities available to *all* children. However, he is expected to be sufficiently in tune with community sentiment, knowledgeable in the law, informed enough about procedure, and sufficiently skilled in case handling to utilize the court as appropriate. Unlike representatives of those "voluntary" and noncorrectional social agencies and institutions which do not wish to use the courts too frequently lest they be publicly perceived as relying upon potent sanctions and authoritative measures, he should be prepared to use such measures when and if available experience and policy suggest that they are desirable. Juvenile police services too often make a virtue of under-use of the courts.

The court's intake service

The juvenile court or the juvenile term of a family court is an institution which houses four or five major functions relevant to the specialized delinquency-oriented intervention system: intake, adjudication of status, disposition planning, direct service, detention. Each deserves separate, if somewhat brief, attention to clarify issues and alternatives relevant to the mission of the total system.

Within a delinquency-specific case service system, whether or not actually located in a court building or in a detention center, there is need for an intake service which considers both whether there is legal sanction to process the case within the delinquency-oriented system as well as whether it is *useful* to do so in the light of community norms and resources and the case situation. First, the intake worker must explore the existence of a *prima facie* case, without seeking the child's admission or denial or himself adjudicating the charge. The parent would ordinarily be present during the interview with the child as would an attorney if requested by the parent. A parent might also be interviewed alone—as might a complainant.

Thus both probation (social work) and legal competence are called for —usually in the form of a trained probation officer who knows the juvenile code and has access to legal consultation. Interviewing and diagnostic skills are needed, and there is a premium on up-to-date knowledge of the service capabilities of other elements in the social service network. The second of the two considerations above ("Is it useful to involve a court?") requires information and judgment.

The outcomes of the process may be several. Given the decision that there is no basis for a petition (a complainant-petitioner should have the right to appeal to a judge for the right to file), a referral to a non-authoritative public service or to a voluntary agency may nonetheless be suggested to the parent. The need for emergency medical or psychiatric service may be recognized—with the judge making the assignment if there is no parental agreement. Even given a technical basis for a petition, parental and complainant agreement on service in the general system may be proposed if this appears advantageous for the particular case. Finally, a petition may be drawn, its form and type varying with the state legal system.

Should a petition be proposed, the intake worker would also prepare for the judge, on the basis of his preliminary assessment and telephone contacts, a recommendation as to the need for detention up to the time of the court adjudication hearing (*see below*) unless the hearing will occur at once. In a well-staffed court, he would have access to a psychiatric consultant in instances of what appeared to be psychiatric emergencies.

Internal coherence is best achieved if supervision of reception and other court "doorway" personnel as well as the actual petition writing are seen as functions of the intake staff; in some courts independent, offense-oriented petition clerks have been known to confuse the process, while insensitive receptionists have made it difficult to believe that the court's intent is to help and rehabilitate.[23]

This general strategy, emphasizing the use of the court only when its authoritative nature carries advantages, yet recognizing the stigma it *must*

---

[23] Alfred J. Kahn, *A Court for Children* (New York: Columbia University Press, 1953), Chap. IV, and *Planning Community Services for Children in Trouble*, Chap. VII.

carry, obviously argues against "informal" supervision and protection—very unclear statuses which may violate rights since there has been no adjudication.

Court disposition—the adjudication of status

The core role of the court, its unique advantage as a community intervention component, is the right to adjudicate. To decide that, in the particular case at hand, circumstances exist, as defined by law, which justify intervention by the state, is to take a drastic step. Yet community policy and case reasoning consider such a step necessary on some occasions. Current conceptions, therefore, place on the adjudication hearing the heavy burden of deciding whether a basis for authoritative intervention in the case exists under law.

For a long period, the concept of the court as playing the role of a kind and helpful parent served as justification for a blurring of adjudication and disposition phases. Little of due process was preserved; children were adjudicated on "belief"; "admissions" were taken informally, often under pressure; lawyers seldom were available, and appeals most rare. Records were confused and incomplete. The reforms of the late nineteen-fifties and nineteen-sixties in this field have stressed that, although the juvenile court or juvenile term of a family court would be destroyed if it became a junior criminal court and introduced all the attendant criminal protections, this does not justify "Star Chamber" proceedings and a dilution of rights. New emphasis is placed on separation of adjudication from disposition (do not plan for the child until the court has taken jurisdiction; do not take jurisdiction in order to carry out a service plan). The child has a right to legal assistance if he wants it even if his parent cannot afford a lawyer. Evidence should be reviewed and witnesses may be cross-examined. All the standards of a fair hearing in a civil case should apply. Adjudication is on the basis of a preponderance of evidence. The judge may seek to bring out the facts, but should not become the prosecutor.[24]

---

[24] It would here be out of place to review the evolving legal precedents, as lawyers enter juvenile court, cases are appealed, and law is "made." Some would even bring a public prosecutor in, to balance the legal aid, and to avoid making the judge play the role of public accuser as well. Others fear this step. Progress is being made in strengthening the adjudication hearing as a judicial process and assuring constitutional protections. Basic materials are found in "Standards for Juvenile and Family Courts"; Margaret K. Rosenheim, Editor, *Justice for the Child* (New York: The Free Press, 1962); Monrad G. Paulsen, "The New York Family Court Act," *Buffalo Law Review*, 12 (June, 1963), 420–441; Oram W. Ketcham, "The Juvenile Court for 1975," *Social Service Review*, 40, No.

The Supreme Court has begun to give the juvenile court much-needed attention, thus accelerating these trends. It observed in one of its first cases:

There is evidence, in fact, that there may be grounds for concern that the child receives the worst of both worlds: that he gets neither the protections accorded to adults nor the solicitous care and regenerative treatment postulated for children.[25]

In a more definitive, historic case in 1967, the Court commented that "unbridled discretion, however benevolently motivated, is frequently a poor substitute for principle and procedure." Furthermore, "the features of the juvenile system which its proponents have asserted are of unique benefit will not be impaired by constitutional domestication." A delinquency hearing, the Court ruled, must measure up to the essentials of due process and a fair hearing. Notice of charges, right to counsel, and right to cross-examination are essential in a juvenile court, as they are whenever the potential for deprivation of liberty is present.[26]

The adjudication, which finds that the child is a "delinquent" or under circumstances demanding the "care and protection" of the state (depending on the provisions of the particular delinquency statute), is a major phase in case processing. A legal basis has been created for deprivation of freedom, if necessary, or for community-based treatment with some authoritative elements (probation or a reporting center). Whether these resources will actually be employed should, of course, depend on individualized assessment of a child's circumstances and a realistic appraisal of the capabilities of the relevant resources. Before discussing disposition, however, some brief reference to detention is necessary.

Detention

Juvenile detention is another component of the delinquency-specific service network. Its function is to provide secure (but not punitive) custody between apprehension or petition-writing and the adjudication hearing, be-

---

3 (September, 1966), 283–288; Alex Elson and Margaret K. Rosenheim, "Justice for the Child at the Grassroots," *American Bar Association Journal* (April, 1965), no pagination; Margaret K. Rosenheim, "The Child and His Day in Court," *Child Welfare*, XLV, No. 1 (January, 1966), 17–27.

For a recent, relevant British review, see W. E. Cavenagh, *Juvenile Courts, the Child and the Law* (Harmondsworth, Middlesex, England: Penguin Books, revised edition, 1967).

[25] *Kent v. United States*, 383 U.S. 541 (1966).

[26] *In the Matter of the Application of Gault*, 387 U.S. 1, 87 Sup. Ct. 1428 (1967).

tween adjudication and disposition, between disposition and transfer to a specialized treatment resource, but only in that limited group of cases in which:

- ☐ it is considered likely that the child will harm himself if permitted to remain at home; or,
- ☐ it is considered highly likely that additional serious offenses will be committed in the interim; or,
- ☐ it is considered highly likely that the child will run away or be removed from the area of court jurisdiction in the interim; or,
- ☐ a disposition has been made and the child is awaiting transfer to an institution involving secure custody.

The judgment as to the use of detention in the predispositional and preadjudicatory phases is in the province of the judge, on the basis of his own observations and the advice of the intake worker. Psychiatric consultation should be available upon request. In cases which arise when the court is not in session, the intake worker (or a special detention intake worker) makes the decision on an interim basis. Large cities should probably have 24-hour court coverage or, at the least, a judge who sits at some time every day, including weekends. In such instances, the court intake worker readily serves as detention intake worker or vice versa.

The history of delinquency services is replete with evidence of detention misuse. Some judges employ it punitively ("Keep him there to learn a lesson while we decide what to do"). Others refer children to detention as a way to assure access to diagnostic resources. (The process of case study is often complicated by removal from the child's normal environment, and is certainly made more costly; besides, secure custody involves questionable deprivation of liberty if not absolutely necessary.) Many children are sent to detention for lack of shelters for dependent and neglected children, stand-by foster boarding homes, or emergency psychiatric facilities. This is obviously poor provision on the part of the community. Some states, such as New York, seek to guard against misuse by statutory definition of the grounds for detention. The experience is that the abuse continues where the alternative resources are not also provided and where judges are not regularly challenged by legal aid or private counsel.

The protection of individual rights also requires administrative or statutory limitations on the length of permissible detention. While there must be variations according to geographic and resource factors, which affect the length of disposition study and planning, the frequency of court hearings, etc., detention should be a matter of days or weeks, at the most, not of months. Long detention is often the source of considerable anti-community resentment in young people who were previously quite amenable to help. Besides, given the fluctuating nature of the detention population, it is difficult to achieve and maintain a wholesome atmosphere under conditions of security. For many young people, prolonged detention may be a very damaging experience of socialization into delinquent norms.

Some of the negative consequences seem better controlled in small detention facilities or detention homes for younger children, rather than in very large structures. To emphasize the temporary nature of the service, facilitate access of the child to the courtroom, and to permit the probation officer carrying out the disposition study to observe and become acquainted with the child, detention centers should be decentralized, each located quite close to the court branch which it services.

The emphasis on court-detention integration also serves to avoid an oft-observed phenomenon: the tendency of workers in some institutions to become proud of their programs, concentrating their energies on program improvement and assuming that they are "good" for a child—forgetting that detention is intended as a brief experience and only for those who absolutely require it.

Administration of detention by the probation department usually contributes to the objective of achieving a close court-detention tie. Under ordinary circumstances, one would not have a separate detention social service department. The probation officer would visit the child in detention and collect relevant observations from the residential and clinical staff. Detention and court social service records would be fully integrated.

None of this would contra-indicate actual operation of housekeeping, medical, and child care aspects of detention programs by the same city or county unit (a public social service department) that is responsible for foster homes, shelters, and so on. Child care skills and special management organization are required. It is at the level of both intake and social study that the integration of detention into court process is essential—to assure appropriate use of detention and its contribution to the total court mission.

Disposition planning

One here approaches a most unsatisfactory aspect of the system. Alternatives have been posed and transitions may be under way. In brief, it has long been assumed that, following adjudication, a judge awaits a social study report by the probation staff and, then, selects the disposition. The situation may be dismissed or discharged (the child needs no further help), the child may be referred to the general service system in the community (potent sanctions are not needed), or he may be placed on probation, committed to a juvenile training school or to an institution or foster home resource, which is not part of the delinquency-specific service system.

Discouraged by high rates of institutional recidivism, probation failure, and voluntary agency inability to follow through, observers have increasingly looked at each phase of the process more carefully. The weakness of dispositional planning in most courts is apparent. Disposition is a job for behavioral experts and few judges are so qualified. If they have been carefully selected and exposed to the special institutes and seminars currently developing, they are better able to use detention, make dispositional decisions, carry out adjudication hearings, and perhaps to interpret case studies submitted by probation officers, so as to choose between institutionalization and a community-based service. This does not qualify them to choose from among a significant number of different institutions involving various degrees of freedom and security, educational or therapeutic emphases, individual or group approaches, small group or large group exposure, and varying lengths of stay.

The assignment is somewhat simpler in smaller jurisdictions, where the judge has ample opportunity to become acquainted with each resource and to telephone institutional directors, clinic heads, and agency administrators as he considers a plan for a child. It is also argued that in larger jurisdictions the judge's limitations are compensated for by the probation officer assigned to the case, who has explored possibilities and developed an appropriate plan. The judge inevitably follows it. Certainly, in small and medium-sized jurisdictions this may be adequate. One wonders why the judge should be in a position to veto a treatment plan made on this basis, however, since he presumably has less access to relevant information than the probation officer. Would it not be wise to formalize the role and place responsibility appropriately?

In the sizeable jurisdictions where a large proportion of all cases originate, even the most competent of probation officers are seldom likely to possess sufficient current information to match child with agency or facility at a given moment. And with staff shortages, many lack time and qualifications.

These circumstances suggest the need, where case volume is large, for a dispositional system under which a panel of experts would develop the fundamental treatment plan. Educators, vocational counselors, social workers, psychologists, psychiatrists, and child care experts would be appropriate panel members. At least two or three people would share each decision, in recognition of the multidisciplinary issues which usually arise, and *share their knowledge* of resources.[27] Reserved for the judge might be the *general* decisions about (*a*) discharge, (*b*) non-authoritative (other-than-probation) referral in the community, (*c*) court-based (probation) treatment, (*d*) institutionalization. At this point, the disposition machinery would take over to make a *specific* plan. The expert panels would draw upon the probation study, clinical reports if available, and other records. Where needed, but not routinely, an observational-study center could be employed. Panel members would have access to constantly-updated information about available institutional space and the right to assign directly to the training school system and to draw upon space in voluntary institutions "purchased" for public use. Their programs would permit routine visits to assure a clear picture of each facility employed.

Under this plan, the court would actually add one tier to its system: adjudication, dispositional hearing for the judge's first level (general) decisions, and dispositional conference (specific plans) with the panel. The degree of formality and resemblance to an adversary procedure would decrease with each stage. At adjudication, as already indicated, there would be legal representation if wished by parent or child. At disposition, with the probation officer's report before him, the judge would be making a decision about deprivation of freedom in a situation in which he already had the right to do so. Parent or child might seek to supplement the probation officer's report and their attorney might make the case for a treatment approach seen as appropriate by the family. But the issue would be expert judgment, not evidence, and the judge would be exercising the discretion which is his right.

The disposition panel would merely hold a group interview with parents and child, or with any of them alone, to test out tentative plans based on study of reports and to interpret and introduce the disposition. Here there would be no need for "outsiders" or representation.

The need for accountability would probably call for a continuing role beyond this point either for the judge or for the panel. A case can be made for both possibilities, and experimentation would appear to be in order.

A specific commitment for a given number of years would smack of punishment and sentence. Yet to protect against abuse, some juvenile statutes now set maximum limits on the period of institutionalization, elimi-

---

[27] We here differ with a recent overseas report which calls for a lay panel. In our perspective, community preferences affect the case service system in many ways but the "promise" of the court demands expert dispositions, a technical matter.

nating the possibility of years or even decades of unnecessary institutional-ization. Recently some statutes have required periodic reports to the court about a child's progress and court permission to extend a stay for "case" reasons. At times, such reports have been processed very routinely; at others, they have been carefully studied to consider whether continued institution-alization was truly desirable for the child. Continued provision for such accountability is needed.

Treatment effectiveness requires easy transfer among institutions, from institution to community-based service, from community-based service to institution. Yet, since some of the facilities—those which are delinquency-specific—may be secure, and since none permits a return home at will, it is necessary to develop a procedure for judge or panel to grant permission to transfer to a more secure facility (increased deprivation of freedom) or from community to institution. Such permission should be required even after parental consent, to avoid the problem of coercion, offer an opportunity for negative opinions, and avoid parental use of institutionalization as a pathological attack upon a child.

Court-based treatment, the further specification of "probation"

Before looking at the transformation of probation into what might be seen as a new stage in the evolution of court-based treatment, it may be useful to comment briefly on the effort to develop psychiatric clinics and mental health facilities in courts.[28]

The early psychological and psychiatric clinics in courts were diagnostic, the notion having been early developed that a judge needed maximum as-sistance in understanding a child in order to help him. Quite naturally, both because clinicians develop their skills best if they both treat and diagnose and because treatment resources were in short supply, such clinics also took on treatment responsibilities. In an era when courts themselves were test-ing their functions and clinical disciplines were refining their methods, a flexible, and perhaps ad hoc, approach was readily justified.

Today a somewhat different picture emerges. A national effort is under way to develop a community psychiatry network and to assure its effective integration with other networks. It is generally agreed that psychiatric treatment clinics need a medical base for operations, and that assurance of continuity of care argues against their fragmentation among other host

---

[28] For more detailed review and further citations, see *Planning Community Services for Children in Trouble*, 266–270, and Henry Machover, "Mental Health Services in the Family Court of the State of New York in the City of New York" (New York: The Ju-dicial Conference, 1966, mimeographed).

institutions. Moreover, each major element in the social service intervention network should be characterized by its intervention specific. This is also a potent reason for not basing full-fledged psychiatric treatment clinics in schools, courts, and employment offices thereby confusing the nature of these several institutions and creating conflicts between clinical-treatment values and those which must govern education, courts, or job offices. Experience therefore suggests the desirability of equipping a juvenile court with a clinical team (preferably one outposted by a community mental health center or treatment clinic, so that the staff members will keep their treatment skills "sharp") whose important but limited assignment would be:

☐ consultation to judges, intake workers, and probation personnel involved in all phases of the work
☐ diagnostic assessments
☐ emergency examinations and help where called for
☐ staff training.

If, at the disposition phase, child or parent requires psychiatric treatment (under medical auspices), the referral should be to the community mental health network, including out-patient clinics, day and night hospitals, etc. Should this not yield enough "control," psychiatric institutional resources may be employed. If court-based treatment is considered appropriate, the assignment would be to the court social service unit, which would not be a treatment "clinic" but would have access to clinical consultation.

The philosophy behind this approach is *that the court must seek itself to develop and house the intervention specific appropriate to its unique role as a facility which works with adjudicated children who cannot withdraw at will, who may be sent to secure institutions if the community-based service effort fails, and who must be kept under control for community protection, during the treatment process.*

For many years the probation departments which sought to elaborate this unique assignment have been caught in a bog compounded of several elements. Major changes are needed if probation is to be converted from a largely meaningless ritual into an effective intervention specific.

The one and same department, often the same staff, has attempted to man intake, carry out predispositional social studies, and "supervise" children "on probation." The latter role has always suffered under the pressure to get new cases into the courtroom and to service the judge with dispositional studies. Treatment is often a meaningless brief reporting routine. While one overall administration might have responsibility for all court social services, there is a strong case for two or three sub-units: intake; social studies and dispositional planning; court-based treatment. The creation of a corps dedicated to treatment innovation in the court context might produce some breakthrough.

Probation had its professional development as a social work discipline at a time when interpersonal influence and clinical intervention were considered the main ways to help individuals. School adjustments, referrals to churches and character-building agencies, and job counseling were attempted, but only peripherally. The "ideal type" probation contact was a leisurely-conducted office interview, part of a series designed to create "insight" in the young offender and, thus, to remove motivation for antisocial conduct. Today the concept of "delinquencies" implies the need for a complex repertoire of inverventions within the court treatment service: individual, group, family, on several different levels and with varied goals. For some young people, role training in the search for and holding of a job is the way to open "opportunity"; others need intensive insight therapy. Family-oriented, multiple-impact therapies will reach some delinquents, while sound, strong leadership and aid in community integration will help others.

Probation long was, and in some places still is, a low-status discipline, intended in fact, if not in court philosophy, to serve as the judge's general errand boy. Without professional status, control of its time, a research base, ability to experiment, or an identity, it could not be expected to have the needed capacity for innovation in a most difficult field. Externally, in professional recognition, training, salaries, job loads, much has improved. Some departments are autonomous, and occasional probation chiefs are almost co-equal with administrative judges—at least, they have a measure of professional autonomy. Conditions for a program "take off" may now exist. Administrative redefinitions will encourage the process.

A true probation "take off" would change the picture to a point where "court treatment services" would become the more appropriate term. The disposition would call for such service if the child was considered to need community-based help under controls. A diversified staff, freed of the intake and social study (disposition) assignment, would include specialists in group therapy, employment role training, less intensive group activities with adolescents, intensive (clinically-oriented) casework, work with family groups, and environmental manipulation. Day reporting centers (plus group counseling), office treatment interviews, group trips, and home services would all be part of the picture.[29]

---

[29] References to new developments in the service repertoire are listed in Kahn, *Planning Community Services* . . . , Chap. X. Research to match delinquent-type and treatment

One might also assume considerable emphasis on community organization activity in the future court services. From what has been said earlier in the chapter, it would follow that "treatment" of certain delinquents requires a major effort to help them find their places in the community which actually has, or is erroneously perceived by them as having, closed them out. In effect, communities which would end several kinds of delinquencies must together solve the problem of finding a place for certain young people in viable roles and of facilitating the transition stages. Court service people, in collaboration with staff and members of local organizations, including those developed in the poverty program, are taking this on. Indeed, the reintegration and reclaiming of alienated youth may well be an ideal type of activity for self-help neighborhood groups. It combines realistic social resource development with socio-therapeutic and political activities.

Court services of this kind would require an interdisciplinary team, perhaps with social work at the core, but with personnel from several fields —and with case aides, former inmates, and volunteers as well.

The loci of this new type of service would be court offices; all-day, afternoon, or weekend "reporting centers" (combining work, recreation, group therapy); neighborhood organization offices; and other community facilities. The service would go where the young people may be seen naturally and given the experiences needed.

Specialized institutions

In most cases the disposition process will result in referral to generalized community-based services or to general institutions and schools serving *all* child welfare needs and clinical treatment requirements. Some cases will be helped best in community-based but court-centered treatment services of the sort described above. Similarly, some will need the help of what are commonly called juvenile training schools, i.e. institutions involving greater control. Easy movement from one to the other will be desirable, with provision to prevent extension of stay without appropriate review, to prevent loss of the child within the system, and to preclude any measures which

---

specifics is reported by: Marguerite Q. Warren, "Community Treatment Project: An Evaluation of Community Treatment for Delinquents," Research Report No. 5 (Sacramento, California: Department of Youth Authority, 1964); Frank Riessman, Jerome Cohen, Arthur Pearl, Editors, *Mental Health of the Poor* (New York: The Free Press of Glencoe, 1964), 478–594; Lamar Empey, "Alternatives to Incarceration," United States Department of Health, Education, and Welfare, Juvenile Delinquency Publication No. 9001 (Washington, D.C.: Government Printing Office, 1967).

involve decreased freedom without occasion for careful consideration and review.

In recent years, the specialized institutional repertoire, if this term may be seen as encompassing all "away from home" dispositions, has increased, both within the delinquency field and in child welfare generally:

☐ work camps
☐ small group residences outside the city
☐ urban residences
☐ urban institutions
☐ educational-vocational settings
☐ psychiatrically-oriented treatment programs
☐ sociologically, value-change-oriented programs.

The major theme of planning efforts might be: each institution type should be or seek to become an intervention specific, a known type of help for identifiable type(s) of child(ren).[30] Or, put differently, through experience and research, "it is necessary both to identify the essence of the treatment impact of each major type of program and to specify the range of children for which it is suitable."[31]

Only the most naïve now fail to recognize, in one way or another, the impact of the living routine, the peer relationships, the informal contacts, the maintenance and clerical personnel on those who are institutionalized. Some group facilities seek to neutralize group processes, which may interfere, and focus on individual treatment, education, and wholesome relationships with adults. Others strive to convert the "peer culture," long an anti-institution, anti-authoritarian force, into an ally in the reform of individuals. Both of these strategies are illustrations of the larger concern with the "away from home," authority-based facility as a "therapeutic milieu."[32]

Similarly, there is general agreement that one should not commit children to out-of-community dispositions unless absolutely necessary, since any period of enforced absence only serves to increase their sense of alienation and exile, which may in some cases be the core problem. Thus, institutional

---

[30] Kahn, *Planning Community Services* . . . , Chap. XI.

[31] *Ibid.*, 425.
A fruitful type of research is reported by Carl F. Jesness, "The Fricot Ranch Study," Research Report No. 47 (Sacramento, California: Department of Youth Authority, 1965).

[32] Illustrative sources are: Howard W. Polsky, *Cottage Six* (New York: Russell Sage Foundation, 1962); Lloyd E. Ohlin and William Lawrence, "Social Interaction Among Clients as a Treatment Problem," *Social Work*, IV, No. 2 (April, 1959), 3–13; Social Science Research Council, "Theoretical Studies in Social Organization of the Prison," Pamphlet No. 15 (New York, 1960).

treatment should carry with it a bias towards relatively brief stays where possible—or longer stays designed for known purposes as appropriate: to complete a school course, solve certain personal problems, permit some problems to be solved at home in one's absence, or achieve specific treatment goals. At the same time, the administrative plan should maximize the likelihood of continuity between institutional and community-based service, assuring a consistency of community stance toward the youngster and the optimum supports for his reintegration as an accepted member upon return.

The specific devices to be adopted for this latter purpose must vary with circumstances in a given city and state, but the following are relevant *possibilities*, all now in operation in some places:

☐ Have treatment continuity reside with the court-based treatment service in all instances of commitment to facilities in the delinquency-specific network (now generally called training schools). The court service worker would retain contact with the child during the away-from-home experience, continue to work on home-related problems, carry specific responsibility for individual, community, and familial aspects of reintegration upon return, and serve as the aftercare worker.

☐ Assure that each institution has both city-based and institutional staff, so that commitment includes the aftercare and case continuity responsibility.

☐ Assign case accountability to a general neighborhood-based social service center, with the responsible worker playing the role outlined above for the court-based treatment service. In addition, a social worker so situated would be concerned with case integration for the family unit in a broader sense than could be possible for a court- or institution-bound service.

These brief summary programming suggestions, both for the transition of probation into more comprehensive, court-based treatment service and for the creation out of training school systems of a network of treatment-specific services away from home, are based on trends in the more developed cities and states and on the newer knowledge of the range of delinquencies and of treatment strategies. The city and state planning personnel concerned with programming in this field have access to guides and standards produced by a variety of federal agencies and the National Council on Crime and Delinquency. Research developments are reported regularly in professional and scientific journals and, most recently, reviewed by the President's Commission on Law Enforcement and the Administration of Justice.

This much said, it is necessary to add that knowledge is limited, treatment technology weak—and community protection is an urgent objective. Thus, delinquency-specific institutional systems will continue to require some essentially custodial security facilities, even though their therapeutic impact is questionable. One can only counsel that such facilities be small and admit only through a well-defined procedure which protects all children. Careful staffing, direction, and inspection are needed to prevent the brutalization and punitive regimes so common to the prison system. Large research investments are essential to decrease and eventually eliminate such evidences of hopelessness.

JUVENILE VS. FAMILY COURTS

It is not necessary for present purposes to consider the relative advantages of distinctive juvenile courts as opposed to more comprehensive family courts, which have jurisdiction over all marital issues and adoption as well as delinquency and neglect. Adequate exploration would require considerable detail and take us beyond the illustrative intent of the present chapter. It may be noted, however, that the realities of family dynamics, under all the types of circumstances mentioned above, are seen by many in the field as presenting a convincing case for a court with comprehensive jurisdiction. Such jurisdiction permits integration of several interdependent legal actions, now often carried on in fragmented fashion. It assures a coherent socialized approach to all family problems in accord with community preferences and has advantages in the deployment of professional resources.

The question is asked whether family or juvenile courts should continue to include, as part of delinquency jurisdiction, the approximately 26 percent of such cases involving activities that are not crimes in adults (truancy, ungovernable behavior, etc.). There is little dispute about the need for court intervention into many such cases, but some observers hold that the delinquency stigma intensifies the problems.

New York has sought to cope with these matters by assigning some of the behavior in question to the "neglect" category, where parental incapacity or acts of omission are involved. The remainder of the children are called "persons in need of supervision," not delinquents, and certain dispositional differences are mandated. Although experience so far is limited, the approach may be useful. We have here maintained that general child care services should be used wherever possible. Since delinquency is now a stigmatized status, perhaps the end of all court labeling except adjudication as "children in need of court services" would be preferable.

"Neglect" jurisdiction per se also requires re-evaluation by communities, although this has not been necessary for present purposes. "Neglect" is generally joined with delinquency jurisdiction in children's and family courts.

In the early years of the juvenile court, when delinquency was seen as a non-stigmatizing category and the court's role defined as "parenting," it was quite logical that such jurisdiction should be added. In fact, before child welfare services were developed in many places, courts also served dependent and handicapped children, and some continue to do so.

In a more planfully developed service system, services to abused and neglected children would be part of general family and child welfare services. The protective casework units, reporting system for child abuse, emergency services, and so on obviously belong in a general social service network, locally based. Community authority is needed at certain points to protect children, and when such authority involves potential or actual infringement on parental rights, court protections are needed for all concerned. Where possible, the jurisdiction over intervention in this fashion should be assigned to a comprehensive family court; where such court does not exist, a children's court with delinquency jurisdiction is probably that institution in the community system most likely to have the appropriate approach to problems and access to needed resources. It is important that the pattern of operations and of supportive resources reflect the fact that the parent—not the child—is the respondent and that the "solutions" require easy access to a network of family and child welfare services, clinical facilities, income supports, and practical services.[33]

THE PLANNING AND COORDINATION BASE

While we have argued that the total repertoire of community responses to the delinquencies requires a delinquency-specific community and institutional treatment system (e.g., the "old" probation and training school services), a strong case has been made for maximum use of *general* (non-delinquency-specific) services and for easy and frequent moving from the more to the less authoritative system as case circumstances permit. The question is thus raised as to the locus and nature of planning structures, coordination machinery, and administrative mechanisms. Special difficulties reside in these issues, and there are no definitive answers based on experience.

Institutional services to delinquents often have been placed in state child welfare departments, while the state juvenile court system may be part of the general city or state court system; and probation is administratively related to courts, child welfare, or correctional departments. Sometimes juve-

---

[33] For detail, see Donald Brieland, "Protective Services and Child Abuse: Implications for Public Child Welfare," *The Social Service Review*, XL, No. 4 (December, 1966), 369–377. Also, Monrad G. Paulsen, "Legal Protections Against Child Abuse," *Children*, 13, No. 2 (March–April, 1966), 42–48.

nile facilities are functions of the department that also administers the adult prison and reformatory system. In some states, during recent decades, divisions for youth or governor's committees for children and youth have developed as the administratively responsible agencies for some or all of these functions, or they may have generalized planning assignments—often without sanction to do more than to "recommend" to the executive or legislative branches.[34]

While city or state organizational patterns must perforce vary, it may be useful to suggest the real alternatives posed by a planning perspective on the issues. There is little doubt that juvenile police are part of a city police function and juvenile or family courts part of a city or state court system. Planning for such services belongs in whichever arms of government are planning police and court services. The complications which often appear to arise with reference to prevention are also readily resolved in the light of the general thrust of this chapter: primary prevention is part of a more comprehensive system and is not delinquency-specific.

Thus the key administrative and planning issues are two:

Should the social services which are court-related be administratively part of and planned by the general community social service system or do they belong in a system with access to more authority: courts or corrections?

Should the delinquency-specific institutions and other away-from-home facilities be conceived as an integral part of family and child welfare or psychiatry, be a separate system, or be administratively related to adult corrections?

Administration and planning of treatment services

The first problem posed does not arise with reference to intake or court social study activities. These are obviously court staff functions and subject to the same planning and administration as other court services. As already suggested, the weakness of probation as a treatment service is related in part to the assumption that these must be part of the same operation.

The search for continuity of care, service innovation, resource differentiation, accountability, and case integration all lead to the conceptualization of delinquency-specific treatment services as part of a more comprehensive neighborhood-based social service system. The probation officers in their new role (and perhaps with a new name) could be assigned from and even based in such services.

On the side of the alternative choice is the fact that the very essence of

---

[34] Kahn, *Planning Community Services* . . . , Chap. XIII.

the delinquency-specific service is its access to potent sanctions. This is so critical in public perception of the service and in the worker stance vis-à-vis client as to justify the conceptualization of corrections as an intervention-specific.

Each of the choices involves a price: some dilution of the potency of the delinquency-specific services on the one hand, and some sacrifice of continuity and case integration, on the other. The obvious, yet informed, conclusion is that planners in a given city or state might consider which price is more readily paid. Only experimentation over time will yield a generalized answer.

Away-from-home services

The same considerations apply to the away-from-home facilities, with the likelihood that separation of general from delinquency-specific facilities will increase the stigma assigned to the latter and contribute to the process which, in the past, usually kept them custodial and unequipped to "treat." On the other hand, failure to differentiate may in some ways handicap the more general network. Either way, experience does argue against administration by adult corrections, a field which is expected to carry a large punitive component and a smaller rehabilitative rationale.

The conclusion, then, might be that experiments in this realm would call for either a complete integration of the delinquency-specific facilities into the general institutional network, or the maintenance of a separate system of juvenile training schools, perhaps by another name, but under the same overall auspices as the general child care and treatment resources. (Experience would suggest that, except in so far as one is dealing with medically-based psychiatric and retardation facilities, traditional mental health, youth, and child welfare system should be merged and planned for as an integrated network.)

Again, monitored experience is needed.

Finally, the disposition of the several issues outlined in this section will carry implications for coordination machinery. To the extent that separate administrative and planning mechanisms are chosen, parallel provision is needed to assure coordination of planning and administration as well as case integration, with the other relevant social service systems.

A FINAL NOTE

The exercise represented by this chapter attempts relevance to the delinquency problem, but all negative-status social problem categories involve similar considerations. Where the goal is rehabilitation and reintegration, then, there is a strong bias against separation and an argument for universalism in the service system. Thus, the approach to prevention and early case screening would tend to favor the general, child development *problems*, not retardation or autism, as the basis for early screening (to choose other illustrations).

On the other hand, community imagery, social control, treatment logic, and the advantages of creating specialized statuses that permit restriction and control ("delinquent," "addict," "neglectful parent," etc.) may at times justify a special case service network for such groups. One must attempt to assure protection of constitutional rights, as well as all necessary devices for continuity, integration, and service specificity within the network, while building and assuring constant employment of doorways into and out of the special system wherever possible or wise. The administrative and planning structures must be developed with this end in view.

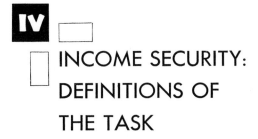

IV

INCOME SECURITY: DEFINITIONS OF THE TASK

THE POVERTY and the delinquency discussions were comprehensive in the sense that they addressed many aspects of planning; in the first instance, there was also considerable attention to the constraints inherent in a political context.

The next chapters deal with fewer of the planning dimensions. None ignores any component in the process completely; *but each concentrates on one or two elements*, in an effort to deepen and to elaborate. This chapter and the next focus on the definition of the task, a much underestimated and often invisible stage in planning.

Out of the interaction of preferences and reality assessment, the interplay between expertise and self-interest, the planning process fixes for itself a definition of the "problem to be solved." Such definition encompasses preliminary conclusions about such issues as etiological forces, conceptualization of the system within which the planning is to take place, and the type of intervention to be established. It sets many of the parameters of the planning outcome. However, as these matters are pursued further, there is feedback which, in turn, may lead to a redefinition of the task. The planning process shapes its "idea sword." Knowledge, values, and strategy remain in constant interaction.[1]

Income security, chosen for this illustration, is a "sector" or field in which economic, political, and moral concerns, cultural inhibitions, and special-interest pleadings are so potent that it may be argued truly that rational planning has no place here at all. Yet, comprehensive and partial planning efforts are almost constantly under way to improve or change basically the

---

[1] See Chapter III in the companion volume, THEORY AND PRACTICE OF SOCIAL PLANNING.

present, admittedly patchwork system. These efforts are well directed. What other field has better potential for coping basically with poverty, underpinning the core guarantees of the American welfare society, and setting the central themes of social policy?

The thesis of the chapter has two facets: the components of what could comprise a rounded income-security[2] system are at present at hand or proposed. However, the alternatives, from among which choices may be made, reflect unreconciled conceptions of the task. The shaping of a sound system, therefore, requires considerable attention to task definition. It is useful to focus on differing views of society and its responsibility and divers conceptions of social priority.

One chapter provides limited space for such ambitious undertakings. We therefore limit the discussion to a sampling from four separate attempts at policy planning and programming in segments of the total income-security field. Other efforts have been made and other approaches have been proposed but need not be included to achieve our illustrative intent. This "case study" effort is introduced by a survey of some strengths and inadequacies in the current operation, and it is followed by a brief discussion of a possible approach to task formulation for comprehensive income security in the United States.[3]

COMPONENTS, COVERAGE, AND GAPS

One should not minimize the progress in building an income-security system in the United States, particularly since 1935. Almost one-third of all United States households received payments from public income-maintenance programs in 1965.

1. The social insurance programs known technically as *Old Age, Survivors, Disability and Health Insurance* (OASDHI), a wage-related, contributory system referred to by the man on the street as "social security," covers practically the entire current labor force, except for those civil servants and government employees in other plans. Employer and employee payroll taxes meet almost all the costs. Receiving retirement benefits, disability insurance, and "life insurance" benefits as survivors at the end of 1967 were 23.7 million individuals, not counting those utilizing hospital and medical benefits under social security.

---

[2] In choosing the term "income security," rather than "income maintenance," "income transfers," or "social assistance," we begin to introduce a point of view.

[3] The illustrative materials cover the period 1966–1968, ending with the 1967 Social Security Amendments (P.L. 90–248) and the intensification in 1968 of the debate about guaranteed income, negative income tax, and children's allowances. In this sense it is a

2. *Unemployment insurance* benefits were going to an average of over 1,027,000 workers each week in late 1967.

3. *Public assistance* included the following totals at the end of 1967, with the federal government contributing $4.5+ billion of $7.8+ billion in costs for all except general assistance cases:

- *Old Age Assistance*   2,070,000
- *Aid to Families with Dependent Children*   3,986,000 children and 1,323,000 adults
- *Aid to the Permanently and Totally Disabled*   646,000
- *Aid to the Blind*   82,600
- *General assistance*   782,000.

4. *Veterans' Pensions* were paid to 5 million veterans and their families or surviving dependents in 1966, some receiving compensation for injury or disability incurred in service and others, permanently and totally disabled, collecting pensions because they were in need.

One central point is immediately relevant: despite the evidence that, as of 1965, at least 19.5 million of 60.5 million households in the United States received some income supports—and notwithstanding over $50 billion in expenditure per year—the components do not add up to an efficient, coherent, and comprehensive system of insurance against major social risks involving need for income. Nor do they offer a basic minimum guarantee for all, or even adequate investment in more limited, specified social goals —if these are the rationales chosen.[4]

To illustrate the gaps, inadequacies, and inconsistencies at the time when the proposals here analyzed were put forth, and not attempting a complete survey, we note the following:

---

coherent "case" relating to task definition. Late 1967 data are reported for the most part, as providing context for the debate.

[4] We shall not discuss here workmen's compensation, a state program of medical care and cash benefits to an injured worker and monetary benefits to his dependents in case of death; medical assistance; railroad and other public retirement systems. These details would round out the chapter but would not change essentially the thrust of the analysis.

For overviews, see: Charles I. Schottland, "Government Economic Programs and Family Life," *Journal of Marriage and the Family*, 29, No. 1 (February, 1967), 71–123. Eveline M. Burns, *Social Security and Public Policy* (New York: McGraw-Hill Book Co., 1956). Margaret S. Gordon, *The Economics of Welfare Policies* (New York: Columbia University Press, 1963). Sar A. Levitan, "Programs in Aid of the Poor" (Kalamazoo, Mich.: The W. E. Upjohn Institute for Employment Research, 1965, pamphlet). Division of Research and Statistics, Social Security Administration, "Social Security Programs in the United States" (Washington, D.C.: Government Printing Office, 1964, pamphlet). "Annual Statistical Supplement, 1966," *Social Security Bulletin* (Washington, D.C.: Department of Health, Education, and Welfare, 1968).

□ There is a large group in the United States lacking adequate basic income, the poverty population.

□ Almost all public assistance recipients are maintained below the poverty level—as defined in the anti-poverty "war." In fact, according to Mollie Orshansky, to depend exclusively for income on OASDHI, or public assistance, or unemployment insurance is almost invariably to know poverty.[5]

□ A large proportion of social security recipients do not, in fact, have other simultaneous income sources and thus are maintained below the poverty level. Half of those who are poor before drawing OASDHI checks are still poor afterward.

□ Many "pensions" recipients or social insurance beneficiaries (for example, unemployment insurance, veterans' pensions, OASDHI) apply for public assistance as well—for lack of adequate grants or exhaustion of entitlement.[6] Four-fifths of wage and salary workers are covered by unemployment insurance, for example, but benefit levels have lagged far behind wages, and many workers exhaust their eligibility before finding new work.

□ The levels of benefits in these programs reflect an obscure relationship between concepts of need, contributions, attribution of responsibility, and a theory of how people are motivated. Failure to adjust grants to the price index or to provide for automatic adjustments often negates any rationale as to grant levels. One could hardly justify grant levels at the end of 1967 whereby, to illustrate, an OASDHI retired worker received $85.37 monthly and a recipient of Aid to the Blind, $89.35, but an adult caring for an AFDC child or the child himself averaged $39.50. The average state unemployment monthly benefit at the time was $167.40—and deemed inadequate!

Congress defines grant levels for social insurance. States formulate their own standards of need for the assistances. Not only are state standards for the latter miserably low (it was assumed in 1966, in 18 states, that a family of four could manage on $45 per person per month or less), but many states pay grants far below their own standards by legislative decision or failure to appropriate sufficient funds. As many as two-thirds of the states often pay less than predetermined minimum needs in the Aid to Families with Dependent Children program.[7]

A considerable fiction is maintained in relation to the nature of entitle-

---

[5] Mollie Orshansky, "More About the Poor in 1964," *Social Security Bulletin*, 29, No. 5 (May, 1966), 3. For 1965, Orshansky estimated that 5 of 6 public assistance recipients were in poverty. See Mollie Orshansky, "Counting the Poor: Before and After Federal Income–Support Programs," Joint Economic Committee, *Old Age Income Assistance*, Part II (Washington, D.C.: Government Printing Office, 1967), 177–231.

[6] See page 126 in re OAA–OASDHI and AFDC–OASDHI overlapping.

[7] Levitan, *op. cit.*, 17. Hilda Siff, "Feeding a Family on a Public Assistance Budget," *Welfare in Review*, 3, No. 5 (May, 1965), 8–10. Charles Lebeaux, "Life on ADC: Budg-

ments, contributions, and equity in various programs. Social insurance stresses the private insurance model and conventional wisdom ignores the many departures from private investment principles: the considerable "blanketing in" by legislation over the years to establish eligibility of new groups despite very limited contributions; a benefit bias in favor of low-wage workers; the continued eligibility of handicapped dependents as they cease to be minors; a general emphasis on need, not contributions, as the basis for computing budgets.[8] Public assistance stresses constant readiness for employment and an administrative structure to check such readiness, even though except for an uncounted subgroup of AFDC mothers, about whom public policy is quite contradictory, there are proportionately few employables on assistance. Veterans' programs relax disability qualifications over the age of sixty-five, and in effect the program responds to need, despite provisions about disability.

Programs are written or administered so as to create consequences which, on the surface at least, do not appear to reflect the public interest. Except in the minority of states adopting the 1965 "AFDC for the unemployed" option, unemployed fathers who have exhausted unemployment insurance may help their families more, financially, by deserting and making them eligible for AFDC rather than for general assistance or nothing at all. Except where experiments were under way, before the 1967 federal amendments, recipients did not help themselves by working and earning sums insufficient to meet their total budget deficits—since all earned money was deducted. (This is the equivalent of a 100 percent tax on earnings of relief recipients.) By contrast, the retirement test for an OASDHI recipient under seventy-two permitted his earning $1,500 per year before benefits were affected, and the limit was raised to $1,680 in 1967.

Public assistance is expected to provide the "ultimate" minimum floor guarantee of income to meet basic needs—yet stigma and other undesirable consequences or the formal obstacles toward eligibility are such that there are at least 8 million potentially eligible, very needy people who do not receive such aid, while almost 8 million do. Half of the poor in the United States receive neither public assistance nor social insurance; in fact, they receive *no* form of public transfer income!

Some of the programs ignore regional differences in cost of living (or in incomes) and are national in every sense (OASDHI). Others depend on

ets of Despair," reprinted in Louis A. Ferman, Joyce L. Kornbluh, and Alan Haber, Editors, *Poverty in America* (Ann Arbor: University of Michigan Press, 1965), 401–410.

[8] Samuel Mencher, "Perspectives on Recent Welfare Legislation, Fore and Aft," *Social Work*, 8, No. 3 (July, 1963), 59–65.

state (unemployment insurance) or local (general assistance) or state-local (AFDC, assistance to the aged, blind, or disabled) decisions. One cannot therefore be certain what the combination of eligibilities in a locale may produce by way of need-meeting grants. Inconsistencies among states in residence laws for assistance complicate the picture.

Heavy costs are incurred in the constant investigation and re-investigation of the eligibility of public assistance caseloads, yet 90 to 95 percent of the loads are made up of the aged, the disabled, young children, and mothers taking care of such children, relatively "stable" statuses, thus raising a question about the use of an individual means test for such recipients.

There are great inconsistencies among the programs (and, within public assistance, among the states) in relatives' responsibility for aid as an alternative to a grant, increase in grants to take account of the needs of spouse or children, vesting of rights to services and aid upon other family members by virtue of the family head's eligibility status. Similarly, some of the programs permit achievement of eligibility by personal contribution and others by status. To dramatize hidden premises, we note Jacobus tenBroek's comment that relatives' responsibility laws require one segment of the population (relatives of applicants) to contribute, i.e., to pay "personal taxation" so as to meet the costs of certain programs that implement general public policy.[9] This can be retrogressive taxation in extreme form. When, in contrast, a state abolishes or diminishes relatives' responsibility—or it is done nationally, as in the instance of the 1965 Medicaid provisions—one is affirming the principle, "once the public has assumed the responsibility, the cost must be derived from publicly apportioned taxation."[10]

Students of social policy in the United States and England[11] have noted the ongoing debate as to whether the goal at this point should be to assure a floor of protection (a "national minimum") against want or to help people maintain previous relative standards under conditions of income interruption, particularly retirement or personal family catastrophe. Clearly, the components of the United States income security "system" do not take us very far along the way in either of these directions. United States social insurance is addressed to interruption or loss of earning power and to other special circumstances, it is true, but the payments are so low that most recipients do not reach a needed minimum without access to other income as well. Public assistance is neither guaranteed nor adequate.

---

[9] Jacobus tenBroek, *California's Dual System of Family Law*, reprinted from the *Stanford Law Review*, 16, Nos. 2, 4 (March, July, 1964) and 17, No. 4 (April, 1965), 634–635.

[10] *Ibid.*, 639.

[11] T. H. Marshall, *Social Policy* (London: Hutchinson University Library, 1965), 100.

Alvin Schorr adds the suggestion of a policy to offer capital for "take off," i.e., basic self-improvement, to the most deprived families; the proposal, to which we shall return, is as yet completely beyond current practice.[12]

Divergencies in income-security philosophies among countries are revealed in the following data, relating to percentage of gross national product expended for social insurance:

Table 3   PERCENTAGE OF GROSS NATIONAL PRODUCT EXPENDED
FOR SOCIAL INSURANCE

Country	Total	OASDI	Sickness and maternity insurance	Unemployment insurance	Work accident insurance	Family allowances
Belgium	13.4	4.7	3.6	1.1	1.0	3.0
France	13.4	3.9	4.1	—	1.1	4.3
Germany (Federal Republic)	14.4	8.1	4.5	.4	.8	.6
Italy	12.0	4.7	2.9	.6	.6	2.9
Luxembourg	13.7	6.3	3.1	—	1.8	2.5
Netherlands	12.0	5.7	3.6	.6	.4	1.7
Sweden	9.2	5.1	2.2	.2	.2	1.6
United Kingdom	10.6	4.2	5.1	.3	.3	.6
United States	4.8	3.6	.1	.7	.3	—

Source: Joint Economic Committee, *European Social Security Systems*, Paper #7, Economic Policies and Practices (Washington, D.C.: Government Printing Office, 1965), 11. Data are for 1962.

The same range is noted if one focuses only on cash assistance for children:

Table 4   PROPORTION OF GROSS NATIONAL PRODUCT ASSIGNED
TO FAMILY OR CHILDREN'S ALLOWANCES

Country	Percentage
United States (AFDC)	0.3
Canada	1.9
Netherlands	3.0
Italy	3.2
France	4.8

Source: Sar A. Levitan, "The Poor in the Work Force," in Chamber of Commerce of the United States, Task Force on Economic Growth and Opportunity, *The Disadvantaged Poor: Education and Employment* (Washington, D.C.: The Chamber of Commerce of the U.S., 1966), 27.

---

[12] Alvin Schorr, *Poor Kids* (New York: Basic Books, 1966).

Obviously the issue is one of policy, not of fiscal capacity.

Much of the present United States system is inadequate and unsatisfactory. In projecting the future there are those who see the need in a high-productivity, technologically sophisticated society to loosen the ties between income and work and to legitimate the dependency of the very old, the young, the students, the homemakers, the child-rearers—by guarantees of, at the least, adequate minimum income. Others doubt that the problems of production and of motivating actual and potential labor force members to contribute to production are issues of the past. Among these, some would therefore retain the work-income tie quite closely and leave the assistance granted by other criteria at minimal levels. Others, somewhat more convinced that the ethic requires a measure of income redistribution, support generous income-security measures but develop rationales relating to the work ethic. They urge fellowships, training grants, child-care grants, and insurance measures covering more "risks," rather than income guarantees as such.

"HAVING THE POWER. . . ," PUBLIC WELFARE IN TRANSITION

In June of 1966, the Advisory Council on Public Welfare submitted to the Secretary of Health, Education, and Welfare the report of a year of hearings, visits, staff work, and discussion, *"Having the Power, We Have the Duty."*[13] Building on the existing public welfare program, yet calling for its expansion and liberalization, the expert panel offered one possible direction for the development of an American income-security system. They were to learn during the subsequent year that, although some of the specific reforms proposed would be considered by the executive and legislative branches, there was apparent rejection of their central premise: that public welfare could be reformed and expanded adequately as, "the channel through which the Government assures each individual and family that their basic living needs will be met."[14]

The response must be seen in context. We have sketched elsewhere an American ethic in which "salvation through work" has continued as a dominant note, personal poverty has aroused immediate suspicion of moral taint, private charity has been trusted as more effective than public bureaucracy, and the receipt of either public or private aid has carried obligations toward self-betterment, personal reform, or at least listening to the advice of one's benefactors.[15]

---

[13] The Advisory Council on Public Welfare, *"Having the Power, We Have the Duty"* (Washington, D.C.: Government Printing Office, 1966).

[14] *Ibid.*, 2.

[15] See Chapter II in the companion volume.

In a broader political and sociological sense, one may demonstrate that nineteenth-century adaptation of two centuries of Elizabethan poor law tradition, whether examined in England or the United States, had the economic and social "functions," generally latent but occasionally manifest, of creating and motivating a mobile labor force and assuring its availability to an expanding industrialism at a cost that could be sustained in a period when the economy required capital accumulation. One may also suggest that sincere personal motivation aside, private charity made possible the excesses and inadequacies of the public system, because special things could be done for those deemed "worthy" victims of tragedy beyond human control. Whether or not such interpretations are accepted, however, the facts are not challenged. Public welfare in the early nineteen-sixties provided a tax-supported ultimate guarantee against starvation; but its characteristics, even after the reforms of 1935 and the greater acceptability which came with mass experience of need, were continuous with nineteenth-century adaptations of Elizabethan poor law tradition:

- an emphasis on local responsibility, including a system of residence laws designed to discourage and decrease applications
- low-level, inadequate grants, below the poverty line
- an investigative approach that assumes that the applicants should not be trusted as much as most other people are trusted
- stigma, invasion of privacy, and loss of the right to complete community participation and self-direction as a consequence of a relief application ("paupers oaths," "man in the house rule," "midnight raids") [16]
- the assumption that all relief recipients need social service counseling and that, indeed, the relief investigator or a voluntary agency representative must always provide simultaneous counseling ("relief as a rehabilitative tool")
- the requirement that certain categories of relatives support the needy, thereby making them ineligible for public aid
- the demand that almost all possible savings and capital resources be exhausted before application for relief is made. [17]

United States public welfare reforms from 1935 to 1962 were in the direction of increasing the federal categories of reimbursement to the states for public assistance, raising the reimbursement levels—largely in response to

---

[16] By mid-1968, Supreme Court rulings had begun to restore some of the constitutional rights upon which administrative practices infringed.

[17] See, for example, "Having the Power . . ."; tenBroek, op. cit.; Richard M. Elman, The Poorhouse State (New York: Pantheon Books, 1966); Julius Horowitz, The Inhabitants (New York: New American Library, 1960); Elizabeth Wickenden and Winifred Bell, Public Welfare, Time for a Change (New York: Columbia University School of Social Work, 1964); Winifred Bell, Aid to Dependent Children (New York: Columbia University Press, 1965).

the cost of living—improving the staffing and training, broadening eligibility within categories, especially AFDC,[18] and constantly reiterating the goal of rehabilitation and training of relief recipients.[19] Advisory Council studies, research, public lobbying, and debate culminated, in 1962, in the most extensive amendments since the enactment of the system in 1935 (Public Welfare Amendments of 1962, P.L. 87–543). Yet after the enthusiasm of the moment, many who sought basic reforms noted that, despite the value of increased federal ceilings for reimbursement and some encouragement to states to combine adult categorical programs, it was more of the same: the amendment of "a primarily outmoded system."[20]

Congress had been told that the relief rolls kept rising and the cycle of poverty was being perpetuated because public welfare departments were not given the supports necessary for adequate social services. Therefore, the heart of the 1962 amendments—if one puts aside an ambiguous mandate to coordinate public assistance and child welfare—was in what may be called the "service" provisions. Recognizing unequivocally for the first time that, apart from the reimbursement of a portion of the funds actually going to recipients, it was also sharing *two* other kinds of expense, the Congress made a separation between administrative costs, in the narrower sense, and the costs of social services. Whereas the previous maximum reimbursement for administrative costs had been 50 percent, the amendments authorized 75 percent reimbursement, through open-end grants, for services to implement the purposes of the Act: casework, community planning to develop local resources, group work, homemakers, volunteer services, foster care for children and family care for adults, training opportunities aimed at self-support for the unemployed, and self-care for the handicapped. These services could be provided directly by the state welfare system or "purchased" from other public agencies such as education or vocational rehabilitation departments. Certain basic services were "prescribed" as essential if a state wished to qualify for the higher reimbursement.

---

[18] The abbreviation ADC was used before 1962, and AFDC after 1962, when coverage of some adults was expanded and the family emphasis of the programs more fully recognized—Aid to *Families* with Dependent Children.

[19] Appendixes containing the reimbursement formulas and chronology are available in the "Annual Statistical Supplement, 1966," *Social Security Bulletin*.

For documentation of the perspectives of the early 'sixties, see *Public Welfare Amendments of 1962*, Hearings Before the Committee on Ways and Means, House of Representatives, February 7, 9, 13, 1962 (Washington, D.C.: Government Printing Office, 1962).

[20] Mencher, *op. cit.*, 59–65.

The states rushed to take advantage of the increased reimbursement, and the then Welfare Administration, aware of shortages of personnel and limitations of resources in many of the states, was generous in its interpretations of standards and requirements. By the time of the first, public, comprehensive report late in 1964, all but one state had elected the prescribed services and increased reimbursement under AFDC, and 38 states had taken the same step for one or more adult categories (Old Age Assistance, Aid to the Blind, Aid to the Permanently and Totally Disabled). Staffs expanded, more and more states created case records in which check lists described client needs, and much staff development work was soon in process. Specialists were appointed to enrich the services. While quantitative outputs could be listed and the advantages of the increased federal funds to clients and states hypothesized, there was little evidence that the results sought by Congress were achieved.[21] Public welfare remained a whipping boy in many parts of the country, apparently "blamed" for children born out of wedlock and unemployed fathers who asked for aid—whereas those in need suffered the continued inadequacies and humiliations of the programs. Some administrators boasted of smaller assistance caseloads, not coping with Mencher's admonition that, "the issue at this time is not the *size* of case loads in public assistance, but whether *we shall have* case loads in public assistance." Had the time not come to face the desirability of separating income maintenance and service functions?[22] And grants continued at well below poverty-line levels.

At this point the Advisory Council on Public Welfare began its work. The appointment of a council in 1964 and a report to the Congress by July 1, 1966, was mandated by the 1962 amendments.[23] In appointing the Council consisting of nationally recognized public welfare leaders, the Secretary of Health, Education, and Welfare assured the program of a sympathetic review and the likelihood of support for increased resources. However, the interim growth of the poverty program and advocacy of a negative income tax placed the 1966 report in broader perspective. Here was a policy planning effort carried out in the midst of a debate about social security, negative income tax, and other approaches. What were its perspectives?

---

[21] Department of Health, Education, and Welfare, "Report to the Bureau of the Budget on the Implementation and Results of the 1962 Amendments to the Public Assistance Titles" (November, 1964, mimeographed).

[22] Mencher, *op. cit.*, 63–64.

[23] In fact, some of the 1962 reforms had cut-off dates as of June 30, 1967, so that evaluation was needed. Among these were the AFDC extension to include unemployed parents,

The Council on the defects of the present system

The Advisory Council announced at the outset that public welfare was prevented both by inadequate legislative mandate and insufficient financial resources from rising to the challenge of serving as ultimate guarantor against poverty and deprivation for all 34 million people in poverty. Then, reflecting the concerns of the anti-poverty war and the civil rights movement, it evaluated public welfare in terms a group sympathetic to public welfare could not have used a few years before.

☐ The Council stated flatly, "Public assistance payments are so low and so uneven that the Government is, by its own standards and definitions, a major source of the poverty on which it has declared unconditional war."

☐ Arbitrary eligibility requirements unrelated to need exclude many from even the inadequate aid available. Special reference was made to residence requirements; various categorical criteria such as age, degree of disability or employability; unrealistic requirements for financial contribution by relatives.

☐ The methods of determining and redetermining eligibility and budgeting procedures are "confusing, onerous, and demeaning for the applicant; complex and time consuming for the worker; and incompatible with the concept of assistance as a legal right."

☐ The lack of adequate social services is a major factor in the perpetuation of crime, illegitimacy, dependency, alienation, etc.[24]

In the course of statistical specification of these inadequacies, the Council reflected elements of several approaches to task definition. On the one hand, it talked of 34 million Americans in poverty during a period of economic growth, stressing the problems of tenant farmers, the aged, and neglected children as "examples of the ways our failure to adapt our institutional structure to changing needs and conditions has taken its toll from those least able to protect themselves." The dependent age groups grow more rapidly than the wage-earning groups in our present population cycle. Measures benefiting most Americans do not reach those at the "bottom of the ladder."[25] One notes here a constant shifting among the "adequate" who are pushed aside by social change, those able to be self-sustaining if helped, and those whose economic dependency must be regarded as permanent and natural.

---

an option enacted in only 22 states by 1967, AFDC payments for foster care in institutions, community work and training programs for unemployed parents, etc.

[24] "Having the Power. . . ."

[25] Ibid., 4–5.

Turning to the assistance caseload of almost 8 million, the Council documents that "most public welfare recipients, with the exception of children and younger adults, cannot realistically be expected ever to become self-sustaining."[26] There is stress on service measures to facilitate self-care, comfort, and security for the aged and the handicapped, training for the small number of fathers who are potentially self-supporting, and child care services plus training for a group of Aid to Families with Dependent Children mothers who, too, may subsequently become self-sufficient. No question is raised as to whether it is effective or efficient to treat all of these groups within a single income-maintenance system—even though there is obviously one public policy toward permanently dependent group and another for the employable group. Nor, despite rumors of a considerable behind-the-scenes debate, does the Council ask in the report whether one system, public welfare, should unite and combine an income and social service program.[27]

The Council's proposals

Not much is said about policy options in the Report, but the Council defines social insurance as the point of departure for assistance. Describing social insurance as "the primary source of economic security for workers and their dependents when earnings are interrupted by circumstances beyond their control," there is a call for more complete unemployment insurance coverage (almost one of every four workers is still not covered) and a plea for more adequate benefit levels. Note is taken of the need for coverage of the risk of temporary disability. Such reference to social insurance and reliance upon it as a base has long been characteristic of reports on public assistance. But the possibility that new forms of social insurance might affect the core assistance load is not discussed: fatherless child insurance, for example. Public assistance is to "recognize fully need, unusual need, and special circumstances."

Thus, despite the reference to the entire poverty population at some points, the Report does not address basically the considerable poverty deriving from low salaries and large families—categories not touched by the insurances and unaided except through inadequate general assistance supplementation in some places.

---

[26] *Ibid.*, 10.

[27] Mencher, "Perspectives on Recent Welfare Legislation. . . ." Gordon Hamilton, "Editorial," *Social Work*, 7, No. 1 (January, 1962). Eveline M. Burns, "What's Wrong with Public Welfare?" *Social Service Review*, 36, No. 2 (June, 1962), 111–122. Alfred J. Kahn, "Social Services in Relation to Income Security," *Social Service Review*, 39, No. 4 (December, 1965), 381–389.

The heart of the *financial recommendations,* formulated within the existing framework, is toward a federal "floor" and greater objectivity in investigations:

- □ a minimum federal standard for public assistance payments, allowing regional variations, since current state levels vary from one-half to one-fourth of subsistence needs (Again, the presentation refers to the total poverty population as its apparent target.)
- □ increased federal participation to help states meet the costs of raising assistance levels
- □ ending the differentiation by categories in rates of aid
- □ simplified budgeting to cut paper work and speed the process.

Such arbitrary eligibility requirements as residence, category, degree of disability, and estimate of employability should be eliminated and only *need* retained as a condition of eligibility. New federal aid formulas, which take adequate account of a state's fiscal capacity, are held out as incentive.

Considerable stress is placed throughout the Report on development within public welfare of comprehensive social services "readily accessible as a matter of right at all times to all who need them." Child welfare services are to have special priority. Just what is meant by the "right" to social services is not made clear. If a justiciable right is intended, too little is said. Nor does the Report discuss whether the public at large will utilize social services rendered by the stigmatized public welfare departments; or, whether the intended objectivity and simplification of eligibility for relief can be protected if social services are intermingled and the risk of administrative discretion retained.

Nevertheless, a section of the Report is dedicated to the "principle of public welfare as a right." A variety of procedural proposals is specified: a clear application process, promptness, legal representation for appeals, an independent appeals system, publication of rights. Unfortunately, there is no detail as to how statutes will guarantee a payment or a service level and just what level is to be selected. Rights are hardly justiciable until this is the case.

The response

The response must have startled the Council and disappointed many public welfare leaders. The Report went far beyond 1962. Yet much had occurred. Interested professionals, scholars, and citizens were debating the negative income tax. Relief clients, organized for the first time by a national Poverty/Rights Action Group,[28] were demanding reforms. Social services

---

[28] "The Welfare Marches," *Trans-action,* 4, No. 2 (December, 1966), 33; Richard A.

were expanding under a variety of administrative auspices. Social work leaders were urging administrative and organizational separation of financial assistance from social services both as necessary to affirm the right to assistance and as a more efficient way to reach people and to deploy manpower. In the meantime, with the encouragement of federal authorities, some public welfare departments were experimenting with simplified affidavit-declaration applications (more like a veteran's pension application, assuming the applicant's honesty), simplifying budgeting, and ending some of the practices which humiliated clients and infringed on their rights. One state court upset residence laws as unconstitutional, and others were expected to follow suit. Soon the matter should reach the Supreme Court. Permission was obtained for experiments in recipients' retaining a portion of their earnings, as an incentive to self-support, while legislation in this regard was presented to the Congress. And federal officials were willing only to propose that states be required to meet their own budgetary standards, without endorsing a national assistance minimum. It appeared as though the Council's major contribution would be to launch legislation continuing the temporary reforms of 1962—a side issue. Even the American Public Welfare Association, the Council's home base, in a sense, would say only that the document was

> the most significant statement currently available containing guidelines for the future development of the public welfare programs and policies in the nation. There should be . . . discussion of these proposals as a means of solidifying the goals expressed therein and choosing from the methods proposed by the Advisory Council and *other possible* methods for achieving these goals.[29]

The core of the hesitation is evident:

> . . . there should be exploration of other money payment programs such as negative income tax, demogrants, family allowances, and an insurance program against additional risks as broadly inclusive as possible, *in order to reduce the need for public assistance to a minimum.*

> It should be clear . . . that eligibility for services is not tied to financial need, nor eligibility for financial assistance dependent on acceptance of services.[30]

Cloward and Frances Fox Piven, "Birth of a Movement," *The Nation*, 204, No. 19 (May 8, 1967), 582–588.

[29] American Public Welfare Association, "A Commentary on the Report of the Advisory Council on Public Welfare" (Chicago: American Public Welfare Association, 1966). (Emphasis supplied.)

[30] *Ibid.* (Emphasis supplied.)

In a period of two years some important changes had occurred. Friends of public welfare and of liberal social policy generally were beginning to consider design of a comprehensive income-security system, *conscious* of the policy implications of the choices made, and to review quite separately the issue of how to organize universal social services. In its stress on rights and support for simplified budgeting and application procedures, the Advisory Council was approaching a negative income tax or income guarantee solution. Its report conceived of public welfare as an ultimate guarantee of a national minimum. Yet the Report's continued reliance on a federal-state-local system, despite the limitation of state-local fiscal capacity and its assumption that one should associate social services with grants, plus the public's suspicions arising from the "poor law heritage," weakened public welfare's case. Similarly, in noting that large numbers of aged recipients and children needed support not premised on the possibility of rehabilitation or employability, but by virtue of their status, the Council was approaching a demogrant principle, a children's allowance or pension for the aged available by virtue only of one's membership in the category, without proof of need. Here, too, however, it has failed to carry its analysis to its conclusion.

Nor were the Council's proposals by-passed only by people favoring more comprehensive and obviously forward-looking conceptions of the task. On the contrary, there were those who, while open to consideration of alternatives, had basic questions about the overall public welfare strategy. They were not sure about adding programs. They saw need for rational analysis and careful staff work, but wanted it less reflective of the public welfare bureaucracy and the social work profession.[31] Even more potent were the views of those in the Congress who sought to curtail governmental expenditures, to strengthen traditional approaches, and to demonstrate that riots in the cities would not yield new social programs. Thus, the policies of 1967 seemed once again to demonstrate the prevalence of a repressive view of public assistance, a preference for below-poverty support given so as not to undermine what were conceived to be the components of motivation to work.[32]

On the one hand, in the spirit of the civil rights revolution, the "welfare rights" movement, and the anti-poverty "war," state courts had begun to upset residence laws, punitive "man-in-the-house" rules, and other infringements on rights due to public assistance status. Simultaneously, new ad-

[31] Gilbert Y. Steiner, *Social Insecurity: The Politics of Welfare* (Chicago: Rand McNally & Company, 1966).

[32] Surprisingly little is actually known about work incentives, etc. at low- or no-income levels.

ministrative protections for clients and simplified budgeting continued to spread.[33] On the other hand, a bipartisan coalition in Congress concluded that it had been misguided by the premises of 1962; social services as designed at that time had not cut relief rolls. In fact, AFDC grew more rapidly than ever as improved agricultural technology (federally funded) speeded up migration from southern farms to northern cities, where industrial technology had developed rapidly and minimized the need for this new unskilled labor force. Indeed, the anti-poverty programs and the new welfare rights movement appeared to decrease the stigma of assistance and to accelerate applications for aid from some groups. And the rate of unmarried motherhood continued high.

Thus, despite the considerable mobilization by proponents of public welfare and governmental anti-poverty efforts, as well as strong opposition by Congressional liberals, Congress passed, at the end of 1967, a series of amendments that seemed to ignore much of the country's overall social welfare thrust of the early 'sixties. They were quite inconsistent with simultaneous developments in anti-poverty, aid to the city, and educational programs. The new legislation (P.L. 90–248) was premised on the conviction that the bulk of the AFDC load could be decreased by training mothers while providing day care for their children. Ignoring data and experience, the Congress decreed that many or most AFDC mothers were trainable and subsequently employable. Readiness to cooperate constituted a re-established "work test," long a "poor law" hallmark. The states were allowed some options in judging the desirability of employment for mothers caring for young children, yet in the background was a related source of pressure upon all: a freeze on federal AFDC reimbursement to that proportion of the state's child-care population being aided on January 1, 1968. A state could refuse new cases, cut average grants, or assume the entire burden of new cases. Work incentives were to be increased by permitting any relief recipient to retain the first $30 of earnings each month and 33 percent of earnings above that, a "ratio" described by the *New York Times* as "so low it provides almost no incentive."[34] New restrictions in the definition of unemployment would further decrease AFDC eligibility with a father in the home.

---

[33] For a review of the issues being litigated and the states involved in 1966–1967, see *Social Security Amendments of 1967*, Hearings before the Committee on Finance, U.S. Senate, in 3 parts (Washington, D.C.: Government Printing Office, 1967), Part 2, 1374–1387. The Supreme Court did not rule definitively on the "man in the house" cases until June, 1968, and did not outlaw residence laws until April, 1969.

[34] In 1962, a blind worker was allowed an exemption of $85 monthly and half of all

Some denied that this was "poor law" revived and called attention to improved social service provisions in the amendments. The problem, they stressed, was the increased financial burden on localities. The issue, they said, was to encourage employment and to facilitate training. AFDC had not "withered away" as the numbers of orphans decreased—the expectation in 1935. Illegitimacy and desertion had replaced the death of the father as the cause of children's dependency, and real financial pressure had given the Congress concern. (Yet although absolute costs had increased, public assistance had not substantially added to its share of the gross national product. And $300 million annually would have permitted states to bring relief levels up to need, with the federal government aiding the poorer states appropriately.)[35]

Obviously there were, in the public debate, varying versions of reality, of human motivation, and of value hierarchies. Temporary administrative and statutory brakes on the punitive 1967 measures resolved nothing. The time had come to face anew the definition of the task in planning the future of public assistance. Nor could one proceed by ignoring the other income-security programs.[36]

INCOME THROUGH SOCIAL INSURANCE

The American Social Security legislation includes in one overall act provision for social insurance and public assistance. Social insurance covers unemployment insurance, retirement, disability, and survivor benefits (and their related provisions for dependents), as well as the recently-enacted hospital and medical coverage. For clarity of understanding, however, and because the several Titles hardly form an integrated and comprehensive system, it is useful to ignore the fact that these programs are authorized in one Act. The man-in-the-street sees unemployment insurance as one thing, public assistance ("the welfare") as a second program, and the several social

---

earned above that. The Economic Opportunity Act in 1964 used these same levels in relation to income for youth-program participants and community-action workers.

[35] Cost estimates are offered by the Department of Health, Education, and Welfare in *Social Security Amendments of 1967*, Part 1, 284. Public assistance represented the following proportion of gross national product in the years indicated: 1.07 percent (1940), .47 percent (1945), .84 percent (1950), .69 percent (1955), .76 percent (1960), and then, respectively, .79, .80, .80, .79, .81, .85 percent for each of the years from 1961 to 1966.

[36] Eveline M. Burns reviewed the issues and elements of choice for a late 1967 conference under the title "The Future Course of Public Welfare," in Victor Weingarten, Editor, *Position Papers for the Governor's Conference on Public Welfare* (Albany: New York State Department of Social Services, 1967).

insurances ("the security") as a third. We shall preserve this distinction in terminology.

In 1965 the system took its longest stride forward since its enactment in 1935: it added hospitalization and medical provisions. Then, in the midst of the nation-wide anti-poverty effort, the question periodically arose: should social security assume a new and more complete role in general income-security strategy, with special reference to the poverty group? Our discussion here concentrates on how the question was answered in discussion and eventual legislative enactment in 1967, for the answers include a variety of perspectives on the income-security task.[37] The relevant materials derive, not from one study or report, but from the record of the total process: articles, research reports, governmental publications, two statutory advisory councils, and the published proceedings of hearings before the House Ways and Means Committee, which initiated the 1967 amendments, and the Senate Finance Committee, which had to cope with a complex "mixed package" from the House.

Coverage

First, for some facts. Social (insurance) security systems, a product of the past century, exist in more or less developed forms in 120 countries.[38] The original 1935 program in the United States offered modest provision for the retired aged and the temporarily unemployed and included lump-sum death benefits. There was gradual addition, over the years, to the risks covered until the program encompassed not only retirement income and death benefits, but also survivor benefits, disability benefits, support for dependents (a group defined somewhat more broadly as the years went by), and finally the hospital and health coverage for the aged. Characteristic of social insurance, there is no test of need or means (except a retirement test for the aged), benefits and rights are clearly specified in the statutes, and there are employer-employee contributions as well as a tax on the self-

---

[37] U.S. Department of Health, Education, and Welfare, "Social Security Programs in the United States" (Washington, D.C.: Government Printing Office, 1968). *The Status of the Social Security Program and Recommendations for Its Improvement,* Report of the Advisory Council on Social Security (Washington, D.C.: Government Printing Office, 1965). *President's Proposals for Revision in the Social Security System,* Hearings Before the Committee on Ways and Means, House of Representatives, Ninetieth Congress, March and April, 1967, 4 volumes (Washington, D.C.: Government Printing Office, 1967). *Social Security Amendments of 1967* (Senate).

[38] Social Security Administration, Office of Research and Statistics, *Social Security Programs Throughout the World, 1967* (Washington, D.C.: Government Printing Office, 1967). Joint Economic Committee, *European Social Security Systems.*

employed to finance the effort. Contributions are accumulated in trust funds. By the nineteen-sixties coverage had become virtually universal for people currently in the labor force; in fact, of those at present reaching the age of sixty-five, almost 95 percent are covered.[39]

In the words of the Commissioner of Social Security, social insurance "relies on the age old tradition of self-help, and, like private pension plans and private insurance, is connected in people's minds with the responsible and prudent management of their own affairs."[40] Or, as put by a recent advisory panel, social insurance "is a method that operates through the individual efforts of the worker and his employer, and thus is in total harmony with general economic incentives to work and save."[41]

Despite early hesitations in some quarters and doubts and debates as each successive group or each new risk was considered, social insurance is obviously universally popular by now in the United States. From most points of view, the system is a magnificent achievement of social policy: coverage, scale, acceptance, efficiency, fiscal soundness, growth, and protection of rights. Those who would extend the use of the approach build on a substantial base, but they must preserve the elements most supporters see as critical, lest this support be lost.

The designers of social insurance may have concentrated only on the capacity of the system to offer at least a minimum subsistence guarantee to low-wage earners, but other advocates considered social insurance as having the characteristics of a comprehensive retirement system; high-wage earners would contribute on a higher wage-base and would subsequently receive higher benefits. One's relative standard of living at retirement would be, in some rough measure, reflective of an earlier relative position. These two conceptions persist, were to reappear in the Congressional hearing of 1967, and are not yet fully resolved. The experience has been that, just as specified minima have been so low as to serve as mere tokens, the earnings maximum on which deductions are made and the top-benefit levels computed have

---

[39] "Social Security Programs in the United States."

The legislation since 1935 is summarized in a series of charts in the *Social Security Bulletin's* "Annual Statistical Supplement."

The statistic given includes special parallel systems for railroad workers and certain public employees.

[40] Robert M. Ball, "Policy Issues in Social Security," *Social Security Bulletin*, 29, No. 6 (June, 1966), 3–9.

[41] *The Status of the Social Security Program and Recommendations for Its Improvement*, 2. A similar point about the compatibility of this form of income maintenance with the ethic is made in Eveline M. Burns, "Social Insurance in Evolution," special supplement, *American Economic Review*, March, 1944.

not, over the years, kept up with the cost of living or with changes in real wages.[42]

There, of course, is no consensus as to desirable levels of retirement income, given the decreased costs and obligations of the aged, yet some advocates wish to sustain previous standards. There is less agreement about levels to be sought through social insurance for the disabled, for survivors in various categories, and for dependents. Ida C. Merriam reported, before the 1967 amendments, that for workers of about average income, the social security retirement level was approximately one-third of preretirement earnings for individuals and 45 percent for couples. For low-wage earners, the retirement income was 75, 80, or even 100 percent of preretirement earnings. Of course, for the worker above the average in earnings, the rate was much lower.

The debate about the role of social insurance in the overall income-security picture rests on differences in the interpretation of these data: should social insurance do more; should social insurance plus private pensions do more? Should one count on private pensions and savings or must social security per se be enough? What is "enough"?

The data are clear and indicate that some people do not receive adequate income through this system. For 1962, two-thirds of the retired couples had retirement incomes below the poverty standard of $2,500, and four-fifths of all single individuals were below the $1,800 standard.[43] At the time of the Congressional analysis, prior to legislative action in 1967, the Social Security Administration estimated that, speaking in terms of total family income and resources available after retirement, 42 percent of all aged were above the poverty-line even without OASDHI benefits, 30 percent were kept above poverty by the addition of benefits to other income, and 28 percent remained in poverty despite benefits.[44]

About one-fourth (and perhaps as many as one-third) of mother-child families trying to manage on survivor benefits, *plus* all other income available to them, are below a very stringent poverty line (and at present 30 percent of paternal orphans do not yet receive benefits). A third of the disabled

---

[42] The wage-base never kept pace. The benefit increases of 1950, 1952, and 1954 exceeded cost of living rises, but those of 1959 and 1965 lagged. In 1967, the debate was whether to approach, equal, or exceed the rise in cost of living. See Saul Waldman, "OASDI Benefits, Prices and Wages: 1966 Experience," *Social Security Bulletin*, 30, No. 6 (June, 1967), 9–12, 36.

[43] Ida C. Merriam, "Overlap of Benefits Under OASDI and Other Programs," *Social Security Bulletin*, 28, No. 4 (April, 1965), 24.

[44] Ida C. Merriam, "Social Security Benefits and Poverty," Social Security Administration, *Research and Statistics Note*, No. 6, February 24, 1967, Table 1.

workers and their dependents who receive benefits are also below the poverty-line.[45]

Because benefit levels were so low, early in 1967 over 7 percent of OASDHI beneficiaries aged sixty-five and over also required public assistance through the Old Age Assistance Program. In fact, of the more than 2 million beneficiaries of old age assistance, over 53 percent were also recipients of OASDHI.[46] Of mothers and children receiving survivior benefits in 1961, 4.5 percent also required assistance through AFDC and constituted 5 to 6 percent of AFDC totals. Later data are not available.

At first glance, one is impressed with the totals of workers who have supplementary coverage through union contract agreements: 50 million with life insurance coverage, 52 million with major medical expense coverage, and 26 million with private retirement income.[47] Yet private industry's employee benefit plans disburse only a little more than one-eighth of the federal public benefit total. Only 15 percent of the aged at present have supplementary pensions through all private schemes, and the most optimistic projections see 30 percent covered by 1980, when more private plans will have matured.[48] Other risks are covered in diverse and incomplete ways, to the extent that data are available. Most plans offer little to survivors.

The 1965 Advisory Council on Social Security noted its view that social security "is designed so as to work in ongoing partnership with voluntary insurance, individual savings and private pension plans."[49] The statement about savings is not meaningful for most workers. Furthermore, one of the least reliable aspects of this strategy is the private pension sector. Coverage, as indicated, is limited; benefits are incomplete and unstandardized. Finally, rights are only partial. For 1962, if one considers all kinds of risks,

---

[45] Erdman Palmore, Gertrude L. Stanley, and Robert H. Cormier, *Widows with Children Under Social Security*, Research Report No. 16, Social Security Administration (Washington, D.C.: Government Printing Office, 1966). Again, these statements describe the situation before the December, 1967, legislation, the "case" in our focus.

[46] *Social Security Bulletin*, 30, No. 5 (May, 1967), 19–20.

[47] Walter W. Kolodrubetz, "Employee-Benefit Plans in 1966," *Social Security Bulletin*, 31, No. 4 (April, 1968), 23–40.
  Also see Eveline M. Burns, "Social Security in America: The Two Systems, Public and Private," in W. Haber, Editor, *Labor in a Changing World* (New York: Basic Books, 1966).

[48] Merriam, "Overlap of Benefits. . . ." Burns, "Social Security in America: The Two Systems, Public and Private," *op. cit.*

[49] *The Status of the Social Security Program. . . .*, 2.

private pension plans included something like 45% of employees in private industry [but] the extent to which workers formally covered by them can count on actually receiving benefits when they retire is unfortunately limited. Not all pension plans are funded. It is common for the employer to reserve the right to terminate, modify, or amend the plan. *Vesting*, namely the worker's right on leaving a given employer before retirement to receive all or part of the benefits purchased on his behalf by the employer's contribution, *is still relatively rare*. And the period of service necessary to quality for reasonably adequate pensions is still quite long. One authority has estimated that not more than half of those currently covered under private pension plans would ever receive a cash benefit because of lack of vesting. [Emphasis supplied.][50]

Issues

What should be expected of social insurance as one looks ahead to somewhat more comprehensive income security in the United States? There may be some hints in the policy issues highlighted by Commissioner Robert Ball when he looked ahead in 1966:[51]

Benefit level. Real wages have improved substantially in recent decades (approximately 50 percent in the 1954–1965 period) without the rise's being reflected in benefit levels. The 7 percent cost-of-living increase applicable in 1959 did not quite restore the 1954 purchasing power of benefits; the 1965 rise of 7 percent did not quite restore the benefits to 1958 purchasing power. The 13 percent increase enacted as a 1967 compromise did not change the pattern. Yet even restoration of earlier levels would not make benefits sufficient for those with no other income sources.[52] The social security benefit level is therefore seen as the critical issue.

---

[50] Burns, "Social Security in America: The Two Systems, Public and Private," *op. cit.* Or see testimony of Wilbur Cohen, Undersecretary of Health, Education, and Welfare, in *President's Proposals for Revision in the Social Security System*, 402:

For millions of workers there are no supplementary pensions and there is little likelihood that there ever will be. Those most apt to be without protection are the least well circumstanced. For most of them, social security will be the only protection in retirement. . . .

. . . There is little justification . . . for retaining the present low level of social security benefits on the theory that private pension plans will achieve adequate income replacement for the total group of the aged.

Detailed background is provided by Walter W. Kolodrubetz, "Growth in Employee Benefit Plans, 1950–1965," *Social Security Bulletin*, 30, No. 4 (April, 1967).

[51] Ball, *op. cit.*

[52] Ball, *op. cit.*; Waldman, *op. cit.*

Automatic adjustments. Civil service and military retirement systems in the United States and social security programs in many countries provide for automatic adjustment of benefits to changes in price levels. Several industries include similar provision in collective bargaining contracts. American social insurance could not provide automatic adjustments without related periodic adjustments of employer-employee contributions and of the benefit base, the maximum amount of salary on which the social security tax is computed and which is considered for benefit purposes. In addition, a general revenue contribution would be needed.

A more complex and controversial benefit plan would tie benefit levels at a given moment to labor-force earning levels ("dynamized benefits"). Retired workers would share the fruits of increased productivity. At various times, there have been variations on these proposals, taking account of changes in cost of living and earning levels in various relationships deriving from the proponent's concern with low-salary or high-salary wage earners, whether the goal is to keep people at their relative retirement positions in the wage scale or not.

Unremarked by Ball in this connection, but very relevant is the fact that no system of automatic adjustments is possible if it must be dependent, as it now is, upon timely legislative enactment. The Congress is subject to considerable interest-group pressures, fiscal and social security perspectives of its leadership, and to all the other components of the legislative bargaining process when, under the present system, it attempts to take account of economic changes since the last amendments. Automatic adjustments would have to be written into law and assigned for administrative action, something not possible unless one overall philosophy of social insurance becomes dominant and Congress is willing to give up some prerogatives. Because this would require that issues currently glossed over be resolved and definition of the task be settled, automatic adjustment is seldom seriously proposed. Its occurrence would be a symptom of a more planful approach generally.

Contribution and benefit base. Whether out of concern for basic benefit levels, cost-of-living or increased-productivity adjustments, or the philosophy of the overall role of a social security system, the discussion rapidly takes one to the contribution and benefit base. Ball sees this as a central issue. If social insurance is to be more than a poverty-line minimum guarantee for all, taxes should be collected and benefits paid on salaries reflecting the range in earning levels. In 1935 it was contemplated that the base established would cover 95 percent of total earnings in covered work. From the very beginning, as earnings have increased and the law has been amended to adjust benefits to living costs, there have been compromises. In

1966, if levels had kept pace with the coverage provided by the 1935 maximum of $3,000, the top benefit base would have been $15,000, not $6,600. The administration's proposal for the 1967 amendments provided only a maximum of $10,800 after 1973. Opponents of a higher base were most expansive about their expectations with regard to private pensions and opposed a public scheme which concerned itself with high-level earners.[53] Congress voted a base of $7,800.

General revenue contribution. Blanketing-in of groups at various times and their rapid achievement of entitlement to benefits, as a matter of public policy, has meant that some subsequent and future beneficiaries have been paid or will be paid benefits at levels less than might have been purchased by their combined employer-employee contributions. Paying full-rate benefits to people who had not made contributions at the actuarial rate or who had made no contributions at all accounted for about one-third of program costs in 1967. How one regards this depends, of course, on whether one considers the employer's share as something which would otherwise have gone to the employee as salary. In either instance, it seems valid to hold that social security as insurance is not quite the same as private insurance. The system redistributes benefits at both ends to reflect policy objectives rather than, as in private insurance, risk experience.

The view taken of current practice by a recent Advisory Council is characteristic:

> The contributions paid by self-employed people above the rates paid by employees are, like employers' contributions to the program, used in large part to help provide protection for low-paid workers, workers with large families and workers who were already on in years when their jobs were first covered. The Council believes that it is reasonable to use the contributions of an employer for general purposes, rather than for the benefit of the particular employees on whose earnings the contributions are based, as long as the employee can in general be said to get his own money's worth. On

---

[53] The issues are even more far reaching. Mr. Ball also notes that failure to raise the base as earnings rise, while imposing a tax as a single percentage rate, places the burden on the lowest-paid workers and makes the taxation regressive. It becomes progressive only if a high contribution and tax base is maintained by constant adjustment. The Canadian and British, who elected to have flat-rate contributions and flat-rate benefits for all, had to gear both levels to what the person with the lowest income could afford. The system proved regressive and inadequate and has been supplemented by a second "tier," which is wage related. Ball, *op. cit.*, 7.

A British government proposal, debated as we write, departs from "flat-rate" premises and—in a major reform—would provide earning-related contributions and benefits. See Department of Health and Social Security, *National Superannuation and Social Insurance* (London: Her Majesty's Stationery Office, Cmnd. 3883).

the other hand, the Council does not believe that self-employed workers should as a rule be charged rates for their own coverage beyond the rates needed to pay for the protection they are provided by the program in order to help meet the costs of the protection provided to others.[54]

Many strict adherents of the private insurance model argue that a given worker should be purchasing coverage equal to the value of his contributions and those of his employer. To the extent that those already retired have their benefits increased to reflect cost-of-living or wage-level changes, general revenue should cover the difference. Similarly, where "blanketing-in" was a matter of public policy, but not actuarially justifiable, it should be paid for out of public revenue.

Those who are not willing to accept the private insurance analogy make an even broader case for a general revenue contribution as a way to implement public objectives without excessive constraints. They argue for a public-employer-employee stake of 1/3:1/3:1/3 or 1/2:1/4:1/4 and refer to practices in many other countries. They cite the precedent of 1965, in the provision that general revenue funds would match the enrollee share of costs of the voluntary medical insurance program, which parallels the hospital insurance provision of Medicare. They also note 1966 legislation making uncovered persons aged seventy-two and over eligible for minimum benefits under certain conditions, with the costs met out of a combination of general revenue and trust funds.[55] Some make the argument in terms of economic policy, noting that trust funds are maintained in government bonds and repaid as needed out of current taxes under any circumstances. Others add that, at least with present coverage maximums, social security payroll taxes are far more regressive than income taxes in the United States. To join social security with the regular tax system (perhaps earmarking a portion) would introduce collection economies while increasing equity. Social security was initiated at a time when far fewer Americans paid income taxes; subsequent tax-system changes make the maintenance of a separate system

---

[54] *The Status of the Social Security Program* . . . , 25. For an elaboration of the view that the private insurance model is not actually applicable to social security and is employed largely for "public relations" reasons, see Joseph A. Pechman, Henry J. Aaron, and Michael Taussig, "The Objectives of Social Security," a reprint (Washington, D.C.: The Brookings Institution, 1968). We agree with this view.

The complexities of the debate are revealed in William G. Bowen, *et al.*, Editors, *The American System of Social Insurance* (New York: McGraw-Hill Book Co., 1968); Joseph A. Pechman, Henry J. Aaron, Michael K. Taussig, *Social Security: Perspectives for Reform* (Washington, D.C.: The Brookings Institution, 1968).

[55] Wilbur J. Cohen, Robert M. Ball, and Robert J. Meyers, "Social Security Payments for Noninsured Persons," *Social Security Bulletin*, 29, No. 9 (September, 1966), 3–9.

inefficient. The case for a general revenue contribution is still independent of the question as to how it would be implemented.[56] The central point is that taxpayers at large, rather than any specific individual, should, through the general tax system, pay to implement governmental social security policy.

What is the policy?

These issues cannot be resolved adequately unless the underlying concepts of the role of social security are faced and the differences considered. Ball, speaking for the social security field, is clear about the perspective from which his formulation of the issues and his recommendations derive. Social insurance is concerned with income interruption. It is *not* conceived as a complete, comprehensive income-transfer system:

> Economic insecurity in a money economy arises in considerable part when earnings stop because of unemployment, retirement in old age, death of the family breadwinner, or disability, either short-term or long-term. No matter how high the level of production, poverty will persist unless there are institutional arrangements for making sure that all have the continuing right to share in consumption when these risks occur. To provide such continuing income is the principal role of social insurance.
>
> Thus we have at hand a widely applicable and widely acceptable instrument. Its objective is not solely the abolition of poverty, but in its operation it does prevent poverty. *It can be used much more effectively for this purpose.* Perhaps one-fourth to one-third of all poverty that exists in the United States could be prevented by the improvement and broader application of the social insurance principle, both in the Federal program I have been talking about and in our Federal-State program of unemployment insurance. Some part of the problem of poverty is best solved by expansion in job opportunities and preparing workers to fit these opportunities. On the other hand, a major part of the problem can best be met by an expansion of insurance against the loss of job income so that retired people, the disabled, widows and orphans, and those between jobs can have an assured and adequate income when not working.[57]

In this perspective, social insurance is seen as the basic mechanism for income distribution to the retired, disabled, unemployed, and to the survivors of covered workers, offering practically universal coverage and reasonable replacement (say, 40 to 50 percent) of loss of earnings. Automatic adjustments, general revenue contributions, and routine adjustments of benefit

---

[56] Eveline M. Burns, "Social Security in Evolution: Towards What?" *Social Service Review,* XXXIX, No. 2 (June, 1965), 129–140.

[57] Ball, *op. cit.,* 9.

and contribution bases to reflect wage levels are the vehicles to achieve this. Those who wish even more adequate retirement levels[58] seek both higher benefit levels within the system (replacing two-thirds of wages, perhaps) and supplementation through more adequate private pension plans.

A more adequate social insurance system could make a major contribution to the reduction of poverty.[59] However, although it replaces "relatively more of low than of high earnings," social insurance "cannot in itself compensate for a lifetime of low earnings."[60] One alternative strategy is to give up the effort to reflect the entire range of earnings and to concentrate on a poverty-level base for all. The British flat-rate system was directed toward this end, but always required supplementation through what in the United States is called public assistance. Recent legislation offers the equivalent of a low-level guaranteed income for the retired aged, adding to social insurance benefits a supplement which is easily requested and obtained, in a manner corresponding to the proposed public assistance "declarations" in this country. (Then, one adds a second tier, somewhat differently managed in Britain, Sweden, and Canada, which does reflect earning levels and differential contributions.)

New risks might be added to social security, too. Norway set the precedent of employing the social insurance mechanism to meet the financial needs of fatherless children who comprise, in this country, the huge Aid to Families with Dependent Children category. In the case of a child born out of wedlock, if no liability for support has been established through the excellent Norwegian administrative and legal machinery and the clear statutory delineation of responsibility, there is available to the child a money benefit, *without means test*, under "Survivors Benefits for Children." This Act, which came into effect in 1958, assures the child born out of wedlock the same grant and status under these circumstances as a child whose father or supporting mother is dead.

For some years here, Alvin Schorr has posed the possibility of a "fatherless child" insurance category under Social Security, i.e., protection against the economic risk of family breakup.[61] The major problem foreseen in the

---

[58] Walter Reuther, President of the United Auto Workers, before the Committee on Ways and Means, House of Representatives, *President's Proposals for Revision in the Social Security System*, 1432.

[59] For estimates and documentation relating to the aged, see Merriam, "Social Security Benefits and Poverty."

[60] *Ibid.*, 8.

[61] Margaret Wynn initiated discussion in England in *Fatherless Familes* (London: Michael Joseph, 1964).

United States is the long tradition that insurance is not possible where the contingency is not completely outside of the control of one of the potential beneficiaries. Plans in Australia and New Zealand provide benefits to deserted, separated, and divorced wives on the same basis as widows following a procedure to prove the separation involuntary or justifiable from the women's point of view.[62] Any American plan would probably require a court determination of such status. In his recent review, Schorr estimates that a program along these lines might at most cover a fourth of all needy children —but would probably help fewer.[63] It, of course, does not meet the needs of many other groups of children and is not a substitute for other measures under consideration. It probably could not include large groups of illegitimate children or those in stable marriages in very poor families. There is little active support for such a program in the United States at present; the issue of whether support should be mobilized by its advocates depends, at least in part, on the evolution of the other possibilities being debated.

The cycle thus constantly returns to the question of the *task* assigned to social insurance. In 1944 Burns noted that, because it was urgent to underscore congruence with the ethic, social insurance would try to remain faithful to the private insurance model, at least initially. Equity and fiscal-actuarial guidelines are dominant in such an atmosphere. Then, as earlier hesitations are overcome and concern for the poorer parts of the population grows, questions of adequacy of benefits and of risks to be covered become predominant.[64] These predictions were correct. By the nineteen-sixties this second phase was almost over. The large questions were being asked. What is the next stage?

In Burns's view, we may soon be prepared to depart from our primary concern with using the income security system to cope with income *interruption* and employ it increasingly to remedy income *deficiency*.[65] Then one may consider whether the social insurance system as originally conceived is the sole or the best device or whether it may be more effective to employ the tax system or some combination of the tax system, social insurance, and new devices. *A plan can be devised if the objectives are clear.*

When the first session of the Ninetieth Congress convened in 1967 and considered modest improvements in public assistance, only to return to a more punitive approach, it also had before it administration proposals for

[62] Alvin Schorr, *Poor Kids*, Chap. 7.

[63] *Ibid.*, 119–120.

[64] Burns, "Social Security in Evolution: Towards What?"

[65] *Ibid.*

significant across-the-board increases in social insurance benefits (15 percent) and related improvements:

- ☐ a $70 minimum grant to retired individuals and $105 for couples, replacing $44 and $66 respectively ($55 and $82.50 were voted)
- ☐ a $100 minimum retirement grant for a worker who has contributed for 25 years (not enacted)
- ☐ an increase from $1,500 to $1,680 in the amount a beneficiary under 72 could earn without reduction in benefits ($1,680 was voted)
- ☐ a gradual increase in the taxable-earnings ceiling from $6,600 until it reached $10,800 in 1973 ($7,800 voted)
- ☐ corresponding tax-schedule changes to finance the increases.

The across-the-board increase voted was 13 percent (P.L. 90–248). In short, there was to be no major departure—no general revenue contribution, no automatic adjustment of benefits in the future, and no raising of taxable bases to levels originally expected. There was to be no clear resolution of whether what is sought is a guaranteed "floor" for all, a system reflecting differential places in the wage scale, a more traditional private insurance model, or a public policy that covers risks not fully met through a contributory system. Long-term unemployment and family breakup for reasons other than the death of a male family head were not to be dealt with as problems through this system. Children born out of wedlock were to be left to public assistance. The child-rearing costs that can make the resources of a wife-earner of moderate means inadequate were not to be considered at this time, or at least in this forum. By Social Security Administration calculations, *none* of the proposals under discussion could take all the aged out of poverty, and the Congress enacted less than what was proposed.[66]

The "disjointed incrementalists" point to social security as evidence of how pragmatism, ad hoc measures, and bargaining create admirable results, and there is no doubt that they are correct.[67] Yet it is also true that holes, gaps, and inadequacies may long be obscured and basic policy thrusts delayed by this method as well.

Champions of current programs note two possibilities:

Further reforms in social *insurance* to raise benefits, increase risks covered, and add general revenue funds could achieve the objectives of the negative income tax or children's allowance advocates by means of an available mechanism.

---

[66] Merriam, "Social Security Benefits and Poverty."

[67] See David Braybrooke and Charles E. Lindblom, A *Strategy of Decision* (New York: The Free Press of Glencoe, 1963), 72.

Basic reforms in public *assistance* based on a national minimum, increased federal financial aid to the states, and substitution of a simple income declaration for the present degrading means tests could have similar effect.

All of this may be true. Yet the enactments of the Congress in 1967 gave proponents of more adequate income security no reason to drop their advocacy of new measures. There was every reason to believe that the Congress would continue to follow the Advisory Council in the view that social security is "a method of *preventing* destitution and poverty rather than relieving these conditions after they occur."[68] Even should the regressions of the 1967 welfare amendments be undone, *"Having the Power. . ."* will not define directions. A vision of a more comprehensive income-security system, which would see social insurance as basic but fill in the other requirements in quite specific fashion, was yet to be offered and accepted.

NEGATIVE INCOME TAX

Clearly the proponents of the social security system as the vehicle for rounding out American income security see the planning task somewhat differently from those who concentrate on the reform of public assistance. The champions of the negative income tax have their unique and by no means unanimous perspectives as well.

A negative income tax in its simplest form is a system of cash payments to people whose incomes fall below the federal personal income tax level. Milton Friedman, a conservative economist, assured the proposal its first widespread hearing in the 'sixties.[69] Friedman, an opponent of graduated taxation to redistribute income and of social security, both of which he sees as infringements on individual freedom, proposed the negative income tax "on purely mechanical grounds." Such a plan would focus on poverty, make costs quite visible, and would be administratively simpler than "the present rag bag of measures." Although worried about possible distortion of the approach to impose a heavy burden on a more prosperous minority, Friedman considered it most promising. He continued to advocate it and suggested quite modest benefits once the anti-poverty effort was launched and income-transfer proposals began to be discussed publicly.

Friedman's main concern is to protect the market as he conceives it and

---

[68] *The Status of the Social Security Program. . .*, 2.

[69] Milton Friedman, *Capitalism and Freedom* (Chicago: University of Chicago Press, 1962). Earlier history of negative income tax is reviewed by Schorr, *op. cit.* A comprehensive overview and sophisticated analysis is offered in Christopher Green, *Negative Taxes and the Poverty Problem* (Washington, D.C.: The Brookings Institution, 1967).

to meet the needs of the poor simply, through an efficient governmental mechanism, if private charity cannot manage to do so. Robert Lampman, who prepared several basic papers for the Office of Economic Opportunity, notes that one can use the proposed mechanism to implement one of several possible concepts of the planning task—and that the details would vary with the somewhat contradictory objectives:[70]

- ☐ to improve tax equity
- ☐ to narrow the poverty-income gap
- ☐ to replace public assistance as a program for delivering income to poor people.

The several plans are best understood in Lampman's total context. Because the thinking represents a major departure in the approach to our tax system, an extended quotation will be helpful:

> Almost all of the poor are now non-taxable under the Federal individual income tax. However, they do pay a considerable part of their incomes under other Federal, State and local taxes. Many possible changes in the income tax law will not affect their incomes. Thus, reducing the positive tax rates, raising the personal exemptions, or increasing the allowable deductions will not help the family that is already non-taxable. A zero tax bill cannot be made less than zero, at least according to conventional thinking on this subject. This means that we tolerate a considerable amount of vertical and horizontal inequity within the non-taxable income range. It means that we let families of the same size pay the same tax—namely, zero—even though their incomes differ widely. Thus, a family of four persons will pay zero tax whether its income is $1 or $3000. It also means that a family of four with a $3000 income pays the same tax—namely, zero—as does a family of eight persons with a $3000 income.
>
> If we are to get at these tax inequities and at the same time to improve the incomes of the poor via the income tax it is necessary to alter the tax law to pay out benefits. This throwing of the tax system into reverse can be done either by the use of tax credits, or by the use of negative tax rates which are to be applied to unused exemptions and deductions or to some other measure of the amount by which actual income falls below a desired standard.
>
> . . . transfers can be thought of as negative taxes and taxes as negative trans-

---

[70] Robert J. Lampman, "Negative Rates Income Taxation" and "Preliminary Report on a Plan for Negative Income Taxation," two mimeographed papers prepared in 1965 for the United States Office of Economic Opportunity. An excellent summary of Lampman's views and the several alternative proposals under discussion is offered by Helen O. Nicol, "Guaranteed Income Maintenance," *Welfare in Review*, 4, No. 4 (April, 1966), 1–10. A general source on proposals discussed in 1967 is the same author's "Guaranteed Income Maintenance: Another Look at the Debate," *Welfare in Review*, 5, No. 1 (June–July, 1967), 1–13.

fers. Hence, it does not seem so strange to contemplate taxing and transferring by this same device. As a matter of fact, the income tax is doing this kind of double duty right now, but principally among the non-poor. For example, the personal exemptions, in effect, transfer tax burdens from those who have children to those who do not. And the medical expense deduction transfers, via a tax reduction or negative tax, an income increase to the sick taxpayer from a well taxpayer. And so on. The transfers in the present tax law are substantial in amount. The personal exemption and minimum standard deduction (total of $700) for a child can be thought of as a children's allowance equal to between $98 and $490 depending upon the taxpayers' marginal tax rate. At $100 per child the tax forgiveness amounts to about $6 billion for all non-poor families. There are also 15 million children in poor families. It is, perhaps, ironic that this "family allowance" written into the tax law diminishes in importance as family income decreases or as family size increases. Consider again the case of a family of four with $3000 of income. The fact that their tax liability is zero means that their second child saved them $98 in taxes. This tax saving may be said to shrink when that family's income falls to below $3000 or when a third child arrives. Either of these possibilities will give rise to redundant or unused exemptions and deductions. For the 35 million poor persons, who have taxable income of about $12 billion in total, we can say that exemptions and deductions afford them a tax saving of 14 percent of $12 billion, or $1.7 billion. However, if they were to get the full tax value of their exemptions and minimum standard deductions it would be a tax saving of 14 percent of about $750 times 35 million, or $3.7 billion. That is $2 billion more than they now save.

Unused exemptions and deductions can be the basis for negative tax payments or positive transfers and it would appear to be consistent with the logic of the income tax to make such payments.[71]

The first negative income tax plan seriously discussed by an official federal advisory group merely would have allowed people to claim 14 percent of their unused exemptions and deductions, 14 percent being the lowest rate in our tax law. The costs (Lampman's estimates are all in 1964 terms) would be $2 billion minus possible public assistance savings out of a gap of $12 billion between 1964 incomes of the poor and the poverty line. Too little money would be paid out to solve much of the poverty problem under this scheme, but from some perspectives, it would increase the equity of the tax system.

Of Lampman's several other, more adequate models, Nicol highlights three as sharpening the choices:

---

[71] Lampman, "Negative Rates Income Taxation," 2–4. Or, see, "Prepared Statement of Professor Robert Lampman," *Income Maintenance Programs*, Hearings Before the Subcommittee on Fiscal Policy, Joint Economic Committee, 2 volumes (Washington, D.C.: Government Printing Office, 1968), I, 149–155.

Fifty-percent plan. This plan simply computes the gap by subtracting a family's total income from the poverty-line income for a family of that particular size and type (urban, rural, etc.) and, then, pays 50 percent of the gap. One would pay only 50 percent of the gap as a way to preserve work incentives, a point to which we shall return. (Cost: $5–8 billion).

One-hundred-percent plan. To fill the total gap under such a plan would probably cost twice the poverty gap in Lampman's view ($24 billion) because of likely reduction in work incentives for people earning below the level and above it to a point where income minus taxes is not much more than the payment under the negative plan. He also predicts political rejection of such proposals by taxpayers because of the unacceptability of a working taxpayer's filling completely the income gap for the non-employed.

Flat-rate plan. Under this plan,

> a flat tax allowance of $750 would be paid to a family up to $1,500 of their original earned income. After their income had reached $1,500, the tax allowance would fall 50 cents for every dollar earned. The allowance would fall to zero when income reached $3,000.

Obviously better suited to those with some income (social insurance or underpaid work) this approach would not help the "poorest of the poor."[72]

Much of Lampman's work, rejecting the 100-percent plan, is a matter of elaborating variations of the 50-percent scheme with reference to the incentive question: What will actually give people most incentive to earn as much as possible and not be content with the support of the negative rate tax? What will be least likely to offer disincentives to those currently self-supporting? To illustrate, one might pay the entire income gap for the first $1,500 and a 50 percent rate on the next $1,500. Or one might pay 75 percent, 50 percent, and 25 percent on successive $1,000 brackets. One might pay 75 percent on the first $500, and 33 percent on the next $1,500. These plans cover substantial, but differing, parts of the poverty gap at some differing cost; and all assume subtraction of public assistance payments. Any one of these plans could be restricted to families with children, but in Lampman's view, this would create a substantial child-rearing incentive for some families.[73]

After analyzing the effects of different possible plans on incentives and disincentives to work, to marry, to have children, to keep a family intact, Lampman wisely concludes:

---

[72] Nicol, "Guaranteed Income Maintenance," 4–5.

[73] Lampman, "Negative Rates. . . ."

Who will get how much benefit out of a negative rates tax plan will depend on the level and pattern of negative rates, the way the tax base is defined, and the way the eligible tax unit is defined. By working with these three variables, the tax policy-maker can put the money where he wants it. . . .[74]

One must make choices among paying some money to the non-poor, concentrating on families with children and ignoring the other 40 percent, and replacing or building upon public assistance.

Green states the choices technically in these terms:

> . . . all transfer-by-taxation contains three basic variables: (1) a guaranteed minimum level of income that varies with family size or family composition or both; (2) a tax rate or rates applied against a tax base; and (3) a breakeven level of income where the tax liability equals the income guarantee. Any two of these variables determine the outcome of the third.[75]

Careful exploration of a number of schemes in relation to the interplay of these variables convinces Green that one could not successfully plan a negative income tax scheme, *except as a supplement to public assistance*, without making relief recipients worse off monetarily.[76] He sees no way to bridge fully the income gap of the poor by such an approach without a serious work disincentive for many others (at least in the immediate future). On the other hand, the negative income tax plan does target transfers sharply where needed, avoids "inefficiency" in redistribution, and is relatively economical as such schemes go. It also recognizes that relatively few of the poor, proportionately, should be viewed as eligible for labor-force participation.

A leading proponent, James Tobin, offers the following approach: a family with no other income would receive a basic annual allowance, perhaps $400 per person. The allowance would be reduced by a specified fraction, perhaps one-third, for every dollar of income received. Thus, a considerable incentive to earn income would remain. Eligibility would end only when a family's regular income reached three times its allowance; those above the "break-even" point would be the taxpayers. Rates immediately above the point would also be adjusted with the incentive problem in mind. OASDHI payments would—or should—be high enough to make recipients ineligible. Income from pensions and unemployment insurance would be

---

[74] *Ibid.*, 28.

[75] Green, *op. cit.*, 62.

[76] *Ibid.*, 91.

regarded as income for purposes of computing possible allowances, but would not be taxable. Public assistance would be eliminated. The total program (see Table 5) could be introduced in stages.[77]

Tobin's plan, of course, assumes changes in the tax structure—as do some of Lampman's options. Schorr notes that one could develop a proposal involving accepting the deduction-exemption system as it now operates. His focus is on aiding children:

> Every family with children under eighteen would be expected to file an income tax return. . . . Any family showing deductions and exemptions in excess of taxable income would receive a cash payment . . . only public assistance payments would be exempted from consideration. . . . For each $600 of deficit, up to the number of child exemptions in the family, a payment of $300 would be made. The payments would arrive in twelve equal monthly installments following the date on which the return was filed. The cost would be met from general revenues. . . .[78]

Both advocates and opponents of the negative income tax are concerned that some of the specifics of administration and other aspects of programming are so important that they may weight the balance against such approach. What is the family unit; could income tax rules apply? What should be the rules about wealth and the use thereof? What constitutes income? Obviously, income tax rules could not be completely applicable or one would subsidize people of considerable means whose "wealth" is not current income or who are supported by close relatives whose taxes are filed sepa-

---

[77] James Tobin, "Improving the Economic Status of the Negro," in *The American Negro, Daedalus*, 94, No. 4, (Fall, 1965), 840–844. Other less-widely discussed guaranteed income programs are offered by Edward Schwartz, whose mechanism is more like Lampman's but who would rely on a federal commission to set levels, and Robert Theobald, who considers it essential at this stage of economic development to separate income-rights from labor market motivations. See summaries in Nicol, "Guaranteed Income Maintenance," and "Guaranteed Income Maintenance: Another Look at the Debate," Edward Schwartz, "A Way to End the Means Test," *Social Work*, 9, No. 3 (July, 1964), 3–12 and reprinted in Ferman, Kornbluh, and Haber, *Poverty in America*, 481–496. Also, Robert Theobald, *Free Men and Free Markets* (Garden City, New York: Doubleday Anchor edition, 1965) and Robert Theobald, Editor, *The Guaranteed Income* (Garden City, New York: Doubleday & Company, 1966). Also, James Tobin, Joseph A. Pechman, and Peter M. Mieszkowski, "Is a Negative Income Tax Practical?" a reprint (Washington, D.C.: The Brookings Institution, 1967) or *The Yale Law Journal*, 77, No. 1 (November, 1967), 1–27. These authors provide detailed specifications for several schemes and cope with the major technical questions. The several schemes are debated in *Income Maintenance Programs*, Hearings Before the Subcommittee on Fiscal Policy, Joint Economic Committee, 2 volumes (Washington, D.C.: Government Printing Office, 1968).

[78] Schorr, *op. cit.*, 132–133.

Table 5 ONE NEGATIVE INCOME TAX PLAN CALCULATED FOR A FAMILY OF FIVE

Income before subsidy or tax liability	PROPOSED SCHEDULE					PRESENT TAX SCHEDULE	
	Guaranteed minimum income ($400 per capita)	Taxable income	Tax rate	Amount of negative or positive tax	Income after subsidy or tax liability	Amount of positive tax	Income after tax
0	$2,000	−$2,000[a]	100%[b]	−$2,000	$2,000	$ 0	$ 0
$1,000	2,000	−1,667[a]	100%[b]	−1,667	2,667	0	1,000
2,000	2,000	−1,333[a]	100%[b]	−1,333	3,333	0	2,000
2,500	2,000	−1,167[a]	100%[b]	−1,167	3,667	0	2,500
3,000	2,000	−1,000[a]	100%[b]	−1,000	4,000	0	3,000
3,700	2,000	−767[a]	100%[b]	−767	4,467	0	3,700
4,000	2,000	−667[a]	100%[b]	−667	4,667	+42	3,958
5,000	2,000	−333[a]	100%[b]	−333	5,333	+185	4,815
6,000	2,000	0[a]		0	6,000	+338	5,662
7,000	2,000	+1,000	33⅓%	+333	6,667	+501	6,499
7,963[c]	2,000	+1,963 / +4,167	33⅓%} 14–19%}	+654	7,309	+654	7,309
8,000	2,000	+4,200	14–19%	+658	7,342	+658	7,342

[a] Negative income tax base, i.e. difference between the guaranteed minimum income and the tax on earnings, which is one-third of earnings.
[b] Negative income tax rate, i.e. percentage applied to negative income tax base to calculate subsidy.
[c] Income level at which tax liability is the same under present and proposed methods of calculation (liability differs slightly due to rounding). The present tax schedule applies to income in excess of this level.

Source: Library of Congress Legislative Service, Memo, "The Negative Income tax and Other Welfare Proposals to Guarantee an Annual Income," 1967, 11.

rately. The negative income tax requires a revised means test, special forms; the income tax form would not suffice. How does one take into account regional or urban-rural differences in the cost of living? Assuming that people are paid their benefits in advance on the basis of declarations of expected income (rather than on returns for the past year), how does one recover overpayment from people at this income level? Could a negative-tax payment start at any time the way public assistance does? If one uses the federal tax system and its annual base, how does one account for changes in family income in mid-year? Would one refer to public assistance to take account of unexpected illness and other emergencies? These problems are complex. Green considers them amenable to solution; others do not.

But the ultimate issue remains: should one propose a negative income tax approach even though the analysis suggests that, given the interplay of variables listed above, it could not pay enough to meet the needs of the very poor, thus necessitating some state-local administrative plan for assistance as well? As put by a conference of experts: "a negative tax would supplement, rather than substitute for, present public transfer and service programs."[79] There are those who see no problem in this: relieved of the basic burden, the states, it is contended, could then supplement and provide the "last resort" program. Other proponents of the negative income tax, as the debate continued into late 1968, had decided, in fact, to concentrate on the working poor, those not receiving public assistance but unable to manage because of low wages, irregular work, or too many children to feed. The major New Jersey negative income tax "experiment" launched late in 1968 took this group as its main population.

At this point, friends of reformed public assistance note that solution of some of the programming problems in negative income tax plans eventually brings one to a pattern of administration, in which the negative income tax meets the reformed and humane public assistance program: both call for a simple statement of means as related to prescheduled tables of minimum guarantees; the application is taken at face value and benefits are paid; subsamples are investigated and verified. Thus, the issue between reformed public assistance and a new negative income tax system becomes a matter of determining whether the Department of the Treasury would be more efficient than the Department of Health, Education, and Welfare; whether the public-assistance stigma and the intertwining of money payments and social services can or cannot now be overcome to offer money as a justiciable right through public welfare; and whether there are advantages in retaining

---

[79] Green, op. cit., 168.

a state-federal-local system in contrast to creating a centralized system of negative taxes, supplemented by public assistance. (By mid-1968, the Secretary of Health, Education, and Welfare had proposed federal operation of assistance to assure uniformity.)

As one pursues these considerations and their bases in preferences, administrative science, and political theory, and as one analyzes the several plans, which have been much debated, it becomes very clear that the issues for solution with reference to the negative income tax are not primarily fiscal or technical. Basically, the question is one of objectives or, in our vocabulary, of definition of the task. The champions of various proposals talk past one another, not coming to grips with the same issues. To cope adequately with the negative income tax, the Commission on Income Maintenance Programs, appointed by President Lyndon Johnson and scheduled to report late in 1969, would need to decide just what problem it was attempting to solve and at what cost.

CHILDREN'S ALLOWANCES

Schorr has provided in *Poor Kids*[80] one of the most systematic illustrations of the tie between definition of the task and policy-programming choices. He does not choose among children's allowances, fatherless-child insurance, or negative income tax as the priority new component for American income security, but he uses his yardstick to evaluate each. He assumes continuous improvements in social security and public assistance along the lines already described. For our present purposes, his analysis of children's allowances may be emphasized. His backing for such allowances as part of a comprehensive program has been stated in other contexts.

The point of departure is sharp and clear: children are at the center of vision and the aim is to assure them an income. As an income-security measure, children's allowances have both the advantage and disadvantage of being limited to families with children. Beyond meeting elemental need is the matter of "how the program fits into children's lives." Here Schorr develops his distinctive perspective:

> . . . poor children in the United States are poorly sheltered, many of them do not eat adequately, and their medical care is insufficient. Their right to an intact family is compromised. Their recreational and personal needs are not met. They do not even benefit from proper education.[81]

---

[80] *Op. cit.*

[81] *Ibid.*, 15.

Millions of children are so deprived: one-third in homes of men who have regular work, one-third in the homes of men without regular work, and one-third in homes headed by women. The high poverty-risks are in large families, broken families, families in which the head has poor earning capacity; these three categories have considerable overlap, covering three out of four poor children. Economic growth alone will not solve the child poverty problem.[82]

Piecing together available research and plausibilities, and building upon a British tradition, Schorr develops a theory of the family cycle and its relationship to income, looking at the reciprocal relationships of marriage, birth, job choice, the opportunity and models available to children—and the effects of all these on ending the poverty cycle. He concludes that for a family to "take off" from poverty it needs more than mere subsistence.

> Take-off for poor families requires surplus money for investment in self-improvement, as well as the skill and drive more usually asked of them. . . . If it does not . . . provide some surplus . . . it is not a functional anti-poverty program.[83]

Here, then, is a clearly formulated definition of the planning task for an income security program focused on long-term eradication of poverty. It is very much in the spirit of what the nineteen-sixties has come to know as an "opportunity" strategy. The planning is kept realistic: while guaranteed income as proposed by Theobald may come eventually, one has to assume, for the next decade or two at least, a preference for income from work and continued concern for work motivation. Nor, given precedent and current concepts of the poverty gap, is a program costing more than one percent of current national income likely to be enacted. Programs costing $8 to $14 billion may be discussed but will be resisted.

Schorr looks at various points in the life cycle to see where investments might most profitably be made. Adequate money when a marriage begins and at the birth of the first child might provide a degree of needed stability. It might, too, be used to improve the job preparation of young fathers and their job-choices. A third critical stage in the cycle comes for those with four or five children, who feel a "family-cycle squeeze" when compelled to

---

[82] *Ibid.*, 20.

By 1967, the picture was: of 10.7 million children in poverty, 4.2 million lived with a family head who worked all year, 3.7 million with a family head who worked part of the year, and 2 million with a "not disabled" head who did not work. The remainder, 0.8 million, lived with aged or disabled heads. "Progressing Against Poverty," Note No. 24, Research and Statistics Note, Social Security Administration, December 10, 1968, Table 7.

[83] Schorr, *op. cit.*, 47.

cope with the conflict of aspiration and need in large families. Another stage, for some, is breakdown: divorce, separation, and desertion.

Proposals for income security may be appraised with reference to the provision of "social capital" for the necessary "take off" at the critical life-cycle points. Schorr begins with a social insurance proposal. Fatherless-child insurance aids the orphaned, but will not sustain an intact family at the critical points early in marriage when access to money affects a mother's ability to concentrate on child care. Nor does it cope with the financial problem of the young marriage in which the man is trying to complete school or to develop a career strategy—and is limited by financial responsibilities for children. It would probably not cover children born out of wedlock. Negative income tax, whether Schorr's version or one of the other proposals, could in theory give the needed boost at several critical points in the cycle, particularly when in "mid-term" a family is trying to rear four or more children—but Schorr doubts that payments under any plan which might be enacted would be large enough to make critical impact. One in effect would need to do better than fill 50 percent of the deficit between available income and the poverty-line—and, as one does this, serious work disincentives do develop both for the completely self-supporting at marginal levels and for those receiving some aid who must work to improve their situation.

This brings Schorr to the family or children's allowance, an almost universal measure among industrialized countries, aimed at that poverty traceable to the size of the family: "three out of five poor children are members of families with four or more children."[84] In fact, large families have lower incomes than small families, and the program of children's allowances may be conceptualized as helping them cope with their competitive disadvantage in improving their situation.

A family allowance is what Burns[85] calls a demogrant, a payment to a segment of the population based on status. Payments are made in this instance to a family for its children, whether or not there is need. There are no eligibility conditions other than being a child. Plans differ from country to country: allowances may be paid to first, second, third, fourth children, or to all children. The grant may be very small or relatively significant. It is considered an income *supplement*, not complete support for a child. A means test of a sort may be introduced, but usually is not. The check generally is paid to the mother. Most often termed family allowances, such

[84] *Ibid.*, 147.

[85] Burns, *Social Security and Public Policy*, 88–93.

demogrants were paid, at last report, in 62 countries, including 27 in Western Europe, 20 in Africa, Canada in North America, 6 in South America, 3 in the Middle East, and several elsewhere. Their major development took place between World War II and 1960. Although all large industrialized countries except the United States make these grants, many developing countries also have adopted such allowances. The two main patterns of family-allowance programs are: allowances which are a right by virtue of residence in a country (14 countries); and allowances as a condition of the employment relationship (thus adjusting income to family size). Financing ranges from general revenue coverage to employer contributions.[86]

From among all the possibilities and with his concept of the planning task very much in mind, Schorr devises a children's allowance scheme focused on critical family-cycle points. Rather than the usual uniform or almost uniform rates for all children—which would permit grants too modest to achieve the desired results within the expenditure limits deemed reasonable—Schorr proposes allowances biased in favor of children under six. A payment of $50 per month out of general revenue would be paid to the mother for each child in this age group, income tax exemptions for children would be eliminated, and the benefit would be taxable.[87]

Schorr's analysis of this so-called preschool allowance suggests that it is the best targeted of all the possible strategies—if one begins with his judgments as to the critical stages for financial intervention, assumes expenditures not much larger than the 1964 poverty gap ($12 billion), and agrees that the society will not at this time enact an income program significantly departing from our work ethic or endangering work motivation. Schorr knows that traditionally labor unions in the United States have feared children's allowances as affecting bargaining strategies, but his preschool emphasis precludes that problem. He recognizes that the public has always worried about the possible incentives such allowances might offer for childbearing, but, after analyzing available demographic evidence, he suggests that, at the least, one can say that no such effect has been demonstrated anywhere; it is almost certain from available studies that there is no such effect.

Preschool allowances at the proposed level would achieve Schorr's goal of a small income surplus in the family above the bare minimum of needs when the children are very young, the marriage's character is in balance, and the husband's occupational pattern is being shaped. Because the grant would

---

[86] *Social Security Programs Throughout the World, 1967*, xxvii, xxviii.

[87] Schorr, *op. cit.*, 151.

go to intact families as well as to unmarried mothers, children would be reached who would not be covered by fatherless-child insurance. Much of Schorr's case rests on the assumption that a poverty-free experience in the first six years of a child's life could do much for him and his parents to encourage a "take off" from poverty.

The needs of children over six are thus sacrificed to keep the program's costs within reason. Schorr would make up for this by investing heavily in school-based health, social, and educational services—and raising public assistance grants for the children over six. If this is not acceptable, he poses the less satisfactory alternative of $25 a month for children up to six and $10 a month for children from six to eighteen.

Schorr knows that the opponents of continued fragmentation would prefer to end categories rather than add a new categorical program. However, the realities of politics, i.e., assembling backing for a program, and the ethic appear to involve tying "to each new program an acceptable, unique quality (old age, widowhood, disability)" rather than building on "their vexatious common quality (need)."[88] If and when the society accepts a publicly-assured, non-means-tested guaranteed income for all, he would drop a special program for "kids." In the long interim children continue as the only sizable population group for whom there is no satisfactory plan.

We cannot here do justice to Schorr's consideration of the possible effects of each of the proposed measures on each stage of the family cycle. He illustrates in rich detail how clarity of objectives offers yardsticks, which go beyond internal program criteria or considerations of cost. He computes the portion of the poverty gap covered by each option. He demonstrates how, where knowledge is incomplete, one may make optimum use of available research. Children's allowances are particularly attractive because they skirt entirely the work-incentive question—the allowances are a right for *all*; they do not introduce differences between poor and rich children; they move current tax exemption and deduction allowances to an early point in the life cycle; they readjust federal transfer systems in favor of "poor kids." Administration becomes a very simple matter. But most important: "If we eliminated poverty for families with children in 1964, fewer than a third of those counted poor would remain poor."[89] Those who would not be reached thus—the poor aged, the disabled, the unemployed—would be reached by raising social security benefit levels. Hence, focused income

---

[88] Schorr, *ibid.*, 97.

[89] *Ibid.*, 170.

maintenance planning for children leads to the question of a comprehensive plan.

There are other major advocates of family and children's allowances; Schorr was chosen in illustration because of the clarity of his definition of the task and the derivation therefrom of policy perspectives and programming guides. Daniel P. Moynihan has proposed a relatively small allowance, being concerned basically with the family focus of this scheme as opposed to other forms of income maintenance. Participants in a conference of experts on the subject stressed the validity of children's allowances to combat child poverty. They did note that universal benefits without a means test inevitably do involve "inefficiency" in the sense that one must distribute to and then collect large sums from the non-poor. In this connection, Harvey Brazer of the University of Michigan has proposed a recoupment tax on such allowances, i.e., a special tax to take much of the allowance away from those deemed not to need it, thus keeping the grants more closely focused on need and decreasing overall costs while avoiding an initial means test. The Council of Economic Advisors has proposed consideration of a grant to households with poor children, a "children's minimum income allowance," among the next round of income-maintenance measures.[90] Mollie Orshansky, of the Research Department of the Social Security Administration, has computed the costs and potential accomplishments of various programs, focused specially on children in poverty. (See Table 6.) Again the need to define the planning task is manifest.[91]

Finally, one should note that none of the serious scholars who have investigated the matter[92] considers children's allowances as posing a serious problem in encouraging a rise in the birth rate. All acknowledge, however, that public concern with the issue is a serious obstacle to devising a plan.

COMPREHENSIVE INCOME SECURITY

David Bazelon has argued that the modern American, as compensation for what he has sacrificed to large organization and bureaucracy and as a prerequisite to individual freedom, has a right to a decent standard of liv-

---

[90] 1968 Economic Report of the President and Annual Report of the Council of Economic Advisors (Washington, D.C.: Government Printing Office, 1968), 147.

[91] See Eveline M. Burns, Editor, Children's Allowances and the Economic Welfare of Children (New York: Citizens' Committee for Children, 1968). The Brazer scheme is included. Also see James C. Vadakin, Children, Poverty, and Family Allowances (New York: Basic Books, 1968).

[92] See Green, Burns, Schorr.

ing.[93] Some of the proponents of new income-security measures would agree with Bazelon; others have more modest perspectives. What has become clear in our selective illustrations is that the debate among the alternatives, and for different options within each of the several possible major new thrusts, assumes different definitions of the task. Since, at the highest levels, Americans are currently attempting systematic policy planning for income security, the first choices should therefore be choices of objectives.

We hold that the several components here reviewed in some detail and the additional elements mentioned only in passing might be approached as possible segments of an income-security system—and that policy and programming could emerge from a serious dialogue about task. Some policy-makers argue for coping separately with each of the interventions: the public accepts social security and supports its reforms from self-interest; one draws upon humanitarian and charitable impulses with reference to public assistance; perhaps now one could enact children's allowances by calling for sympathy for "poor kids." This, it is true, is how social policy measures generally grow in the West; it is consistent with our ethic's anti-planning bias. But it is also true that the separate interventions increasingly impinge upon one another, that the gaps among them are serious, and that a status-linked categorical system (in which the rights component is strong in social security and weak in public assistance) creates many negative effects.

The time may have arrived in the United States when it is useful to conceptualize the components as one income-security system and to seek coherence. This does not preclude separate lobbying and enactments, to the degree that the political arm wishes to involve different constituencies. It does call for an overall vision, so that informed recommendations may be made with a view to those decisions about risks, eligibility, financing, and administration which are involved in translating objectives into program.

The debate about the task is in fact under way. Inspired by the realization that the anti-poverty effort was truncated without an income-security component, various governmental task forces, voluntary organizations, and individual scholars began to address the matter actively in the mid-sixties. Several views have been cited.

One could begin with first principles and line up all the choices in deductive fashion as do Dahl and Lindblom. But even where such exercise

---

[93] David Bazelon, *The Paper Economy* (New York: Vintage Books, 1965), especially Chap. 16.

Table 6 COST AND ANTI-POVERTY EFFECT ON FAMILIES WITH CHILDREN
UNDER 18 OF FOUR SPECIFIED MONTHLY ALLOWANCE-
PAYMENTS FOR CHILDREN IN 1965

	$25		$50	
Payment program	Every child	Third and subsequent children	Every child	Third and subsequent children
Program cost				
Payment (in billions)	$20.9	$ 6.7	$41.2	$13.3
Tax recovery potential (in billions)	$ 9.6	$ 2.6	$12.7	$ 3.5
Eliminating exemption[a]	6.5	1.8	6.5	1.8
Tax on the allowance	3.1	.8	6.2	1.7
Reduction in poverty status of families with children				
Payments to the poor (in billions)	$ 4.2	$ 1.9	$ 8.4	$ 3.9
Percent of families removed from poverty:				
Total	36.2	15.2	64.3	28.7
With male head	40.7	18.9	67.7	33.0
With female head	27.8	8.3	58.3	21.2
Percent of children in families removed from poverty:				
Total children	45.4	24.9	77.0	46.4
In families with male head	50.4	29.9	79.8	51.3
In families with female head	34.7	14.3	71.8	37.3
Percent of persons in families removed from poverty:				
Total persons[b]	35.4	17.9	61.0	33.9
In families with male head	37.0	20.0	59.9	34.6
In families with female head	30.9	12.2	64.0	31.9

[a] Eliminating $600 exemption and minimum standard deduction for children receiving allowance.
[b] Based on total of 27.1 million persons in poor families including persons in families with no children.
Source: Prepared by the Social Security Administration as background material for Citizens' Committee for Children, Conference on Children's Allowances, October, 1967. See Eveline M. Burns, Editor, *Children's Allowances and the Economic Welfare of Children* (New York: Citizens' Committee for Children, 1968).

might prove impractical, one cannot avoid asking: how will the society distribute claims; how much redistribution is intended? The answers, in turn, guide one with reference to the several different variables in the equation:

☐ the *"size* of shares," and "the direction and speed of change in size of shares"

☐ *what* is divided up (income, leisure, free services, particular goods, earned or unearned income, wealth, income at the start of life or at retirement)

☐ *standards* to be attained (equality, meeting need, protecting physical subsistence, minimum consumption of certain kinds, personal integrity, political stability, social harmony, etc.)

Table 6   COST AND ANTI-POVERTY EFFECT ON FAMILIES WITH CHILDREN
UNDER 18 OF FOUR SPECIFIED MONTHLY ALLOWANCE-
PAYMENTS FOR CHILDREN IN 1965 (cont.)

	$25		$50	
Payment program	Every child	Third and subsequent children	Every child	Third and subsequent children
Reduction in low-income status of families with children				
Payments to the poor and near poor (in billions)	$ 6.0	$ 2.7	$12.0	$ 5.4
Percent of families removed from low-income status:				
Total	27.2	9.6	53.6	20.3
With male head	32.4	12.3	59.2	24.8
With female head	14.1	3.1	40.0	9.5
Percent of children in families removed from low-income status:				
Total children	32.6	15.9	64.5	33.8
In families with male head	50.4	29.9	79.8	51.3
In families with female head	34.7	14.3	71.8	37.3
Percent of persons in families removed from low-income status:				
Total persons[b]	36.8	16.9	66.7	33.9
In families with male head	14.7	4.6	47.8	14.4
In families with female head	31.3	13.8	62.0	29.0

[a] Eliminating $600 exemption and minimum standard deduction for children receiving allowance.
[b] Based on total of 27.1 million persons in poor families including persons in families with no children.
Source: Prepared by the Social Security Administration as background material for Citizens' Committee for Children, Conference on Children's Allowances, October, 1967. See Eveline M. Burns, Editor, *Children's Allowances and the Economic Welfare of Children* (New York: Citizens' Committee for Children, 1968).

□ on *whom* redistribution is to focus: individuals, families, children, particular individuals (widows), particular groups (farmers)
□ *purposes* to be emphasized (consumption, status, security, control, increased earning capacity).[94]

These overlapping elements, summarized from a more complete presentation, are somewhat familiar. Some, but not all, appear in different language in our discussion of social security, public assistance, children's allowances, and the negative income tax. While the policy dialogue, whether in a planning office, task force, citizens' organization, or legislative forum, cannot be as extensive as full absorption of all the Dahl-Lindblom dimensions

---

[94] Robert A. Dahl and Charles E. Lindblom, Chap. 5, "Social Processes for Economizing," *Politics, Economics, and Welfare* (New York: Harper & Row Torchbook paper edition, 1963).

might inspire, it should be as comprehensive as the assessment of social reality dictates. To the mother in extreme need the "fine points" may not matter because, "government money is government money."[95] Yet those in a position to consider competing demands upon resources and alternative strategies do need to ask: What alternative definitions of the task make sense in the United States today given subgroup preferences and the economic and social realities? Proponents of a given view are called upon to spell out as comprehensive a strategy as possible. We merely *illustrate* one hypothesis to suggest a level of argument.

An hypothesis of the planning task

With no claim to originality, but merely combining elements offered by others, we summarize, by way of illustration, one view of a comprehensive income security planning task upon which policy and programming specifics might be elaborated. Much is left unsaid, since a full overview involves basic value and preference questions.

The first premise is that the requirements of productivity, our value system, and current motivational patterns demand protection of the primacy of work as a source of income. Fiscal and monetary policies ("demand management") should be focused on a full-employment economy and jobs for the employable—with employability defined and redefined to include the labor force needed at a given moment. Minimum wages in this view should be raised as much as possible, but closing out of jobs where machines are not so effective as workers should be avoided. "Dirty work" should be well paid, on the assumption that it must be done and, if adequately valued, will become less stigmatized.[96]

It is thus concluded, with no evidence here cited, that Theobald's proposals are, at the least, premature. Technology and automation have not yet created a situation requiring substantial measures to separate work and consumption rights.[97] This does not mean that the society must not constantly decide who is to be regarded as "legitimately dependent" and supported by virtue of such status at least at an above-poverty or subsistence level. One type of device may thus meet the needs of the graduate student

---

[95] *Examination of the War on Poverty* (Senate), I, 34.

[96] See Herbert Gans, "Income Grants and 'Dirty Work,'" *The Public Interest*, No. 6 (Winter, 1967), 110–113.

[97] Theobald, *Free Men and Free Markets*. The contrary evidence is summarized in National Commission on Technology, Automation and Economic Progress, *Technology and the American Economy* (Washington, D.C.: Government Printing Office, 1966).

or theoretical mathematician (scholarships and fellowships). Other devices are needed for the retired aged, the handicapped, school-age children, and mothers who care for them.

The work ethic, and a scheme based on it, also assumes that work will be available to those ready and able to work. Thus, in addition to demand management policies, government should indeed become an "employer of last resort," as has been proposed.[98] Real work at adequate wages is required in such programs, not the usual work-test, work-training, or punitive-work offerings, which have historically characterized welfare work programs.

Our approach assumes that, given the availability of work, and adequate manpower policy to assure training and placement, most employable persons will meet their economic needs through work and work-related schemes. Both wage levels and income security measures will also take account of available resources for "collective consumption," or what we have called "social utilities." Public health, education, recreation, housing, and social service programs, as well as public transportation, cultural resources, and voluntary associational activities have considerable impact on the amount of cash needed by the individual.[99] It is probably not an exaggeration to affirm that "the smoothest road to more equalization is through aids to education, occupational and professional training, mobility and health, all of which have the effect of equalizing earning opportunities."[100]

Next, facing the inadequacies of available income maintenance measures, with special reference to benefit levels, uncovered subgroups, the problems of the large family, gaps, and different approaches to rights, one might attempt reforms and innovations aimed at entitlement, adequacy, and comprehensiveness. Universalism would be emphasized, but not to the point of completely eradicating categories. Some of the Dahl-Lindblom questions must be answered to set benefit levels. We assume a readiness to support modest redistributional measures through the tax system—aimed not at equality but at *equity*, seeking to assure

- ☐ that everyone has enough income for subsistence (measured by a rising poverty-line);
- ☐ that money is available to facilitate access to opportunity on the part of the deprived;

---

[98] See *Technology and the American Economy* or A *"Freedom Budget"* for All Americans (New York: A. Philip Randolph Institute, 1966).

[99] Some policy perspectives on these matters are offered in the companion volume, Chapters V, VI, and VII.

[100] Dahl and Lindblom, *op. cit.*, 441.

☐ that in some way retirement, disability, and survivor benefits are scaled in relation to previous wage levels so as to sustain work motivation.

The non-stigmatic component in an income-security design—and this must mean the entire program—should go beyond the old concern with interruptions in earnings, toward taking responsibility for *deprivation*, too. It might seek a subsistence-level, national minimum for all, reflecting current productivity and living standards. And it might begin with the three groups about which there is most agreement and least worry over motivation: the retired, the disabled, and children.

Social insurance (with the possibility of collections through the general income tax mechanism and certainly with some general revenue contributions as a redistributional measure and for the sake of efficiency) would be the foundation of such an income-security system and could meet the basic needs of those without competitive handicaps. Eventually all the aged and disabled should be covered. All socially recognized "legitimate" risks of interrupted income would be included. The minimum grant would keep one above a constantly rising poverty-line, reflecting cost-of-living revisions and increased productivity. Unemployment coverage would be expanded considerably and include dependents.

Recognizing the special problem of large families, broken families, and children born out of wedlock, income deficiencies which affect children and the need for "take off" could very well be met by a demogrant, a children's allowance. Such allowance could be conceived in precisely the sense proposed by Schorr: as an income counterpart to the opportunity programs, designed to guarantee that poor children generally, particularly poor children in large families, begin their life experiences on terms which permit the breaking of the cycle of deprivation. When financing is feasible, one would wish to include children through the age of sixteen or eighteen, on the terms Schorr offered for the first six years of life. Grants should go beyond basic food and shelter needs and provide a bit of "surplus." Brazer's recoupment proposals, to recover children's allowance grants from those who do not need them, would allow a universal benefit at reasonable cost.

In a larger sense, children's allowances may also be seen as an essential counterpart of a wage policy. Since wages are not related to family size or need, it is essential that income security be geared to the situation of the low-wage earner.

New provision will be needed to reflect the capacities and aspirations of the wage earners above the minimal level. Here is required either an expansion and reform of private pension schemes, including "vesting," or revised perspectives in social security, whereby quite a high contribution base and an additional social security tax offer entry to further benefits—to approximate the retirement incomes proposed by some union advocates. In short, through this "second tier," the goal of the above-average earner is sought: "a more comfortable and adequate level of replacement."[101] To achieve this, it will be necessary to face squarely present limitations of private schemes.

A renewal social security system related to interrupted income and the dependency of the aged, plus demogrants for children, would not eliminate the need for a "safety net" or "last resort" program for the unprotected —even though far fewer would fall into such a net. There will remain those without social insurance rights in special circumstances, or with unusual needs. Lord Beveridge has said, "The essential condition for freedom and responsibility for the citizen is avoidance by the State of any form of means test in dealing with the citizens."[102] Yet a "safety net" or "last resort" program does require a means test; and there has been little success in avoiding degradation in such programs thus far, even when they stress rights. One should recall, however, that every income tax return is also a means test. The issue is the test's universality, whether it impinges on privacy and rights, whether it is demeaning in its very process. Since a "last resort" device is essential in a total income-security system, the problem will have to be faced directly.

Certainly nothing currently known about incentives[103] argues against a "safety net" program—or the entire system outlined. The final protection and ultimate guarantee could be either a simplified, objectified, better-guaranteed, higher level, noncategorical public assistance or a poverty-line-keyed negative income tax. The choice could be between a federal or a state-local system, between Treasury or Health, Education, and Welfare administration (although recent proposals that all public assistance be federalized also remove this distinction, at least in part). For given a federal minimum and a rights conception, assured of a simple application which assumes applicant honesty until experience shows otherwise, these become the chief issues between negative income tax and public assistance. In either instance, social service administration is no longer integrated with relief-eligibility questions. In both cases, a means test of a kind will be present, and the question will be whether current shame, stigma, and infringement on rights

---

[101] Cohen, *President's Proposals for Revision in the Social Security System*, 401–403.

[102] William Beveridge, "Foreword," Charles Schottland, *The Social Security Program in the United States* (New York: Appleton-Century-Crofts, 1963).

[103] Dahl and Lindblom, *op. cit.*, 161.

in public assistance can be ended or whether one needs a new program to achieve new public acceptability and improved self-concepts for recipients.

Whatever the choice, the requirement for a federal minimum, the April, 1969, ruling that residence laws are unconstitutional—because they undermine the right to mobility—and the realities of state-local fiscal capacities will demand new methods of financing and a new federal role.[104] In sum, the entire income-security system requires national design and support, whatever the administrative options for some components.

This brief run-through does not constitute a complete, rounded task definition: it does not adequately probe the specific requirements of the minimum guarantee, a second tier, a "safety net," "take off," funding—with special reference to the degree of redistribution to be sought and achieved and to the operational definitions of equity in various programs. We have not even mentioned costs, financing, tax system recovery, pace, or interrelations of the components. These illustrative paragraphs are merely the beginning of an approach to a comprehensive income-security system related to broader fiscal and manpower policy. Once the notion of system is accepted and the components of comprehensiveness specified, alternatives will certainly be proposed and the older assumptions challenged further. For this is the essential point: in this day more than unrelated programs is required; an income-security *system* is necessary. And the design of a system forces one to define the planning task.

---

[104] Indeed, such a role was under active consideration as this volume went to press.

THE SOCIAL PLANNER
AND THE CITY:
THE "TASK" IN
PERSPECTIVE

FROM 1934 to 1937 the federal government, through public agencies, carried out a program of clearing slums and blighted areas and rehousing the resident families. The assignment was turned over to the cities for the period 1937 to 1949. Then, for almost twenty years, despite the increased scope and range of the legislation passed, private enterprise was the major and preferred instrument of public policy. And throughout the nineteen-sixties there was widespread agreement that, despite notable accomplishments, the outcome was far from satisfactory. Some participants and observers considered it a monumental failure. Critics complained especially about the injustices of relocation and the insufficiency in quantity and lack of quality of low-cost housing. Others questioned whether the entire enterprise was aimed at the right targets in an even more fundamental sense.

Among the latter, Charles Abrams, expert and sympathetic friend of the public housing program, phrased his perspective in these terms:

> Urban renewal puts the cart before the horse. If cities could have better schools, recreation and environments, if they could cut their tax levies and provide their needed improvements from their revenues, and if they could be made pleasanter, safer, more interesting and more convenient places in which to live and work, the demand for city living and housing would appear automatically in many areas. Mortgage money without FHA or FNMA assistance would become more plentiful, and private builders and merchants would scramble for the profit opportunities available. Urban renewal could then become a more constructive tool for assembling land, replanning

obsolete layouts, and providing recreation, schools, housing, and other amenities to new, well-planned neighborhoods.[1]

In short, true renewal of the city cannot be conceived merely in terms of clearing blight and building new commercial and residential centers plus public housing. In a basic sense it is an economic, social, educational, and physical process of planning and programming. Nothing less will do. However, in the past far less has been undertaken.

At about the time that the riots of 1967 reached some fifty to one hundred-fifty American city ghettos (depending upon what one counted), politicians, planners, and citizens-at-large seemed to be converging in increasing number on the view that physical rebuilding of the city is of limited significance unless it attends to social concerns; and that city planning cannot address itself only to clearance, relocation, and rebuilding; it is in the most complete sense a comprehensive process requiring a general social policy, a political and economic context.

Those who would act in accord with this perspective find it most difficult; the translation of these principles into policies and programs introduces a variety of complex dilemmas and bares the poverty of available intellectual, political, and material resources. Here, therefore, we pose some of the difficulties in the way of progress in this field and note the direction in which solutions might be sought.

From the point of view of the structure of concepts introduced to clarify the planning process, this chapter illustrates *the difficulty of settling upon a planning task or defining a system appropriate for planning.* The experience calls for a very broad systems perspective, but the very process of broadening decreases availability of sanction and leverage and carries one to realms in which the state of the art is primitive. Furthermore, an expansive concept of the task introduces complex and controversial political, administrative, and policy issues.

By placing this "case" discussion in the context of the summer and fall of 1967 and the first half of 1968, it becomes possible to identify with the search for direction of those administrators who were attempting to launch the Model Cities Program, a major federal departure, and of the members of Congress who through hearings and staff study sought to *define the task* and to shape a federal policy for the cities.[2]

---

[1] Charles Abrams, *The City is the Frontier* (New York: Harper & Row, 1965), 179–180.

[2] See *Examination of the War on Poverty*, Hearings Before the Subcommittee on Employment, Manpower, and Poverty of the Committee on Labor and Public Welfare, United States Senate, in 22 parts (Washington, D.C.: Government Printing Office, 1967);

Our premise is that task definition is so critical a planning phase as to deserve considerable clarification here, at the expense of other aspects of urban planning. The federal-city relationship problems, central to the housing and renewal program, are thus by-passed; but questions of coordination among related departments are discussed below. Furthermore, both to simplify the presentation and because detail would not change the burden of the theme, little will be said, except in a peripheral sense, about urban racial ghettos per se and the alternative strategies for coping with them; the problem of city planning in a universe of fragmented interest groups; other aspects of intergovernmental issues (city-region-state); the problem of the city's financial base; the evolution of "megalopolis" as it affects planning;[3] or of the state of physical building and planning technology as these influence the universe of the feasible.[4]

PROBLEMS, NEEDS, AND TRENDS

It has been said of the modern city that:

The micro-organisms in the soil no longer exist; the original animal inhabitants have largely been banished. Only a few members of the plant kingdom represent the original members of the limited ecology. The rivers are foul; the atmosphere is polluted; the original configuration of the land is only rarely in evidence; climate and micro-climate have retrogressed so that the external micro-climate is more violent than was the case before the establishment of the city. . . . Floods alternate with drought. . . . The epidemiologist speaks of neuroses, lung cancer, heart and renal disease, ulcers, the stress diseases, as the badges of urban conditions. . . .

Whatever triumphs there are to be seen in the modern city as an institution it is only with great difficulty that one can see any vestige of triumph in the modern city as a physical environment.[5]

also, *The Federal Role in Urban Affairs*, Hearings Before the Subcommittee on Executive Reorganization of the Committee on Government Operations, United States Senate, in 21 parts (Washington, D.C.: Government Printing Office, 1967); Subcommittee on Urban Affairs, Joint Economic Committee, *Urban America: Goals and Problems* (Washington, D.C.: Government Printing Office, 1967).

[3] Jean Gottman, *Megalopolis* (Cambridge, Mass.: The M.I.T. Press, 1961).

[4] See Henry B. Schecter and Bernard Horn, "Technology, Automation and Economic Progress in Housing and Urban Development" in National Commission on Technology, Automation and Economic Progress, *Applying Technology to Unmet Needs*, constituting Appendix Volume V of *Technology and the American Economy* (Washington, D.C.: Government Printing Office, 1966), 13–29. Also, *The Federal Role in Urban Affairs*, Part 16, 3314–3342.

[5] Ian L. McHarg, "Man and Environment," in Leonard J. Duhl, Editor, *The Urban Condition* (New York: Basic Books, 1963), 48–49. Also see, H. Wentworth Eldredge, Edi-

However, even those few who have recognized that "the city is at least an ecological regression"[6] and the many more who have perceived and suffered the city's social problems and wondered about the lasting significance of its alleged cultural accomplishments assume that urbanism will remain our way of life and will dominate human culture in the future. It will encompass Constantinos Doxiadis' "ecumenopolis," the universal, globe-covering settlement of the future.[7] For the nature of modern technology, communication, and economic organization mandates urbanism to an ever-increasing degree. Within the pattern, man may live by preferences and styles based in agrarian reality and myth,[8] but even his suburban detached house, "greenbelt," or weekend hideaway is set in the context of an urban, metropolitan, and even megalopolitan development. The United States was 70 percent urban, in a technical sense, following one type of definition, as of 1960, and was expected to be 80 percent urban within a decade. Projections place 180 million people in 216 cities in 1985; this was the total population in 1960. As early as 1960, 52 million Americans lived in 16 urbanized areas, and 96 million (53 percent of the population) were concentrated in 213 urbanized areas covering only 0.7 percent of the country's land.[9] There are as many city "slum people" as farm people.[10] This degree of urbanization is a product of the past one hundred years.

That the planning challenge is a world-wide one is suggested in the fact that, at conservative estimate, more than half of the world's people will probably be living in cities of 100,000 or more by 1990; already, of the 250 cities throughout the world with populations of 500,000 or more, nearly half are located in the so-called developing countries. While many of these agglomerations were founded in agricultural and mercantile economies, their continued growth and viability is based on their role in the industrial process. Calcutta, India's metropolitan area of 7 million people, may serve as illustration.[11]

---

tor, *Taming Megalopolis*, 2 volumes (Garden City, New York: Doubleday & Co., Anchor Books edition, 1967), especially Volume 1.

[6] McHarg, *op. cit.*, 49.

[7] C. A. Doxiadis, *Urban Renewal and the Future of the American City* (Chicago: Public Administration Service, 1966), Parts D and E.

[8] Daniel J. Elazar, "Are We a Nation of Cities?", *The Public Interest*, No. 4 (Summer, 1966), 42–58.

[9] Kingsley Davis, "The Urbanization of the Human Population," *Scientific American*, special issue: *Cities*, 213, No. 3 (September, 1965), 41.

[10] Whitney Young in *The Federal Role in Urban Affairs*, Part 14, 2945.

[11] Davis, *op. cit.*; and Nivomal K. Bose, "Calcutta: A Premature Metropolis," in *Scientific American*, special issue: *Cities*, 90–102.

The civilization is and is expected to continue to be urban. The city, its center, is clearly in trouble. However, there are major differences in assessment of the character of that trouble, particularly as one moves from the need to provide clean water, dispose more efficiently of garbage, purify the air, facilitate traffic flow, and make the setting more aesthetically attractive. Ultimately the specific diagnosis of social ills grows out of the diagnostician's concept of the good life and his view of the desirable degree of formal intervention into primary and secondary institutions.

Some urban reformers and planners put major emphasis on the deficiencies of physical conditions, the crowding of the land, the number of persons per room, the toilet facilities, the windows, the central heating, the conditions of buildings.[12] Others, for whom Nathan Glazer is a foremost spokesman, note that these are relative matters as among countries and over time.[13] Louis Winnick illustrates changing conceptions of "need":

The urban slum building of the 1890's was typically a dumb-bell tenement with tiny windowless bedrooms in which up to twenty families shared a toilet. Today a dwelling unit is marked as substandard if it lacks a private bathroom for each family. In the 1890's a dwelling unit could contain three or four persons per room before it was regarded as overcrowded; in 1950 the standard of 1.51 persons was more generally accepted; by 1960 it had become 1.01. The average block on the Lower East Side today has far lower density than before World War I; Harlem is not nearly as jam-packed today as it was in the 1930's and 40's. The present slum buildings of Harlem were the middle-class and even luxury apartments of prior generations. Structurally, they are solid masonry buildings with windows in every room, a major reason why rehabilitation rather than replacement has become an acceptable means of ministering to the housing needs of the poverty class. The average quality of the American housing inventory has been steadily rising but not as fast as our standards of what constitutes acceptable housing.[14]

American slums are physically far better than many city sectors elsewhere which are not considered slums at all. Parts of Tokyo serve as primary illustration. The Watts area in California, which exploded in 1966, shocking

---

[12] Whitney Young told a Congressional Committee that, if all the United States population were as overcrowded as the people on the several worst blocks in Harlem, all of the United States population could be fitted into three of New York City's five boroughs. *The Federal Role in Urban Affairs*, Part 14, 2945.

[13] Nathan Glazer, "Housing Policy and the Family," *Journal of Marriage and the Family*, 29, No. 1 (February, 1967), 140–163; his "The Renewal of Cities," *Scientific American*, special issue: *Cities*, 194–208; and "Housing Problems and Housing Policies," *The Public Interest*, No. 7 (Spring, 1967), 21–51.

[14] Louis Winnick, "Housing and Urban Development: The Private Foundation's Role" (New York: The Ford Foundation, 1965, pamphlet), 4.

Americans and dramatizing the crisis of the cities, did not externally meet many of the expectations of a blighted area; to the casual visitor, Watts looked like a pleasant lower-middle-class district.[15] It was certainly in better shape physically than many calm, stable, lower-class settlements. The research evidence on the relationship between poor physical housing and social consequences, such as individual growth and development, is by no means definitive. The effects are clearest where the housing is *grossly inadequate*; for housing above this level, many of the effects appear to be more obviously related to *symbolic* interpretation of the housing type or locale as meaning degradation, than to the direct physical consequences of daily experience in a particular type of dwelling.[16]

There are those who place more stress on lacks in "collective consumption goods" or social utilities, the sources of urban amenity: schools, parks, transportation, playgrounds, libraries, parking space, health centers, and the like. Other critics, of a more sociological or psychological bent, see the city's problem as one of conquering anonymity, lack of personal stake in the community, isolation, worthlessness, Émile Durkheim's *anomie*. Yet another group of participants in the debate, for whom Jane Jacobs is an articulate spokesman, poses the goals of permitting "spontaneous self-diversification," enriched living, and mutual stimulation.[17]

In the view of still other observers, the city "crisis" and the poverty problem are substantially a racial crisis. The city is in difficulty because society has not coped with inequality and discrimination. The city cannot find the solution to its problems unless those with a major stake, the residents of the ghettos, shape such solutions. Thus far, in this view, the city has failed to allow such residents their proper role and hence the situation deteriorates.

For each indictment, there are public prosecutors galore—as well as serious research students who point to the facts, note cultural contrasts, and question what often seem like oversimplified correlations. For example,

A number of sociological studies in western metropolises of North America and Western Europe have shown that family ties remain very much

---

[15] Calvin S. Hamilton, Director of Los Angeles Planning Commission, in "Comments," in William R. Ewald, Jr., *Environment for Man* (Bloomington: Indiana University Press, 1967), 249.

[16] Glazer, in "Housing Policy and the Family," appraises the research literature. The basic source is Alvin Schorr, *Slums and Social Insecurity* (Washington, D.C.: Government Printing Office, 1963).

W. C. Loring concludes that, "The social sciences report definite grist for the planners' mill mainly on *extreme* conditions," and he urges planner–public health–social science collaboration to clarify the facts in "Comments," in Ewald, *op. cit.*, 53.

[17] Jane Jacobs, *The Death and Life of Great American Cities* (New York: Vintage Books paper edition, 1963).

alive and that a considerable amount of informal community organization can be found even in the slums.[18]

Similarly, Gottman, who gave great visibility to the Northeastern United States *Megalopolis* as a center of intensive urbanism and the locus of major cities, concludes

> the picture of Megalopolis is not as dark as the outspoken pessimists and frequent protests would seem to paint it. . . . It is, *on the average,* the richest, best educated, best housed, and best serviced group of similar size . . . in the world.[19]

Future growth and abundance, in this perspective, require major governmental reform on all levels, administrative reorganization, new instruments for coordination, reassignment of revenue resources, and a redistribution of city functions over a wider terrain.

On one level the many advocates, critics, and dreamers of different persuasions meet, urging the humanization of the urban environment and the assurance of effective discharge of the city's special function as "a complex receptacle for maximizing the possibilities of human intercourse and passing on the contents of civilization."[20] However, in the daily arena of federal bureaucratic programming, of competition for funds, of local housing and zoning department efforts to develop and implement long-range plans and specific projects, the diverse emphases are not always compatible, and the several schools of thought advance different priorities. Groups compete and work at cross-purposes at a given moment. Emphases shift over time. Some give highest priority to improved housing; others see it as following from other social gains.

What have been the planner's approaches to the city historically?[21] He began of course by concentrating on fortifications and drainage. Later he laid out streets, markets, and malls. When further government intervention into the process began, he advised on land use and concentrated on zoning

---

[18] Hans Blumenfeld, "The Modern Metropolis," *Scientific American,* special issue: *Cities,* 69. Or, with reference to conventional wisdom about suburbs, see Herbert Gans, *The Levittowners* (New York: Pantheon Books, 1967).

[19] Gottman, *op. cit.,* 15.

[20] Lewis Mumford, *The City in History* (New York: Harcourt, Brace and World, 1961), 87.

[21] Jacobs lists some of the planning "classics," not here discussed, in her footnote on page 17, *op. cit.,* referring to Ebenezer Howard, Mumford, Patrick Geddes, Catherine Bauer, Raymond Unwin, Le Corbusier, Clarence Stein.

A somewhat different overview and extensive bibliography are offered by John L. Hancock, "Planners in the Changing American City," *Journal of the American Institute of Planners,* XXXIII, No. 5 (September, 1967), 290–303.

laws and regulations of various sorts. In the United States, the philosophy was laissez faire and the interventions limited. Early urban planning in this country "was concerned purely with the design and aesthetic nature of municipal artifacts." The "city beautiful" concepts of the early twentieth century concentrated on broad avenues and boulevards designed for beauty, not for traffic flow. Public construction of civic centers aimed at monumentality, not at efficient governmental operations. By the second and third decades of the century, American urban planners were in search of efficiency: street patterns for rapid vehicular movement, zoning to protect land values and "good" neighborhoods; but each component was autonomous. Even the emphasis of the 'thirties on the quality of housing and the recognition of the deleterious effects of slums on occupants did not take one much beyond a concern with physical improvement: light, air, windows, room size, etc. But for the first time, too, there was some recognition of and attention to the gap between housing costs and the incomes of many city dwellers.[22]

Certainly, in each phase, there were occasional instances in which very broad social concerns guided some of the decisions, but for the most part these were secondary. The major exceptions came from the utopians, the dreamers who devised, on paper, model communities and cities of the future, and the visionaries such as Ebenezer Howard who saw their plans implemented on a small scale. More recently, the planner has turned to renewal and public housing, topics which we shall subsequently address; a few of his colleagues have considered systematically such matters as how building style and height affect children's play habits or social interaction among adults, and they have developed schemes to implement their conclusions. Ideologically, many have favored something called comprehensive development planning, but the range of interpretation has been very wide, varying from megalopolis, to New Towns, to specific renewal projects, to model housing-shopping-industry units within cities or on a city-size scale. There also has been widespread, although by no means unanimous, appreciation of the fact that urban areas "are constantly altering in economic and social composition and in physical form." Thus, one no longer creates and attempts to implement a desired image: "planning has moved from picture to continuing process."[23]

---

[22] The above is summarized after Chester A. Rapkin, "A Brief Summary of Recent Development in Urban Planning Research and Practice in the United States," as presented at a meeting of the Economic Commission for Europe, publication pending.

[23] The quotations, *ibid*.

Interestingly, at the very moment that broader social policy motivations, such as accomplishing racial or social-class integration through housing or overcoming anomie through general community planning, began increasingly to concern some mid-twentieth-century planners, the physical planning emphases also began to encompass new concerns: how does one enhance urban amenity, protect the pedestrian, purify the air, decrease noise, add to recreational opportunity? Can one develop a concept of city design on a "human" scale?

To the extent that journals and books, public pronouncements and proposals, practice theory, and education may serve as indicators, the majority of city planning remains physical in a constricted sense, with frequent rhetorical gestures toward broader values. Yet the portion of city planning that might be described as "socially aware" physical planning and the segment that involves encasing the physical into a broader social perspective continue to grow.[24] Public authorities turned increasingly to social scientists, social planners, "urbanists," and social policy specialists, as they confronted the problem of the city in the last years of the decade. Mumford at one time seemed a voice in the wilderness, but his goals, if couched in grandiose terms, were hardly strange by the time the country had begun to evolve new concepts of the city planning task:

> The recovery of the essential activities and values that first were incorporated in the ancient cities . . . is . . . a primary condition for the further development of the city in our time. . . . the human dialogue, the drama, the living circle of mates and associates, the society of friends. These sustain the growth and reproduction of human culture, and without them the whole elaborate structure becomes meaningless. . . .
>
> . . . The positive functions of the city cannot be performed without creating new institutional arrangements. . . .
>
> . . . The task of the coming city . . . is to put the highest concern of man at the center of all his activities; to unite the scattered fragments of the human personality, turning artificially dismembered men . . . into complete human beings. . . .[25]

ACCOMPLISHMENTS AND FAILURES

To the point of enactment of the Model Cities (Demonstration Cities and Metropolitan Development Act of 1966, P.L. 89–754) and rent supple-

---

[24] One optimistic overview is offered in Bernard J. Frieden, "The Changing Prospects for Social Planning," *Journal of the American Institute of Planners*, XXXIII, No. 5 (September, 1967), 311–323.

[25] Mumford, *op. cit.*, 569, 571, 573.

mentation programs, the United States had tried a number of loosely inter-related strategies with reference to the city. On balance, despite disputes about appropriateness and efficacy, the accomplishments have been significant. These federally employed approaches have included

☐ federal credit mechanisms
☐ federal mortgage insurance
☐ federally supported public housing
☐ comprehensive urban renewal.[26]

A bitter debate about accomplishments and alleged evils emanating from these efforts has raged throughout the 'sixties. There is a well-documented history of slums and blighted areas cleared out; of city centers renewed for public purposes, business, and housing; of public housing and publicly-aided, middle-income housing built; of street and highway realignment made possible by renewal; of reconstruction of the tax base in the centers of cities; of new sewage and water systems added.[27] The largest complaint has been that, on balance, the federal program is "socialism for the rich and private enterprise for the poor."[28] While credit and mortgage insurance

---

[26] The Home Owners' Loan Corporation, established in 1933, functioned until 1951, saving homes through re-financing. The National Housing Act of 1934 provided government insurance for long-term residential mortgages and created the Federal Housing Administration (which helped over 5 million Americans to buy houses by 1960). The several "G.I. Bills," the Home Loan Bank Board, the Federal National Mortgage Association have facilitated, guaranteed, and insured loans for home building and purchase; these units were eventually joined in the Housing and Home Finance Agency which, in turn, became part of a new Department of Housing and Urban Development (1965). From 1937, recognizing that FHA insurance of mortgages largely aided middle-income families, Congress established authority for modest aid for low-rent housing and slum clearance. This was consolidated and expanded, with broader public housing provisions and the beginning of urban redevelopment and renewal, in the Housing Act of 1949. The 1954 legislation expanded federal participation in slum clearance, urban renewal, and planned redevelopment. The legislation in 1949 and 1954 also expanded earlier modest support for housing renovation and modernization, as part of the fight against blight. Model cities and rent supplementation were authorized in 1965 but the process of implementation and Congressional fights over appropriations delayed them as viable innovations until late in 1967, as far as localities were concerned. For program detail and statistics, see *Federal Role in Urban Affairs*, Part 1 and Appendix volume to Part 1.

[27] For example, the several Glazer articles cited above; Doxiadis, *op. cit.*; Abrams, *op. cit.*; *Federal Role in Urban Affairs*, Part 1 and Appendix to Part 1. Unfortunately there are few cost/benefit studies of the sort proposed by Jerome Rothenberg and few conceptual analyses of true sophistication and disinterested character. See Jerome Rothenberg, "Urban Renewal Programs," in Robert Dorfman, Editor, *Measuring Benefits of Government Programs* (Washington, D.C.: The Brookings Institution, 1965), 292–366. Also, Jerome Rothenberg, *An Analysis of Urban Renewal* (Washington, D.C.: The Brookings Institution, 1967).

[28] Abrams, *op. cit.*, 236.

aids have made possible and have backed on a substantial scale the entire post–World War II suburban development of single-family detached houses for the middle class, little direct help has been given the slum dweller. According to the severest critics, the program for slum renewal has relied substantially on the speculation by private enterprise in slum clearance and rebuilding. The government has financed such speculation and often protected private enterprise in the process without specifying the social purpose for which the risk is socialized.[29]

Foes of the program acknowledge that slums have been cleared but note that there has not been an adequate housing program for the people displaced in the effort. The "score" may be impressive with reference to the number of dwelling units constructed, for the number taken down, but analysis shows that much of the new housing was not available to the evicted because of increased cost, location, time of availability, or racial discrimination.

Experts have debated the quality and results of the mandated relocation program, and studies have produced conflicting conclusions.[30] By minimal, formal criteria, perhaps, and if one deals only with those who waited to be relocated and could be interviewed on follow-up, the record is good.

---

[29] *Ibid.*, 179, 236.

By 1967, according to a variety of estimates, the federal government had built some 700,000 public housing units in programs launched in 1937. The Federal Housing Administration's various efforts had helped 235,000 families in low-income and middle-income projects. The totals are to be contrasted with 9 million suburban families aided by FHA to buy homes and 28 million enabled to secure low-cost loans for home improvement.

[30] Among the best known sources are Martin Anderson, *The Federal Bulldozer* (Cambridge, Mass.: The M.I.T. Press, 1964); Herbert J. Gans, "The Failure of Urban Renewal," *Commentary*, 39, No. 4 (April, 1965), 29–37; the response to Gans by George M. Raymond and Malcolm Rivlin and his rebuttal in *Commentary*, 40, No. 1 (July, 1965), 72–80; Chester Hartman, "The Limitations of Public Housing: Relocation Choices in a Working-Class Community," *Journal of the American Institute of Planners*, XXIX, No. 4 (November, 1963), 283–296; Chester Hartman, "The Housing of Relocated Families," *Journal of the American Institute of Planners*, XXX, No. 4 (November, 1964), 266–286.

Also see Abrams, *op. cit.*; and Peter Marris, "A Report on Urban Renewal in the United States," in Duhl, *op. cit.*, 113–134; as well as, "A Comment on 'The Housing of Relocated Families,'" by Edward J. Logue and the Hartman rejoinder in the *Journal of the American Institute of Planners*, XXXI, No. 4 (November, 1965), 338–343. Also, "The Housing of Relocated Families: Summary of a Bureau of the Census Survey of Families Recently Displaced from Urban Renewal Sites," as reprinted in *Federal Role in Urban Affairs*, Part 1, 101–111. And, Paul L. Neibanck, *The Elderly in Older Urban Areas* and *Relocation, from Obstacle to Opportunity* (Philadelphia: Institute for Environmental Studies, University of Pennsylvania, 1965 and 1968).

More careful analyses and some follow-up experiences of displaced "cohorts" of residents support the protests that, for the most part, renewal has been carried out without fair and humane relocation. According to some observers, relocation could not have been satisfactory unless new low-income public housing had gone up on a large scale and in the selfsame neighborhoods while the clearance and demolition went on. This is probably an over-statement of the case, but certainly far more appropriate provision was frequently needed and was generally lacking.

The acknowledgement of the unsatisfactory results is contained in the new emphasis, beginning in the mid-sixties, on housing rehabilitation and on vest-pocket projects. Early in 1968 the Administration in Washington sought to increase substantially the scale of federally-aided housing construction for low-income families and for the very poor. Administrative devices were also being invented to stabilize public housing and to hold the more successful residents. These approaches tended at least to some degree to confirm three additional aspects of the indictment. First, it was held that relocation was often "Negro removal" from the center of the city. Second, it was noted that much good, usable housing was being knocked down. Finally, it was asserted, renewal destroys neighborhoods and community life and eliminates those elements which make streets centers of interest and primary group experience. These consequences defeat the basic social goals of city planning and housing policy.[31]

Closely related to questions about renewal were the attacks on those low-income public housing projects which were constructed, whether with federal, state, or local funds: short-cuts and economies decreased comfort and created an institutional atmosphere; income ceilings required that the successful and upwardly mobile move out and thus thwarted the development of neighborhood stability; stigma resulted from income ceilings, investigations, and rules and regulations of a kind not permissible in private housing; lack of amenity tended to discourage applications from, or hasten departures of, those with alternatives. In many places, public housing became a community of the most disadvantaged Negroes.[32] Nonetheless, noted proponents, many public housing units did not at all resemble the stereotype of the "high-rise" slum. Most became attractive, normally-clean dwellings; in fact, most public housing has long waiting lists and, hence, must be desirable in some ways.

---

[31] See Herbert Gans, The Urban Villagers (New York: The Free Press, 1962); Jacobs, op. cit.

[32] For an oft-cited extreme "horror" story, see Lee Rainwater, "The Lessons of Pruitt-Igoe," The Public Interest, No. 8 (Summer, 1967), 116–126.

For most observers, the real problem is the inadequate supply of low-cost housing, public or private. The amount of public housing does not begin to approximate need, yet the private market economy cannot, in any view, be expected to produce new housing for the poorer members of the community—unless new tax and credit incentives are discovered and considered desirable.[33]

On a quite different level, not listed among major federal approaches, but for a brief period the center of interdepartmental attention, was a "concerted services" program, which sought coordinated social services and emphasized personal and family rehabilitation for those in public housing.[34] The program was continuous with a tradition that goes back to the 'thirties and which defined the social objectives of public housing policies as improvement of tenants by outside community agencies concerned with their "outside" behavior, and efforts to improve public housing tenants as tenants.[35]

The scale of operation was small, a major defect in the eyes of some people. To others, the basic issue was whether the assignment of social services particularly to public housing residents did not create an institutional atmosphere and welfare-stigma that was self-defeating. More fundamentally, perhaps, were not social services being offered as a substitute for income?[36]

On balance, the claims and counterclaims with reference to renewal, relocation, and public housing derive from varied expectations and goals. To members of different publics, the renewal program, for example, was a program of slum clearance, reclaiming of blighted areas, upgrading of substandard housing, remodeling of "downtown," construction of public build-

---

[33] Of course, referring not to *new* housing alone but to the total supply, much standard housing is in fact provided by the private-housing market at low rentals. In New York City, in 1965, three-quarters of all private rental housing carrying a gross rent of under $40 per month, and 90 percent with rents of $40–$59 per month, were considered standard by census enumerators. Together, these two categories constitute one out of every seven rental-housing units in the City. Chester Rapkin, *The Private Rental Housing Market in New York City, 1965* (New York: The City Rent and Rehabilitation Administration, 1966).

[34] Joint Task Force on Health, Education, and Welfare Services and Housing, "Services for Families Living in Public Housing" (Washington, D.C.: Government Printing Office, 1963, pamphlet); and I. Jack Fasteau and Abner D. Silverman, "Two Year Progress Report" (Washington, D.C.: Government Printing Office, 1965, pamphlet).

[35] The Buffalo Housing Authority's indoctrination, inspection, and demonstration program may serve as illustration. See Harry W. Reynolds, Jr., "Public Housing and Social Values in an American City," *Social Service Review*, XXXIX, No. 2 (June, 1965), 157–164.

[36] Rainwater, *op. cit.*

ings, solution of traffic problems, house preservation.[37] In truth, *much has been accomplished and much provision made. Yet it is a mere shadow of what is needed, when measured against the problem of the cities, and it does not begin to attack what some see as the core problems. Many of the undesirable results are balanced by real meeting of needs, it is true; yet the negative impact on the very poor, on Negroes, on marginal businesses has been devastating.*[38]

By the mid-sixties, it was poverty, social unrest, and racial friction, as well as physical obsolescence, the decline of the city's economic base, and spatial restrictions, which demanded attention. It was obvious to all that existing programs offered too few resources for the residents in the areas to be cleared. But it was also obvious that a search for significant improvement demanded new perspectives on the city.[39] A new federal department, Housing and Urban Development (HUD), had been created by Presidential initiative and eventual Congressional agreement to coordinate fragmented efforts and provide new guidelines for the task. Certainly, the opportunity would be there; in the next forty years, both for renewal and to keep up with population growth, the United States will need to construct as much housing as has been produced in the entire history of this nation.[40] The question, thus, is whether the construction will or will not become the occasion, in the deepest sense, of human and social renewal.

PHYSICAL PLANNING, SOCIALLY INFORMED

Traditionally, housing policy at its best has concerned itself with housing availability and accessibility. Marshall's formulation is characteristic:

> The task of housing policy is to estimate as accurately as possible the present and future demands for houses, to wrestle with the physical problems of production, and to manipulate the financial circumstances governing supply and demand as far as is necessary to ensure that houses are made available as fast as the state of the national economy permits, of the kind

---

[37] Doxiadis, *op. cit.*

[38] Also see, Glazer, in *Scientific American*, special issue: *Cities*, 198.

[39] The community renewal program, enacted in 1959 as an amendment to the 1949 housing act, was actually the transitional stage, speaking statutorily—even though it was virtually unnoticed for two years. By 1965, 125 cities were drawing upon the funds and displaying the broader substantive concerns of social welfare, education, transportation, as well as traditional urban renewal aspects. See Ira M. Robinson, "Beyond the Middle-Range Planning Bridge," *Journal of the American Institute of Planners*, XXXI, No. 4 (November, 1965), 304–312.

[40] Robert Weaver, remarks to the press, New York, 1964.

that the population desires, in the places where they are going to be wanted and at prices the people can afford to pay. And in doing this it must have regard to the liberty of the individual, the rights of property, and the principles of social justice.[41]

As we have seen, programs to date have yet to approach these goals. Yet there have always been those who have striven to assure that the physical plans for houses, projects, communities, even cities, would be socially informed in an additional sense.

In theory, physical planners and architects always attend to social dimensions, since preferences and evaluations always derive from individuals and from various social units. Few practitioners in the field would quarrel with the premise that:

No species can exist without an environment, no species can exist in an environment of its exclusive creation, no species can survive, save as a non-disruptive member of an ecological community. Every member must adjust to other members of the community and to the environment in order to survive. Man is not excluded from the test. Man must learn this prime ecological lesson of interdependence.[42]

Many citizens and professional observers would concur that:

Man is now in the position of actually creating the total world in which he lives. . . . In creating this world he is actually determining *what kind of an organism* he will be.[43]

But city- and house-building are technology, and we do not know much about social consequences of specific decisions. Thus, to agree on the principle of interdependence does not create a housing policy or tell one whether to invest in high-rise buildings or to permit people to enact their obvious preferences for detached single-family dwellings in relatively uniform suburban areas. Glazer has shown how difficult it is to make housing policy "work" so as to implement objectives for the American family: first, because we are far from agreed as a people about such objectives; second, because it is in no sense clear just which policies best implement the goals, and whether one can or should attempt to enact policies which certainly do not reflect the free-market behavior of most Americans.

In addition, the diffusion of responsibilities often precludes concern with social dimensions. The highway designer, for example, is responsive to a

---

[41] T. H. Marshall, *Social Policy* (London: Hutchinson University Library, 1965), 152–153.

[42] McHarg, *op. cit.*, 57–58.

[43] Edward T. Hall, "The Hidden Dimension," in *Urban America: Goals and Problems*, 3.

cost-benefit analysis, which does not consider the human costs of his cross-city artery (or of the aesthetic results of certain countryside routings). The slum dweller often pays an added price in destroyed neighborhoods as a result of what appear to be inevitable "economic" arguments.[44]

Yet planners generally do want their physical plans to be "socially informed." The major interpretation of the goal is usually that one must attend to parking, open space, children's play areas, shopping, and neighborhood schools. Sometimes the list includes community day care and workshop, club room, and social-center space in public or nonprofit projects. (Federal legislation mandated this.) Public Health stations and special facilities for the aged may also be offered. It is not that planners do not have wider ambitions as well: traffic-free walks, open space of several kinds, spots for repose and relaxation, facilities to promote interaction and interest. Except for large-scale renewal, or a New Town, or a "satellite city," the planner can seldom go quite this far. The more utopian among them suggest new patterning of work–daily living–recreation–transportation, but dispersion of authority and planning seldom allow even partial implementation. In effect, when one combines (a) the realities of a market economy and a circumscribed public sector; (b) dispersion of governmental authority; and (c) institutional independence, the meshing prerequisite to the more ambitious undertakings does not occur. "Model Cities," an attempt to create an exception, is discussed below.

Nor should the problem be attributed only to the lack of technical capacity or of comprehensive sanction and power. As soon as one seeks to realize social goals through broad physical interventions, difficult questions of preferences and interest-group conflict are opened up.[45] Should one support or

---

[44] We deal elsewhere, especially in Chapter XII of the companion volume, with the more basic difficulties of comprehensive planning generally as affected by wide diffusion of and conflicts among power groups on vital issues. In the public housing field particularly, the limiting conditions placed on the "opportunity area" for planning as a result of many prior decisions are described in a dramatic "case" in Martin Meyerson and Edward C. Banfield, *Politics, Planning and the Public Interest* (Glencoe, Ill.: The Free Press, 1955).

[45] One type of preference study is discussed in Janet S. Reiner, Everett Reimer, Thomas A. Reiner, "Client Analysis and the Planning of Public Programs," *Journal of the American Institute of Planners*, XXIX, No. 4 (November, 1963), 270–282; also see, Richard A. Lamanna, "Value Consensus Among Urban Residents," *ibid.*, XXX, No. 4 (November, 1964), 317–323. It would appear possible to clarify preferences and achieve consensus on "livability values."

For contradictions between most peoples' preferences and the "designer's paradise," see William Michelson, "Most People Don't Want What Architects Want," *Transaction*, 5, No. 8 (July–August, 1968), 37–43.

allow degrees of ethnic, class, or religious homogeneity in residential patterns? If so, does this not upset elementary premises of many socially informed physical planners? If so, is it legal thus to employ federal mortgage guarantees and support? Whose preferences are to be weighted, to what degree, as between national policy thrust and local community development? Or, in another domain, how does one resolve conflicts deriving from application of aesthetic criteria on the one hand and social criteria on the other? How is each set to be weighted?

It may very well be that goal diffusion is so great as to preclude any extensive and long-range infusion of physical planning with social concerns. Yet, given awareness of the urgency of social problems and eager to realize aspirations for a more satisfactory living environment, the society seems determined to attempt it. Perhaps the first prerequisite to success is the recognition that, as long as the task is defined as the production of a physical plan, albeit a socially informed one, the parameters are too narrow. Perhaps there is a way to conceive of the whole in social terms; increasingly there are those who ask whether the time has not arrived to see physical planning as a facet of a total strategy to facilitate and enhance social living. Thus, the question is rephrased: What are the implications of placing the physical planning of developments, renewal areas, and whole cities into a social context?

CITY RENEWAL AS SOCIAL PLANNING

Physical-locational planning is increasingly socially informed as social problems and social change become major objects of public concern. Planners come to recognize that they cannot attend only to the construction of buildings and the layout of streets and subdivisions. Nonetheless, physical elements may set the pace.[46]

The case for shifting to a basically social point of departure is made strongly and frequently in the literature and on public platforms. First, there is the fact, already noted, that one cannot assume the automatic achievement of social ends through physical means. While connections exist (design of streets and buildings may cut crime), little is known about them. Unless one begins with social goals, these occasional insights are lost. Second, and more basically, the social milieu is more important to people than the physical, and a "deteriorated" community soon lets its new project

---

[46] Demetrius Iatridis, "Social Scientists in Physical Development Planning: A Practitioner's Viewpoint," *International Social Science Journal*, XVIII, No. 4 (1966), 480–484.

building fall into disrepair, whereas a "competent" settlement may overcome a physical environment.[47] This does not mean that one does not need more and better housing for the poor, indeed, for the large portion of the population that will not fare well under a free-market system of producing and distributing domiciles. It does mean, however, that the physically-oriented city planner cannot avoid becoming more modest about his own contribution and attending or collaborating with those who attend basic social concerns.

Melvin Webber supports this direction for city planning. He notes that, before expenditure of resources for "municipal facilities," people with low incomes would rather see resources assigned to occupational retraining, empathetic teachers, compatible school curricula, professionalization of low-skill service jobs, removal of racial bars, and increased employment opportunity. ". . . Planning for the locational and physical aspects of our cities must therefore be conducted in concert with planning for all other programs that governmental and non-governmental agencies conduct." The city planner becomes, in his view, the practical-idealistic integrator of the specialized disciplines. The larger social tasks are primary; only some aspects of the city as a complex social system are expressed or reached by physical-locational strategies.[48] In terms preferred by architects and specialists in urban design, he and others put it thus:

> The artifactual city, apart from visual qualities, holds meaning for inhabitants only as it opens or closes economic or social opportunities. A plan for the physical city has utility only as part of a means-end continuum that causally relates artifactual city to the socio-economic-political city.[49]

In the mid-sixties, the social planning "wing" of the American Institute of Planners, the sociologists, political scientists, and social workers who tried to interrelate physical planning and the renewal of the city to fundamental social trends and major social problems, began to "build out" from social policy stances. They had various priority social goals, to:

☐ open opportunity
☐ promote social mobility

---

[47] Illustrated with reference to Tokyo's "non-slum" impoverished community by Nathan Glazer, "Slum Dwellings Do Not Make a Slum," in the *New York Times* Magazine, November 21, 1965, 55.

[48] Melvin Webber, "Comprehensive Planning and Social Responsibility: Toward an AIP Consensus on the Profession's Role and Purpose," *Journal of the American Institute of Planners*, XXIX, No. 4 (November, 1963), 235.

[49] Melvin Webber, "The Prospects for Policies Planning," in Duhl, *op. cit.*, 328.

☐ facilitate racial integration
☐ improve intergroup relations
☐ assure maximum feasible participation of the disadvantaged in the major social institutions
☐ facilitate development of indigenous institutions and facilities under local control by black ghetto residents.

The formulations and stances varied, but the intent was clearly to redress the balance. They argued that physical renewal failed, hurt, was irrelevant, or was overrated; the essence of planning was to be found in the worlds of local political power, education, work, health, and group participation. From this perspective, one should renew major social institutions as one renewed cities, or the latter would be a doomed process.[50]

In this view, one can no longer make decisions about land use, transportation, housing, and community facilities without "debate and decision about the goals of urban life and the values and ends toward which the urban environment is to be shaped."[51] Nor can one ignore questions of politics and institutional control when some Negroes, who feel "closed out" by the society, burn their neighborhoods and attack all symbols of "legitimate" power.

Once voices in the wilderness, the advocates of "relocating" physical planning to its rightful place in the context of an overall political and social strategy began to achieve serious attention late in the nineteen-sixties. The events surrounding the anti-poverty war and the civil rights revolution dramatized the need to do more for the cities than clear slums and build new facilities and housing. Recognition that the cores of cities were in decline, and that white populations were everywhere decreasing in proportion, defining the central city as an undesirable living milieu, clarified some of the ramifications of the issue. The summer riots, which began in a few cities and within a few years took on massive proportions, had, by the summer of 1967, made the "problem of the city" and the "domestic crisis" synonymous phrases. By the time the country had experienced the shock of the assassination of the Reverend Martin Luther King, Jr., in 1968, the lesson had been absorbed. When a National Advisory Commission on Civil Disorders, a voluntary Urban Coalition, and a United States Senate Subcom-

---

[50] See, the several Webber sources already cited; Herbert Gans, *People and Plans* (New York: Basic Books, 1968); Paul Davidoff, "Advocacy and Pluralism in Planning," *Journal of the American Institute of Planners*, XXX, No. 4 (November, 1965), 336; Harvey S. Perloff and Henry Cohen, *Urban Research and Education in the New York Metropolitan Region*, 2 volumes (New York: Regional Plan Association, 1965); Abrams, *op. cit.*

[51] Webber, "The Prospects for Policies Planning," in Duhl, *op. cit.*, 97.

mittee, each in its own fashion, studied the problem and evaluated previous efforts, there was consensus that the problem of the city was certainly no less one of jobs and training than of urban renewal, no less one of education and income security than of public housing. Law enforcement was not to be minimized, but its success depended upon the broader social measures.[52] *One could no longer think of urban design except in relation to that social policy responsive to the Negro revolt, the anti-poverty commitment, and the general domestic and foreign thrust of the country.*

Interestingly enough, community renewal staffs and city planners arrived at a similar perspective even when they did not begin with a stake in solving social problems. Experience with the interdependence of public policies showed them that planners, even if more narrowly committed, must be concerned with the effects on renewal programs and overall city plans of many other governmental decisions. For example, the federal income tax policy is germane (how is interest on a mortgage treated—as contrasted with apartment rent?), as are the national monetary policy (will borrowing be easy for builders or buyers?), local real property tax assessment policy (which strategy is cheaper, renovation or reconstruction?), state of the local economy (is labor entering or leaving, will the tax base support amenities?), the income ranges of different population groups (what range of rentals needs to be accommodated and how does this compare with the housing stock?), and code enforcement (what motivation is there to renovate, to comply, etc.?). The answers determine some aspects of the renewal program "mix" but do not account for all variables. As social purposes come to the forefront, and recognizing that "buildings don't have problems, only people do," one conceives of the total public intervention, not renewal alone, for achieving the public purposes sought.[53]

MODEL CITIES

The Demonstration Cities program, renamed Model Cities, represents the first formal, national effort to implement a policy which seeks to place house building, residence rehabilitation, relocation, and renewal in the broader context of a total social strategy. It is not clear, at the present writing, whether the program will be given enough support and leverage for a true trial—or whether its goals are realistic. Among the blockages, limitations, problems, and doubts are:

---

[52] See *The Federal Role in Urban Affairs; Examination of the War Against Poverty* (Senate); Otto Kerner, Chairman, *Report of the National Advisory Commission on Civil Disorders* (New York: Bantam Books, 1968).

[53] Robinson, *op. cit.*

☐ the fact that the responsible federal bureaucracy is staffed by personnel long wedded to older concepts of renewal, home building, land use, and housing economics;

☐ the fact that the Congress, in its ambivalence, votes appropriations, which do not match legislative authorization, and so delays appropriations each year as to make decent local-level programming extremely difficult;

☐ the sheer complexity of the assignment, covering a field in which there is relatively little experience;

☐ a scale of appropriation which, in large metropolitan areas, will cover only neighborhoods and districts—while the objective sought may require full participation by a city as such;

☐ the need to orchestrate a wide variety of federal-state-local social welfare and manpower interventions, broadly defined, through an administrative structure which, despite some delegation by the Chief Executive, may lack, in the politician's term, adequate "clout."

Each of these problems will be elaborated briefly after summary of the program itself.

The Demonstration Cities and Metropolitan Development Act of 1966 began with a statement of perspective: "Improving the quality of urban life is the most critical domestic problem facing the United States." More specifically, the objective is to:

rebuild or revitalize large slum and blighted areas; expand housing, job and income opportunities; reduce dependence on welfare payments; improve educational facilities and programs, combat disease and ill health; reduce the incidence of crime and delinquency; enhance recreational and cultural opportunities; establish better access between homes and jobs; and generally to improve living conditions for the people who live in such areas.

Here, then, is a comprehensive listing of agenda topics critical to the humanization of the urban environment and the community life it sustains. The instruments authorized are grants, through the Department of Housing and Urban Development (HUD), to enable cities to plan, develop, and carry out comprehensive city demonstration programs. Such programs are to bring together on a "massive scale" the tools, projects, and activities available to "improve dramatically the living environment in slum and blighted areas and open the doors of opportunity to their residents."[54] The

---

[54] This official interpretation by the Assistant Secretary of the Department of Housing and Urban Development responsible for the program and his Special Assistant thus sees physical renewal and social goals as components of one goal. See H. Ralph Taylor and George A. Williams, "Comments on the Demonstration Cities Program," *Journal of the American Institute of Planners*, XXXII, No. 6 (November, 1966), 366–376. Our interpretation follows Taylor-Williams, the "official" HUD summary of the Act, and sub-

problem-to-be-solved is seen by the HUD strategists as: (a) the project-centered, isolated nature of federal programs in education, manpower, housing, health, mental health, social security, public assistance, and poverty, and such isolation's precluding integration at the local service-delivery point; (b) the separate channels through which programs operate, thus ignoring obvious interrelationships and failing to coordinate goals; (c) the gaps which occur when programs are tailored to grant requirements, rather than to local needs.

To solve these difficulties the legislation calls upon the applicant-locality to design and program a comprehensive effort, which will pull together federal aids of many kinds as well as local public and private resources for what Taylor and Williams describe as "a coordinated and concerted attack on the hard-core problems of entire neighborhoods or sections of cities." Locally-planned coordination is intended to correct federal "project-itis" and competition. The applicant must describe the administrative machinery to be established and clarify its capabilities with reference to the goals.

In effect, the demonstration city agency is expected to coordinate urban renewal, education, anti-poverty, public housing, public assistance, building inspection, health, and manpower programs, since such coordination is essential to the goals. If such conditions are met so as to merit a designation as a "Model City," the locality becomes eligible for considerable financial aid to spell out its plan, carry out its projects, meet the problem of local "matching funds," and administer the entire effort.[55]

In general, plans to be completed within five years are encouraged. Such possibilities are mentioned as open space, airports, libraries, hospitals, water supply, and sewage facilities. Additional urban renewal funds are also provided (and technical amendments both strengthen protections for the relocated and seek to assure adequate low- and middle-income housing, if

---

sequent guidelines. Also see, Department of Housing and Urban Development, *Improving the Quality of Urban Life: A Program Guide to Model Neighborhoods in Demonstration Cities* (Washington, D.C.: Government Printing Office, 1967). A revision under the same title was issued in 1968 after the "first round" of grants.

[55] As originally passed, the Act specified that, when designated as a Model City, the municipality (or two or more jointly), county, or other body (or two or more acting jointly) with general governmental powers becomes eligible for (a) up to 80 percent of the costs of specifying and elaborating over a 6- to 12-month period the comprehensive plan outlined in the application; (b) special demonstration grant funds of up to 80 percent of the non-federal contribution to federal grant-in-aid programs which are "packaged" into the proposal; (c) up to 80 percent of administrative costs. Furthermore, (d) certain supplementary funds covering up to 20 percent of the cost may be used to fill the gaps between specific existing federal programs and the total endeavor deemed necessary by the locality. Grants may also be made for relocation costs not otherwise federally aided. Subsequent amendments are not relevant to the purpose of this chapter.

the renewal is to be residential). Two things are thus achieved: there is great incentive for the locality to use federal funds in coordinated fashion; there is assistance to meet the problem of raising adequate local matching money to activate full federal funding under a given program—or to finance activities not specified under existing legislation. The initial guidelines stress (a) an undertaking of "sufficient magnitude" to make "substantial impact"; (b) "widespread citizen participation in the program";[56] (c) maximum opportunity for employment of area residents in all phases; (d) enlarged work and training opportunities to contribute to a well-balanced city; (e) substantial increase in the supply of low-cost and moderate-cost housing and in the choices available to people of all income levels; (f) adequate commercial and public employment facilities. There must be a relocation plan which meets urban renewal regulations and is coordinated with the housing program.

Finally, there is emphasis on action-oriented planning, tied to specific programming and scheduling and designed to be launched rapidly. (In fact, delays in federal processing and funding kept hundreds of applicant-cities waiting.)

Much programming and administrative initiative is thus left to the locality. In fact, applicants are told that planning grants will go only to cities which show understanding of causes and solutions to problems. Grants for implementation will be awarded competitively "to programs which exceed statutory standards or which contain substantial innovation either in program or in intergovernmental cooperation."[57] But the Department of Housing and Urban Development, of course, retains the right to approve applications. Since the initial legislation and funding permitted approval of only a portion of the applications generated, HUD's detailed and suggestive guidelines were a potent force in setting parameters and in pointing to desirable outlooks.[58]

The guidelines and interpretive materials tell localities that the applica-

[56] Model Cities was the first major national legislation to borrow and adopt the antipoverty war's "maximum feasible participation" doctrine. See Chapter II. The "second round" instructions asked planning-grant applicants to defer specific programming in favor of analysis of problems and creation of a strong working coalition, public and voluntary, and including state agencies.

[57] Improving the Quality of Urban Life, 2.

[58] For example, see the analysis in Model Cities Administration, Program Characteristics of Model Cities (Washington, D.C.: Department of Housing and Urban Development, 1967, mimeographed). The general problem of local initiative vis-à-vis federal funding is discussed in Chapter VI.

tions most likely to have favorable review are the products of "practical dreamers," characterized by new solutions to problems, new techniques for housing rehabilitation, experimental approaches to taxation, new building codes, new construction techniques and materials, new designs, and new forms of resident involvement. Provision must be made to measure the impact of the effort on specific social problems; for example, school drop-out rates, infant mortality, and the size of the poverty group. Here, in short, is a program dedicated to the proposition that: "Problems of the physical environment must be seen as a social problem."[59] Or, in President Johnson's words:

> The problem is people and the quality of lives they lead. We want to build not just housing units, but neighborhoods; not just to construct schools, but to educate children; not just to raise income, but create beauty and end the poisoning of our environment.

In short, formal national policy had inevitably completed the cycle from an emphasis on the physical to a recognition that our goals are social and that physical plans are instrumental. Now the issue had become: was all of this seriously meant; could it be achieved; was the repertoire equal to the task?

By early 1968, a total of 75 out of 193 applications was approved and grants totaling $12 million for planning allocated; Congress had authorized $312 million for supplemental grants. (The second-round quota was to be approximately 75 cities.) The approved plans were noteworthy in their general emphasis on unemployment, underemployment, poverty, and discrimination against minority group members as the core of the problem addressed. Urban ghettos were to be dealt with comprehensively. There was major concern with coordination, human resource investment, and building rehabilitation—as opposed to relocation—as strategies. Evidence of a strong executive,[60] participation by all community elements in the planning (including civil rights groups, tenant associations, and organizations of the poor), and the intention to create a competent well-staffed planning instrument characterized the successful applications. In many ways the approved plans were closer to anti-poverty strategies than to renewal traditions.

The Model Cities administrators sought quick transitions from overall

---

[59] Taylor and Williams, op. cit., 367.

[60] The local chief executive—mayor or city manager—is the only source of essential leadership for the complex process of pulling together the components. Even where Model Cities planning is delegated to a sub-unit, to a neighborhood corporation, or an anti-poverty community-action program, local government retains ultimate responsibility and veto power. Thus the 1968 anti-poverty issue of the local prerogatives does not arise.

plans to programs. They could impose such requirements on localities, but could not themselves cope with the vagaries of the Congressional appropriation process and the political maneuverings, which first decreased funding to an unmanageable level and, then, responded to urban riots by coming closer to Administration requests.

To match the enthusiasm of successful applicants there were the serious reservations of skeptics and doubters. Several issues persisted. For example, Model Cities applicants commit themselves to increasing the supply of moderate- and low-income housing, while urban renewal continues to decrease the supply. Will the emphasis upon poor and disadvantaged people not require other programs for everyone else, perpetuating what we might call stigmatized particularism? Can the coordination sought be achieved when separate federal, state, local, and private bureaucracies, with their own political support and constituencies, continue to run all the separate programs listed above as the targets for coordination? To James Q. Wilson, the Model Cities Act is no guarantee of coordination, but it may challenge such bureaucracies to put social goals ahead of physical objectives and may create a new coalition to fight for them.[61]

Many observers, who acknowledge that it will be some years before one actually knows whether the Model Cities program makes a difference, hold that it is clear that the present scale of funding will be too modest for the intended impact. For 1968, President Johnson urged granting $622 million for Model Cities and $40 million for rent supplements. The Congress voted $312 million to Model Cities and $10 million for rent supplements. By 1969 the appropriation was $625 million for Model Cities and $30 million for supplements. At the same time, agricultural subsidies totaled over $5 billion and highway subsidies many times that annually. The long-term instability of even such a level of grants and of the concept of Model Cities was a cause for concern, despite the increases in fiscal 1969.[62]

Some critics claim that on the surface, at least, the program does not assure an emphasis on area, neighborhood, and building rehabilitation to end the moving out of poor people.[63] Yet the guidelines are clear: "The overall emphasis of the physical improvement activity . . . is on rehabilitation."[64] It remains far from certain that adequate impact can be achieved

---

[61] James Q. Wilson in "Comments on the Demonstration Cities Program," *op. cit.*, 371–373.

[62] Wheaton, *ibid.*, 368.

[63] Kaplan, *ibid.*, 370.

[64] *Improving the Quality of Urban Life*, 6.

by even a comprehensive thrust in sections of a city (three neighborhoods in New York) or small cities; do we not really require a regional or metropolitan effort to achieve the objectives given? Furthermore, should one assume that city renewal is always the answer; why not a large New Towns effort along with Model Cities, to determine if the goals are best achieved with a fresh start? Congress was long unwilling to approve this.[65] Can one really undertake "comprehensive planning for urban living" without heed to the regional job-opportunity structure and other aspects of the regional economy, without transportation and land-use planning in the broader frame? The Model Cities Act "acknowledges" this, but does it have adequate leverage? In the aftermath of the summer, 1967, and spring, 1968, riots, large-scale job programs were quite independently conceived.

Even within the program's own framework, difficult questions are raised. Planners often encounter the need for choices among desirable but potentially incompatible goals. Is the commitment to new building technology compatible with employment for area residents? Can sound citizen participation be generated at a pace which meets the need for speed in programming?[66] Will localities, whose preferences in effect defeated some of the goals of renewal–relocation–public housing, do better with Model Cities possibilities? Should hopes be pinned on local government agencies, which tend to be problem-avoiding institutions?[67] Is it reasonable to expect local government to coordinate a diversity of federal programs whose sponsoring departments often are unable to achieve a modus operandi in Washington?

PARALLEL PROPOSALS AND DILEMMAS

Before, during, and after the Model Cities "take off," and long before its impact could be perceived, other planners and housing experts called for additional, often parallel, measures to complete the new program for cities. Many have focused on correction of defects in renewal, relocation, and public housing. They have tried to plan ways to redress the program balance in favor of the poor and of minority group members, to stabilize public housing and increase the supply, to facilitate home ownership at low-income levels, to "save" the city's cultural and commercial core, to revitalize neigh-

---

[65] Wheaton, "Comments on the Demonstration Cities Program," *op. cit.*, 368–369. Title IV of P.L. 90–448 represented a major breakthrough.

[66] Bernard J. Frieden, *ibid.*, 375. In New York's three areas, Negroes and Puerto Ricans battled for control of local machinery and jobs. The process was repeated elsewhere.

[67] See "Comment: Planning for Model Cities," by Robert Montgomery, in *Trans-action*, 4, No. 8 (July/August, 1967), 2.

borhoods, to encourage regional development, and to attend to consumer preferences. These are not, of course, necessarily mutually compatible preoccupations.

Some experts concentrate on the quality of urban living, with reference to physical amenity, noting that this dimension is usually underplayed. It is, for example, now technically possible to handle and process metropolitan waste so as to recover much of value, even fresh water; to electrify public transport so as to clean the air; to discourage motor traffic by restriction while making public transportation attractive; and to make power far from residential concentrations, thus keeping city air clean. These are obviously significant concerns, consistent, but sometimes in competition for funds, with renewal programs.

Among those who do not believe that the Model Cities program has all the answers, several urge much more attention to goals and objectives as a preliminary to planning. Proposals range from creation of goals commissions to sophisticated social science studies of consumer preferences.[68] City plans would, in these approaches, deal with goals, objectives, and priorities; and maximum programming detail would be reserved for neighborhoods.

Jane Jacobs and her adherents do not address most macro-issues, but are united in their determination that the sum total of housing and city planning policy not defeat their primary value of neighborhood diversity. An interesting, safe, stimulating neighborhood for young and old alike, in this view, must encourage multiple uses, short blocks, buildings of varied ages, and dense concentrations of people. Obviously, these are not criteria for all areas, but explicit is the generalized notion that

> . . . The main responsibility of city planning and design should be to develop . . . cities that are congenial for the range of unofficial plans, ideas and opportunities to flourish, along with the flourishing of public enterprises.[69]

This philosophy, while inspired and inspiring, does not suggest specific pathways to meet immediate needs. It considers urban design, not a complete program for the city—and seems peripheral to some.

Economic realities and the required scale of operations demand more attention to specific governmental programs. There is widespread agreement

---

[68] Charles Abrams has proposed a Goals Commission of leading citizens on several occasions. The study of preference has been investigated by several scholars. See footnote on page 172.

For a goals "position" see Lyle C. Fitch, "Eight Goals for an Urbanizing America," in *The Conscience of the City*, constituting *Daedalus*, 97, No. 4 (Fall, 1968), 1141–1164.

[69] Jacobs, *op. cit.*, 241.

that the balance must be shifted, through national and local financial incentives and technological breakthrough, to housing rehabilitation, in contrast to relocation and razing. The arguments are persuasive, given the social goals of the housing programs, but we do not as yet know the conditions under which rehabilitation is financially attractive to private money or the extent of public funding or tax-abatement incentive needed to make rehabilitation a significant program.

Where public housing continues to develop, some planners are seeking ways to transfer ownership to low-income tenants on a cooperative basis, hoping thereby to stabilize these new social milieux, encourage better maintenance, and "change the image" of such public housing. New administrative measures, including rents scaled to income, are also used to retain the more successful public housing tenants. Others continue to urge public programs to facilitate purchase of single-family houses by the very poor. Almost all surveys show that most people would prefer to live in single-family houses and away from the center of things. Interest subsidies, inexpensive, long-term guaranteed loans, and "sweat equity" (the poor buyer does some of the work himself as a "down payment") are among the relatively small-scale devices in need of expansion.

In 1966, the federal government proposed and eventually won limited Congressional approval for a rent-subsidy program similar to successful programs in many other countries. At a defined income level and household size, a family is deemed to be making maximum efforts when it pays a specified portion of income in rent, usually 20 to 25 percent. The government subsidizes the rent to the going market rate, in accord with family size.

This small-scale rent-subsidy program is seen as an experiment to permit very-low-income families to locate in middle-income housing. Anti-poverty and racial integration efforts are joined to the housing program. However, the program is considered by many experts to have a larger potential in relieving the housing shortage. Widely applied it could shift many low-income families to a rental level at which private enterprise might be attracted to rehabilitate or build housing, thus adding significantly to the housing supply and decreasing reliance on massive public housing projects. On the other hand, its disadvantages, the means tests involved, the "backlash" of resentment of unsubsidized families just above the subsidy level, and the general incompatibility with the national ethic of a program that provides a family with a higher living standard and housing status than it has earned, make it doubtful that the Congress will permit rent subsidies to be more than token experiments in the near future. It may prove easier to win support for increased interest-subsidies, for which families within defined income levels are eligible if their monthly payments exceed 20 percent of income. The program was enacted as part of the Housing and Urban Development Act of 1968 (P.L. 90–448) but initial appropriations were limited. Since it reflects apparent consumer preference and may in effect confine purchases to areas of inexpensive housing one might predict popularity and acceptance for this program.

Some of the most experienced of planners doubt that enough leverage exists to reconstruct adequately, achieve balance and choices, and provide amenities under renewal or rehabilitation programs alone—even if accompanied by rent subsidies. They urge that cities and suburbs be seen in relation to one another, since there is no other way to deal successfully with such problems as transportation, the tax base, schools, and welfare costs. The inner city cannot be restored without establishment of new communities on the outskirts. A suburb cannot survive without a vital city.

In the perspective of general strategies to assure the viability of the future megalopolis or any intensively settled region, in fact, there is serious need for an overall policy of population dispersion. Many who have looked ahead are serious proponents of well-planned New Towns or "satellite cities" on the British, Swedish, or Dutch models, balanced among residential, industrial, commercial, recreational, and civic uses, diversified in population, and adequately served by transportation ties to cities. Each New Town becomes a strategically located growth point.[70] Only use of public power to assemble land and assure the open space between such sites will permit a significant scale of development in more than a few show places, however, despite the usefulness of the New Town loan guarantees authorized in 1968 and available in 1969. City renewal may also permit utilization of the concept of "New Towns" in town.[71]

But city-suburb planning or a thrust toward regionalism, while strongly favored by the advocates of efficiency and comprehensiveness, contain a political problem. Many in the Negro community see little possibility of their own achievement of satisfactory economic and social status except from the political base of locally controlled institutions and businesses. Their view of "black power" calls for a slowing down of the thrust toward

---

[70] To illustrate, an imaginative plan for California is contained in Governor's Advisory Commission on Housing Problems, *Report on Housing in California* (Sacramento: California State Printing Office, 1963), 60–62. Or see Symposium, "Creating New Communities," *Journal of the American Institute of Planners*, XXXIII, No. 6 (November, 1967).

[71] Chester Rapkin, "New Towns for America: From Picture to Process," *The Journal of Finance*, XXII, No. 2 (May, 1967), 208–219. Harvey Perloff, "New Towns Intown," *Journal of the American Institute of Planners*, XXXII, No. 3 (May, 1966), 155–160.

integration in favor of local black businesses, decentralized and locally controlled schools, black-controlled "Model Cities" boards, and political machines which offer a foothold to indigenous politicians. Since the deteriorated cores of many metropolitan areas are currently peopled by Negroes and since many cities are expected to have Negro voting majorities or very strong minorities in the coming decade, planning for regionalism or urban-suburban junctures threatens to block new Negro power at the moment that it becomes possible. Thus, the planning problem faces new complexity: can one achieve the coordination and efficiency of the larger units without blocking legitimate goals of "newly-enfranchised" local groups? It may be that local power and competence—a stake in the now-deteriorated areas —are the most important ingredients in ending the anomie, hatred-of-neighborhood, and detachment out of which local lawlessness and deterioration are conceived. Yet it is also true that the city is unlikely to become viable for the black man unless it is also so for the white. Few more knotty problems have ever confronted American politics and political science, and the planner obviously must choose his direction in terms of how this issue may be resolved.

Of special interest, in the period from 1966 to 1968, was the extent to which liberal members of the United States Senate, representing both parties, sought to accelerate the housing and renewal program by facilitating large-scale investment by private business in construction of low-cost housing and in rehabilitation of buildings. Ignoring the criticism that the inadequate treatment of the very poor derived from excessive reliance on publicly "protected" private investment, these proponents sought programs on a new scale, through far greater tax incentives and other public aid, using the devices of intermediate nonprofit corporate groups in the localities or direct appeals for participation of large corporations. HUD saw this as completely appropriate and not in conflict with the general public effort. At the same time, President Johnson prevailed upon private enterprise, particularly insurance companies, to invest substantially in ghetto and low-income housing.

The need for a maximum effort to harness the talents of American industry is evident. Thus all such approaches deserve real support, if it is agreed that private enterprise should prove itself each step of the way and not coast as a preferred agent.[72] Such a role has not been earned through past performance. It may be true that industry will provide the breakthrough, if housing and city building are made truly profitable, whereas they have been marginal investments so far. Perhaps the alternative proposal of a

---

[72] Abrams, *op. cit.*, 257.

public-private corporation, to clear, relocate, build, rent, or sell housing, may be an even more useful instrument, since it will be somewhat more free of market constraints and biases.

Housing programs require adequate lead time and cannot achieve results overnight. The new approaches had enjoyed only modest beginnings by mid-1968. Appropriations and further enactments (P.L. 90–448) promised accelerated new public housing construction and rehabilitation, increased rent supplements, an interest-rate subsidy for low-income house purchases much like rent supplements, New Towns aid, and more adequate Model Cities funding. Yet it was not clear that dramatic results could be expected from the new programs. Many experts have noted that, notwithstanding the advances in methodology of residential construction since World War II, the country lacks a housing industry in the full sense; the independent efforts of thousands of small-scale entrepeneurs simply do not add up to enough. The ways have not yet been found to apply the mass-production methods of automobile manufacture to the construction of low-cost housing— whether because of scale of enterprise, inadequate incentive to attract industrial ingenuity, rigidity of labor union requirements, or the multiplicity of governmental jurisdictions, which make it difficult to "assemble" the required policy, tax supports, building and construction codes, and the required land. And total federal appropriations are limited.

On the assumption that megalopolis will grow and that city plans must relate to regional designs, the Gottmans, Abrams, Mumfords, Doxiadis, and Logues offer models for city units which may become modules, in larger patterns, for cities and towns, which are in turn sound units in even larger regions, allowing for open space, transportation, and diversity of living choices for all social groups. All warn that present paths lead to further decline; but few have more than attractive hypotheses as to the sanctions, funds, and plans to be "mixed" to produce the desired outcome. All are ideologically committed to neighborhood self-direction, yet there is little precedent to encourage the process. Some concentrate on proposals for massive transportation and for land-use development plans which encompass metropolitan regions; others give priority to social policy. Many proclaim that man is to be the measure of all policy.

There remain many unused or partially-used tools. Once the policy thrust is clear, federal subsidies could be redirected and federal tools redeployed. Thus federal financial aids or guarantees could be limited to urban renewal and New Town areas—and could have as prerequisite a regional open space and transportation plan. A change in rules could transfer savings and loan association funds to the guarantee of mortgages for multiple dwellings. Antitrust regulations could be relaxed to facilitate private industry's collaboration.[73] Renewal and clearance programs could be applied to wipe out industrial slums, create industrial facilities in New Towns, build large middle-income communities—and so on.[74] Even more basic tax policies and more extensive direct and indirect subsidies could be developed to encourage the pattern sought.[75]

But as soon as one begins to consider tax policy, industrial development, transportation, city dispersion within the region, cooperation of local governments to plan growth, mobilization of big industry on either a profit or a public service basis—all fields in which excellent proposals exist both to improve the housing supply and to humanize the city—the dilemmas faced by planners vis-à-vis the city become all too clear. Reference to the situation after the summer, 1967, riots in American cities poses the issues most sharply.

When the United States Senate hearings, the voluntary committees of the Urban Coalition, the experts of the National Advisory Commission on Civil Disorders, and the editorial writers of major dailies sought ways to improve the cities of the nation, or at least to enforce the law and to discourage ghetto riots, they began to deal in considerable detail with:

☐ large-scale efforts to create jobs, some emphasizing the voluntary sector and others seeing the government as "employer of last resort," absorbing many workers in public service occupations;

☐ relating the unemployment of unskilled ghetto residents to the need to rehabilitate housing and to build public housing (not quite reconciling the absorption of unskilled labor with the parallel need to upgrade and increase mass-production technology in building);

☐ ways of assuring an income floor, food, or a guaranteed income to some categories of the poor (and thus opening up many questions relating to income transfers, benefits in kind, the character of the public welfare program, etc.);

☐ the general problem of the city's financial base, its revenue sources, its relationships with federal government and with the state, including the proposal that the federal government free city funds for "legitimate" charges by itself financing all poverty-related programs (thus confronting major issues of intergovernmental relations and federalism);

☐ all of the specific issues of housing policy and strategy, ranging from the

---

[73] This was partially enacted in mid-1968.

[74] Bernard Weissbourd, "Segregation, Subsidies and Megalopolis" (Santa Barbara, California: Center for the Study of Democratic Institutions, an "Occasional Paper," 1964).

[75] Planners in the United States do not, of course, have the basic authority to regulate land use and the schedule of development, which has long since been common in Western European statutes.

adequacy of the public housing program, to the wisdom of renewal and relocation, the possibility of more rehabilitation, and the proposals for large-scale rent subsidies;

☐ "a national migration policy to direct the flow of people which now eddies haphazardly from rural backwater to city slum; a national land policy to plan the development of future suburbs and new towns; a national housing policy with much tougher controls over land speculators and featherbedding construction unions";

☐ the various tax, credit, and labor policies that might increase investment in or availability of mortgage money for housing or that might facilitate application of modern technology to building;

☐ the total range of anti-poverty programs and their need for expansion, revision, and improvement the better to contribute to the goals sought;

☐ questions of police and national guard training and practice, with particular reference to problems of riot control.[76]

In a more basic sense, these program areas and the options they offer introduce some of the most complex and controversial policy issues facing government at present: the relative reliance on the market; the degree of redistribution in social policy; the uses of tax power for more than revenue purposes; the redefinition of federal-state-local relations; the new balance between centralization and decentralization of government; the strategy for offering opportunity to previously-deprived minority groups; the readiness to undertake public land purchase on a large scale and to use powers of eminent domain in new ways to achieve allegedly benign social objectives. Also at stake is the hierarchy of values, which will guide choices along such dimensions as maximizing individual choices, assuring consumer participation in planning, assuring maximum results for minimum expenditure, or utilizing the private sector as a major instrument.

SYSTEM AND TASK

Here in this extensive listing one sees the ultimate dilemma. We have noted how United States planners and officials gradually expanded the concept of the housing field until some among them were willing to locate renewal *and* housing programs in the general context of social planning and policy. Some were focusing on problems of the poor, others on the implications of megalopolis. Many participants in the dialogue indicated no aware-

---

[76] For illustration of how the search for urban peace led a Senate subcommittee into anti-poverty policy, income security, law and order, housing and renewal, and related fields, see *The Federal Role in Urban Affairs.*

The new approaches of big business along these lines are described in "Business and the Urban Crisis," constituting *Fortune,* LXXVII, No. 1 (January, 1968).

The quotation re migration is from a *New York Times* editorial, February 23, 1968.

ness that these were somewhat different and occasionally contradictory points of departure. Once a general social policy frame is attempted for housing and renewal from either perspective, however, one opens up almost all fields-sectors in social planning and confronts basic questions relative to goals for the family, the quality of community life sought, and much more.[77]

In 1966, given an expansive definition, one could count 238 federal programs relating to urban affairs in the Departments of Housing and Urban Development, Commerce, Labor, Interior, Agriculture, and Health, Education, and Welfare.[78] Does the city planner, turned social planner, have the sanction, organizational base, and capability needed for so inclusive a role? Would assignment to him of such broad responsibility be useful? In August, 1966, recognizing the widespread governmental involvement through many departments in programs important to the improvement of cities and the solution of community and metropolitan development problems, President Johnson sought a coordinating device. An executive order was issued designating the Secretary of Housing and Urban Development as "convenor" of the federal agencies and departments involved so as to "provide a forum"; "promote cooperation"; obtain advice with reference to cooperation with state and local agencies offering technical help and encouraging comprehensive planning; identify urban problems.[79] Subsequently, the authority was utilized to launch interdepartmental activity in 14 cities to establish multi-service centers and to facilitate "packaging" of Model Cities proposals. However, given the range of issues relevant to city life and its future, as listed above, it is no surprise that coordination was essentially marginal, despite the Secretary's positive comments. The interdepartmental activity did not approach the range of concerns listed above, nor could the Secretary of Housing and Urban Development do very much more than convene "equals" and hope for success in bargaining—with an occasional executive "assist" when some matters became urgent in the public view.

It was apparent that the Director of the Office of Economic Opportunity had a convenor role of sorts, too. When a Senate Subcommittee asked about

---

[77] Several years ago, Scott Greer analyzed the problems of urban renewal as related to the presence of three sets of aims which, while not contradictory, are not identical and result in different emphases. He thus illustrates the problem of task definition within one specific program. Scott Greer, *Urban Renewal and American Cities* (Indianapolis: Bobbs-Merrill Company, 1965).

[78] *Federal Role in Urban Affairs*, Part 13, 2652.

[79] The White House, "Executive Order," August 11, 1966.

this, Housing and Urban Development responded that its role is to "take the initiative in bringing to bear resources of the Federal Establishment in attacking urban problems; both in Washington and in the field." The Office of Economic Opportunity, on the other hand, "is authorized to promote cooperation toward achievement of consistent policies, practices and procedures that relate specifically to antipoverty programs."[80] The response, of course, ignores the fact that all current analyses of the problems of the city see the two tasks as similar to a degree approaching congruence. Indeed, even on the local level, Model Cities boards and anti-poverty community-action groups were in competition in many cities by early 1969, and it was difficult to conceptualize distinct roles. Nor does the above "clarification" cope with the obvious stake of the Department of Health, Education, and Welfare, particularly its units concerned with education, health, mental health, pollution, water supply, and income transfers.

Ultimately, one faces the fact that the United States does not have an executive level or legislative social planning instrument that is superordinate. Thus coordinate departments seek to cooperate and to bargain, often allowing one another the "lead" in fields of a given unit's central interest but sharing the rest. State and local agencies perceive a minimum of coordination and much confusion and competition in vital areas. It requires little investigation to disclose wastage, gaps, and ineffectiveness. Efforts by the Bureau of the Budget improve the situation but are not enough to solve the problem.[81]

For, in reality, the case is "proved" several times over. To cope with the problems of the city is to cope with the core domestic problems of the society. In the terms employed in the present work, this requires nothing less than a social planning instrument in Washington, undertaking for the domestic sector what the National Security Council attempts for foreign affairs—but probably through a device in the executive or legislative branch, or devices in both—closely tied to budgeting and at a level of authority above any single department head. There cannot be, for the city, a "Department of Everything," but policy planning and coordination are unavoidable in Washington.[82]

President Richard M. Nixon created a Council for Urban Affairs by Exec-

[80] *Federal Role in Urban Affairs*, Appendix to Part 1, 101–102.

[81] See testimony by Charles L. Schultze, Director of the Bureau of the Budget, *Federal Role in Urban Affairs*, 20, 4258 ff.

[82] *Ibid.*

utive Order on January 23, 1969, assigning it an advisory, monitoring, and coordinating role. The language of the order opens up many possibilities, but it is not yet clear how the role will develop.

Corresponding planning instruments are needed for state and city governments as well, and there is room to experiment with regional devices crossing state lines. Individual departments and bureaus at all governmental levels also require their own planning staffs, as indicated elsewhere.[83] Current confusion, overlapping, and vacuums will not be eliminated, unless we face the fact that *the concern with the city underscores the urgency of comprehensive social planning tailored to the American scene, but the existing instrumentalities of city planning are not adequate for the broader planning and policy assignment.*

Is there, then, no role for the social planner in housing? Has the entire process of "socialization" of housing policy been in error? On the contrary: the process was an essential part of the development whereby Americans have come to realize that to cope with the city is not merely to produce bricks and mortar, but to deal with the basic issues of the society—including the status of racial minorities. However, now that the case is made and the need for appropriate broad planning instruments underscored, it is also useful to consider the scope of a field for *specific* planning, which we have seen as "a housing, renewal and relocation system, characterized by introduction of nonmarket considerations into the provision of housing and development of community facilities."[84] Such a field, taking its place along with fields such as income maintenance, the medical system, corrections, and education, becomes a major unit within the total social sector, to be coordinated and interrelated through the instrumentalities mentioned above. Staffed by a "coalition" of architects, design specialists, and physical planners; economists, other social scientists; transportation, water pollution, and sanitation experts; social welfare specialists, *the planning arm of a housing-renewal-relocation system*, would deal with:

☐ the elements of traditional housing policy, as listed in the Marshall quotation above (enough, accessible, adequate, diverse housing, offering choices), and including such specific programs as renewal, relocation, rehabilitation, rent supplements, New Towns in town, public housing;

☐ assuring that physical planning is aesthetically and socially informed, in the sense of our earlier discussion;

☐ the translation of human preferences, goals for groups and the family,

---

[83] Chapter XI in the companion volume.

[84] In the companion volume, page 164.

the search for diversity and enrichment into implications for city planning;

☐ the planning of satellite cities and New Towns or new regional patterns, as these affect daily living;

☐ the monitoring of the accomplishments and consequences of policies.

The urban physical planners in the coalition "would take on a new importance and responsibility. In the total spectrum of public planning they would become the custodians, representatives, and advocates of a humane physical environment."[85] In Hans Blumenfeld's terms, as distinguished from socio-economic planning, "physical city planning . . . designs the spatial framework for the life of urban society."[86]

In addition to planning location of highways and other public facilities, with reference to community functional and social patterns, and identifying areas for conservation and renewal—major roles not at all to be denigrated in an attempt to specify and delimit the field—physical planners also would bring "social and economic problems to the attention of appropriate authorities"[87] and be part of a comprehensive effort at solution. Within this effort, roles would be specified.

It will take pragmatism and imagination to produce viable system boundaries, but they are needed to permit escape from global definitions which offer no guidance at all—as we have now escaped from restrictive concepts which ignore the critical variables. A central idea in any ultimate task definition of such planning might be that one should seek, not *an* optimum environment, but, rather, ever-changing optimum environments. It is not necessary to choose city or suburb, renovated core or New Town, high-rise dwelling or private house. The planner seeks to expand, not contract, the options.[88] Is this, after all, not the true heart of the ethic? As Sophocles declared, "A city that is of one man only is no city."[89]

---

[85] Corwin R. Mocine, "Urban Physical Planning and the 'New Planning,' " *Journal of the American Institute of Planners*, XXXII, No. 4 (July, 1966), 236.

[86] Paul D. Speiregan, Editor, *The Modern Metropolis: Selected Essays by Hans Blumenfeld* (Cambridge, Mass.: The M.I.T. Press, 1967), 18. Or see Hans Blumenfeld, "The Role of Design," *Journal of the American Institute of Planners*, XXXIII, No. 5 (September, 1967), 304–310.

[87] Mocine, *op. cit.*

[88] Bertram Gross and René Dubos, in Ewald, *Environment for Man;* Abrams, *The City is the Frontier, op. cit.*, 204; Weissbourd, *op. cit.*, 19.

[89] Quoted by Mumford, *op. cit.*, 117.

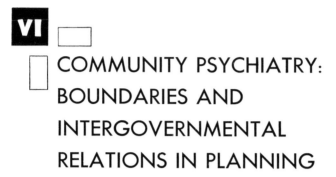

COMMUNITY PSYCHIATRY: BOUNDARIES AND INTERGOVERNMENTAL RELATIONS IN PLANNING

By LONG tradition, and quite generally, services to the mentally ill have been a state responsibility in this country. When national efforts were launched, after World War II, to update psychiatric services, it was possible to devise guidelines and to tie them to financial incentives, with the alleged purpose of encouraging states to develop new approaches. However, because the concepts of the problem and its treatment emphasized treatment in one's *locality*, state planners were urged to incorporate measures which would maximize service localization or decentralization. Thus, the issue was whether the planning system devised could implement national policy and free local creativity, while employing state government as intermediary. All of this was addressed to a field of practice in which validated knowledge was limited and which had not begun to resolve some of the most complex boundary problems in the entire social welfare system.

The boundary problem is our point of departure here: how adequate definition of boundaries might help to focus state and local planning in this one social welfare arena.[1] Then the central problems of national leverage and state-local initiative in planning are considered.

The community psychiatry or community mental health expert will recognize that this must be a lengthy chapter, while still, in many senses,

---

[1] The first part of this chapter employs part of the development in the author's "Planning and Practice Perspectives on the Boundaries of Community Psychiatry," in Leigh M. Roberts *et al.*, Editors, *Community Psychiatry* (Madison: University of Wisconsin Press, 1966), 165–181. A basic bibliography is offered in David S. Sanders, "A Bookshelf on Mental Health," *American Journal of Public Health*, 55, No. 4 (April, 1965), 502–509.

incomplete. The boundaries problem is addressed without full summarization of the scientific status of medical and non-medical interventions in relation to mental illness. The planning output of the Joint Commission on Mental Illness and Health is assessed in terms of the reports and several pieces of legislation and not with reference to internal effects of the process on the National Institute of Mental Health and the related professional groups. Indeed, the planning output is described by means of its final report; many major ideas, which were placed "in the hopper" only to be by-passed, are treated as though they did not exist. Nor is the entire professional interest-group struggle between medical and non-medical mental health personnel adequately covered.

Although the author writes from the conviction that more complete coverage along these latter lines would merely buttress the basic thesis, general agreement with such conclusion is not necessary. The major purpose, again, is to illustrate planning concepts and issues, not to preëmpt a large and developing field. The student who follows the bibliographic leads will encounter the other ramifications of community psychiatry in their fuller complexity.

PART ONE: BOUNDARIES

Delinquents, unmarried mothers, school dropouts, autistic children, unhappy adults, narcotic addicts, ambulatory schizophrenics, and many others have become the deliberate targets of community mental health centers and related programs, or of their own volition have crowded the newly-opened doors.[2] Since (a) clinicians, particularly psychiatrists, are the key helpers in a mental health center, (b) the center is the primary helping agency for many of these people, and (c) its service is community-based in the sense that it is outside of a hospital and is not private practice, the center is defined as a community mental health resource. What the clinician does in the center is then defined either as community psychiatry or as community mental health. All of this seems clear and natural. Why, then, should we be concerned with boundaries in this field?[3]

The claims of community psychiatry are not everywhere acknowledged or accepted. Other institutions often operate on somewhat different assumptions about the service system, as do potential users. Some children's courts believe that *they* provide the central service for delinquents, dropouts, and

---

[2] Leopold Bellak, Editor, *Handbook of Community Psychiatry and Community Mental Health* (New York: Grune & Stratton, 1964).

[3] The general discussion of the boundaries problem as a planning issue appears in the companion volume, Chapter V.

unmarried mothers. Certain specialized agencies believe that they provide the primary aid for unmarried mothers, while youth counseling and employment programs make a major bid for dropouts, for "potential" or "reformed" delinquents, and occasionally even for unmarried mothers. Furthermore, on those occasions when employment, court, or unmarried mothers' agencies do want a mental health center to take over one of their cases, their concept of the case may not coincide with that of the center.

Were all of this merely a problem of jurisdiction, it could be resolved by mediation procedures, arbitration, and court decisions. In the world of competitive funding, interprofessional power rivalry, and political involvement in social welfare, this is precisely what sometimes may be necessary. If the matter is pursued, however, it will be discovered that there are substantive issues involved that may permit rational processes to enter. Indeed it is urgent that such processes enter. For the boundaries issue, we have argued, both reflects and creates problems, and the way in which it is handled makes a substantial difference to those whom the practitioner would help.

The term "intervention system" has been suggested for a segment of the social welfare structure (thus excluding the family or private enterprise) that plays a role in improving or maintaining people's incomes, health, or social functioning. Intervention systems—for example, income maintenance, corrections, and education—generally coincide with social institutions or large organizations. The boundaries question, from a planning perspective, is one of defining the divisions between intervention systems at a given moment *so as to optimize the use of knowledge, sanction, and competence and to maximize the ability of potential users to draw upon the service.* Tasks must then be subdivided among agencies and services within the system, and provision made for case integration.

Should community psychiatry be considered an intervention system in this sense? If so, what are its boundaries? What is its essential core? How should people be enabled to distinguish between community psychiatry and its peripheral, supportive, and housekeeping functions, the noise and static that often obscure the essence of a social institution? If community psychiatry is the system, what is community mental health? Should the system perhaps be seen as a community mental health system? What is the relationship of all this to social psychiatry? Discussion of the latter question offers a beginning.

SOCIAL PSYCHIATRY AND COMMUNITY PSYCHIATRY

There is confusion over the term "social psychiatry." Some of the professional literature tends to leave social psychiatry's boundaries with community psychiatry uncertain, stressing only their common ground. Stephen E. Goldston[4] has assembled a series of efforts at definition that demonstrate this imprecision and an overlapping natural in an evolving field; but a number of authorities have begun to converge in their statements of the distinction between the two. Fredrick C. Redlich and M. P. Pepper see social psychiatry as

> the study of psychiatric disorders and psychiatric therapy, hopefully including prevention, within a social setting. This implies that social psychiatry is defined as an exploration of social systems and culture and their impact on psychiatric phenomena rather than as a type of psychiatric practice.

Maxwell Jones states, "In its widest sense the term implies the social factors associated with the living experiences of psychiatric patients or potential patients, whether in hospital or in the outside world." The staff of the Langley Porter Neuropsychiatric Institute believe social psychiatry to be: "that part of psychiatry concerned with various aspects of society as it relates to emotional disturbance. Insofar as it is similar to social psychology, its emphasis is probably more theoretical than practical."[5]

In the vocabulary of the present discussion, social psychiatry is not an intervention system. It is a *field of theory and an area of research*, and it exists at the point where psychiatric theory and social science converge. The term "community psychiatry," on the other hand, clearly implies a service or practice. Whereas some consider community psychiatry itself to be an intervention system (usually conceived of as part of medicine), others consider it to be a professional discipline within an intervention system, which they designate as "community mental health." Sometimes the specific usage grows out of imprecise language, but at other times it reflects a conviction that community psychiatry finds its characteristic outlet through an institutional base, with broad preventive orientations, which goes far beyond the medical domain.

THE SEARCH FOR BOUNDARIES

The effort to define community psychiatry generally begins with differentiation between it and traditional clinical psychiatry. The clinical psychiatrist characteristically operates through a personal relationship with an

---

[4] "Selected Definitions," in "Appendix" of Stephen E. Goldston, Editor, *Concepts of Community Psychiatry* (Washington, D.C.: Department of Health, Education, and Welfare, 1965).

[5] *Ibid.*

individual patient.[6] His arena of activity may be the office, clinic, hospital. The term "case psychiatry" more accurately describes this activity.

"Community psychiatry" is the term most often used to describe the psychiatrist's other-than-case-practice roles. The community psychiatrist is, for example, described by Duhl as the one

> concerned with optimizing the adaptive potential and psychosocial life skills, as well as lessening the amount of pathology, in population groups (communities, functional groups, etc.) by population-wide programs of prevention, case finding, case treatment, and rehabilitation. The individual becomes important not only as an individual problem but also as a flag of a more general psychiatric need of a population group.[7]

The staff of the Langley Porter Neuropsychiatric Institute, who go even further in stressing prevention and viewing treatment in this context, describe community psychiatry as

> that subspecialty of psychiatry which directs its attention and efforts to community mental health problems. Its tools are consultation, in-service training, general public education; its targets, key groups and individuals in the community whose behavior and attitudes have broad influence over the lives of others; its goals, to reduce significantly the number of seriously disturbed individuals and to decrease the extent of malfunctioning of a significant number of those people designated as emotionally disturbed.[8]

The problem of boundaries becomes apparent as one pursues the definition further. Caplan, for example, states

> Community psychiatry is based upon the acceptance by psychiatrists of responsibility for dealing with all the *mentally disordered* within the confines of a community. The responsibility focuses upon current cases, but also spreads to *potential cases* through programs of primary prevention. [Emphases added.][9]

We must first consider the term "mentally disordered," which implies more than psychiatric illness; it apparently extends to those who are maladjusted in work, play, and school, or at home. Are any areas of difficulty in role enactment or social living omitted? The phrase "potential cases," when coupled with the category "mentally disordered," would seem to in-

---

[6] Gerald Caplan, Editor, *Prevention of Mental Disorders in Children* (New York: Basic Books, 1961), and his "Community Psychiatry—Introduction and Overview," in Goldston, *op. cit.*

[7] Leonard J. Duhl, in Goldston, *op. cit.*, "Appendix."

[8] *Ibid.*

[9] Caplan, "Community Psychiatry . . . ," 4.

clude all members of society born and unborn. The reference to community would seem to exclude only hospitalized patients not on aftercare status.

To follow this direction is to include within community psychiatry almost all efforts to improve social life and affect social problems, as well as psychiatric treatment given outside of private practice—and probably some of that, too. Is this expansive definition useful, or would a more modest delimitation facilitate the organization of psychiatric services and the overall task of community planning? Is it, in fact, possible to cope with the boundaries problem by reference to *problems* or *goals*—the larger components of the definitions quoted? Our general review suggests that the clarity of boundaries requires more than this.

Dimensions relevant to resolution of a boundaries issue have been proposed earlier.[10] One does not know exactly how to weight each, but it is apparent that the debate about community psychiatry is premised on contradictory concepts of the phenomena being treated, different definitions of what is known about *how* to serve or treat (treatment method), and somewhat different assessments of social *sanctions* as they affect the decisions. It is a debate somewhat inhibited by the social power of the psychiatric-medical group.

Clearly, it is in the realm of *direct service* that this field can make its most serious bid as an intervention system, even if the domain in which it assumes service responsibility is staked out illogically. In general, as a product of a complex social control and social definitional process, some deviance is defined as mental disorder. Such definition, in turn, places the problem in the hands of the medically-based psychiatrist. Whatever is not defined as mental disorder is not a target of the psychiatric direct service-intervention system and may be left to the correctional agencies, non-medical social services (*Chapter VII*), or other appropriate agencies.

Thus, the state of the art is such that one should not expect the term "mental disorder" to do more than tell us what many people assign to psychiatry and what psychiatrists accept. Inevitably, others make counterclaims. Thus some delinquents, unmarried mothers, drug addicts, and unhappy people generally are the objects and the rejectees of a number of systems.

For present purposes, however, what is essential is the notion that the psychiatrist works with what he and many others see as mental disorder; and the ultimate responsibility is assigned to this subspecialty within medicine, even though the discipline experiments with non-medical modes of

---

[10] See pages 158–165 in the companion volume.

intervention or uses interventions which some people consider non-medical and others assign to a broadly conceived view of medical science.

Especially relevant is the fact that professional knowledge and experience in the psychiatric subsection of the medical system document the necessity of new modes of service organization: decentralization, emphasis on community-based treatment, and continuity of care from clinic to general hospital to psychiatric hospital to halfway house to aftercare. Operational requirements of services are so conceived that this system must have strong social science support, and its staff should be drawn from a variety of interrelated professions. The new emphases inherent in these services justify the inclusion of the word "community" in "community mental health" and "community psychiatry," but do not change the fact that the parameters of these fields are determined by what psychiatry and social control mechanisms converge upon as justifiably belonging to a *medical* subspecialty.

The key to the boundaries of the medical system in its psychiatric subspecialty is this: Where medical control and responsibility are required for an intervention or where professional and public definitions, self-perceptions, and institutional rules support it, the service is provided under the auspices of community psychiatry. Otherwise one turns to counseling, guidance, and other activities within the general non-medical social services system.

Needless to say, the definition of medicine implied here acknowledges the interaction between individual and environment, psyche and social systems. Community psychiatry can only be part of a medical practice which in the fullest sense is bio-socio-cultural.

If we follow this line of reasoning, the distinctions made at the outset between community psychiatry and case psychiatry no longer hold. A possible exception, however, may be the occasional private practitioner who, in his office, acts as though a patient has no identity other than that manifested within the office and will need no services or institutional supports for change other than those that exist in the psychiatrist's private sanctum.

Duhl reminds us that

> Disease must be seen not as an independent entity but rather something that is intricately tied to the individual, the host of the disease, and to the particular social setting within which both the disease and the individual's development occur. . . . [At] some point or another, as a result of a very special combination of circumstances of host, environment, and the significant etiological factors, the disease is said to begin.[11]

---

[11] Leonard J. Duhl, "The Psychiatric Evolution," in Goldston, *op. cit.*

In this sense, *all* psychiatry is or should be part of the system of community psychiatry. To consider relationship contexts in working on a case basis is to intervene in systems that extend beyond the psyche of any single individual: this is true even where the formulation of a case is completely organic. And it is inevitable in dealing with broad areas of social deviance, in response to which the community enacts, through the symbolism of labeling, a variety of value choices and social control patterns.[12]

The ideological bias of community psychiatry, although not the majority of its actual practice, is toward intervention designed to affect populations. Primary and secondary preventive measures and interventions, in the public health sense of the term, may include direct environmental manipulations. Team members may seek indirectly to affect the social environment through staff training and consultation, among other educational endeavors, and through contributions to administration or organization policy. In general, aspirations are greater than achievements.

Thus the realm of community psychiatry may be considered to encompass a total patient and out-patient system, many types of community-based service, provision for case integration and continuity of care, and the means for assuring adequate ties with the general medical system. In addition, community psychiatry, as do all intervention systems, needs administrative structures and arrangements for policy, planning, and social action to help it develop and protect its domain, assure support, and implement new ideas.

Community psychiatry is involved in other types of activity as well. Some community psychiatrists now have a part in designing policies and programs in secondary institutions (schools, industry, or the Peace Corps) whose aim is to maximize individual development and adjustment. Others have contributed to the formulation of broad social policy with regard, for example, to air raid drills and the search for peace.

Obviously, other social groupings and professions also enter into these realms of activity. Substantial questions have been raised as to the competence of community psychiatry in such arenas and as to whether members of the community psychiatry team could not better pursue these goals in other ways.

It may be possible, eventually, to distinguish between the activities which should be carried out under the auspices of community psychiatry and those in which the community psychiatrist should participate as expert or consultant, perhaps under other than psychiatric or even medical administrative structures. It is too soon to spell out principles for making this distinc-

---

[12] David Mechanic, "Community Psychiatry: Some Sociological Perspectives and Implications," in Roberts, *op. cit.*, 207–208.

tion, but the central question is the relevance of available professional knowledge, competence, and sanction and the sufficiency of the primary institutional context, i.e., the medical system. At many points, of course, too often unrecognized, the community psychiatry professional should be seen as acting as citizen, not expert.

Much could be said about the knowledge and competence required for any community psychiatric practice. In general, performance of *service network tasks* assumes clinical competence supplemented by a social science approach to case analysis and intervention and to organizational planning. Policy and prevention tasks, on the other hand, even when narrowly defined or when performed in support of more direct service, may not require a high level of clinical competence, but would seem to demand a mastery of the clinical knowledge unique to this medical specialty. Such knowledge would be buttressed by more emphasis on political science, organizational theory, and change theory than is needed for case services. Since, no matter which group dominates, any intervention system is manned by representatives of several professions and disciplines, these requirements, despite their breadth, are not unreasonable. However, they suggest that a broadly conceived community psychiatry requires subspecialization and recognition that some roles are not primarily for those trained only as doctors.

Shared clinical knowledge and identification with a common task enable community psychiatry staffs in the direct service network and teams in the broader assignments jointly to contribute to a total effort.

In suggesting a community psychiatry intervention system whose activities range from treatment to formulation of some aspects of public policy, we may seem to be condoning some of the definitions we rejected earlier. Focusing on the core knowledge, skills, values, and sanctions growing out of the psychiatric base, however, facilitates the designation of boundaries. The most difficult area to delimit, that involving broad policy extrapolations, will actually prove to be self-limiting as the community learns to make distinctions for itself. A psychiatrist whose practice requires some social science buttressing does not thereby become the most competent of social policy experts in all areas. A community psychiatry facility is not acceptable to the public as the major planning or policy instrument for many domains of living—despite expansive pronouncements—since most citizens consider what psychiatrists have to offer as specialized expertise in the pathological.

COMMUNITY MENTAL HEALTH

There are those who would assign all the broader so-called preventive and enhancement activities not to community psychiatry—which they see only as a professional field—but to the realm of what they would define as *community mental health*. But this designation is too vague to be practical.

To the extent that community psychiatric knowledge is the core of an intervention or action, the activities relevant to that intervention should be considered part of a community psychiatry intervention system or subsystem. The phrase "community mental health" program or activity may be more usefully employed to designate that more general coalition of people and organizations that comes together around social goals. Included are many loosely interrelated components from several intervention systems and social institutions joined together for the purpose. All of this has its significance, but it is something other than community psychiatric practice.

There are desirable forms of provision in many fields, to be sought because they enrich life and contribute to social goals and the realization of widely held values. These goals include income maintenance and provision of educational opportunities, leisure-time resources, day care and homemaker facilities, a specified level of housing, cultural opportunities, and public health protection. Each represents a projection from strongly held values and a societal definition of what people of a given era require. Each is believed to contribute to the good life. None is adequately formulated if developed only as a means of avoiding pathology, illness, and maladjustment. The prevention concept is inadequate: what should be considered are provision and enhancement.

The subgoals in these fields have been elaborated by their participants, and mutual planning is now being carried on through many formal and informal citizen and professional groupings, which may be seen as social action coalitions.

Where does psychiatry enter? The mental health movement is one of several arenas in which such reform coalitions are formed. During the nineteen-fifties, it became an increasingly popular arena for this purpose because of a general tendency in our culture to humanize and even to "psychologize" our approach to most social institutions. We stress such goals as individual adjustment, happiness, and enhancement, whereas, at one time, the only issue was adequate and efficient production.

However, just as mental health represents far more than the opposite of mental illness, this generalized movement for social betterment represents more than community psychiatry. Community psychiatrists make a contribution; but non-clinicians—informed citizens, clergymen, educators, social scientists, planners, rehabilitation personnel, and others—play their parts. The impact of primary (family) and secondary institutions (church, school, job, or club) on human adjustment and functioning is in special focus.

In this sense, the community mental health movement is just emerging, and its future is uncertain. The knowledge, skill, and acceptability of this activity should not be overestimated, nor should the number of its accomplishments. Parallel goals are to some extent defined as substantially in other fields—religion, tenant protection, civil rights, politics, adult recreation —and experiments are being carried out with organizational vehicles based on locale (neighborhood organization) rather than on professional identity. Many on the community psychiatry team utilize these other outlets in their search for contributions to the good life.

To put it in different terms, the boundaries of community mental health's preventive role are broad and inclusive. *Despite customary usage, community mental health is more a social movement or goal formulation than an intervention system.* It is one of a series of overlapping arenas in which those seeking the good life act. It has few claims to monopoly, or even to success, and its adherents wisely hedge their bets by trying a variety of outlets. There is, in fact, clear evidence that our society has moved away from this sort of approach to a social action rationale, as seen in the recent emphasis on "poverty," "urban crisis," and inequality rather than on "maladjustment." None of this need be seen as a threat to community psychiatry. Its basic task remains, since the heart of the *expertise* and know-how is in the community psychiatry system, more modestly conceived. This system seeks to establish the character of its *expertise*, or at least the domain actually assigned it, and then tries to utilize its true competence in the total range of activities.

The analysis has been presented with full appreciation of the fact that federal statutes do not define community mental health and other terms as they have been defined here or elsewhere in the relevant literature. We face inconsistency and illogic. There is, after all, a National Institute of *Mental Health* (not community psychiatry). More important, we face legislative mandates and funding incentives to states—and through states, to localities—to plan "community mental health" services. In fact, with considerable federal financial aid and conceptual guidance, planning has been carried out on this basis, funding authorized, and programming launched. And, in part because the boundary question is not resolved, there is tentativeness and confusion throughout.

"NON-MEDICAL" MODELS

It may appear to some as though this view of the boundaries question is tied unduly to the status quo, ignoring limitations in knowledge and interventive failures. On the contrary. We begin with awareness of the primitive state of knowledge of mental illness, the lack of clarity as to the meaning of prevention, the confusion of classification and diagnosis.

One might cite many authorities or research reviews: Little is definitive despite all the leads (whether genetic, fetal damage, brain damage, pathology in blood or endocrine systems, family relationships, stress, social variables, social change, or cultural factors). The lack of specificity in labeling-diagnosis is one major problem; the tendency to permit environmental components to contaminate the diagnostic process is another.[13]

Given a situation in which knowledge "is so inadequate in the field of mental disease that practical control programs are no more than conjectural,"[14] one must make strategic choices.

On the one hand, it is urgent that funding sources and research institutions give sympathetic support and aid to those who would begin with the most basic of questions about psychiatry as a social movement, about society vis-à-vis the deviant, and so on.[15] On the other, those whose immediate responsibility is to aid the currently suffering need recall that, since there are in reality many mental illnesses, not a unified disease amenable to the "presumed panacea" of individual psychotherapy, a many-faceted treatment and control strategy is appropriate.[16] The design of such strategy is a complicated matter for, as Kingsley Davis was the first to emphasize, whatever the causes of mental disease, the criteria remain social.[17] No other "disease" is so involved with interpersonal relations, vocational and social factors. None has so complex a social overlay in which the total symptom picture is

---

[13] *Causes of Mental Disorders: A Review of Epidemiological Knowledge, 1959* (New York: Milbank Memorial Fund, 1961).

[14] Richard J. Plunkett and John E. Gordon, *Epidemiology and Mental Illness* (New York: Basic Books, 1960), 17. Or note the authoritative view that "current knowledge about prevention of mental illness is roughly the same percentage of the potential whole as was the case in the prevention of communicable diseases some one hundred years ago when public health workers began their laborious climb toward efficient, scientific control." John D. Porterfield, "The Place of Primary Prevention Services," in *Programs for Community Mental Health* (New York: Milbank Memorial Fund, 1957), 185.

[15] Leonard Schatzman and Anselm Strauss, "A Sociology of Psychiatry: A Perspective and Some Organizing Foci," *Social Problems*, 14, No. 1 (Summer, 1966), 3–16.

[16] Paul Lemkau, Comment, in *Progress and Problems of Community Mental Health Services* (New York: Milbank Memorial Fund, 1959), 96–97.

[17] Kingsley Davis, "Mental Hygiene and the Class Structure," in Herman D. Stein and Richard A. Cloward, Editors, *Social Perspectives on Behavior* (Glencoe, Ill.: The Free Press, 1958), 331–340. The Davis article originally appeared in 1938.

shaped by control methods and community response (as research into social organization of mental hospitals has shown).[18]

The interventive repertoire and the experiments should range very widely. For example, there is need for far more serious investment in biological research and experimentation; early findings suggest that, at least with reference to the schizophrenias, an approach via blood chemistry may be more productive than any yet followed.

Then, there can and should be continued major emphasis, such as has developed since World War II, on that community psychiatric approach sketched above which, while based in medicine and organized along lines of a medical model, conceives of medicine broadly. Drugs may be used to relieve tension or to create the possibility for communication under the latter approaches, but the core treatment may be with reference to role, self-image, interpersonal competence, or other aspects of milieu. M. Brewster Smith sees the essence of "community mental health" in these terms:

> The . . . revolution throws off the constraints of the doctor-patient medical model—the idea that mental disorder is a *private* misery—and relates the trouble, and the cure to the entire web of social and personal relationships in which the individual is caught.[19]

Thus, whether seen as a broadly conceived medical strategy—psychoanalysis, for example, aligns itself with medicine—or as non-medical models of intervention, under community psychiatry, one would provide a full range of new and yet-to-emerge approaches.

At the outer boundaries, however, the question arises as to whether all non-medical intervention models are usefully conceived as related to community psychiatry or may be hampered by such relationship:

> It may be that mental health problems are largely problems of civic irresponsibility, and that they will diminish as new codes of behavior are clarified in conjunction with research. Mental illness is a difficulty of integration that leads to troubled and troublesome behavior. Research indicates that a comparatively small percentage of the mentally ill suffer from organic deficiencies. The significant determiners seem to lie in conflicts early in life, or in confusion and conflict resulting from later exposure to vague or contradictory norms of conduct.
>
> Some inner stress can be kept within tolerable limits by the administration of drugs. More enduring results often come from prolonged psycho-

---

[18] Alfred H. Stanton and Morris S. Schwartz, *The Mental Hospital* (New York: Basic Books, 1954).

[19] M. Brewster Smith, "The Revolution in Mental-Health Care—A 'Bold New Approach?' " *Trans-action*, 5, No. 5 (April, 1968), 19.

therapy. Symptoms can frequently be dealt with by means of group programs that bring moral pressure to bear on the nonconformer and lead to the suppression of objectionable behavior. The latter results obviously depend on the clarifying of expected norms and the mobilization of positive and negative sanctions by the social environment.[20]

Optimum progress would require that non-medical approaches be taken both under psychiatric auspices and also quite independently. Certainly, with Leonard S. Cottrell, Jr., one would wish to go well beyond community psychiatry in developing broader explanatory models for social problems and more comprehensive strategies for society.[21] There are distinct disadvantages *to launching this latter effort under a community psychiatry and community mental health banner* or, at least, in so limiting it.

The conclusions of the boundaries exploration may be summarized briefly:

☐ Mental health is a cause or movement, not an intervention system.

☐ We should, therefore, concentrate on specification and improvement of community psychiatry as an intervention system.

☐ Community psychiatry works with what it and society assign to medical intervention under the general heading of mental disorder.

☐ However, whether under an expansive view of medicine or a flexible view of community psychiatry, it is obvious that there must be room for non-medical models of intervention and non-medical professionals in the system.

☐ Even this approach has limitations and dangers. Psychiatry cannot claim to place its umbrella over all attacks on social problems and deviance. Much of social research, policy, and planning in this general realm belongs in other domains and to other professions—while psychiatry concentrates on its core treatment and control assignments.

Whether or not this view of the boundaries question is satisfactory to all, it is certainly the case that community psychiatry in the United States today, while sometimes labeled community mental health, is engaged in a large-scale, federal-state-local planning effort. The second part of the chapter explores limited aspects of that effort to highlight planning questions, with special focus on intergovernmental relations. For, community psychiatric planning shares a characteristic with many other fields: the federal structure

---

[20] Harold D. Lasswell, "Do We Need Social Observatories?" *Saturday Review*, August 5, 1967, 50.
[21] Leonard S. Cottrell, Jr., "Social Planning, the Competent Community and Mental Health," in *Urban America and the Planning of Mental Health Services* (New York: Group for the Advancement of Psychiatry, 1964), 391–402.

may attempt rational strategies, but the localization and adaptation must take place on a lower level.

PART TWO: INTERGOVERNMENTAL RELATIONS AND PLANNING

Since the early nineteen-sixties, the federal government and the various states have been engaged in a large enterprise defined as community mental health planning, although, perhaps, as we shall see, this enterprise does not meet some of the criteria for an optimum effort. For lack of systematic data, and in the light of the scope and scale of the enterprise, one may attempt only a few impressionistic highlights which contribute to general understanding of problems and choices in social planning. Some clarity may be achieved by artificial separation of several aspects and an arbitrary skipping over of others.

Major attention will therefore be directed, in sequence, to

☐ the Joint Commission on Mental Illness and Health, 1955–1960
☐ the so-called comprehensive state planning, supported by federal funds, 1963–1965
☐ the legislation to support construction and staffing of community mental health centers, 1963, 1965, 1967, and the hospital improvement grants launched in 1963
☐ the potential impact of the Congressional mandate for comprehensive health planning, 1966–1968.

The following important phases are ignored or mentioned briefly in passing:

☐ federal training, research, and demonstration grants
☐ planning and support for work in mental retardation[22]
☐ trends in the general financing of medical care and their impact on this field
☐ the transition in care from a largely public (state) to a new public-private system.

THE JOINT COMMISSION DEFINES THE TASK

The new era in United States treatment of the mentally ill began with the 1946 authorization for the establishment of the National Institute of Mental Health. From 1948 the Institute employed resources allotted it to stimulate training, research, and innovation. The first serious attack in well over one hundred years on the isolation and quarantine of mental patients was underway.

---

[22] The major boundaries issue between "mental health" and "retardation" cannot be long ignored if local wastage and fragmentation are to be controlled.

To cope more basically with this massive problem, consolidate the gains, accelerate constructive trends, seek economic means of coping, and develop overall strategy, the Congress passed the Mental Health Study Act of 1955 establishing a Joint Commission on Mental Illness and Health. An intensive study was to provide the basis for a national mental health program. Thirty-six major professional and civic organizations joined in the effort. The general report was published in 1961. Staff reports to the director were to offer the most comprehensive view of mental illness and the most complete inventory of resources available to that time.[23]

Staff, advisory committees, task forces, and consultants thus had access to an assessment of the "reality" and projections; resource, knowledge, facility, and manpower inventories; perspectives on helpful innovations and research and cost estimates. They knew where theory, knowledge, and technology were weakest—and where the repertoire had strength. Public attitudes and practices were assessed and preferences estimated. But the Joint Commission could only publish its scientific reports for the academic and professional community and offer its recommendations to the National Institute of Mental Health (informally) and to the Congress (officially). It was not a planning body in the executive branch. It could *recommend* policy and programs, but not *enact* them. In fact, as a meeting ground of many interests, it did not sharply define all alternatives or seek to shape an exact policy, leaving what proved to be serious ambiguities. Furthermore, it was a national operation in a field in which service was largely state rendered. There were no state, regional, or local committees. The Commission could not "program" except in the most general sense. Something between a study group and a legislative instrument, it went as far as it could with its sanction and typified many semi-official policy planning exercises in the American federal system. By its very nature it was best equipped to *define* the planning task and programming possibilities. As we shall see, however,

---

[23] All volumes, except the last, were published in New York by Basic Books in the years indicated. Each is a "report to the director" except for the final report, *Action for Mental Health* (1961). The latter was widely circulated in a paperback edition, but the other volumes had modest distribution:

Marie Jahoda, *Current Concepts of Positive Mental Health* (1958); Rashi Fein, *Economics of Mental Illness* (1958); George W. Albee, *Mental Health Manpower Trends* (1959); Gerald Gurin, Joseph Veroff, and Sheila Feld, *Americans View Their Mental Health* (1960); Reginald Robinson, David F. DeMarche, and Mildred K. Wagle, *Community Resources in Mental Health* (1960); Richard J. Plunkett and John E. Gordon, *Epidemiology and Mental Illness* (1960); Wesley Allinsmith and George W. Goethals, *The Role of Schools in Mental Health* (1962); Richard V. McCann, *The Churches and Mental Health* (1962). And, Morris S. Schwartz and Charlotte Green Schwartz, *Social Approaches to Mental Patient Care* (New York: Columbia University Press, 1964).

perhaps because it did not budget or program, the interpretation placed on its task perspective was not fully acceptable to those carrying direct responsibility for federal involvement.[24]

The Commission began from the fact that, despite marked improvements in some places, no group of hospital patients in the country fared so poorly as did those residing in mental hospitals, if one judged by such indices as expenditure, personnel numbers and qualifications, or patient flow.[25] In 1964, for example, the per diem expenditure per patient in 22 states was under $6.00 in mental hospitals. The general hospital per diem average was over $40.00. More moving to most Commission members, perhaps, was the fact that despite signs of improvement in the physical care of many mentally ill patients, there were still many mental hospitals which were, to use Albert Deutsch's title, *The Shame of the States*. The majority, even of those offering decent physical and, perhaps, general medical care, were essentially custodial. Eighteen percent could not meet the health and safety standards of their own state agencies; even the physical custody was inadequate! Half the patients were in hospitals housing over three thousand patients, a size which of itself seemed to defeat treatment. A "typical" patient shared a ward with fifty or more others, covering a wide range of ages and diagnoses, lacking privacy, often mistreated and provided with few meaningful activities. New therapeutic approaches, staffing patterns, and philosophies that excited psychiatric leadership had not penetrated to most mental hospitals —or were beyond their grasp for lack of funds and personnel: ". . . more than half of the patients in most State hospitals receive no active treatment of any kind designed to improve their mental condition."

Adult psychiatric clinic resources and child guidance clinics were absorbing large monetary and personnel commitments but, for the most part, did not deal with the most severely ill, with those who reached state hospitals.

---

[24] To appraise the Joint Commission as a planning operation for the purposes of this chapter is not to ignore the fact that there were those who did not so define its role—or that it may have had, in a sociological sense, the latent function of containing the middle-class orientation of the child guidance movement and private psychiatry.

Some of the problems discussed in Part One probably are the product of the effort to reconcile the middle-class, non-psychosis emphasis of such groups as the National Association for Mental Health with the concerns of those related to the state hospital system and its mass of psychotic and overwhelmingly lower-class patients. There is also the issue of interrelating the groups of psychiatrists aligned with each. As already indicated, we have arbitrarily by-passed such issues in favor of concentration on the two illustrative foci in this chapter.

Dr. Howard Freeman has helped clarify these points.

[25] The summary is an interpretation based on *Action for Mental Health*; the Commission per se did not necessarily endorse findings in all the resource volumes.

In fact, there were many community treatment resources, but each facility had its own doorways and channeling mechanisms, many of them reflecting class, ethnic, educational, and cultural "preference" and "bias." In no sense could one speak of a "system of care"—yet the problems were so complex that disjointed attacks could not possibly achieve significant effect. The perspective of ever-mounting mental hospital populations was frightening to contemplate.

One could explain the mis-treatment or non-treatment of hundreds of thousands of citizens only in terms of the dynamics of rejection. Available data plus speculation add up to the hypothesis that one tolerates much "eccentricity" in home and community and one refuses, if at all possible, to see it as mental illness.[26] Then, when the burden is heavy and the behavior of the afflicted no longer tolerable, one recognizes the deviation as mental illness and the labeling is accompanied by a desire for banishment. The dynamic answer is a remote, seldom-visited mental hospital. The family "closes ranks," achieves a new adjustment, and leaves little or no social space for the member who has been "extruded." The hospital, in turn, responding to the latent public charge to contain and to hide these "annoying" citizens, creates a neglectful and even deterrent and punitive atmosphere. Much of the mental hospital research of the nineteen-fifties disclosed that the grotesque, hostile, withdrawn, and irresponsible patterns characterizing hospitalized psychotics were products, not of the illness, in any biological or medical sense, but rather of the organizational and interpersonal milieu in which patients were "contained and the role expectations which they confronted."[27]

By the early nineteen-fifties tranquilizing drugs had begun to change the whole situation. Management became less of a problem; restraints could be decreased—and patient response to more humane treatment perceived. The psychiatric field had begun to re-learn the lessons of the "moral treatment" period late in the eighteenth and early in the nineteenth century: even if one could not "cure" mental illness, one could avoid complicating

---

[26] *Ibid.*, Chap. 3. For recent bibliography on attitudes toward the mentally ill, see the summary paper by Derek L. Phillips, "Public Identification and Acceptance of the Mentally Ill," *Journal of the American Public Health Association*, 56, No. 5 (May, 1966), 755–763. Or see Harold P. Halpert, "Surveys of Public Opinions and Attitudes About Mental Illness," *Public Health Reports*, 80, No. 7 (July, 1965), 589–597. The rejection thesis was communicated most clearly by Elaine Cumming and John Cumming, *Closed Ranks* (Cambridge, Mass.: Harvard University Press, 1957).

[27] "As hospitals become less like prisons and more like 'therapeutic communities' much of the pathology is relieved . . . ," The American Public Health Association, *Mental Disorders: A Guide to Control Methods* (New York, 1962), 2.

it and could support self-recovery in some patients. By the time the Commission had completed its work, one-third of all the hospitalized mentally ill were receiving tranquilizers, and the parallel development of "open wards," "open hospitals," and "milieu treatment" was well under way.

The Commission did not ignore efforts at prevention of mental illness and all of the psychiatric investment in early detection, treatment, and help in social agencies, schools, guidance clinics, religious institutions, and other sites. Much of its research and publication program was very broad. Nor did it minimize the need for emergency homemaker aids, child care facilities, adequate child welfare and public assistance programs. However, it saw the boundaries of basic preventive work as vague and results uncertain. Most important, *it conceptualized the planning task as one of ending the rejection of the severely mentally ill and their subsequent condemnation to long-term damaging custodial care by both the general public and the responsible professions.* Referring to "mental hygiene," where we in the previous section used the more current term "mental health," the Commission was explicit:

> We have assumed that the mental hygiene movement has diverted attention from the core problem of major mental illness. It is our purpose to redirect attention to the possibilities of improving the mental health of the mentally ill. It is not our purpose to dismiss the many [preventive] measures. . . . But our main concern here, in recommendations for a program attacking mental illness, is with varying levels of service beginning with secondary prevention—early treatment of beginning disturbance to ward off more serious illness, if possible,—and continuing through intensive and protracted treatment of the acutely and chronically ill.[28]

After elaborating in great detail how the federal government might support and accelerate the research tasks of adding to knowledge and interventive possibilities in this field, the Commission then proceeded to spell out the creation of a continuous, case-accountable, integrated service network designed to keep the majority of the mentally ill in the social mainstream if possible, avoid banishment and rejection, assure at-home or near-home brief care, and convert the typical mental hospital into a treatment facility. The basic principle guiding the development was to eliminate obviously harmful practice and to recognize that among the services of practical value were many which were simply "humane" or "social." One must take a broad view of "what constitutes and who can do treatment."

Detail is not here possible. To be included in the total approach were

---

[28] *Action for Mental Health*, 242–243.

components which were then known only to the few, but have subsequently become very familiar:

- □ emergency and acute treatment services, including home visiting and general hospital psychiatric resources
- □ expanded resources for treatment of acutely ill mental patients in community clinics, general hospitals, mental hospitals—including easy movement between and among facilities
- □ community clinics as the main line of defense to decrease the need for prolonged or repeated hospitalization—offering aftercare as well as acute services
- □ incorporation of the general hospital system into the system of care for the mentally ill by assurance of psychiatric beds and out-patient resources
- □ conversion of "smaller" state hospitals from custodial into intensive treatment centers for the mentally ill (one thousand beds or less) and concentration of all new state hospital construction on provision of "these smaller, intensive treatment centers"
- □ gradual conversion of larger mental hospitals over a ten-year period "into centers for long-term and combined care of chronic diseases, including mental illness," the theory being that long-term care cannot be eliminated, but that such approach would appropriately end separation of the mentally ill while using vocational and physical rehabilitation personnel efficiently
- □ an emphasis on short-term institutionalization, to decrease negative effects inherent in separation from family and community, minimize the closing out of the hospitalized member, and hasten adjustment in the home and community
- □ provision of many resources to support the mentally ill in the community as alternatives to or as rapid follow-up from a general and mental hospital experience for psychiatric illness: day and night hospitals, aftercare and rehabilitation services, public health psychiatric nursing services, foster family care, convalescent nursing homes, work programs, expatient groups, contacts with volunteers
- □ a public information program to convey knowledge and understanding of mental illness and to support the treatment expansion needed (rather than focus on "prevention," an elusive goal which seems to divert attention from the ill who need help).

These, in brief, were to be the directions. Costs and manpower requirements were estimated on the assumption of national quantitative targets for mental health centers, hospitals, and so on—and on the premise of a new funding pattern. Implicit was to be the restoration of care of the mentally ill to the mainstream of medical practice; for example, voluntary admission should become the preferred method of entering psychiatric services and court commitment the exception. To implement a practice of maintaining the mentally ill as family members and citizens and to end the philosophy of "casting out" it would be necessary at each phase to emphasize *local* responsibility in the face of a century-long tradition that the state, not the locality, was accountable for the mentally ill.

The Commission's report was affirmed by 42 members and repudiated by none. Three added partial dissents, with one member questioning particularly the proposal that large mental hospitals be converted into centers of long-term care for all types of chronically ill patients. The report closed with a recommendation that a group be assigned the task of writing legislation and specifying standards.

STATE PLANNING AS COMMUNITY ORGANIZATION

Action for Mental Health was presented to the Congress in December, 1960. The President appointed a Cabinet-level committee to make recommendations to him. An ad hoc committee, which had been appointed by the Surgeon General in response to requests from state authorities for guidelines for state planning, submitted its final report in January, 1961, having utilized some of the documentation prepared for the Commission.[29] It said, ". . . each state must approach its planning individually." The pressure for more detailed, state-level planning continued and was expressed at conferences of state mental health authorities and the 1962 Governors' Conference. The Congress responded in the Appropriations Acts for the Department of Health, Education, and Welfare. The states were granted $4.2 million for fiscal 1963, and a similar sum was added later for fiscal 1964 to develop state plans. Such plans were to be available by September, 1965. It was to be a one-time effort, at least in so far as federal funds were committed.

The outcome was a large, national community organization effort in mental health, plus a modest degree of specific policy planning and programming in a few states.

The federal guidelines called for development of comprehensive programs which would "provide a broad spectrum of mental health services emphasizing a continuum of care, . . . coordination among all relevant community resources, . . . prevention of mental illnesses, and . . . promotion of mental health."[30] There was no stand on the "task" definition of the Joint Com-

---

[29] *Planning of Facilities for Mental Health Services*, Report of the Surgeon General's Ad Hoc Committee on Planning for Mental Health Facilities, Public Health Service Publication No. 808 (Washington, D.C.: Government Printing Office, 1961).

[30] National Institute of Mental Health, "Guidelines for the Federal Grant-in-Aid Program to Support Mental Health Planning," January, 1963.

mission. States were told that the planning should consider prevention, diagnosis, treatment, rehabilitation, education, and consultation and should attend to services in institutions and in the community and be concerned with all age groups. Mental health components of social problems were deemed relevant (aging, alcoholism, delinquency, etc.). Research, training, legislation, financing, equipment, and personnel were all considered appropriate topics. Public-voluntary and interdepartmental coordination were emphasized. And, as a starting point, "States were encouraged to assess population, needs and resources, identifying gaps so that program objectives [might] . . . be selected, priorities among these objectives determined, methods chosen, and resources allocated."

In applying for the planning funds, states specified a variety of structures for planning and many different patterns were acceptable. In effect, the mandate was to take the Joint Commission study group approach down to the state level and to widen the participation of professionals and citizens. There was no precedent to decree that one structure was more adequate than another. Many states set up regional and local committees and task forces. Citizen participation was more easily assured than expert professional staffing. Interdepartmental committees and study groups were activated. In 22 states the governors were more or less involved.

When the process had ended one could point to

- □ the participation of over 25,000 citizens
- □ over 400 federally-financed staff members for the process
- □ a considerable amount of survey work and inventorying
- □ a variety of special studies
- □ hundreds of "recommendations"
- □ a small number of interdepartmental planning and coordinating structures
- □ increased planning activity in this field in some states
- □ final reports to Washington from all but one state.

But it was also clear that the process was in most places one of involvement, education, communication, and coordination, rather than long-term planning in a formal sense. Throughout the country, constituencies were created or mobilized for psychiatric services. Governors and legislators in many states were impressed with the degree of public support generated and appropriations were thereby affected. States in some instances subdivided and regionalized their territories for planning purposes, a long-term gain for subsequent programming. Ongoing public and voluntary efforts to create new service forms were encouraged and supported by the overall process.

Many of the assets of the process were in the community organization and political, rather than formal, planning aspects. Few of the state reports stated a clear conception of the task and even fewer went from policy to programming. There was little quantification and specification of goals and only rarely precise scheduling. The few exceptions were outstanding: states with planning units, which built upon the community organization and produced five- or ten-year plans. Even here, the major influence was either a state's previous legislative and planning experience or the subsequent mental health center and hospital improvement legislation described below, not the planning grants per se.

Where serious, specific planning was attempted, unresolved questions arose as to respective state and local prerogatives: was the local board a state instrument, "localizing" the services in a restricted sense—or was there to be true decentralization? If the latter, where would the locality obtain funds? Few localities could do more than advise, request, or recommend.

Thus, in effect, the planning grants of 1963 and 1964 filled the gap between the stance of the Joint Commission and general levels of knowledge and commitment. Ideas were communicated, groups organized, problems noted. The national leadership had not been prepared truly to mandate or encourage executive-level planning in the states, nor were the states to receive "free" funds to implement such planning.[31] All available internal National Institute of Mental Health documentation suggests that what was sought was localization and variation *on centrally articulated themes* and not a fully elaborated planning process. Nowhere was there much confidence in the capacities of most states to cope alone or anew with the basic issues confronted by the Joint Commission. Nor did states show any readiness to turn block grants over to regions or localities. The states, in fact, were not urged to do more than identify themselves in the most general sense with the Commission perspectives on the need to update care of the mentally ill and to strengthen prevention. Although *Action for Mental Health* was cir-

---

[31] The state planning process has not been systematically studied. Several summaries, largely the work of Dorothea L. Dolan of the National Institute of Mental Health, are available: "State Mental Health Planning Grant Proposals, 1963," *Digest* (National Clearinghouse for Mental Health Information, Department of Health, Education, and Welfare); "Progress Reports on State Mental Health Planning, 1964," *ibid.*, 1964 (Washington, D.C.: Government Printing Office, 1964); *State Recommendations in Final Reports on Comprehensive Mental Health Planning* (Washington, D.C.: National Institute of Mental Health, 1966, mimeographed). The reports are filed with the National Institute of Mental Health. For an ambitious, printed state report see New York's six-volume *A Plan for a Comprehensive Mental Health and Mental Retardation Program for New York State* (Albany: Department of Mental Hygiene, 1965).

culated widely, it is doubtful that the other report volumes were reviewed by many of those who led or participated in the state process. Furthermore, as we shall see, higher priority directives arrived from Washington before the planning had gone very far.

MENTAL HEALTH CENTERS AND HOSPITAL IMPROVEMENT: INITIATIVE AT THE TOP

Centers

A casual reader might have seen in *Action for Mental Health* a general plea for new perspectives on curability and control of mental illness; a strategy to end "rejection"; and a series of proposals to strengthen local services, including those in general hospitals, so as to eliminate or decrease long-term custodial hospitalization of the mentally ill. As has been noted, however, "one can find what he wants somewhere in the manuscript of the final document" because this is a very extensive committee report.[32] To the National Institute leadership and to state mental health authorities, debating as to the relative balance to be struck between an investment in improving state mental hospitals and a more basic thrust to build a community-based mental health service system, the "main emphasis of the report was on the upgrading of the state mental hospital system to a therapeutic level."[33] And this was an error in the view of federal leadership.

National Institute of Mental Health personnel, working with the Cabinet Committee, were able to convince the Administration that the Joint Commission had been wrong. A more radical departure, something likely to cut the rate of hospitalization, was needed: "After a year they emerged with the mental health center as the bold new approach."[34] The White House staff debated the relative merits of a state mental hospital or a community mental health center emphasis in a federal program. It explored costs, financing, staffing, and relationships. To those on the "inside," President Kennedy's historic Presidential message on mental health and mental retardation in February, 1963, was a rebuttal of the Joint Commission. The theme with reference to the mentally ill was clear (for present purposes,

---

[32] Dr. Bertram S. Brown, Chief, Community Mental Health Facilities Branch of National Institute of Mental Health, "The Impact of the New Federal Mental Health Legislation on the State Mental Hospital System," presented before the Northeast State Governments' Conference, 1964, mimeographed.

[33] *Ibid.*

[34] *Ibid.*

we ignore the mental retardation sections of the message and of subsequent legislation):

> If we launch a broad new mental health program now, it will be possible within a decade or two to reduce the number of patients now under custodial care by 50 percent or more. Many more mentally ill can be helped to remain in their own homes without hardship to themselves or their families. Those who are hospitalized can be helped to return to their own communities. All but a small proportion can be restored to useful life. We can spare them and their families much of the misery which mental illness now entails. We can save public funds, and we can conserve our manpower resources. . . .
>
> . . . reliance on the cold mercy of custodial isolation will be supplanted by the open warmth of community concern and capability. Emphasis on prevention, treatment and rehabilitation will be substituted for a desultory interest in confining patients in an institution to wither away.[35]

The new thrust did not "reject" the mental hospital as a program component, but was an effort to create a new hub for the system. Local and immediately-available resources were to respond to psychiatric need and, encompassing all necessary components (prevention, diagnosis, out-patient and in-patient treatment facilities, rehabilitation, education, consultation), were to seek a major breakthrough. The emphasis was on an integrated complex of facilities and services. A community mental health center (CMHC) was to be a *function*, not a *place*. Two thousand centers would be sought over a ten-to-fifteen-year period. To emphasize the new outlook, there were to be special inducements to affiliate centers with or locate them in general hospitals. Psychiatry would be restored to general medicine, just as the mentally ill were to be returned to the human community.

In passing the Mental Retardation Facilities and Community Mental Health Centers Construction Act late in 1963, the Congress endorsed this new perspective (P.L. 88–164). Up to $150 million was authorized for a three-year period beginning July, 1964, to *construct* approximately 145 community mental health centers.[36] To qualify, a state was to submit an overall state mental health center plan, which designated a single agency to administer the plan, provided an advisory council, set up a construction program, and specified a system to determine priorities. Then, individual

---

[35] The basic data about hospitalization trends and costs, about the inadequacy of mental hospitals, and the case for "maintaining the patient in contact with his home and total environment [to] . . . accelerate his recovery" are summarized in Robert H. Felix, "Breakthrough in Mental Illness," *Health, Education, and Welfare Indicators*, November, 1963, xxlv–xlvi. Dr. Felix was then Director of the National Institute of Mental Health.

[36] The 1967 three-year extension authorized another $180 million. (P.L. 90–31).

project applications could be forwarded to Washington for approval through the designated state agency.

On the surface, the ongoing comprehensive state planning process was to be relied upon. Indeed, the second state comprehensive planning appropriation of $4.2 million was also authorized by the Eighty-eighth Congress. However, in effect, the states perceived clearly that Congress had made a critical decision. There were now funds for centers. The inevitable occurred. The visibility of centers increased in state planning. Planning staffs were diverted from the comprehensive effort to permit states to apply for center funds; the states were being "told," at least symbolically, that they could *program* centers—but that the fundamental policy planning had been done. States, in turn, had to convey a similar message to localities. Some of them thus developed state-wide community mental health center plans in the executive branch, apart from the ongoing mental health planning process described in the previous section.

The theory had been that the output of comprehensive state mental health planning could and would suggest the national specifications for the centers and for the related rules and regulations. The law stated quite specifically that a state's mental health center plan was to be "consistent with the comprehensive mental health planning of the state." But with appropriations made and time pressures facing the administrative apparatus, the National Institute of Mental Health took its cues from the Cabinet committee and the previously completed staff work. State "comprehensive planning" reports were after the fact. Centers were the major component —whether or not state planners so concluded. On the critical question of the elements of a community mental health center there was no waiting for the states' contribution. To qualify for federal funds a center had to include the following as "essential elements": in-patient services; out-patient services; partial hospitalization services, to include at least a day hospital; 24-hour emergency services; consultation and education services.[37] Where the new facility itself would not offer all these components, it was called upon to demonstrate that it was part of a community program that did include all of them. Not mandated but also sought in the total program, if not in the facility to be constructed, were: diagnostic services, rehabilitation services, community pre-care and aftercare (foster homes, home visiting, halfway houses), training, research, and evaluation.

The designers of the approach, well aware of the spectacular increase in numbers of out-patient clinics from 600 in the nineteen-fifties to 1,500 by

---

[37] P.L. 88–164, part 54.212.

1963, were determined to fashion an out-patient system that would not ignore the potential mental hospital patient. Acquainted with innovations in day and night hospitals, rehabilitation services, emergency aid, home care, and the like, the planners recognized, too, that current service-delivery modes left all of these innovations as fragmented entities, not as components of an integrated strategy for each case. Their view of the center, then, was in context of a desire to achieve a service-delivery system oriented toward accountability, integration, and responsibility. A requirement that a center serve a specific geographic area (with a population of from 75,000 to 200,000) was designed to end the "picking and choosing" of "hopeful," "motivated," or "cooperative" cases, which seemed always to close out the very ill. Continuity of care was a constant theme. Patient-centered, not system-centered, organization was stressed.[38]

Later, many would argue that a distillation of state experience would have classified differently the essential and the recommended components. Certainly, to the point of the writing of the regulations, "not a single facility exemplifying the community mental health center [had] . . . been subjected to rigorously controlled investigation.[39] In fact, the consensus four and a half years after the Kennedy message was that the "pure type" community mental health center which was posited in law and regulation did not yet exist.

As an aside, one might also note that the choice of the word *center* was at the very least unfortunate if a new *function* was sought, since "it evokes the image of physical structures."[40] The intent was to construct those buildings (facilities) actually needed to complete a center (service system). But the impact of the word chosen, plus considerable legislative specification with reference to the construction aspects of the physical facilities needed for the centers, had the inevitable consequence: there was much

---

[38] For a perspective on the National Institute's thinking, see Ruth I. Knee, "A Conceptual and Practical Approach to Community Mental Health—The Social Worker's Role" (Washington, D.C.: National Institute of Mental Health, 1967, mimeographed). Also Robert H. Felix, "A Model for Comprehensive Mental Health Centers," *Journal of the American Public Health Association*, 54, No. 12 (December, 1964), 1964–1969.

[39] Raymond M. Glasscote *et al.*, *The Community Mental Health Center: An Analysis of Existing Models* (Washington, D.C.: Joint Information Service, 1964), 11.

[40] *Ibid.*, 10. Also see Raymond Glasscote and Charles Kanno, *Comprehensive Psychiatric Programs: A Survey of 234 Facilities* (Washington, D.C.: Joint Information Service, undated [1963?]). The Joint Information Service, publisher of the two paperbound reports here cited, is a service of the American Psychiatric Association and the National Association for Mental Health.

preoccupation with the creation of new service locations and perhaps far less grasp of the essence of the functions and the strategy for their implementation.

To an extent, another reality may have made this inevitable. The federal government traditionally did not provide the states with funds to operate facilities for patients, and legislators did not propose to do so in this instance. Congress deleted proposals for operational grants. Thus, in specifying "essential elements" the National Institute was using a construction grant to achieve a program objective—there being no program money. When it responded to further urging a year later, the Congress approved funding for initial staffing of the centers (P.L. 89–105). Here, too, the directive sought to introduce program objectives. In short, this was largely a construction program, with the NIMH staff constantly seeking to use construction-money incentives to achieve program goals and to add staffing funds for similar reasons. There was awareness that the construction grants might become the National Institute of Mental Health equivalent of post office construction funds, sought for many extraneous reasons, and that, if the center concept were lost, the new facilities could become, in the nineteen-seventies, the new custodial network within community psychiatry.

The three-year, $150-million mental health center construction authorization of 1963 (federal share of 1/3 to 2/3) was joined by staffing authorization totaling $7.5 million in P.L. 89–105 of 1965 ($19.5 million for 1965, $29.5 million for 1966, $34 million for 1967, $37 million for 1968). A deceasing scale of 75 to 30 percent reimbursement was specified (continuation grants would extend to 1972).[41] Funding for staffing could be requested simultaneously with construction funds, but the majority of applicants were not prepared to do so. State authorities were expected to screen an application before it was processed by the regional office and in Washington.

Hospital improvement

But this was not to be the entire federal program. There were those who challenged the community mental health center strategy from the start. Not that they opposed the new community services and philosophy—but how did one know that these would decrease the flow to state hospitals? Did one not need to give priority to the .5 million people actually in such hospitals at one time, or to the 1.6 million receiving some form of in-patient

---

[41] The 1967 extension added $58 million to the authorization and substituted 1970 as the cut-off date for new grants.

or out-patient services in public mental hospitals in 1962?[42] Might it not be that untapped need for out-patient and preventive service would simply fill up the centers' caseloads without affecting the hospitals? Besides, under any perspective, would there not be hundreds of thousands of people in state mental hospitals for a long time; should one not do something about them? One might project 2,000 centers, but the Congress had appropriated money for only 145, and even these would take years to get into effective operation and would then require considerable yet-to-be-voted state appropriations, while populations would still be growing and released patients be returning to hospitals in large numbers. Finally, could mental health centers really work if one did not stimulate the simultaneous reform of mental hospitals to become part of the total system? There can be no center in the sense conceived without an intensive in-patient treatment program as one component.

Having achieved its goal of shifting the locus of new endeavor to the mental health center, the National Institute of Mental Health was willing to take advantage of a variety of positive political factors and to encourage the same session of Congress to enact what became the modest Hospital Improvement Grant Program. In this context hospital reform could be shaped to the overall purposes which had resulted in the center emphasis. The appropriations—to be contrasted with authorization for the centers —were, for fiscal 1964, $6 million; fiscal 1965, $12 million. The expectation was a $6-million increase annually to a rate of $36 million for fiscal 1969. The average annual award per institution would be about $83,000; and, by 1969, all eligible institutions for the mentally ill listed in 1966, some 430 in number, would have been covered.[43] No support could exceed ten years.

What was expected of these grants? First, we might note, the program was not new. Amendments in 1956 to the National Mental Health Act had created the so-called "Title V grants," enabling the National Institute to fund, through direct project grants, "experiments, demonstrations, studies and research projects," which would improve the care of the mentally ill. By late 1963, several hundred such projects were being supported. Increas-

---

[42] Statistics and trends are summarized and sources cited in Wilbur J. Cohen et al., "New Approaches to Mental Retardation and Mental Illness," Health, Education, and Welfare Indicators, November, 1963, xv–xxxiii. Also see Morton Kramer, Some Implications of Trends in the Usage of Psychiatric Facilities for Community Mental Health Programs and Related Research, Public Health Service Publication No. 1434 (Washington, D.C.: Government Printing Office, 1966).

[43] By 1968, this had become an unrealistic perspective.

ingly significant numbers of the projects had been directed to "open door" and "open ward" hospital experiments, to work on the "therapeutic milieu," to new staffing patterns, to rehabilitation and aftercare—indeed, to the redefinition of the mental hospital as a component in the community service system. The new program converted administrative practice into Congressional policy, increased substantially the level of funding, and offered a time perspective.

Over the next several years, guidelines and directives were to emphasize treatment, training, and rehabilitation for the long-stay, more severely ill patients. Some hospitals concentrated on the creation or improvement of treatment services for special groups (children or the aged); others "broke down" large hospitals and experimented with reorganizing large units into sub-units serving specified geographic areas and coordinated with local community clinic services.[44] There was much attention to introduction of new therapeutic program elements into custodial settings of long standing which had offered no possibility of individualization in the past: milieu therapy, educational programs, day and night hospitals, work therapy, family treatment, and individual psychotherapy.

The Hospital Improvement Program (HIP) was on a small scale in comparison to the centers program and was not a basic support enterprise. The federal strategy was to employ a project approach to achieve maximum change with a relatively small investment, adding up to less than 5 percent of state hospital budgets at the most ($10 million of federal funds were defining directions for $300 million of state funds). Parallel legislation for support of mental hospital in-service training (IT), also passed in 1963, was to back up the effort. This program, with a maximum grant of $25,000 per hospital per year, was assigned $3.3 million for the first year. Both HIP and IT grantees have assigned the bulk of their funds to salaries for new positions.

The NIMH leadership's long-term perspective on the Hospital Improvement Program had been reflected in the 1963 message from President Kennedy

> Until the Community Mental Health Centers Program develops fully, it is imperative that the quality of care in existing State mental institutions be improved. By strengthening their therapeutic services, by becoming open institutions serving their local communities, many such institutions can perform a valuable transitional role. The Federal Government can assist

---

[44] Milbank Memorial Fund, *Decentralization of Psychiatric Services and Continuity of Care* (New York, 1962). Also Ernest M. Gruenberg, *Evaluating the Effectiveness of Mental Health Services* (New York: Milbank Memorial Fund, 1966).

materially by encouraging State mental institutions to undertake intensive demonstration and pilot projects to improve the quality of care, and to provide inservice training for personnel manning these institutions.[45]

The key departure from the Joint Commission's stance, as seen by those at the federal policy end, was a general effort to support those aspects of hospital improvement which would convert the state hospitals from the sole or the major resources in their respective states into components "of a larger network or system." Workshops, conferences, and consultations, through which NIMH staff aided in the preparation of Hospital Improvement and In-Service Training applications by the institutions, highlighted efforts to reshape hospitals until they were easily entered and left, hopeful about their patients, and often well integrated with local day and night facilities, out-patient help, general medical care, private psychiatry, aftercare, and rehabilitation.[46]

Individual institutions prepare their own HIP applications, after utilizing available consultation; however, an application must be accompanied by an endorsement from the administrator of the state agency responsible for the institution. Such endorsement must specify how the proposed improvement project is integrated into and coordinated with the agency's overall planning and with the state's comprehensive planning for mental health (and retardation). Regional NIMH staff offers consultation to individual hospitals and to state agencies, but applications are processed by staff in Washington. In effect, the mechanism creates opportunities for state, for institutions, and for local leadership, within the framework of general federal philosophy, and strives for coordination of hospital improvement and community mental health centers. Several years of experience have revealed a flexible federal stance. Although the federal preference is to see the improved hospital as a center component and not to convert a hospital per se into a community mental health center locus, in actual practice:

---

[45] Quoted in Brown, *op. cit.*, 8.

[46] By contrast, British community psychiatry, which concentrates on psychotic patients, is built around extended activities of mental hospitals which secure the cooperation of the local health authority and the general practitioners in the area. Services are hospital directed and concentrate on treatment, rehabilitation, and follow-up. The out-patient clinic or center has not become the locus. Richard W. Anderson, "British Community Psychiatry and its Implications for American Planning," *Community Mental Health Journal*, 1, No. 3 (Fall, 1965), 223–232. Many American reforms were in the same direction prior to 1963, and some of those who reacted negatively to President Kennedy's message favored the facing of the hospital toward the community, while it served as fulcrum of an in-patient, out-patient, and ex-patient system.

Some grants focus on the hospital, not on the system. Such grants assume that large hospitals will be with us for a long time, but that the custodial and often dehumanizing atmosphere should be eliminated and the treatment accessibility of those long-term patients and new arrivals who are able to respond should be maximized.

Some grants are premised on assuring that the hospital becomes a treatment component in a community-oriented system.

Some Hospital Improvement grants are premised on converting state hospitals into nuclei of community mental health centers for their areas.

To eradicate that organizational separatism which might perpetuate the custodial, "dumping-ground," conception of hospitals, NIMH designated one overall administrative unit to provide help and leadership to the two major program components:

> The Clinical Facilities Section is the focal point within the Institute for study of trends in mental hospitals, community mental health programs and for planning and initiating programs designed to improve the quality of care provided in public mental hospitals, to create and expand community alternatives to hospitalization, and to facilitate the integration of mental hospitals and other treatment facilities into the broader and more comprehensive community mental health programs. *Currently, the highest priority for the Section, in the achievement of the goals of the national mental health program, is the exploration of approaches to the improvement of mental hospitals and the on-going implementation of the Hospital Improvement Project Grant Program.*[47]

Administrative practice thus blurred the 1963 debate: it did not have to be *either* hospitals *or* centers, even though centers were planned on a major scale and HIP as a minor note.[48] Yet, to a degree, sub-units, within NIMH, tended to reflect some of the initial differences and preferences. It was not clear just how much integration of planning occurred in the states either. There was evidence of both token and serious application clearances with relation to overall state plans, of unified and of separated administration auspices for the two components. Planning logic was upset (but estimates are not possible as to quantitative frequency) where mental hospitals continued to be state operated and mental health centers were the responsibili-

---

[47] Internal National Institute of Mental Health document, February 1, 1965. The unit was no longer operative after further reorganization in 1968. The coordination objective remains.

[48] The process remains a dynamic one. By mid-1968 HIP grants were leveling off, earlier projections seemed excessive and the centers could be seen as the only "real" thrust. Furthermore, the effects of Medicare and Medicaid funds on the states were such as to decrease considerably the leverage of the limited HIP grants vis-à-vis state planning.

ties of local government or private organizations. Also, as William Ryan has noted, the extensive community mental health board system, in many states the vehicle for locally-based community services, was neither administratively nor operationally tied in any formal fashion to state hospital operations.[49]

In short, the basic National Institute of Mental Health policy was pervasive. Community mental health center funding and promotion had become by far the major agency activity. Efforts of state hospitals to become mental health centers were discouraged and general hospitals were encouraged. Unlike Great Britain's, the United States program assumed that secondary prevention was known to be effective in relation to severe mental illness, and there was no longer presumptive need for hospital-based medical treatment for all psychotics. Relatively more attention was being assigned neurotic and nonpsychotic patients than the Joint Commission had apparently contemplated. The Joint Commission's notions about the eventual merger of state hospitals with other services for the chronically ill were abandoned in favor of a view that some percentage of the severely ill (perhaps 15 percent, it was thought in 1967) might require long-term hospitalization and that the facilities would be needed for such special groups as alcoholics and narcotics addicts, too. The state hospital made considerably smaller (with shifts occurring several times in estimates of optimum size) would be converted to fill this role.

To some extent during the first several years, the perspectives became more tentative than the rhetoric of 1963 suggested, as staff faced the fact that there was little firm information. General hospital psychiatric patients were increasing in numbers to the point where they exceeded populations resident in state hospitals; but were these the same patients? There was significant evidence that the group constituting the long-time custodial load in state hospitals was much under-represented in general hospitals.[50] Similarly, while evidence from specific places was impressive, with reference to the characteristics of center populations as contrasted with traditional out-patient clinics, it was not known whether the center caseloads as a whole were truly integrated with or similar to mental hospital loads. There was some concern that the old selectivities were still operative. Emphasis was

---

[49] William Ryan, "State-Local Relationships in Community Mental Health" (Boston: Massachusetts Committee on Children and Youth, 1967, mimeographed).

[50] Morton Kramer, "Epidemiology, Biostatistics, and Mental Health Planning," in Russell R. Monroe, Gerald D. Klee, Eugene B. Brody, Editors, *Psychiatric Epidemiology and Mental Health Planning* (Washington, D.C.: American Psychiatric Association, 1967), 15–23.

placed on obtaining adequate "patient-flow" data but this would not be readily made available.

The available statistical data continued to show declines in the average daily resident patient population of state hospitals. Analysis revealed such declines to be the product of increases in net releases (not reductions in admissions or excessive increases in deaths).[51] However, one could not apportion the trend among increased use of more effective drugs, new state hospital philosophies or programs, and the impact of centers. Furthermore, whatever the causes, the developing rates of decline would not achieve President Kennedy's goal of a 50-percent decrease in the mental hospital population by 1973 or 1983—and it was not clear whence new leverage could be sought.[52]

Legislators and officials often must rely on less basic evidence. By many "external" criteria the program has "taken" successfully: numbers of applications filed, building or program improvements inaugurated, range of proposals, training programs initiated, consultation used.

From a planning perspective one notes again that the major initiative was and is federal: within definable parameters, localities and states may program and give vent to "creativity" involving limited federal funds. The NIMH facilitates conferences, workshops, and visits to stimulate state and local innovation and adaptation within the framework supplied. Since the states are paying most of the bill for mental illness, they actually have great autonomy, but the small federal increment has proven to be very potent. What began as comprehensive state planning has quickly become programming for community mental health center and hospital improvement programs, placed in state planning frameworks. To the extent that a state had sought federal funds or respected federal leadership—and most states apparently did—it did not have an open-end planning situation. Nor was there evidence that many states wanted more autonomy. There was no sign of stifled creativity or of fine initiatives lost. There was some evidence of formal compliance for funding, followed by considerable operational independence. There was also some degree of autonomy in the larger states that had previously set their own direction (California and New York, for example). For those favoring strong federal policy and program initiatives, the pattern was quite satisfactory. Such supporters, in fact, tended to consider that the policy was not clear enough and that the need to provide geographic balance in center and hospital improvement

---

[51] *Ibid.*

[52] *Ibid.* There was a 20 percent decline from 1957 to 1967.

allocations and to distribute to each state at least the minima assigned blunted the edge of the federal programs as instruments of change.[53]

One aspect of the difference between the center and hospital improvement programs, subject to a variety of interpretations, may be worthy of note in a discussion of planning strategy. Hospital improvement requires no local matching, involves modest sums, and assures each complying hospital access to a grant. The center program demands an increasing local commitment, with the federal share tapering off rapidly, but it offers large sums. Both programs are in a project-grant format: there are one or more federal reviews and quite detailed guidelines.

The small number of states equipped to define the planning task for themselves, to analyze trends, and to experiment did wonder if the federal activity really encouraged state planning or utilized modest subsidies to divert it. Dr. Paul Hoch had spoken for them early in 1963 in response to President Kennedy's message; backing the broad purposes of the new approach to mental illness, Hoch still questioned the predetermined objective, the community mental health center, which seemed to negate the utility of a state planning process. Would such centers truly replace mental hospitals? Did projections really support the expectation of a 50-percent decrease in census in such hospitals? Should not one take the chronicity of severe mental illness into account; 80 percent of such patients may respond to modern drugs and related therapies, but half of these will relapse. Should one assume, in the modern urban environment, that families could tolerate the disruptive behavior of the psychotic at home? What basis was there for the National Institute's "premise" that all acute cases can be treated, that chronic cases are "hopeless," that one should therefore invest so heavily in services for the acutely ill? Federal funding was limited and of limited duration, and too inflexible to serve state purposes; nor was it clear that all federal funds would channel through the official state agencies.[54]

Others went even further, asking if the federal definition of the planning task, whether in the Joint Commission version or in the subsequent legislation, was not tied to premises relevant in some cultural environments but not necessarily universal: would all relatives re-admit the mentally ill; would all general practitioners play their assigned roles?[55]

---

[53] A somewhat different perspective on planning questions raised by the federal program is offered in Elizabeth R. Smith, "Current Issues in Mental Health Planning," *Community Mental Health Journal*, 2, No. 1 (Spring, 1966), 73–77.

[54] Paul Hoch, *Mental Hygiene News* (Albany, New York: New York State Department of Mental Hygiene, April and December, 1963).

[55] Elaine and John Cumming, "Some Questions on Community Care," *Canada's Mental Health*, XIII, No. 6 (November–December, 1965), 7–12.

The United States effort was based on a definition of the task rooted in a humanistic ethic, but not scientifically validated. Project planning and a categorical approach had limited the states' choices. Yet, as never before, the rituals of planning were very much in the picture. How should this be assessed?

INTERGOVERNMENTAL RELATIONS AND PLANNING

The basic issues are more profound than the mental health center–hospital debate. Planning in the field of community mental health encompasses a situation in which there was and is considerable federal interest in promoting planning and in advocating new program emphases. Success depends on state-local involvement and investment. The question arises as to whether the two motives are compatible. There is, at this writing, no basis for final evaluation of the process by any fundamental criteria related to the welfare of the ill and the disturbed. Nor are all the returns in as yet from the viewpoints of community organization or rational planning theory. However, examined as a "case," the twenty-year segment of federal-state-local interplay does serve to define and illuminate a number of significant issues and to clarify some possibilities.

The Joint Commission did all of the "homework" quite exhaustively, defined the planning task somewhat ambiguously, and suggested a Congressional strategy. A Cabinet committee, supporting the dominant National Institute of Public Health viewpoint, advised somewhat different emphases to the President. Out of this came the legislation for community mental health center construction, which utilized grants for facilities as leverage to shape service operations, and the legislation for Hospital Improvement, redefining the state mental hospital as a component of a new kind of psychiatric service system. The former effort was also supported by staffing grants and the latter by in-service training grants. In short, a federal study group had been followed (and partially negated) by executive level planning and Congressional action. Much of that activity referred to the Joint Commission as point of departure and sanction, nonetheless.

As part of this process, the states received $8.4 million for one-time planning activity, which was expected to contribute to the national process of policy development and programming, but did not do so on any large scale. Nor was state activity detailed, disciplined, or specific enough to be described as state *programming* in the context of national policy. What, then, was it? What should state-level planning be, in a federal system, in a field like community mental health?

The reports seem clear that, within the context of national policy, the so-called state planning process was, at its best, a successful community organization effort: educating, motivating, winning support. It probably was more than worth the funds, as viewed from any perspective. And because, when the limits of the general national policy were tested, they were actually found to be quite flexible and somewhat opportunistic, a few states used planning funds to go their own way and many merely complied superficially with the national policy directive. But, except for several well-staffed states which were embarked on their own program, there was extraordinarily little systematic planning on the state and local level, and it is far from clear that there should or could have been.

In the American federal system, some programs are federally operated directly (Old Age, Survivors, Disability and Health Insurance) and some are state and local operations under clear and specific federal policy, which allows some previously submitted and approved local options and variations at the program level (public assistance for various categories). In many other fields, however, there are no ongoing operational funds or there are limited grants of operational and staffing funds, perhaps capital construction aid, and often project monies. In such fields there tends to be an emphasis on localization, decentralization, and lower-level planning. Community mental health planning is illustrative, but one might point as well to vocational rehabilitation, services to the aging, the anti-poverty program, or the activities from 1961 through 1964 of the President's Committee on Delinquency and Youth Crime.

Here there are difficult choices. One might apply to the federal-state relationship equally well Ryan's formulation of the dilemma with reference to state and local roles:

> The arguments for resting primary responsibility at the state level are simple and compelling: efficiency and uniformity. From the administrative point of view, it is unquestionably more efficient to have a state-wide authority, with a small number of high-quality staff persons charged with developing and maintaining local programs. Ideally, such a centrally administered program should be less costly and should insure standards of quality in local services. In addition, centralization can more effectively guarantee that local services conform to current concepts and, perhaps even more important, can act to insure an even distribution of services to all parts of the state.
>
> Decentralized responsibility for operating community mental health programs is justified on different grounds: responsiveness and involvement. The argument here is that locally administered services can be tailored to meet the particular pattern of local needs and can respond more swiftly and effectively to changes in local conditions. Furthermore, resting responsibility at the local level insures the very important element of local involvement.

The philosophy underlying decentralization can be simply stated: a community mental health program should be, not only *in* the community, but an integral part *of* the community.[56]

True localization or decentralization would provide block funds (lump sums) or formula grants on the assurance of some state planning, but would avoid imposing very detailed definitions of the planning task or specific programming. Yet this can occur only if (*a*) the federal government decides as a general matter of policy to return a specific portion of tax revenue funds to the states, as proposed by Walter Heller and others, or (*b*) if there is sufficient faith in local decision-making or conviction about its importance to justify the risk of the relatively uncontrolled block or formula grants for specific fields of activity. Occasionally, as in the instance of the anti-poverty effort enacted in 1964, the latter condition has prevailed. The program may mandate grants based on the most general statements of local intent, on the assumption that the problem-to-be-solved demands local freedom to plan. Of course, in the anti-poverty instance, Congress had begun by 1966 to impose restrictions and to assign increasingly large proportions of Community Action Program monies to specified activities. By 1967 Congress was engaged in a debate as to whether localities should be allowed any Community Action monies not specifically assigned to defined program categories. (*See Chapter II.*)

For the most part, when it enacts a program, Congress also legislates a definition of the task, which is recorded and available in the legislative history and which shapes the guidelines prepared by the federal bureaucracy. In other words, Washington staff are to do more than write checks. Indeed, if the Congress did not follow such an approach, major question would arise about its sense of responsibility.

Does this, then, mean that all reference to lower-level planning is pretense in those fields in which Congress has not decided to distribute funds on a no-strings attached formula basis? To examine the record is to discover that it quite often is. The problem, however, is not necessarily one of a federal "octopus" usurping states' rights, but rather that of a reality faced by the Congress and of decisions democratically made: one is often dealing with fields in which overriding considerations of national policy, or the ability of people at the national level to provide clear positive direction, have been joined to national fiscal capability. The legislators would quite properly consider it incompetence if, at that point, one financed open-ended state-level planning as though there were no federal preconceptions.

---

[56] Ryan, *op. cit.*, 1.

Yet it is also true that in a country as diverse and sprawling as the United States one needs state planning and programming as well as local planning and programming to shape services to regions and their people and to maximize the effect of expenditures.[57] Furthermore, to cope with bureaucracy, bigness, specialization, and social distance, service-delivery systems need in many ways to be localized. All of this remains true even where Congress has defined intent or thrust.

The solution, then, is not necessarily to eliminate national policy planning and programming. Such planning and programming may be essential to the general policy goal. When this is the case, however, clear directions should be enunciated, technical staff work should be strengthened, and political considerations should not be permitted to distill the product so often. Equivocal national policy and competing "guidelines" are self-defeating substantively, if politically strategic. What is also needed in such instances—and has so long been absent in the community mental health planning process—is a serious effort at the same time to define *appropriate* state and local-level policy and programming concerns. Here there was a void in the comprehensive legislation calling for reference to state plans when applications were submitted for centers or for hospital improvement. Not knowing what was appropriate, and not instructed as to what was relevant, most states produced "catalogues" or comprehensive "shopping lists" in the guise of plans, and then proceeded to write applications which would assure the available grants.

It would not be feasible here to settle what are appropriate issues at each level, since *this, too, is a planning question,* but we may illustrate the approach with some hypothetical formulations; none is complete. For the moment, we do not question the premise that quite specific overall policy needs to be set at the federal level in the particular subfield we have surveyed.

National-level policy
☐ relative emphasis on the very disturbed and the mildly disturbed
☐ relative stress on community-based or institutional treatment services
☐ perspective on separation or integration of mental illness with general medical care
☐ is this a "community psychiatry" or "community mental health" system, in the sense of Part I of this chapter?
☐ are voluntary services to be included in the system and publicly funded?

---

[57] For a political science rationale relative to "non-centralization" as basic to the American system, see Daniel J. Elazar, "The Outlook for Creative Federalism," Public Education Papers, No. 3 (Philadelphia: Temple University Center for the study of Federalism, 1968).

National-level programming
- [ ] levels of expenditure
- [ ] patterns of funding, timing, minimum standards
- [ ] decisions relative to work with states, regions, cities

State-level policy
- [ ] role of region or locality in a particular state
- [ ] roles of various state departments and agencies in view of the program concept as adapted to the state
- [ ] role of the voluntary—in the context of federal options
- [ ] local and district service-delivery models to be deemed appropriate
- [ ] experiments particularly strategic for this state
- [ ] ways of relating to and making the most of federal offerings

State-level programming
- [ ] details re financing, timing, manpower, and service delivery
- [ ] administrative patterns vis-à-vis locality
- [ ] evaluation and feedback, both to suit state policy evaluation and programming needs and to report as appropriate to the federal agency.

It would, of course, be necessary similarly to work out local-level policy and programming dimensions, with emphasis on the latter.

To such redistribution of prerogatives, it would be important to add considerable flexibility for grant programs such as that for centers.

One might have expected a very different outcome had federal and state comprehensive community mental health planning been launched with guidelines focused on the *discovery* of policy and planning arenas uniquely suited to the other levels. In saying this we do not disregard the complexity of such endeavor; states do not wish in all instances to relegate to the Washington level all the policy-programming areas the former might preëmpt or consider to be mandated. The federal bureaucracy in turn may not be prepared to relinquish to the states what the latter consider to be their domains, for fear that legislative intent will be subverted or bureaucratic prerogatives curtailed. Moreover, a well-defined series of distinctions as to state-federal-local prerogatives and a resulting chain of relationships may close out the possibility of direct federal-city dealings on a project basis, an approach found essential in several fields in the nineteen-sixties to circumvent state conservatism or a tendency to shortchange the cities.

Since the purpose here is illustrative, we merely mention the financial aspect of intergovernmental relations in planning in mental health, but in practice it is a major consideration. If service in a state hospital involves little or no local costs, while mental health centers or other community care are largely financial burdens on the locality, extraneous factors enter into decision-making, and the impulse will be to resist emphasis on local service commitments. The planners of the new thrusts in community mental health have had to cope with this difficulty—with only limited success.[58] It may be that the recent inclusion of costs of services to the mentally ill in Medicare and Medicaid benefits and in private health insurance may eventually offer the leverage necessary for changes in the existing pattern of financing.[59]

A program structured in the manner of the community mental health center effort creates another financial dilemma. If there is a local fund-matching requirement, to be met by local government completely or shared with the state, the effect is to engage local (or state) fiscal capacity for the given field once federal participation tapers off. In the instance of community mental health centers, the tapering off follows quite quickly. Thus a generous federal matching arrangement can prove to be another element in decreasing the freedom for policy or program initiative on the lower level.

COMPREHENSIVE HEALTH PLANNING CHANGES THE FRAME

Before the above-described process had gone very far, the enactment of P.L. 89–749 late in 1966 launched a new stage in health planning in the United States and revived the issues outlined. "The Congress finds that comprehensive planning for health services, health manpower, and health facilities is essential at every level of government. . . ."[60] Federal health programs had been categorical, focused on specific diseases and problems. President Lyndon Johnson said in a special message in March, 1966, "This leads to an unnecessarily rigid and compartmentalized approach . . . special health problems occur in some parts of our Nation and not in others." As

---

[58] For example, see Hyman Forstenzer, "Planning and Evaluation of Community Mental Health Programs," in Goldston, *op. cit.*, 143–144.

[59] Ruth Knee of the National Institute of Mental Health has provided unpublished materials; at this writing, the evidence is developing that the impact may be major. See, for example, Alan I. Levenson, Bertram S. Brown, and Ruth I. Knee, "The Joint Role of Public and Private Hospitals in Community Mental Health"; and Richard N. Elwell, "Medicare—A Means for Merging Pathways to Service," both in *Hospitals: Journal of the American Hospital Association*, 42 (February 1, 1968), 12–16; 17–20. Note that pages 1–59 constitute a complete section on planning and construction of mental health center facilities as well.

[60] P.L. 89–749 (1966), Sec. 26. A good legislative summary is provided by James H. Cavanaugh and William McC. Hiscock, "Comprehensive Health Planning and Public Health Service Act of 1966 (P.L. 89–749)," *Health, Education, and Welfare Indicators*, January, 1967, 9–18.
P.L. 90–174 extended the grants for three years as follows:
1968 $205 million
1969   256 million
1970   284 million

expressed by the Surgeon General, "Depending on how you count them, there are from 40 to 100 different programs involved in the flow [of federal funds, into any given state], stemming from many federal agencies."[61] The federal government was contributing to construction and resource creation (medical schools and hospitals); research; manpower development; direct service (vendor payment programs on behalf of the individuals); and categorical programs aimed at specific disease targets. Although two large independent endeavors in addition to the community mental health program were encouraging planning, they were unrelated to each other and to the many categorical efforts; these were hospital planning (backed by the Hill-Burton legislation) and regional medical planning focused on heart-stroke-cancer (P.L. 89–239 of 1965).

The new legislation proclaimed the national commitment in general terms to "promoting and assuring the highest level of health attainable for every person" and noted that the goal "required intergovernmental collaboration, official and voluntary efforts." Federal financial backing was offered to help marshal all resources "without interference with existing patterns of private professional practice. . . ."[62]

Several instruments were to be employed: (1) grants to states for ongoing comprehensive health planning, involving designation of a planning agency meeting specified criteria and assurance of periodic plan updating; (2) project grants for area-wide health planning to cover regions, metropolitan areas, and local areas—but to be checked against state plans; (3) project grants for training, studies, and demonstrations which would contribute to planning capabilities; (4) grants to states for comprehensive health services, such services to be related to the state plans (thus consolidating many categorical efforts); (5) project grants to public or private agencies, also to be related to such plans. The last two types of grants were authorized appropriations of $62.5 million each for fiscal 1968. The several planning efforts (state formula grants, area-wide projects, and training demonstrations) were to have up to $24 million over two years. The intent was clear: a state planning *process* was to be encouraged, a planning *structure* created, and federal funds for support of basic public health services—very broadly defined—and of special projects under a variety of auspices would be channeled in accord with such process. The hospital construction planning was to be retained (most states had created independent authorities

---

[61] William H. Stewart, "Partnership for Planning" (Washington, D.C.: Public Health Service, 1966, processed), 10–11.

[62] P.L. 89–749, Sec. 2c.

for this), as was the regional heart-stroke-cancer planning (assigned largely to the voluntary sector and to medical schools). But the emphasis on coordination of and with these efforts was considerable. Categorical planning was not to be undermined—community mental health was guaranteed at least 15 percent of a state's allotment by the legislation—but it was expected to be integrated into the whole.

In contrast to the community mental health planning endeavor reviewed above, several structural and content aspects of what became known as the "partnership-for-health-planning" are of interest. First, while certain realms of activity are protected (hospital construction, heart-stroke-cancer, mental health), there is emphasis in the act and in the guidelines and regulations on freeing the states from once rigid categories. As the Surgeon General said, at the very time when National Institute of Mental Health funding was being sharply targeted in the light of federal policy:

> Unstated but implicit is the attempt to break down unnecessary restrictive barriers among categories; to provide for priority demonstration and decision at a level closer to the needs of the people; and thus to use this instrument as a means for reorienting federal-state relations—and by extension all relationships—within the health field.[63]

In the future both formula and project grants, which had previously been a matter of federal approval of specific state applications and which had been shaped to meet federal guidelines, would be spent in accordance with plans made by the state.[64] Federal guidelines were now to be focused on planning structure and process and on generalized goals, not on program content or operations.

Thus the states have a real assignment. This is not "make work." They are to decide what combination of old and new components should be packaged for their use. Funds are available for state initiative and innovation. Moreover the definition of public health is so broad as to permit significant innovation, especially with reference to environmental programs. Finally, it is clear that the flexibility applies to the delivery mechanism as well as to program substance; the policy is to reach all population elements,

---

[63] Stewart, *op. cit.*, 10.

[64] The Surgeon General's interpretation is as follows: "Now, the state will be able to plan its use of health services money. . . . Obviously the granting of these funds will be dependent upon a state plan which shows what the state intends to do. This plan, in turn, must be related to the comprehensive plan. The important thing is that there is now a range of choice within the structure of formula grants for health services." Stewart, *op. cit.*, 14. Also see, Robert L. Smith, "Comment," in Stewart, *op. cit.*, 32.

with special attention to the disadvantaged. The area grants allow initiative on other levels than that of a state capital.

Nor is the planning structure meant to be a one-time, amorphous committee process; planning support is to be continuous. The structural options reveal sophisticated appreciation of what is involved, and the intent is to create an ongoing planning operation and a staff capable of effective programming and feedback analysis. The planning agency may be (a) an agency or commission in the governor's office—either limited to health or assigned a broader role; (b) an interdepartmental agency or board representing all departments with health responsibilities; (c) an existing state agency with major health responsibility.[65] The application, under P.L. 89–749, must present convincing evidence that staffing and prerogatives are adequate for programming, budgeting, assembling and analyzing relevant information, and promoting coordination. The agency must plan for "planning capability." The role conceived is well put in a policy statement from the Public Health Service:

> The Agency should establish and maintain a continuing process for developing and adopting recommendations to guide the organization, financing and provision of health services, facilities and manpower. Over a period of time, as revised and interrelated within a comprehensive framework of study, problem identification, goal establishment and priority determination, these recommendations will form the basis for a comprehensive State health plan.

Considerable emphasis is placed upon creation of a state-wide advisory mechanism (a "health planning council") in which "consumers," who are defined in the regulations, will hold the majority of membership. This is to be an approach in which the state "calls the shots" and in which consumer interests, especially interests of underprivileged consumers, are to have special attention.

To dramatize the nature of the shift in the locus of decisions, "The Regional Offices will be where the action is."[66] Washington will develop overall policy and will create tools. It will assist regional directors in the early phase. But the entire grant procedure and approval structure will be placed in the regions. Here, too, localization and diversity will be enhanced.

---

[65] New York, to illustrate, established a Health Planning Commission by executive order. A nine-man interdepartmental body, the Commission is advised by a Council and relates to the overall State Office of Planning Coordination.

[66] Stewart, *op. cit.*, 17.

In short, comprehensive health planning (here summarized very briefly and without the wealth of detail specified in the act and subsequent regulations and guides) affirms an intergovernmental approach not followed in the community mental health field. Considerably larger financial stakes and many more interests are involved. On the assumption that, despite long and difficult struggles in some states around the designation of a planning body, the philosophy of the act and of the promulgated regulations will be translated successfully into operational reality—*something which cannot be gauged at this writing*—one might ask whether a rationale exists for the difference between the community mental health planning approach and this more general approach to the planning of all health services. None is specified in the relevant literature. Implied, however, is the view that there is at the state level the competence to plan and program so as to meet the state situation more satisfactorily than what would occur through continuation of federal categorical specifications. It is also assumed that people in the United States will eventually have better health services if public health programs are permitted the diversity that this approach could create. Obviously the drafters of the strategy believed it validated by experience, just as those who allowed the states much less leverage, in the contrasting community mental health approach, felt that more detailed federal specification and narrower parameters for local planners were essential. The authors of this new system of federal-state relationships in the health field knew the old theory, of course, that categorical programs win constituencies and maximize appropriations. They had apparently decided, however, that integration and decentralization had become more important values under current conditions. Perhaps they believed that shared professional goals and ethics would protect the general policy thrust in the states even if decision-making were decentralized, so that the risk of losing the national goal was minimized. It remains to be seen whether one or another of these approaches is confirmed in the long run—and whether the differences between them are justified by the unique character of community mental health.

Although a core budget of no less than 15 percent of the total allocation is protected for it, community mental health is to be included in comprehensive health planning. Thus, the boundary question is also revived. On the one hand, a vehicle exists for implementing the objective of bringing psychiatry back into medicine. Comprehensive health planning should certainly·facilitate the process of strengthening the general practitioner's role in treating psychiatric illness, expanding general hospital psychiatric resources, and planning for psychiatric services in the new local service-delivery systems, particularly in the neighborhoods.[67] On the other hand, community psychiatry may not be in a position fully to call the tune as to how the re-integration is to occur; to the extent that non-medical models of practice are contemplated, backing may become somewhat more difficult to obtain in a comprehensive health system dominated by medicine.

From the boundaries perspective taken in the first section of the present chapter, the positives far outweigh the negatives. The core community psychiatry role is part of medicine and ought to be planned in such relationship. The entire case for the community mental health center (localization, keeping the mentally ill related to the community, home and neighborhood emergency services, general practitioner case accountability, encouraging acceptance of mental illness as a "normal" phenomenon not requiring banishment, etc.) also argues for a broader multipurpose doorway. If comprehensive health planning increases the pace of development of neighborhood multipurpose health centers or of multipurpose health centers in the context of multipurpose neighborhood social service centers or complexes, much will have been gained. Then it would not be essential that the emotional or developmental problem be fully assessed as belonging in the counseling sphere, retardation center, community psychiatry program, or in the clinic or office of the internist or endocrinologist. A competent multidisciplinary team could avoid premature and biased channeling (see the next chapter), assure assessment and a system of accountability, and provide appropriate expertise and case integration. Several different patterns have been proposed, and others would certainly emerge in the course of a truly decentralized planning process. In effect, program planning or field planning must be a component of system planning (medical and health services). Comprehensive health planning may provide a model for other aspects of social welfare as well.

It may also be noted—parenthetically, since the detail would not here be

---

[67] That this is not unreasonable is noted in a Canadian report to the effect that "integration of psychiatry with other health services is being favored." C. A. Roberts, "Community Psychiatry—Integration or More Specialization," *Canadian Mental Health*, XIII, No. 6 (November–December, 1965), 5. Canada's closest equivalent to *Action for Mental Health* urged that one organization deal with mental and physical illness. J. S. Tyhurst et al., *More for the Mind* (Toronto: The Canadian Mental Health Association, 1963).

British traditions and service patterns also favor integration of general medical and mental health services. See Ernest M. Gruenberg, Editor, *Evaluating the Effectiveness of Mental Health Services*, especially comment by Dr. Sydney Brandon, on pages 99–100.

An official United States report in 1961 placed major emphasis on establishing community-based mental health facilities "as part of a coordinated system of statewide health services." *Planning of Facilities for Mental Health Services*, v.

relevant—that the Medicare and Medicaid amendments to the Social Security Act in 1965 also have had the effect of partially returning services for the mentally ill to medicine generally. While there are some special limitations on benefits to the mentally ill, much is provided. As new patterns of payment develop, the mentally ill patient is also in a new relationship to the treatment facility, and this, too, will affect what were for so long custodial centers for the exiled.

FINAL COMMENTS

This "case" review, however incomplete, does suggest several other issues and illustrates additional problems which deserve at least passing mention.

Unanticipated consequences.[68]   Those who focused on the mentally ill and their restoration to the world of men paid all too little attention to the effect of the easier return of psychotics to the community or to their added entrances and exits from hospitals. Leaving aside the occasional outrageous crime perpetrated by individuals in this category, regarding it perhaps as the necessary risk for the reform, much like the accident rates that are the price of highway traffic, we do note another daily, less dramatic, but perhaps ultimately higher price. We refer to the mentally ill mothers in the tens of thousands who now return to the community to resume care of their children, arriving and departing in the lives of these children—offering more or less mothering and sound care—or the terrible neglect and trauma that mental illness can also bring. The strategists of the modern community mental health programs did not foresee these effects; day care, shelters, emergency protective resources, and the like were discussed only after the effects had been felt, and these services have not yet become available in significant volume.[69] Nor do those who plan mothers' treatments fully visualize yet the family consequences of their case decisions.

Similarly, who anticipated and considered how to deal with the tens of thousands of schizophrenics who could not bear children while in custodial settings but who are now in the communities, fully capable of fathering and mothering in the biological sense? Whether one considers genetic or developmental factors, it is clear that there are unanticipated risks here. Thus far there is little public discussion of possible policy implications.[70]

---

[68] See the companion volume, Chapter V.

[69] Of course, there were those on the NIMH staff or otherwise involved in the process who did raise such questions; we refer to what entered into law and policy at the start.

[70] For some of the unanticipated consequences of the community care emphasis and an elaboration of the view that residing outside a hospital is not necessarily synonymous with participating in community life, see Howard Freeman and Ozzie Simmons, *The Mental Patient Comes Home* (New York: John Wiley & Sons, 1963).

Another hazard was also unrecognized. If mental health centers are the uniform facility and if, despite formal intent, there is emphasis on construction without matching program capacity, will one create a new version of the universal custodial facility, under a new euphemism? Or, if advocates unrealistically proclaim that there is no longer a need for long-term care for the mentally ill, will we break up the state hospital system, placing its components in new organizational locations, only to discover the need to reinvent the institution some years from now?

Analyzing the British experience, Richard M. Titmuss has looked behind generalized goals and intent to the emerging service pattern and commented,

> . . . At present we are drifting into a situation in which, by shifting the emphasis from the institution to the community . . . , we are transferring the care of the mentally ill from trained staff to an untrained, or an ill-equipped staff, or no staff at all. . . .[71]

Planners will want to weigh the realities on which they construct their design and avoid fadism and extremes when the facts call for experiment and pragmatism.

The basis for choices. The community mental health planning experience would appear to argue for more realism about the foundations of our choices. The planning of 1963 involved the abandonment of the most economical forms of psychiatric hospital care, at about $6.00 per day, and the substitution of forms costing $25.00 to $50.00 per day.[72] Several types of out-patient care, not always carrying clear price tags, were also proposed.[73] Many of these were quite economical. Yet decisions were made about all of these elements and their combinations on the basis of very little systematic evaluative data: very modest experiments or case reports, often from abroad. Cost-benefit data did not exist. Titmuss has commented on

---

[71] Richard M. Titmuss, "Community Care of the Mentally Ill: Some British Observations," Supplement No. 49, *Canada's Mental Health*, XIII, No. 6 (November–December, 1965), 7. In some places in both Britain and the United States one may question the characterization of institution staff as "trained."

[72] Paul Hoch in *Mental Hygiene News* (Albany, New York: New York State Department of Mental Hygiene), December, 1963, 6.

[73] Fort Logen (Colorado) Mental Health Center costs were estimated as follows in 1961:

In-patient	$20.00 per day
Day hospital	12.00 " "
Evening hospital	6.00 " "
Halfway house	14.00 " "
Out-patient	8.00 " week (1 or more visits)
Family care	140.00 " month

SOURCE: Raymond M. Glasscote *et al.*, *The Community Health Center: An Analysis of Existing Models* (Washington, D.C.: Joint Information Service), 146.

the naive assumption . . . that community care is inevitably economically cheaper than institutional care. . . . There is obviously much work to be done by social scientists in examining the actual social costs and benefits of community care, and this should also take into account alternative uses of time by families of the mentally ill.[74]

Situations of this kind are and remain unavoidable in social policy and programming. Social goals and ideology certainly take over in the absence of objective data—and often in spite of such data. Again, under such circumstances, the bias of the planner should be toward experimentation and diversity rather than premature uniformity and closure. All things being equal—and one does not know after-the-fact if they were—one would choose the strategy of comprehensive health planning rather than that adopted in community mental health.

Planning context. The entire analysis also suggests that federal social sector planning per se requires more systematic organization and coordination. The discrepancy between comprehensive health planning as a strategy and community mental health is perhaps the product, not of alternative hypotheses each deliberately pursued and watched, but of interest-group pressures or spastic intervention, which do not fully examine experience and commitments.

Despite the experience of the Joint Commission on Mental Illness and Health and its limited linear relationship to the substance of federal community psychiatry interventions, the Congress responded to a variety of pressures, in 1965, and authorized funds which, by plan, were used to create a two-year Joint Commission on Mental Health of Children. Again separated from the executive branch and the operating department, this large study group followed the methods of its predecessor. It could do little more than produce "recommendations," which, again, would or would not win support when a more authentic executive-branch planning process was launched.

But, even more, the evidence is accumulating that segmented sectorial planning is not enough: viz., the search for non-medical as well as medical models of mental health intervention; the need for neighborhood multipurpose doorways to health, mental health, and social services generally; the interplay between income security, housing policy, and health—to cite only a few examples. The largest lesson of community mental health planning and, indeed, of health planning, is that it must remain truncated in the absence of a more systematic overall method of addressing the social field.

---

[74] Titmuss, *op. cit.*, 3

THE DELIVERY OF
SOCIAL SERVICES AT
THE LOCAL LEVEL:
BOUNDARIES IN
PROGRAMMING

THE COMMUNITY psychiatry discussion suggested that a planning process may need to give major attention to boundaries issues as a policy matter where there is ambiguity about or dissatisfaction with the status of the "art" and "science" upon which the interventions are based. The present chapter illustrates how a broad policy premise—the need for accessible, general, non-medical social services at the local level—does not resolve all programming dilemmas. In any attempt to translate such overall policy into what we have called parameters of programming,[1] one confronts organizational questions, practice issues, and loyalties to specific systems of specialized agencies.

The special programming question here is the hierarchical organization of social services, with the focus on the foundation of the system at the local level. Further programming details are not specified since staffing, budget, locations, and the rest must be developed with reference to a particular locale.

The reader will note at once that, in this discussion, the planner is advocate, advancing a point of view about the nature and urgency of the problem to be solved, the limitations of available provision, and the direction a solution must take. While never a neutral technician, the planner enters into various fields with differing degrees of involvement. Here he draws upon

---

[1] See Chapter VII in the companion volume.

positions previously taken, solutions strongly advanced. Specific programming strategies are offered.

The interdependence of social policy instruments is again noted. One cannot consider social services at the local level, particularly insofar as these may utilize or be based in a public welfare system, except as one builds upon specific assumptions about the system of income maintenance. To some degree at least, income and social services are complementary. Certainly the pattern of organization is affected by the nature of the public assistance delivery system.

The point of departure is the commitment to assuring access to social services and the consequences thereof.[2] How, in effect, does such commitment help determine what the neighborhood social service pattern might look like? One might approach the topic deductively, deriving a system from principles of organization and practice and producing a comprehensive design *de novo*. An alternative, quite common, and somewhat more developmental pattern of analysis is chosen and may thus illustrate a context in which the incrementalist may claim that his is the obvious way to plan. In effect, it is here argued that the independent systems of family and child welfare services, which have been historically very important in the United States, have been made obsolete by the growth of knowledge and a shifting social scene. As the system boundaries are readjusted, in response to such trends and in the light of related developments in public assistance and other social service fields, one emerges with new formulation of programming options. However, only a synoptic strategy will meet our objectives.

Several other countries, with Great Britain in the lead, have been involved in a similar re-evaluation.[3] The issues are universal; while specific solutions depend on context, some general principles appear to emerge.

---

[2] Chapter X in the companion volume.

[3] For background, see Richard M. Titmuss, "The Welfare Complex in a Changing Society," *The Milbank Memorial Fund Quarterly*, XLV, No. 1 (January, 1967), 9–24; or, his *Commitment to Welfare* (New York: Pantheon Books, 1968), 72–84. Scottish Education Department and Scottish Home and Health Department, *Social Work and the Community* (Edinburgh: Her Majesty's Stationery Office, 1966, Cmnd. 3065). *Report of The Committee on Local Authority and Allied Personal Social Services*, Frederic Seebohm, Esq., Chairman (London: Her Majesty's Stationery Office, 1968, Cmnd. 3703).

We shall from time to time employ the term introduced by the British, "*personal* social services," to suggest the general service encompassing family and child welfare and service to detached individuals, the aged, adolescents, etc. "General" may be a more suitable term in the United States.

THE PROBLEMS ADDRESSED

The point of departure is the broadly unsatisfactory status of general, non-medical, and nonmonetary social services, whether one means by the term (a) the traditional family counseling and child welfare services rendered by affiliates of the Family Service Association of America and the Child Welfare League of America and by public welfare departments; (b) more general personal counseling and casework—to include social services to youth, to the aged, to persons in marital difficulty; (c) resources and facilities such as day care, homemakers, and "meals-on-wheels"; or (d) information and referral services. There are major difficulties in the quantity of service available (coverage), quality of service (ability to accomplish the designated purpose), delivery of services (access, integration, accountability, suitability), as well as in the implications of use for the client's self-image and social status. To be somewhat more specific, but not detailed:

1. *There is not enough service.* Family casework service, the front line in family counseling, is rendered by over 300 member social agencies of the Family Service Association of America. Fewer than 150,000 families receive ongoing intensive service from these agencies in the course of a year. Only about 60 percent of United States families reside within family agency territories, and the "coverage" is limited to about three caseworkers per 100,000 population.[4] Scale, geographic concentration, and known difficulty in reaching many among the most disorganized mean that the family agency system does not provide many families in need of help with what it is set up to offer.

On the other hand, public welfare departments, seeking since 1962 to develop competent and generally available social services to prevent or cope with dependency, have found themselves unable to solve problems of manpower, public image, or of ties to their public assistance responsibilities. With rare exceptions, Americans in need of personal counseling, but not financial aid, do not think of their public welfare departments. They turn to such departments for child welfare service, homemakers, or day care in many jurisdictions, but the means tests and stigma turn them away in other areas.

Nor is coverage provided by the loosely-defined "marriage counseling" movement. Its roster of psychologists, educators, social workers, sociologists,

---

[4] Department of Systems and Statistics, Family Service Agency of America, *Family Service Statistics*, September, 1967, Part III.

ministers, psychiatrists, and lawyers renders a quantitatively far less visible service than do the family service agencies.

Child welfare services, another element, are suffering from major and constant shortage in foster homes; group care; shelter and other interim care; adoptive homes for certain categories of children in specified places; protective services; so-called preventive services, ranging from family case-work to homemakers, home aid service, and day care. Close to one-fifth of all United States counties do not yet have public child welfare services and many others have only token services.

The long stays of children in crowded temporary shelters and interim facilities in several parts of the country, the backing-up of well children in hospital wards because of insufficient child welfare resources, the use of second- and third-best solutions for lack of needed services may be charac-terized as a national urban child welfare crisis.[5]

In some thousand units, small and large, anti-poverty neighborhood groups are attempting to fill in some of the service gaps. They have tended to concentrate on child care, employment referral, job training, and group educational activities—at all levels of adequacy and accessibility. In general, the gap in skilled counseling and intensive child welfare has not been filled —even though general accessibility may have been improved and a measure of potent case and policy advocacy introduced in some places.

2. *Many social services carry a stigma in their use.* For understandable, but no longer defensible, historical reasons much that exists by way of serv-ice is premised on the inability of the potential user to determine his own needs or to take advantage of what is available. There is also a strong under-current of suspicion that those who require help from or use publicly-supported social services have disabilities beyond the illness, handicap, need, or situation that makes the service appropriate. The "hidden" disabilities are conceived as residing in the realm of heredity, endowment, or morality. In short, there is latent or at times conscious identification with the heritage from sixteenth- and seventeenth-century "poor law," and the charity organ-ization tradition of the late-nineteenth century, which associates use of public services with moral defect. Thus, whether or not fully articulated, there is a deterrent, punitive, niggardly character to public social services in many parts of the United States, which is generally considered to be appro-priate.

[5] Alfred J. Kahn, "The Social Scene and the Planning of Services for Children," *Social Work*, 7, No. 3 (July, 1962), and "Child Welfare: Trends and Directions," *Child Wel-fare*, 41, No. 10 (December, 1962); William Ryan and Laura Morris, *Child Welfare Problems and Potentials* (Boston: Massachusetts Committee for Children and Youth, 1967).

This tradition is reinforced by the long association of public social serv-ices with public assistance, which has many aspects of stigma and punish-ment embedded in it. Until the "spill off" from the anti-poverty effort and the civil rights revolution launched a series of legal challenges, client pro-tests, and administrative reforms late in 1966, public welfare in its adminis-trative procedures infringed routinely on privacy, constitutional rights, statu-tory guarantees, and human dignity. Public perception and administrative practice have not yet begun to overtake recent efforts to reconstitute public welfare, and the elements of stigma and deterrence are still strong.

3. *Access to services is difficult, especially for the uneducated and the poor.* Certain of the services (family casework, child guidance) tended in the past to "disengage" themselves from poor people and to develop meth-ods of helping, concepts of client participation, and an organizational pat-tern of service which did not connect with the needs, problems, and ways of taking help of significant elements of the population. This was long ignored because services were in short supply and were kept fully utilized by those who did "fit in." On the other hand, the better educated in the skilled-working class, lower-middle class, and middle class have learned to make the most of the nonstigmatizing components of the social welfare system. In fact, there are some fields of service, such as advanced education, in which the middle class benefits most from the programs of the welfare state.

An interesting and not accidental pattern has thus developed, whereby the very poor have been served, if reached at all, by a system of deterrent-oriented social services related to public assistance and the state mental hospital systems; and the somewhat more advantaged have been the major objects of the largely voluntary family service, child welfare, and child guid-ance movements. The existence of this "dual system" of social service has come into question in the context of general expansion of public child wel-fare, family social service, and child guidance—and the new public commit-ments of the nineteen-sixties to equity and opportunity—but it is far from overcome.

As we have noted elsewhere in some detail, it is difficult for those with-out much formal education who do not have a private lawyer or personal secretary to learn about or to take advantage of many of the benefits, rights, entitlements, facilities, and opportunities available.[6] In fact, without special

---

[6] Lola M. Irelan, Editor, "Low Income Life Styles," Welfare Administration Report No. 14 (Washington, D.C.: Government Printing Office, 1966). Alfred J. Kahn *et al.*, *Neighborhood Information Centers: A Study and Some Proposals* (New York: Colum-bia University School of Social Work, 1966). Also see the companion volume, Chap-ter X.

provision, so-called target groups in the governmental anti-poverty effort do not even get to know about programs designed expressly for them.

On a very elementary level, there are mothers unable to use medical facilities or to apply for available help for lack of a place to leave their children for a few hours or for lack of carfare. In a somewhat more complex realm, many of those most in need of service lack access, not for absence of knowledge, but for inability to cope with bureaucratic rigidity. They need advocates and assistance in asserting their rights.

Educational and financial differentials aside, however, there is need to face the fact that highly developed specialization, the inevitable bureaucratization of large-scale programs, and the complexity inherent in a system composed of federal, state, local, and voluntary components demand some attention to the problem of access. Very few persons alone can negotiate successfully the maze which intervenes between them and a considerable number of basic services. Specific proposals already outlined[7] need to be related to other requirements at the local level.

4. *There is inadequate provision for case integration and case accountability.* Here, again is a much-documented problem.[8]

To illustrate from the children's field, Maurice Hunt has said:

> In many communities, agencies serving children are so specialized and their services are so fragmented that no one seems to be concerned with the whole family or even the whole child. Too often, when a child needs a change in service—as from the home of a relative to a foster home—the change results in a change in the child's worker and even a shift to an entirely different agency.[9]

Interventions to help sick and disorganized people are often very complex. They demand the carefully concerted efforts of a number of specialists and services. The continuity to be established must be concerned at times with services rendered simultaneously by a number of specialists to the same or to different family members. (Public assistance, probation, adult psychiatric clinic, and school social work could be involved at a given moment in a typical case.) Equally important is case continuity over time, as when a child moves from the care of the school attendance department, to the judge

---

[7] Chapter X in the companion volume.

[8] See Chapter X in the companion volume; also, Alfred J. Kahn, *Planning Community Services for Children in Trouble* (New York: Columbia University Press, 1963); Ryan and Morris, *op. cit.*

[9] Maurice O. Hunt, "Progress and Issues in Child Welfare Services," *Children*, 12, No. 2 (March–April, 1965), 60.

in a juvenile court, to probation, to a treatment institution, and then back to the community.

Two closely interrelated requirements must be met in the solution. First, there is the necessity of "meshing" the simultaneous service interventions or those rendered over time. Then, there is the problem of assuring that the client or user is not lost in the gap among or between the several services: being referred somewhere but never arriving, dropping out after a poor contact and not being followed up. Who, in short, is responsible for continuity of community *concern* in a case from the time of its identification as a case needing attention to the time when there is a decision that the case may be dropped safely? This is the substance of case accountability. Where will it be located in the locality?

5. *Specialization, bureaucratization, and historical accident have created some service boundaries which are inherently dysfunctional.* Efforts to open service access and to achieve both case integration and case accountability carry a doubly heavy burden. Even desirable specialization and necessary bureaucratization create large obstacles to be overcome at the point of service delivery. If, beyond this, there are boundaries which negate the essence of the service goal—as will be suggested with reference to family and child welfare later in this chapter—the assignment becomes unrealistic. The result is inefficiency at the operational level and ineffectiveness with reference to the objectives.

To add together problems of boundaries, access, integration, and accountability is to conclude that there is, in fact, no comprehensive *network* or *system* of local social services. The complex problems and needs addressed often demand a system in which basic functions are defined and assigned. Nothing less can carry out potent interventions. But the reality is a patchwork, lacking design, not offering coverage, and developing in terms of its own dynamics.

When, in 1965 and 1966, community representatives in poverty neighborhoods were permitted to influence the planning of service to meet needs and to participate in the rendering of such services, considerable priority was given throughout the country to what became known as multi-service centers or one-stop neighborhood centers and to the "urban broker" or "social broker" services. These programs were designed particularly to cope both with problems of access and problems of dysfunctional service fragmentation, two of the concerns here highlighted.[10] They are premised on the creation of a more responsive service system.

---

[10] Robert Perlman and David Jones, *Neighborhood Service Centers* (Washington, D.C.: Government Printing Office, 1967).

6. *The balance between resources and facilities, on the one hand, and diagnostically-rendered case services, on the other, may be inappropriate, given current social realities.* This is a subject discussed at some length elsewhere.[11] It has special relevance to family and child welfare and to services to the aged, fields under discussion in this chapter. The two particular questions to be faced are these. What type of planning group or lobby is needed to address this issue and to promote more satisfactory balance? Can one develop a pattern of organization, focused on service delivery, which will permit adequate consideration of the use of resources and facilities, which are generally available at user option and do not assume user disability (social utilities), prior to or in balanced relationship with diagnostically-rendered case services?

7. *Manpower shortages in the relevant professional fields are serious.* Statistical details are plentiful, and projections of the output of social work manpower with full professional qualifications (the Master of Science degree) for the next decade are not reassuring.[12] Yet it is the graduate social worker who is seen as the front-line service worker in family and child welfare. Is there a service-delivery strategy to utilize available manpower more effectively and take advantage of the potentially greater availability of relatively untrained staff, so as to meet obligations and needs for service?

8. *There are major gaps between the case service model and the service as actually rendered.* This is a quality problem. Again, the documentation is extensive and detail is here unnecessary; only brief illustration is given.

In many places, foster homes are of low quality; and foster home care becomes a succession of placement and replacement, with increasing upset for the children involved. Institutions seek to achieve a "therapeutic milieu"; this goal is often negated by staff turnover and control practices that lead the children to experience something quite different from the program described in an agency's brochures. Or, the reality of resource and personnel shortages converts the detailed and expensive diagnostic process and careful matching of child and foster care resource into a meaningless ritual. Race, age, handicap, or sex alone often determines the actual case disposition, whatever the findings of the careful "study."

Similarly, looking beyond family service agency statistics, one notes an apparent inability of agencies to meet many applicants on a level meaning-

---

[11] In the companion volume, Chapter VI.

[12] *Closing the Gap in Social Work Manpower*, Report of the Departmental Task Force on Social Work Education and Manpower, Department of Health, Education, and Welfare (Washington, D.C.: Government Printing Office, 1965).

ful to them. Disregarding the rhetoric of reports and professional papers, one finds that a very small percentage of those who ask for help obtain either the service requested or what the agency would describe as its characteristic service. People drop out, are referred but go nowhere, or are rejected in surprisingly large numbers.

9. *Processes are already under way that affect the service-delivery system with reference to many of the elements here in focus. There is need to consider seriously the implications and interrelations of the several trends.* More specifically, experiments are under way with "social brokerage" services in anti-poverty and other urban development programs. Several kinds of multi-service and one-stop neighborhood centers are in operation or proposed under a variety of types of administrative and governmental auspices and functional program sponsorship.[13]

In addition, the United States public welfare system was long premised on the combination of social service and public assistance programs, with the latter inevitably defining tone, eligibility, and public perception. Child welfare services have had more or less separate identity, depending on place, and include a large voluntary (nonpublic) service component in some instances. Except for adoption services, child welfare services, in fact, partake of some of the public view of public social services and suffer some of the disabilities of stigma. Now there is considerable movement as a result of new administrative requirements nationally; court challenges to traditional practice, carried out as a result of the expanding local legal services launched in the anti-poverty effort; client self-organization; and general national interest in new forms of income support for the needy. While new income guarantees are being considered, administration of public assistance is being simplified and objectified to decrease or eliminate the most degrading aspects of the current means test and to eliminate much of the administrative discretion which has entered into determinations of eligibility. There are many consequences. For one, there is the question of deployment of the manpower now devoted to detailed eligibility study and careful policing—in a system generally considered outmoded. Should the granting of aid and the rendering of social service, locally, reside in the same worker, the same bureau, the same department? Some jurisdictions have already begun to separate public assistance administratively from public social services operations, and the Department of Health, Education, and Welfare has done so nationally. Does this gradual freeing of public welfare social services from

---

[13] For a summary, Edward J. O'Donnell, "The Neighborhood Service Center," *Welfare in Review*, 6, No. 1 (January–February, 1968), 11–21.

their historical ties to public assistance eligibility carry the possibility of new relationships to child welfare, delinquency services, community mental health services, service to the aging—fields that previously have projected independent local social service developments? The present chapter focuses on implications for the local service-delivery system.

The field of community mental health occasions special concern and illustrates with great clarity the need for local social service planning.[14] Leaders in psychiatry and federal officials have encouraged a very broad concept, going well beyond psychiatry and its therapeutic allies. Subsequent federal legislation offering aid for the construction and staffing of community mental health centers and for the modernization of state mental hospital programs has supported a similar perspective. As a result of all this, the community mental health leadership throughout the country has been involved in developing a comprehensive social service network, integrated with a medical specialty (psychiatry) and ignoring the implications of the parallel effort to reorganize non-medical helping services, perhaps in multi-service centers.

There are here, then, concern and opportunity. How is the subject to be approached? What are the options for local social service delivery? Some suggestions are implicit in the recent experience of family and child welfare in the United States.[15] The programming stance of the chapter is that a social service system or network in the full sense is essential, that separate, occasionally interrelated islands of service will no longer serve.

CHILD WELFARE AND THE WELFARE OF CHILDREN

The urban child care crisis in the United States has already been summarized briefly. It is a crisis which reflects the inadequacy of current public policy for children; the unsatisfactory development of education, health, income security, housing, and general social utility services; as well as major problems in the case service network.[16]

---

[14] See Chapter VI in this volume.

[15] The question of organizing local-level social services could as readily be introduced by more detailed examination of services to the aged or of trends in the restructuring of public assistance. Given the scope of family and child welfare services, the method here chosen does serve to open up the general subject. At the same time it is the occasion for introducing into the volume materials from two of the major fields of social service, historically.

[16] For further detail, documentation, and bibliographical sources, see Alfred J. Kahn, "The Social Scene and the Planning of Services . . ." and "Child Welfare . . . ," as well as Alfred J. Kahn, "Planning for the Welfare of Children," *The Social Welfare Forum,* 1966 (New York: Columbia University Press, 1966), 165–187; and *Our Troubled Chil-*

While adequate documentation or discussion of solutions must take one well beyond this chapter's focus on local social service delivery, it is relevant to note that the inadequacies here to be addressed are to some degree a problem of inappropriate system boundaries and of an effort to attach to child welfare services more than that system can carry. Thus, the restructuring of local case services must be a component of a larger re-examination of planning for the welfare of children. The latter aspect will be summarized briefly.

The so-called child welfare system in the United States consists of state child welfare agencies (which are often combined with state public assistance agencies in public welfare departments and which sometimes actually operate child welfare services on the local level directly); child welfare agencies operated by local governments under the general supervision of state agencies; voluntary child welfare agencies, both sectarian and nonsectarian, operating on the local level; a national, voluntary, coordinating, and standard-setting agency, the Child Welfare League of America (CWLA); a federal agency assigned research, leadership, coordination, and some funding responsibility for some social services and health services to children, the United States Children's Bureau. It takes little to establish that this group of organizations and agencies cannot and does not take on broad responsibility to prevent family breakdown or parent-child problems, nor does it undertake planning for the welfare of all children, despite occasional exuberance and its related rhetoric. Statutory charges, public expectations, tradition, client needs, and funding patterns have created a program of case services plus occasional "developmental" and "preventive" forays. Ninety percent of total expenditures in child welfare service agencies is devoted to substitute care arrangements for children who are unable to remain with their families or who do not have families.

Child poverty was virtually ignored by these agencies until the antipoverty effort of the 'sixties, despite the known linkage between poverty and family breakup. Parent education and adolescent social services (except for unmarried mothers) were beyond their scope. Educational, health, and mental health planning for children was in other hands. Even the develop-

dren—*Our Community's Challenge*, Proceedings of a Conference Sponsored by the Edwin Gould Foundation (New York: Columbia University Press, 1967). Shirley Jenkins and Mignon Sauber, *Paths to Child Placement* (New York: Community Council of Greater New York, 1966). David Fanshel, "Child Welfare," in Henry S. Maas, Editor, *Five Fields of Social Service: Reviews of Research* (New York: National Association of Social Workers, 1966), 85–143. Miriam Norris and Barbara Wallace, Editors, *The Known and Unknown in Child Welfare Research: An Appraisal* (New York: National Association of Social Workers, 1965). Ryan and Morris, *op. cit.*

ment of preventive casework services to children in their own homes, day care, and emergency homemakers was on an almost-token basis before 1962. American child welfare was largely a program of foster home care, adoption, institutional care, and services to unmarried mothers. Child welfare meant case services, not the welfare of all children.

What had developed reflected a basic type of institutional wisdom about social reality, but its implications were not fully perceived. "Child welfare" is not a viable unit for basic prevention of family difficulties, for organizing income security, or for operating social utilities.

The child welfare movement could not have been expected to become other than a case service network. Just as primary prevention of family disruption or breakdown cannot be conceived as the province of one organization, since it involves all of society in a basic sense, so is the enhancement of child development (what else could be meant by "primary prevention" enthusiasts in child welfare?) a task which ramifies throughout our society. In fact, it is probably coterminal with family welfare, with an added ingredient related to the adequate development of our educational system.

This reality does not preclude the existence of national, state, or local children's "watchdog" agencies or lobbies. Some agencies' constant preoccupation with the impact of societal developments on children, and their evaluation of services directed particularly to children, is necessary so that plans may be proposed, reforms initiated, and budgets supported. Indeed, the Children's Bureau has done much in this field over the years.

An international group asked itself whether child welfare should be an independent "sector" in planning, or whether children could be served adequately by examining how their interests were met in the several sectors: food, health, education, housing, income security, industrial planning, fiscal and monetary policy, and so on. The review concluded:

> Neither a separate governmental sector for children nor a separate section of the plan for children is called for, but rather a deliberate analysis of the investment and consumption expenditures required for the protection and development of children and youth, within and cutting across sectors in relation to the development objectives of the nation and its available resources.
>
> Planning for the interests of children and youth would be aided by the expression and stimulation of public awareness through a national group composed of governmental as well as non-governmental leaders, who would serve to highlight the needs of children and youth and help in the formulation of policy for them.[17]

---

[17] Herman D. Stein, Editor, *Planning for the Needs of Children in Developing Countries,* Report of a Roundtable Conference (New York: United Nations Children's Fund, 1965), 79–80.

Thus, one would argue for a United States Children's Bureau, a Child Welfare League, or a local Citizens' Committee for Children in a planning or "watchdog" role but not as pre-empting all program activity tied to the welfare of children. Such groups would be most useful if they concerned themselves as much with income maintenance, housing, education, health, and child development generally as they do now with case services for those in difficulty. Their constituency would be "all the children" and not merely those needing substitute care or new homes.

Turning from the general policy and planning field to the provision of resources (social utilities) needed by families to help with child rearing, as well as therapeutic, remedial, and substitute care services in the instance of family difficulty and failure, the experience in the United States is as follows:

Far too many of the needed resources and facilities relevant to all families as child-rearing supports have been defined as "case" services, to be reached through a diagnostic doorway. The result has been a degree of stigma, plus insufficient quantitative expansion. Day care serves as illustration.

An artificial separation of child welfare case services (casework, foster home care, institutional services, services to unmarried mothers) from the parallel family social services may lead to excessive emphasis on child-parent separation.

Inadequate attention to research findings and a degree of professional rigidity may overemphasize a limited number of substitute-care approaches, closing out possibilities which may be more readily developed.

All of these issues merit elaboration, as we gradually and indirectly approach the question with which the chapter began: the planning of locally-based general social services.

Social utilities. Social utilities[18] are or should be available to all at the initiative of the user who chooses them (i.e., a "drop-in" community center) or who has access to them by virtue of a socially-recognized status (meals-on-wheels for the aging who live alone). Case services, by contrast, are reached through a "diagnostic" doorway; an expert evaluates the potential user's need.

Some social services are basically facilitating and take account of organizational specialization and bureaucratization, on the one hand, and of people's differential capacities to cope with complexity and to take advantage of what is available, on the other. Included are information, advice, referral, liaison, and advocacy activities in both specialized and multipurpose agencies. The question arises as to whether one would organize such services especially for

---

[18] See the companion volume, Chapter VI.

children. The issue then becomes one of whether a generalized information and facilitation service can be "open" to children. Obviously, since young children are represented by parents and since problems of children are intertwined with parental problems, any broad system of information and referral should address families, not children alone. An argument could be made for a special-purpose entry point to service and advice for adolescents, who are often determined to maintain a separate identity from their parents and have certain unique problems. Given resources for a special system, one might consider such services at central points or in high-need neighborhoods —rather than attempt to parallel completely the general system with one for adolescents. At some levels, the two systems would be united, and in some locations they might share space.

Facilitating and liaison services are an attempt at a bureaucratized solution to a problem inevitable in bureaucracies. Other social utilities may address another function, one which grows out of recognition of what family and other interpersonal relationships become under industrialization and urbanization.

In effect, from the day when it became apparent that the unit family could not do everything related to production, socialization, education and training, cultural enrichment, maintenance of motivation, and facilitation of family formation, the process of developing institutional substitutes for primary functions was under way. What characterizes our present situation is the quantitative change. If we wish to protect some of our core values and to assure intimate primary group experiences and the fruits thereof, we must find other institutional vehicles for some of the functions of the family, the traditional neighborhood, the extended family, the peer group, and the religious institution.

The thesis is simple. Social change creates new prerequisites for adequate socialization and role training in industrial communities. Since these are recognizable as meeting functional requirements of the broader society, they ought to be socially created. There should be no personal defect implied in the need for the service and no penalty involved in its use. Such social inventions designed to meet the normal needs of people arising from their situations and roles in modern social life might be thought of as "developmental provision." Full comprehension of the circumstances of and the demands upon a mother, an adolescent, retired adult, or a child without one parent is a starting point in planning such provision.

Thus day care programs are needed for young children—younger children than would have been released from the shelter of the family ten years ago. Or we could sustain old people in the community by a diversity of communal provisions (meals-on-wheels and home-helps are two illustrations), where the intimate family is no longer available for such service and support.

This is only a beginning. Consider some of the major life transitions and what primary group institutions once offered and still seek to offer in many places so as to assist people through them: entry into elementary school, the beginning of adolescence, the transition to the world of work, the early days of marriage, the period of pregnancy, the early days with a first baby, adjustment to the death of a spouse, retirement, old age. These are normal, everyday, universal experiences, and the institutional efforts to help people adapt to them represent social wisdom and communal self-interest, not charity or sympathy for "victims."

The potential responses range from group counseling and education for parents whose children enter school, through organized activities for adolescents—including coffee houses and "hang-outs," to work guidance and counseling services, to family life education and counseling (including group activities for "young marrieds")—down to specialized services for older people.

Day care (or better, child development centers) and homemakers are very high-priority developmental services. A degree of inventiveness might now be applied to form and name for a related program, the short-term or emergency baby-sitter. Is it not time that the city dweller has access to a resource more routinely available and reliable than the teenage baby-sitter or the neighborhood exchange arrangement for a function whose requirements grow out of current living conditions? Is it necessary to spell out the consequences for personal health (parents need rest, change, diversion), involvement in children's education (parents need to attend parent-teacher meetings and adult classes), emotional security (children and parents need to be comfortable about the substitute arrangement for brief periods for shopping or clinic visits, or longer periods several times a week), deriving from the fact that some mothers never have secure arrangements for care of their children no matter how urgent the other demands upon them? Facilities can and should be located in parks, shopping areas, and in conjunction with other major facilities (as a medical center).

Priorities must vary from place to place. Several sections of the United States could profitably devote resources to

☐ new types of family (or adolescent) vacation resources
☐ new opportunities for peer experiences for adolescents, including group trips, cultural-educational activity, camping
☐ new supports for induction of young people into married life and help

after birth of a first child (to include information and guidance in furnishing and maintaining an apartment, furniture loans or grants, practical nurse's aid after a child's birth, consumer information, more adequate family planning information).

It requires no complex analysis to suggest that these social utilities need a local point of access general enough to serve all of a family's requirements without segmentation by age group or problem. In fact, the homemaker who keeps the family routine going so that children remain in school and a father at work after a mother's emergency hospitalization can hardly be categorized only as part of a child welfare service system. Nor is it useful to have one such homemakers service for the aged and another for families with children.

All of this may appear logical and obvious, yet it does not reflect past service experience. Day care, homemaker services, camps, and other "utilities" were developed by a case-oriented child welfare system bound, on the one hand, by an economy of scarcity and, on the other, by a view of people (true of many of their cases but not of the modal family) as needing special help and outside intercession between them and resources. As a result, the resources were stigmatized and defined by the community as appropriate only for people who could not cope; hence, they were not developed on the scale merited by a social utility.

The new organizational approach to be outlined would permit a fresh start.

Case services. Case services without basic income, health, education, and housing provision are in constant danger of confusing the problem and the intervention needed. Thus, despite all protestations to the contrary, a clearly observable path leads from family poverty to child placement. The situation can be corrected far more readily by a more adequate program of income transfers than by seeking to increase the competence of those who render case services. It is for this reason that we have discussed the wisdom of integrating concern for child welfare into sectorial planning and the creation of watchdog groups—as well as social utilities.

Second, case service decisions at a point where there are too few or inappropriate options may be dysfunctional. There is some evidence that, because of the general unrelatedness of family services to child welfare services and because the latter are largely substitute care and placement services—devoting a proportionately modest share of energies to "family saving"—the child welfare system is "biased" in favor of a placement outcome.

Or, in other terms, there are grounds for concern that the same situation that enters a child welfare agency may end up in foster home care, an institution, or adoption, whereas, in a family service agency, it might have become a family treatment case; a child or maternal treatment case, in a child guidance clinic; or something else in another agency. These are not absolute patterns, but they operate to a degree greater than that allowed by mere chance. Thus, if the goal is to minimize the possibility of family breakup unless it is truly unavoidable, *one would want to create a case service system in which more options could operate.* In fact, one might wish to create a system biased against placement, in the sense that the system assumes the appropriateness of community-based solutions in the first instance.

This is not to deny the expertise of a child welfare worker who selects foster homes, matches child and foster parents, or processes an adoption application. It does suggest that these specializations should be reachable through a more general service with access to other options—and specialists —as well.

The reform of case services in child welfare should begin by providing a broader "frame" at the entry point, thus assuring automatic consideration of solutions to the family problem based on preserving or strengthening the ties of children and parents where separation may now occur. Attention must also be given to the problems of case accountability and service integration.[19] Particularly in instances of family disruption, there is the likelihood of many agencies being involved. And since a child may move through a network of shelters, income sources, diagnostic facilities, and several types of substitute care, responsibility for continuity may become blurred and the original purpose of the parent-child separation may be forgotten.

Finally, the interventive repertoire itself needs expansion, innovation, and increased flexibility—a subject beyond our immediate scope, except for brief illustration. Having re-established the primacy of family-oriented preventive services and basic income-security programs, policy planners and programmers should also face the fact that many traditional professional tenets are challengeable—and research justifies more willingness to experiment.

> Children obviously need warm, intimate primary relationships with their parents or substitute adults if they are to mature satisfactorily.
>
> The congregate institutions condemned in the 1930's did not then and do not now offer adequate environments for healthy growth.
>
> This does not mean that available foster family care is superior to "family groups" in agency-sponsored homes or to small institutions with small cottage groupings and high staff-child ratios.
>
> These latter types of group care are obviously superior to those congregate

---

[19] See Chapter X in the companion volume.

temporary shelters in a few large cities, where children wait for long periods for foster family care that does not materialize.

The history of children separated from their parents is often a sorry one. Since long "temporary care" and many replacements are common, one should pause before any decision is made to separate parent from child—if there is choice. Temporary, emergency, and "first" placements often start irreversible processes. Great attention, therefore, should be given to protecting the family unit through emergency resources (baby-sitters, homemakers, etc.) and a vast expansion in family-oriented casework services, *preferably closely related to the organization that makes child placement decisions.*

Foster home and adoptive home processing is very much affected by what is available at the time. One cannot therefore count on the process per se to protect children who are placed.

While data about what occurs to separated children (and basic social values) should leave all child welfare workers biased against placement, some placement is essential; to avoid it is also to harm children.

If a child belongs to a category in which the chances for adoption are low (because of age, race, physical characteristics, behavior), a stable, long-term group residence plan may be better for him than a long period of holding out for adoption while he lives in unwholesome interim foster family or shelter arrangements.

Peer group dynamics may be constructively used with adolescents whose interpersonal relationships are an extremely difficult vehicle of change. Group programs—for residential arrangements and for the structuring of treatment—may be *preferred* arrangements in some cases just as individual, family plans are vital to others.[20]

A comprehensive review of child welfare research suggests that the limited state of present knowledge and emerging data, which are contrary to "conventional wisdom" in this field of practice, may justify even more extensive departures:

- Do good placement and therapeutic service actually reverse the effect of parent-child separation? [If not, even more stress should be placed on avoiding placement.]
- Does the separated child have a *unique* psychiatric syndrome? [If not, a greater diversity of arrangements for care is needed.]
- Do we know the earmarks of a potentially good foster parent or adoptive parent? [If not, why are the criteria so rigid?]
- Is a child who can cope with either institution or foster home always better off in a foster home? [If not, will it not be easier to provide care?]

---

[20] Kahn, "Child Welfare: Trends and Directions," 471.

· Can the decision process in separation be made more rational? [If so, what organizational means are needed?][21]

Everywhere there is new experimentation with group and small-institution care. Agencies are renting and purchasing apartments and hiring couples or individuals to staff them. The traditionally rigid boundaries between foster care and adoption are being reviewed, with experimentation in converting foster care to adoptive status and subsidizing the exploratory period in adoptive homes—for "hard to place" children. By re-defining foster parents as agency employees, where desirable, and paying them adequately, new resources are being opened for substitute care. More adequate and more differentiated group care is also being developed.[22]

Promising, but also a source of concern to the child welfare field, is the possibility of developing emergency services (homemakers), day care, and even foster home apartments in the context of local anti-poverty programs and other types of neighborhood self-help efforts. Help for deprived children is an attractive and appropriate objective for such groups, and federal funding has permitted hiring of local nonprofessional aides to provide such services. If this new manpower resource can be successfully harnessed, sound standards developed and implemented, and professional guidance assured, the shortage in the child care field could be alleviated.

These child welfare trends hold significant implications for the organization of social services at the local level. Brief review of developments in family counseling services will expand the picture.

AMERICAN FAMILY SERVICES AS CASEWORK

The network of voluntary family service agencies affiliated with the Family Service Association of America immediately comes to mind as a possible nucleus or building block for a system of locally-based social services. Although many counties do not now have coverage, and while even the "covered" counties often have very small staffs, token service, or long waiting

---

[21] The research questions are posed by David Fanshel, *op. cit.* The bracketed comments are mine.

[22] See Beatrice L. Garrett *et al.*, "Meeting the Crisis in Foster Family Care," *Children,* 13, No. 1 (January–February, 1966), 2–15. Draza Kline, "The Validity of Long-Term Foster Family Care Service," *Child Welfare,* XLIV, No. 4 (April, 1965), 185–195. Note Barbara Wootton's comment: ". . . as much good may be done by running the institution better as by leaving the children at home." Or, we might add, as by using unstable and inadequate foster home arrangements. Barbara Wootton, *Social Science and Social Pathology* (New York: The Macmillan Company, 1959), 155.

lists, consideration of the role of family agencies in an emerging pattern is obviously relevant. The family agency field is the locus of much of the best development in social work method and education, is a center of strong and impressive social work professionalization, and has a noteworthy tradition of service and accomplishment.[23] Yet, as in the case of the children's field, we must raise questions about the relationship of prevention to case services; and we find it urgent to explore the viability of the current service pattern —no matter how admirably it has performed in the past.

The core planning issue may be introduced by examining an earlier, and now at least partially discarded, effort of the field to look at itself. Several years ago the Family Service Association of America (FSAA) assembled a national committee and charged it with consideration of the function of a family service agency in the modern world. As is often the case when planning begins with the perspective of a given, well-organized, functional field and is carried on by people heavily committed to an existing pattern, very little that was new emerged. The report, *Range and Emphases of a Family Service Program*,[24] offers a useful case lesson.

The committee must have had access to the data about the "thin" coverage by voluntary family agencies, but such data got no detailed attention in the report. There was little acknowledgment of the current status and potential future role of public welfare offices as family service centers. And, while some comments were offered on family problems in the United States, there was certainly no systematic compilation and analysis. Parallel and related counseling services were ignored. The committee had before it proposals for new emphases based on (*a*) severity of social problems (more work to focus on delinquency), (*b*) need to maximize coverage (group education), (*c*) need to increase prevention (unspecified), and (*d*) urgency of flexibility (more experimentation). However, the central point of departure was: what is our expertise and what function has been expected of us?

Here is the dilemma. Obviously, when planning the relationships of psychiatric to school social work programs, for example, or of group services to community organization, one wants to know the core of expertise, the intervention specific. Periodically, however, there is also need to go back to basics:

---

[23] For a statement of method, as developed out of the family field, see Florence Hollis, *Casework: A Psychosocial Therapy* (New York: Random House, 1964); and Helen Harris Perlman, *Social Casework: A Problem-Solving Process* (Chicago: University of Chicago Press, 1957).

[24] Family Service Association of America, *Range and Emphases of a Family Service Program* (New York, 1963). For a general review of family service, see Scott Briar, "Family Services," in Maas, *op. cit.*, 9–50; contains extensive bibliography.

what are the social problems to be addressed, the social functions to be discharged—and where does this system of service fit in? Or, in the language of
our earlier chapters, the definition of the planning task must concern itself
with problems, trends, goals, values, and not merely with available resources,
structure, tradition, and technology.

The committee that produced *Range and Emphases* did not raise the
larger questions about task. Noting that family service agencies had traditionally offered casework services to help resolve family problems, it re-
emphasized the rendering of casework as the function of the agency.

> The chief function of the agency, therefore, is to provide casework and re-
> lated services to families whose functioning is impaired by strains in their
> interpersonal relationships.
>
> [Furthermore] To determine whether a complementary service should be
> established or continued, and the proportion of agency funds and profes-
> sional time that should be allocated to it, the following criteria are sug-
> gested as relevant: (1) the relatedness of the particular service to casework
> objectives and its value in furthering treatment. . . . (5) the importance of
> keeping the casework treatment program in the central position. . . .[25]

With this as a given, not much that is new emerges. The results are star-
tling when examined from a planning perspective.

The consensus reported is

> the central purpose of the family service agency is to contribute to har-
> monious family relationships, to strengthen the positive in family life, and
> to promote healthy personality development and satisfactory social func-
> tioning of various family members.

Yet the national network of agencies dedicated to strengthening family
life announces that this can and is to be accomplished by the traditional
method, casework. It is as though a network of health clinics should an-
nounce that theirs was a profession of antibiotic dispensers. The conviction that a social task requires a flexible interventive repertoire that is
constantly improving—and hence changing—is lost. (A certain number of
peripheral gestures in this direction are obviously not meant to affect the
report's central thrust.)

The agencies, while talking periodically of prevention of family breakdown, and while pre-empting the prevention assignment in their publicity,
actually undertake what is essentially a treatment role. Clearly this leaves
much of the announced task undone. (Again, there are references to fam-

---

[25] Family Service Association, *Range and Emphases*, 12–13, 15.

ily life education as supplementary activity, but casework treatment is the core and has the major claim on resources.)

The experimentation proposed in group treatment is still within the context of the pattern of agency service as dictated by a casework focus and the hiring of a casework-trained staff, so the extent of potential innovation is limited.

There is an announced commitment to serve a population cross-section, ignoring the quite obvious selective distribution of problems among population groups. Coupled with the prior commitment to casework, this could mean that, if extremely disorganized poor families cannot do well with casework, the family agency would serve more middle-class families, for whom the method has somewhat more attractiveness. (It is not that the poor do not enter or are not referred: the process is such that they do not long "survive" in the internal selective procedure by which clients are sorted out for extended service.) A rationale thus is developed for what some have called the family agency's "estrangement" from the poor and what others have seen as its lack of relevance to urban ghettos.[26]

All of these and related points could be elaborated, but this is not necessary, since the planning issue is now before us. The sponsoring agency itself, FSAA, has moved beyond the *Range and Emphases* report. For present purposes, the problem is posed: if more basic measures are sought, what are the options? Suppose one were to create a national study group to look at the family in the United States and consider its problems and needs. Such a study group would take a very broad look at American society and how our pattern of industrialization, urbanization, suburbanization, mobility, longevity, retirement, education, adolescent peer life, and religion impose certain requirements upon the family. It would also examine evidence of problems or circumstances facing the family in discharging such requirements or functions: family breakaway by young adolescents, out-of-wedlock birth of children, marriage breakup and failure, mothers in the labor market, parent-parent and parent-child relationship problems, personal adjustment problems related to family failure, and so on. It would note the prevalence, location, and characteristics of

---

[26] Richard A. Cloward and Irwin Epstein, "Private Social Welfare's Disengagement from the Poor: The Case of Family Adjustment Agencies," in Mayer N. Zald, Editor, *Social Welfare Institutions* (New York: John Wiley & Sons, 1965), 623–643. Kenneth B. Clark, *Dark Ghetto* (New York: Harper & Row, 1965), 50. Jona Rosenfeld, "Strangeness Between Helper and Client," *Social Service Review*, 38, No. 1 (March, 1964), 17–25.

Basic data are reported by Dorothy Fahs Beck, *Patterns in Use of Family Agency Service* (New York: Family Service Association of America, 1962).

high-risk marriages, family structures that create problems for children, and family types that trouble the community in a variety of ways.[27]

Such a group would soon decide that the family is so basic and so peculiar an institution by virtue of its pervasiveness and general acceptability as fundamental to social organization, that we cannot assign to any one network of agencies the task of primary prevention of breakdown. To enhance and protect family life is in some respects in the realm of foreign policy, economic policy, political policy, and all those basic factors that affect the role, status, stability, and valuation of the family and its members who perform in various ways.

What is legitimate within the social welfare sector, however, is to plan how one delivers to the family those *resources and facilities* (social utilities) and income supports designed to strengthen the family as it is currently expected to function and, also, how to offer the *case services* essential to those family members and groups experiencing difficulty in functioning. In addition, one might wish to see a family *lobby*, or lobbies, established to concern itself with tax policy, and general legislation as well as social service planning from a family perspective.

The creation of a family lobby and social action groups concerned with consumer protections and related matters is beyond the scope of the present chapter, but the subject is relevant and vital. The experience with FSAA does not encourage one in the belief that a network of case service agencies can or will perform this role. A preoccupation with treatment methods does not combine well with social policy and social action activities—if the FSAA history or the experience of child guidance clinics is indicative. In the past, such agencies have often been so dominated by clinically-oriented people and so weak in their research, policy development, and promotional capacities as to minimize their role. Serious consideration, therefore, should be given to the means of creating an alliance of voluntary groups at different governmental levels that might serve as a family lobby—a function known in other countries but surprisingly underdeveloped in the United States, where lobbying has generally reached its most intensive level of development.

---

[27] For a review of what is now known about the family and for extensive bibliography, see John A. Clausen, "Family Structure, Socialization, and Personality," in Lois Wladis Hoffman and Martin L. Hoffman, Editors, *Review of Child Development Research*, 2 volumes (New York: Russell Sage Foundation; I, 1964; II, 1966), II, 1–53.

A conceptual approach to guide family service is offered by Nelson N. Foote and Leonard S. Cottrell, Jr., *Identity and Interpersonal Competence* (Chicago: University of Chicago Press, 1955).

The question of planning, legislating, and implementing income maintenance policy and seeking the creation of needed social utilities that offer
developmental support to the family is also a major one for social policy.
Many voluntary groups and political bodies may be expected to concern
themselves with such matters. Certainly, those who "treat" and "serve"
families in trouble are in a position to spot trends and highlight needs.
Theirs is a significant, not a sole or leadership, role in this field.

One then turns to family-oriented case services, services to serve families in difficulty or under stress. The interest may be in problems which
reflect deep-seated personality difficulties in family members, complex
interpersonal relationship problems, transitory situational emergencies,
and stress or long-term environmental deprivations. The etiology may be
genetic and developmental, environmental, interpersonal, cultural—or,
more usually, a complex combination of these. In considering a system of
case services it becomes abundantly clear, as the child welfare leadership group recently noted, that

> services for children in their own homes cannot be defined specifically and
> exclusively as a child welfare service. . . . services that contribute to the wel-
> fare of children living with their families and to the *improvement of family
> life* . . . include a range of services, offered in a variety of settings, under
> public, voluntary, nonsectarian and religious auspices, such as protective,
> homemaker and day care services for children, public assistance, family serv-
> ices, school social work, public health and medical services, mental health
> and psychiatric services, court services, group work services, recreation pro-
> grams, services in public housing, settlement and neighborhood centers.[28]

As much should be said by the family field. Services contributing to
"the improvement of family life" ramify well beyond the scope of a case
service agency. Money, social utilities, and medical care are involved.
And, with reference to advice-guidance-counseling-casework, there is
little logic for the separation of family service from child welfare. For that
matter, is there convincing argument for developing separately social
services for the aged or adolescents?

The rationale for thinking of a new integrated general or case service
system, which could not be called a *family* service because it must also
serve the single, the separated, and the widowed, is also strengthened by
experimentation and research related to the interventive repertoire.

---

[28] Joseph H. Reid, "Foreword" in Child Welfare League of America, "Social Work
Service for Children in their Own Homes" (New York, 1967, pamphlet). (Emphasis
added.)

Working out from the original one-to-one casework base, many family agencies came to recognize that, at least in some situations, this was hardly an optimum helping strategy. While some formulated the issue quite traditionally ("the other family members are part of the patient's 'reality' "), other agencies went much further ("the *client* is the family *group* as a whole; internal family dynamics decide who actually comes to the agency, but this is not even necessarily the sickest family member"). Still other investigators noted that earlier assumptions about the nuclear family were false: to deal with a woman in marital conflict is to start an interactional process, for example, which may ramify beyond immediate family into a family business, extended kinship network, or a club of "cousins." Thus, the unit interview must now be seen as having ramifications well beyond the wife's psyche or her relationship with her husband and children.

The result of these and similar insights has been a considerable effort to develop relevant group methods—and to consider anew when it is desirable to "treat" a person, when to encourage mutually more advantageous accommodations, when to avoid and ignore problems, when to focus on environmental and "reality" problems alone.[29] Some of the experimentation has come from the family agencies themselves, some from adult mental health clinics and private psychotherapy. Much of the most successful work has involved new, more comprehensive, diagnostic assessments. To a lesser, but significant, degree, treatment approaches have changed, too—but the challenge of using the new knowledge and commitment has proven complex.

There is thus new attention being directed to (a) treating all family members conjointly: they are seen together, at the same time, by the same therapist(s); (b) conjoint diagnosis followed by individual treatment by collaborating therapists; (c) having family members seen individually by closely collaborating therapists; (d) working with one member and

---

[29] The following is merely a sampling: Nathan Ackerman, *The Psychodynamics of Family Life* (New York: Basic Books, 1958); Hope J. Leichter, William E. Mitchell, *et al.*, *Kinship and Casework* (New York: Russell Sage Foundation, 1967); Seymour Fisher and David Mendell, "The Communication of Neurotic Patterns Over Two or Three Generations," in Norman W. Bell and Ezra T. Vogel, *A Modern Introduction to the Family* (Glencoe, Ill.: The Free Press, 1960), 612 ff.; Robert MacGregor *et al.*, *Multiple Impact Therapy with Families* (New York: McGraw-Hill Book Company, 1964); Ludwig Geismar and Michael A. LaSorte, *Understanding the Multi-problem Family* (New York: Association Press, 1964); Otto Pollack and Donald Brieland, "The Midwest Seminar on Family Diagnosis and Treatment," *Social Casework*, XLII, No. 7 (July, 1961), 319–324. Many of the departures and related research are reviewed by Briar, *op. cit.*, 28–50.

seeing the others occasionally to assure "non-interference," if it should be found diagnostically viable.[30]

The notion that the *family* agency works with those under stress to preserve family life has also loosened up under pressure of other developments. Practical social services and counseling to the aged and to many "single" people of any age have obviously become very important in most cities. In a few places, the occasion of divorce or contemplated divorce has provided for a significant case-finding and service opportunity. The move into New Towns or "developments" has occasionally been seized as opportunity for "preventive" work.

While still not common, group therapy is no longer rare in the family agency. Family life education is accepted as a legitimate, if secondary, activity, and there is recognition of the importance of homemakers, day care, adoption, and other child care services—whatever the administrative auspices dictated by the local resource picture.

In recent years, great emphasis has been placed on the development of crisis-oriented emergency counseling services—paralleling similar developments in psychiatric clinics.[31] Significantly, too, the poverty-related Project Enable, carried out as a collaborative enterprise of the FSAA, the Child Study Association of America, and the National Urban League in more than 60 communities in 25 states and funded by the Office of Economic Opportunity in 1965–1966, did surmount old boundaries and intervention strategies. Reflecting neighborhood "demand" as perceived by the League, an agency that concentrates on parent education joined with a casework service to create a group education program, encompassing both educational and community self-help rather than individually-oriented therapeutic objectives. Specially trained local residents were employed as aides.

Never before had so many family agencies accepted public funding for services and concentrated in so extensive a non-casework enterprise.[32] At the same time, many other family agencies began to develop cooperative programs in conjunction with anti-poverty efforts. The rigidity and singleness of pattern described above began to give way.

---

[30] Don D. Jackson and Virginia Satir, "A Review of Psychiatric Developments in Family Diagnosis and Therapy," in Nathan W. Ackerman *et al.*, *Exploring the Base for Family Therapy* (New York: Family Service Association of America, 1961), 29–51.

[31] Howard Parad, "Time and Crisis" (Unpublished doctoral dissertation, Columbia University School of Social Work, 1967).

[32] See "Project Enable," constituting a special issue of *Social Casework*, XLVIII, No. 3 (December, 1967).

Should this process continue, family agencies will no longer perceive of the "modal" client—the one who receives intensive and extended service—as a verbalizing, insight-seeking, anxious office visitor who, for 50 minutes each week, seeks to relive and reconstruct his life-view. They will recognize the reality: that *most* of their cases require brief service and cannot use or are not reached by such help.[33] Alfred Kadushin's picture of "multi-problem" and hard-to-reach cases will be found relevant to an increasingly large portion of the load.

> The research orientation to the therapeutic relationship with this client regards him as tending to externalize problems, to show little anxiety and guilt, to be impulsive, to be oriented to the present and concerned with immediate gratification, to be neither introspective nor highly self-conscious, to see problems in terms of environmental stress and deprivation, in conflict with the environment, rather than in terms of intrapsychic or interpersonal conflicts. He seeks solutions to problems motorically in physical handling rather than in conceptualizing and verbalizing problem situations. He has little capacity for communication. He relates to the environment either in a passive dependent manner or in an aggressive, exploitive manner and identifies the agency with the school, the legal apparatus, and so on, as part of the structure of social sanctions and social control which has alien values and demands, is not to be trusted, and to which he need not be loyal. His orientation to his situation is fatalistic. This suggests that he has little confidence that he has any control over the environment and little hope that he can do anything in a deliberate, planful manner to improve his situation in an unpredictable world.[34]

Clearly, the children's field is prepared for growth and change as it seeks to strengthen "preventive" casework services to children in their own homes and to encourage the expansion of services generally through federal aid to the states. It will be in a position to collaborate with the new initiatives in the service repertoire of the family agencies should there be agreement as to the need for a new local service configuration. Several of the other potential components also deserve at least brief mention.

THE MARRIAGE COUNSELING MOVEMENT

While child welfare and family social service are essentially "social work" movements, a marriage counseling field based in psychology, education, and sociology, with significant participation from psychiatry, social

---

[33] Briar, *op. cit.*

[34] Alfred Kadushin, "Introduction of New Orientations in Child Welfare Research," in Norris and Wallace, Editors, *op. cit.*, 33; also contains extensive references to major studies of work with "multi-problem families."

work, and the ministry, turns for organized leadership and research orientations to the American Association of Marriage Counselors (AAMC) and the National Council on Family Relations (NCFR). The latter, sociologically oriented, publishes the *Journal of Marriage and Family Living.*

The AAMC (500 members) overlaps in membership with the family service field. It concentrates on improving therapeutic practice, offering no new local service models and no significant degree of coverage. The NCFR would like to become a family lobby; its chief accomplishments to date are in research and publication. Neither points to a new local service pattern or precludes an effort to plan one.[35]

RELATED SOCIAL SERVICE DEVELOPMENTS

The planner of a new pattern of general social services must look beyond family and child welfare. For one thing, public welfare is now separating the administration of public assistance from the rendering of generally available social services.

The direction is described by a former top official in the Department of Health, Education, and Welfare:

> The trend is clearly towards making quality services available and readily accessible to all those who need them. . . . Solvency in itself is no barrier to need. The financially well-off also have social problems, yet some services are not available at any price. We are gradually accepting the premise that these needs too must be served.[36]

At the same time, serious exploration of the needs of the aged suggests either the expansion of general social services to encompass them (since their problems must often be coped with in "extended family" context) or the coordination of specialized services for the aged with a general system. Also, many in- and out-patient psychiatric and medical services seek transfer to a locally-based, general social work service in the final transition to full community functioning—or to provide an ongoing supportive relationship for those not likely to "recover" fully. Finally, expanded social services to adolescents, tied to employment counseling, on the one hand,

---

[35] See *Journal of Marriage and Family Living*, published by National Council on Family Relations; Harold T. Christensen, Editor, *Handbook of Marriage and the Family* (Chicago: Rand McNally, 1964); E. M. Naob *et al., Marriage Counseling in Medical Practice* (Chapel Hill: University of North Carolina Press, 1964).

[36] Lisle C. Carter, Jr., "Optimum Social Welfare through Planning, Participation, and Manpower," *Health, Education, and Welfare Indicators*, January, 1967, 25. For detail, see Chapter IV in the present work.

and to family interventions, on the other, need to be seen as part of a total system.

These goals are quite compatible with the general service which would emerge out of a combination of family and child welfare. *In fact, the latter two systems, plus public welfare, services for the aged, and a variety of aftercare responsibilities (mental hospitals, several types of institutions), could provide the components of a new, locally-based, general social service office—which might provide the much needed ingredients of accountability and social integration.* Internal administrative reorganization in the Department of Health, Education, and Welfare has created, in its Social and Rehabilitation Service, a possible national locus for such development.

A recent Scottish "White Paper" and the British Seebohm Report go beyond this.[37] In the British instance, it was the logic of an attempt to move child welfare toward increased family-preventive activity[38] that created the occasion and leverage for considering even more extensive reforms.

A relatively recent ingredient encouraging the review of basic patterns in the United States is the network of some thousand anti-poverty service centers, more or less guided by locally-based committees and neighborhood corporations, and stressing social utilities, liaison services, and community self-help.[39] In the short run, poverty-specific enterprises were defensible and served to dramatize the need for change both in the pattern of local social services and their control and in the interventive repertoire. In the long run, they should help reshape the general social service system into a universal program not carrying the stigma of poverty. The experience of these centers, only partially assembled to date, seems to strengthen the case for a general, readily accessible, quite flexible local entry point to social services—with some "outreach characteristics," at least for the uneducated and deprived. It also suggests that each decision about functions, structure, and auspices carries "costs" and "benefits" in terms of attractiveness, community perception, staff role, and development of specific activities.[40]

---

[37] Scottish Education Department and Scottish Home and Health Department, *Social Work and the Community; Report of The Committee on Local Authority and Allied Personal Social Services;* Titmuss, "The Welfare Complex in a Changing Society," which contains listing of relevant background reports and studies. Also see, "Welfare for Everyone," *The Economist* (London), XIII, No. 22 (February 19, 1966), 684–685.

[38] Aryeh Leissner, *Family Advice Services* (London: Longmans, Green & Co., 1967).

[39] See Chapter II.

[40] Perlman and Jones, *op. cit.;* Kahn *et al., Neighborhood Information Centers.*

FAMILY LIFE EDUCATION AND SOCIAL UTILITIES

Both child welfare and family agencies have conducted family life education programs, with the latter giving the effort more serious, yet still limited, attention. If one begins to visualize a new pattern of social service on the local level that builds upon but eradicates the dysfunctional boundaries between these two movements, the place of family life education must be faced. In effect, what is involved is the larger question of the relationship between case services and social utilities. Put more generally, should the new local social service center be conceived as a place for case treatment services or does it also have a developmental role relevant to all?

In his authoritative review of the family life education field, Orville G. Brim, Jr., reminds us that, as a subdivision of adult education, parent education is aimed at helping the parent to become competent and independent in his role. Although the knowledge-base on which such programs rest is limited and the values from which they derive guidance are elusive, it does seem clear that the objectives of role development and independence demand an ecletic approach and the selection of a variety of community contexts for the effort. As much may be said for premarital educational efforts. These generalizations hold with reference both to formally organized courses and one-time educational experiences and to the informal efforts of many persons in contact with parents (teachers, doctors, nurses, social workers, etc.).[41]

Thus, while one would certainly see the new local social service center as a suitable location for such programs, it is not likely to seek or obtain a monopoly. Adult education, health, mental health, church, union, and related programs have legitimate roles. At present, programs in family agencies often are counseling and less-intensive group therapeutic endeavors. A broader educational role must be based on achievement of community perception of the center as developmental as well as therapeutic. If there is interest in primary and secondary preventive activity and allegiance to a flexible interventive repertoire, such an image would be worthy of cultivation.

From this it would follow that the center could also be the entry point or even administrative headquarters for homemaker services, home-helps, meals-on-wheels, and other social utilities that facilitate family functioning

---

[41] Orville G. Brim, Jr., *Education for Child Rearing* (New York: Russell Sage Foundation, 1959). Also see, Ivor Kraft and Catherine S. Chilman, "Helping Low-Income Families through Parent Education: A Survey of Research" (Washington, D.C.: Government Printing Office, 1966).

and the older citizen's independent living in the community. Although in the past family and children's agencies have sponsored such programs on a small scale, such services were seen as supportive of case services only. Complex intake procedures prevailed. If, while some diagnostically-assigned resources remain relevant, there is agreement that many of these resources are utilities available by status, expansion and simplified eligibility become essential.

It is routine in some countries to assign to the retired several hours a week of home-help service and access to meals-on-wheels, friendly visitors, and other resources that keep the isolated older person out of an institution. Social security and health insurance schemes often finance the measures. Depending on ultimate federal decisions in the United States and the involvement of specific state and local agencies in administration, one might visualize either public or voluntary central service agencies or expansion through contracts with a variety of outlets, some of them, perhaps, profit-making organizations. Access would be facilitated if locally-based social service centers forwarded applications for the service, provided recipients with "vouchers" (should such approach develop), or were outlets for the actual local operation. The latter approach would maximize use of volunteers and adaptation to local needs.

A similar approach may be taken with reference to day care.[42] It may be assumed that education and group service programs will provide the basic utility, the child development service, while case-oriented social service agencies and mental health centers tend toward therapeutic efforts. However, the local social service center should certainly offer access to this utility as well.[43]

SOCIAL SERVICES AT THE LOCAL LEVEL—THE TASK

We have discussed in some detail the specialized child welfare and family service movements and have made brief reference to new thrusts

---

[42] Anna B. Mayer and Alfred J. Kahn, *Day Care as a Social Instrument* (New York: Columbia University School of Social Work, 1965).

[43] This, too, does not preclude experimentation with commercial operation in which competing, profit-making sponsors or nonprofit organizations vie for "vouchers" available to the parent who needs the service. The parent then becomes a consumer in the market. In the case of a utility, any individual of the designated status gets the voucher upon application. Case service vouchers are supplied only by diagnostic agencies. While rare at this writing, it does seem possible that social service planners in the future may well seek more consumer autonomy and increased efficiency through such resort to market mechanisms. "Trial balloon" proposals were offered in "Services for People," Report of the Task Force on Organization of Social Services (Washington, D.C.: U.S. Department of Health, Education, and Welfare, 1968).

in public welfare, to marriage counseling, and to the expanding neighborhood services growing out of the anti-poverty program, noting the case for their integration at the level at which the family is met. The new location, it has been held, should also offer access to social utilities and might even administer some.

In an earlier discussion of programming, the need for improved access to services, rights, and benefits and for much more efficient channeling has been outlined, and both the neighborhood information center and the outposted "polyvalent worker" have been described as possible contributors to a solution. The latter was also seen as relevant to the search for case integration and accountability.[44]

One might look in some detail at delinquency programs or services to the aged as well, but such examination would merely multiply the illustrations. The basic elements for consideration in a possible local social service pattern are already before us. Quite specifically, what are to be the relationships among (*a*) the new access and channeling machinery (neighborhood information center or polyvalent worker); (*b*) the basic integration and accountability devices; (*c*) the obvious need to review the boundaries of family and child welfare, public welfare, and social services to the aged, to adolescents, and to single people; (*d*) the new multifunction neighborhood centers under anti-poverty, housing, anti-delinquency, and health auspices; and (*e*) the locally-based outlets for basic social utilities? What, in short, is to be the local social service picture—and what are the relationships between the services close to home and those covering larger geographic areas?

THE CASE FOR DECENTRALIZATION

It will be argued in the remainder of this chapter that, if the goal is to develop a service-delivery approach that improves access, facilitates feedback so as to adapt to user preference and priority, and maximizes case integration and accountability, the base of the total social service system should be in the neighborhood. Furthermore, if one wants to minimize child placement, affirm family relationships and roles, and make a contribution to wholesome child development, old boundaries must be dropped. We shall hold that the overall entry to social services should be a general information, referral, and access service. Then the entry point to *case* services should be a general practice or "personal" social worker who renders general counseling, refers to specialists, and assures case integration.

---

[44] Chapter X in the companion volume.

There are fluctuations in economic, governmental, and social planning between an emphasis on increased centralization and a conviction that decentralization is necessary. Obviously, some elements of both are preconditions for sound planning, coordination, and service delivery. Since we have been in an era of service centralization and of selectivity, which has led to the closing out of some groups, there is now need for increased emphasis on and a bias toward a service-delivery system which is highly decentralized at the point at which it meets the user. Some services are too specialized and do not have sufficient user-density at the local level to justify such decentralization. Program coordination, standard protection, evaluation measures all call for considerable centralization for overall program administration, but do not preclude localization of the system of delivery per se.

The basic objective of decentralization in service delivery is to reduce cities and counties, and their services, to "people-sized" scale. Many people cannot encompass and make use of complex, multifaceted programs centrally located; in fact, they cannot even comprehend such services. But a local unit able to individualize, help, and follow a person and to aid him in drawing upon specialties is manageable.

More than service usage is involved, however. The social forces which have created metropolis and megalopolis have conspired to make these large units impersonal places; many individuals do not develop ties or relationships to very large, vaguely bounded areas. There is, therefore, a general search for ways to "break down" cities to human scale for some purposes, on the assumption that people find it easier to relate to a neighborhood or section and to its population. Behind this is the belief that some of the value-vacuum that accompanies urban mobility and changes in family structure will be overcome by neighborhood solidarity. Thus, the organization of services at the neighborhood level has the added purpose of contributing to the search for neighborhood. The process apparently is much enhanced if the decentralization is accompanied by a measure of real local control over some or all aspects of the operation ("power"). There is special interest in decentralization in urban ghetto areas whose residents see local control over facilities and institutions as a precursor of equality. Everywhere on the United States urban scene, there is an effort to determine the measure of such control which is consistent with the general public interest and the responsibility assigned locally elected officials.

Beyond this, there are further elements of the rationale that are more directly tied to social services and their organization. One function of social services almost everywhere is to facilitate use of other services and resources and to help people cope with bureaucracy and complexity. Certainly this is a meaningful undertaking only if launched at an organizational level close to where the users are and attuned to them and to their needs. Otherwise, one has merely created another layer of impersonal bureaucratic structure.

Then, there is the issue of adapting services to cultural and ethnic differences and to the particular local age distributions. Central bureaucracies find this difficult. Locally organized units, *which are permitted certain program options*, may achieve such adaptation. Central standard setting and enforcement must be balanced against this, lest some services so "adapted" become inferior and it is assumed that people in one area do not "need" or "cannot use" what others have.

The community care movement in general medicine, psychiatry, and correctional services is especially relevant to decentralization. Each of these fields sees a local service as a deterrent to institutionalization, defines the institution as a treatment episode that begins close to home, and emphasizes the need for continuity of help in the locality after the return home. Such delegation is meaningful only under one of several decentralized patterns. It demands a worker with a geographic assignment and a caseload small enough to undertake case integration and case accountability responsibilities on a family basis.

Closely connected to these goals is the objective of maximum consumer participation in policy development and service evaluation. Locally organized services permit the creation of local advisory or policy committees and allow local evaluation of impact of service and feedback of suggestions. The movement toward service decentralization does permit increased democratization of social services. (Again the caveat that this must be in the context of central policy and standards, so that legislative objectives are not subverted and so that public funds purchase what they are intended to.)

Also relevant to decentralization is the current interest in opening many service jobs, including jobs in the social services, to the less-educated and the uneducated. This new employment arena develops as jobs previously reserved for credentialed professional workers are re-defined and re-divided. Many of the service assignments are in categories such as child care, welfare aide, homemaker, and teacher aide. These are assignments in which knowledge of neighborhood and of group served *and easy access to user* are distinct assets. For example, local emergency homemaker service would do much to protect families in sudden crisis situations and make child placement unnecessary. Here, decentralization has major virtues.

From another perspective, our society now has the affluence to consider a pattern of universally available basic social services and must address the question of what pattern of organization for delivery would most likely contribute to the objectives sought. For all the reasons cited and *for the convenience of users*, decentralization would seem desirable. *The services sold in the market place always locate locally if volume justifies it.*

Even as one considers the problem of the less densely populated areas and notes the extent to which there is a search for activities, program, and provision that may be the nucleus for "community," one comes to the idea of service decentralization in some planned pattern.

Obviously, of course, this could not apply:

☐ where the need-density is too little to justify a local service unit
☐ to skills or resources so rare that they could not be supplied at the most immediate local level
☐ where the costs of decentralization are so high as to outweigh by far the potential benefits
☐ to services so standardized as to allow no room or need for local variation (money payments?).

What must emerge, eventually is an hierarchical pattern in which

☐ Certain services, facilities, resources, and *responsibilities* reside at *the most immediate local level.*
☐ Other services, facilities, resources, and *responsibilities* (generally more specialized) reside in certain *larger units*—several neighborhoods combined, a district, or a borough.
☐ Still other services, facilities, resources, and responsibilities (quite specialized) reside at a *central governmental level*: county, city, state, regional. The level would also be the locus of program coordination, budgeting, planning, standard-setting, inspection, and certain central services.

It will require considerable trial and error, as well as study of user patterns, to define adequately neighborhood, district, and other units for such purposes and to clarify the measure of policy autonomy, as contrasted with programming flexibility, to be allocated to the lower levels.

THE MAJOR OPTIONS

The programming goal is to create a new type of integrated social service practice, offering the basic counseling and "social brokerage" services, which will join together the components now fragmented among child welfare, family service, public welfare social services, special programs to the aged, and others. The role involves basic counseling, general help to the families or individuals needing it—and a constant drawing upon both social utilities, on the one hand, and more specialized case services, on the other.[45]

The general practitioner as the fulcrum of the system

A locally-based, general practitioner social worker would have the same relationship to the family as does a general medical practitioner. He would refer to, consult with, and support the work of specialists, being ever prepared to pick up the case again as the specialist completed his work.

His would be the major case integration responsibility, focused on the meshing of simultaneous or sequential services and interventions of the total case service system with reference to a single household member or all members. (Obviously, he would exercise discretion, depending on the family situation, to determine whether family members or relatives could carry such responsibility alone.)

Should it be compatible with other systems and their needs, he also would be the obvious aftercare worker for mental hospital and other institutional dischargees. Indeed, as the family's general worker, he (*a*) would always be consulted about commitment, voluntary institutionalization, or foster home placement of a child; (*b*) would constantly be at work on the community and familial factors affecting the potential for a return to the family; (*c*) would assess the appropriateness of the return and would support it.

In addition, in those categories of "clear and present danger" cases, for which case accountability is considered urgent (child abuse and neglect, protective cases in the senior citizen group, mental hospital and juvenile institution parole, etc.), he would be a possible accountability worker.[46]

This combination of basic counseling, liaison, advice, and referral activity is quite consistent with the long tradition of social casework. The role exists in a number of European and Latin American countries in the assignment of the *assistante sociale*, of whom the polyvalent French worker serves as an example. The professionalization of casework in the United States generally has been accompanied by a pattern of segmentation of role that reflects organizational fragmentation. One begins in a specific field of practice, rises in the hierarchy in a field, and transfers to another field. But one is always child welfare worker, family agency social worker, medical social worker, psychiatric social worker, and so on—not a general

---

[45] Referral would be to public and voluntary agencies as well as to profit-making organizations, should such programs expand.

[46] See Chapter X in the companion volume.

(i.e., general practitioner) family worker.[47] Recently, however, as already indicated, "intensive" workers in a variety of agencies, staff of special multi-service units or units serving multi-problem families, and both non-professional and professional staffs of anti-poverty service programs have begun to reshape a "polyvalent" or general practice role. It is reasonable to expect social work education to support the development if the organizational structure for local social service delivery requires it.

What organizational patterns could support this thrust?

The local social service-delivery system, decentralized for the reasons given and concerned with access, case integration, and accountability, would appear to face two major structural options in handling entry and accountability. These, in turn, relate to other options for creating local social service "outposts." Several of the possible resultant combinations are here spelled out; but it is clear that present experience does not yet offer an overwhelming case for any one.[48]

The central choice would seem to be between (a) a neighborhood information (advice, referral, and advocacy) center as the entry point, closely related to a general personal service or case unit for accountability for those families who need special case services, and (b) a "polyvalent" worker available to all families, offering access to information as well as first-line case services. These possibilities and their relative advantages may merit some elaboration. The highly-regarded "multi-service center" approach is not here considered an adequate approach to the major issues.

Functions at the entry point

The choices are best understood if functions are considered before structure. Careful study discloses the following as the essential elements of a neighborhood information and referral service—or the essential information and referral activities of a polyvalent worker, if the second option is chosen.

☐ to provide simple information, such as where something is located or how to get there

---

[47] Alfred J. Kahn, "Social Work Fields of Practice," in Harry L. Lurie, Editor, Encyclopedia of Social Work, Fifteenth Issue (New York: National Association of Social Workers, 1965), 750–755; or Harriet M. Bartlett, Analyzing Social Work Practice by Fields (New York: National Association of Social Workers, 1961).

[48] I am here in the debt of my colleagues on the Task Force on Social Services, United States Department of Health, Education, and Welfare (1966) and the subsequent 1968 Task Force on Organization of Social Services. Also see Carter, op. cit., 24–33. A suggestive summary of British experience, growing out of the decision to expand "preventive" work in child welfare, is reported by Leissner, op. cit. The Seebohm Committee urged a general practice role in Report of The Committee . . . , 160–161.

☐ to provide information about more complex matters, such as the provisions of a law or an agency's function

☐ to clarify the significance of a statute or a provision for a specific person (one aspect of the advice function)

☐ to give advice on how to proceed—not only clarifying the possible, but suggesting a course of action

☐ to steer to an agency or service able to help, merely telling the inquirer what and where the service is, but doing nothing to help him get there

☐ to refer to the right agency, going beyond steering to arrange for an appointment, send a referral letter or summary, facilitating the transition from inquiry to service

☐ to provide a supporting, friendly relationship for those people whose continued welfare requires an occasional dropping in for a friendly chat, often supplemented by information and advice

☐ to help the inquirer with the contact—or to make it for him (Sometimes the inquirer is helped to make the contact with a telephone referral or a letter. At other times the action required involves a letter of inquiry from the information service itself or an attempt to achieve a solution by mail.)

In addition to the above functions, some of the following *may be* encompassed by the information and advice service, each having a price in terms of community image, access to some elements of the population, and response of the agencies rendering service:

☐ to go beyond the presenting problem in helping people (In general, social work services stress the need to see beyond the presenting request and to offer information, advice, referral, or help related to the real problem.)

☐ to carry out formal diagnostic study

☐ to carry out continuing counseling and treatment

☐ to follow through (aggressively if necessary) until the inquirer has his needs or his rights recognized (case-oriented advocacy)

☐ to seek program and policy changes in agencies (policy and program advocacy)

☐ to conduct general community education, where inquiries reveal widespread need for information

☐ to recruit potential clients (outreach)

☐ to monitor and report one's experience with human need and public provision (A well-functioning information and advice service is, indeed, a window on the man-in-the-street.)

☐ to facilitate the self-organization of people with common problems (The intent may be socio-therapeutic, group education, institutional change, or political action.)[49]

---

[49] Kahn *et al.*, *Neighborhood Information Centers*, 112–119.

A neighborhood system based on a neighborhood information center

Under this plan, the neighborhood information center is the pivot. It is available within walking distance or at strategic points on the public transportation system, is very much influenced by the British Citizens' Advice Bureaus, but adapts to the local scene in relation to a possibly greater or lesser degree of case and policy advocacy and a greater or lesser degree of diagnostic competence. It is professionally guided but employs a considerable proportion of "non-credentialed" aides and volunteers. While perhaps based in national functional service systems (antipoverty, public welfare, social insurance), it is locally controlled.[50]

Staff in such a center may provide information and advice to meet many needs, but may also offer direct entry to such social utilities as homemakers and meals-on-wheels and help inquirers fill out forms for other benefits and services (public assistance declarations, social insurance applications, veteran pensions, housing applications, scholarship applications, and the like). The exact way in which this works depends on whether the information center is part of a so-called multi-service center containing "outposts" of such departments and services, is in a cluster of buildings in which such outposts are located, or operates separately. The first makes for coordination and integration, the last for freer advocacy.

Under this pattern, there is also a *neighborhood general social service unit,* staffed by general practitioners, to work intensively with people screened out of the information center, referred directly by other agencies, or self-referred. It should probably serve the territories of from one to five information services, depending on intensity of local need. Its general practitioners, as already stated, combine and re-define roles currently fragmented among child welfare, family service, public welfare social services, and special programs for the aging—as well as some aftercare programs attached to institutions. It is for those who need personal help, treatment, counseling, or substitute care—the diagnostically-based service. It, too, offers entry to utilities and may administer some. This is, by definition, a professional service, but aides and escorts can be used as well. Unlike the family service agency or child welfare office as presently conceived, it has range (family welfare, child welfare, aged, people living alone), carries case integration and accountability responsibility, and organizes itself to assure consideration of all possible options and to avoid premature channeling.

---

[50] *Ibid.*

It may have child welfare experts in the office, and perhaps experts in working with the aging, but it is essentially the "general practitioner" case service. It refers clients to more specialized services that cannot be neighborhood based (a psychiatric clinic, a day hospital) but retains responsibility for case integration.

Depending on local conditions, this personal or general social service office could be developed in the United States out of the voluntary family and children's agencies or out of the public welfare system. If from the former, the voluntary agencies would have to give up the rigidity of their service repertoire (now making them a specialized resource, not a basic service) and undertake case accountability responsibilities. For the public welfare system to develop so, it would have to separate out the public assistance–granting function, which now stigmatizes the entire system, and seek to become a social service operation available to all citizens. The British Seebohm Committee projected a similar, but not identical, development, based on the existing local child welfare and public welfare services.

Since the essence of the pattern is to provide wide geographic coverage, as well as a non-stigmatic service available to all social classes, the guarantee and the financing would have to be public. Local custom, as well as state and federal law, might determine whether, in some instances, the actual service could be rendered on a contract, voucher, or purchase of care basis by a voluntary, nonprofit, or profit-making agency. Public planning and overall auditing would be required to assure fiscal and service accountability in these instances, of course; and one may assume that, in most places, a government department would oversee the actual operation of the network.

Should this occur in the United States, there will be strong incentive to incorporate or assure participation of the family and child welfare agencies in the voluntary sector. For a variety of historical reasons, their levels of staff preparation and experience exceed those in public welfare and anti-poverty programs.

On the negative side, some observers note that this proposed approach creates an intermediate layer of screening (the information center) between the individual and access to personal help in the form of case services. The second option is addressed to this situation.

A system based on an all-purpose family social worker
This option is inspired by the French social work pattern.[51] French law

---

[51] Alvin L. Schorr, *Social Security and Social Services in France* (Washington, D.C.: Government Printing Office, 1965).

requires that each *départment* (region) establish a Committee of Liaison and Coordination to work out a plan for the area and have it approved by the *Conseil Superieur de Service Social*. Each family is assured "coverage" by a general family worker who may derive from the social services of the municipality, the social security office, the health department, or a voluntary agency. Families need not accept a worker—or agency—if they do not wish to do so. Coordination, case integration, and general implementation of the scheme is the line responsibility of a local supervisor of coordination, elected by the social workers involved. The overall city-wide responsibility is in the hands of the Director of the Service of Coordination who is responsible to a committee chaired by the Mayor. General family workers are assigned, usually on a geographic basis, in a ratio of about one worker per 400 families. The social worker knows who is on his list. The families know where the worker may be located and that they have a right to his service. (An analogy might be the family physician who has a list of people who have elected him under a group health plan.) Case integration is stressed: "No work may be done twice."[52]

Under this plan, the general or polyvalent worker may be "detached," housed in a settlement, a health center, or other local building, or he may be located in a local service center or multi-service center with other polyvalent workers and some outpost services and specialists. He is close by, a frequent visitor, and locally known. Unlike the first option—in which the individual or family is on caseload only after referral—the potential client is always "assigned." When he comes to the office, he knows whom to see. In an emergency, he knows whom to telephone.

The polyvalent or general family social worker *combines* the functions of the worker in the neighborhood information center and the caseworker in the general case service unit. He offers information, advice and referral, opens the doorway to certain social utilities available by status, but *also* does the basic individual counseling and casework. He is the case integration and accountability worker, even when referral to a more specialized and intensive diagnostically-based case service must be initiated. His referrals are accepted by such specialized services.

Clearly the general family social worker must be a well-trained professional person. As indicated, the pattern is not viable in the United States without reforms in social work education. Today, United States family social workers are "specialists," much as are medical social workers, psychiatric workers, etc. Reforms would also be needed for the other option,

[52] *Ibid.*, 33.

to create a general practice unit that does not also serve the information function.

A variation on this pattern would assign case aide (less than Master of Science, professional degree) personnel to the polyvalent social work role. The assignment would involve all of the neighborhood information center functions and only the simplest personal counseling and emotional support. Then there would be referral to a local personal case service unit with better-trained personnel—as in the instance of the first option—for other needs.

The general or polyvalent worker plan is attractive in view of its obvious focus on coverage and access. American experience does not clarify whether it is viable from the point of view of concept of the role (one worker serving as access to the system and as the case-accountable professional in relation to all family services), whether the extensive manpower demands involved in professional staffing are in any sense realistic or whether it would not be wiser to base the system in neighborhood centers if untrained or partially-trained staff are to be used.

Concepts of a multi-service or one-stop center

Much of the interest in decentralization has tended to focus on the notion of a multi-service or one-stop center. It is often suggested that both the information and basic counseling services be located in such centers. Examination of experience reveals that a number of concepts of multi-service centers prevail and that the evidence of impact is uncertain. In effect, such centers address a number of different objectives.[53] Most began with the goal of improving access to services. They were responding to claims that services were "disengaged" from the poor, that social workers had middle-class expectations that closed out some clients, that the service modes in some agencies were inappropriate to the priorities of many people in difficulty (especially in their preoccupation with counseling and insight-type therapies for people in need of very concrete help with daily living and access to practical resources).

Potentially in conflict with such goals were two other goals. Demonstration programs under the President's Committee on Delinquency and Youth Crime and the anti-poverty effort also were based on the belief that the decrease of delinquency and conquest of poverty required an increase in community "competence," which could be achieved by successful organization of the previously disinherited. Such organization would

---

[53] Perlman and Jones, *op. cit.*

aim at making public agencies, service bureaucracies, and the local government more responsive to neighborhood needs. In this sense it would be socio-therapeutic and achieve practical, useful reforms at the same time. Some advocates went beyond this, conceiving of the task as one of organizing the poor or racially-discriminated-against to achieve their just share of political power.

An additional goal assigned the multi-service centers was actually first, chronologically, but tended to fade from formal rationales as the anti-poverty program gained momentum. In brief, multi-service centers were created because of the recognition that the most disorganized families needed the persistent, reaching-out and the well-integrated service of a host of agencies over a period of time, and that they were best helped if in the hands of a skilled practitioner who took on such responsibilities. These centers contained agency outposts to facilitate coordination and case integration for "multi-problem" families. They were not expected to serve the "average" neighborhood case and meet the total neighborhood volume.

Since multi-service centers have addressed several or all of these goals, with varied degrees of emphasis and without full consideration of the mutual compatibility of some functions, it is not surprising that many different types of programs are manifest under the general banner. There are no pure types but several of the emphases may be described:

Multi-service centers as outposts. The average citizen is far from and finds it difficult to reach the housing application office, the employment office, the visiting nurse center, and so on. A multi-service center may offer easy access for consulting with representatives of such agencies or applying for their service. In effect, the center offers outposts of public and voluntary agencies.

This is a useful and valid pattern. It tends to have limited development because many of the services cannot be encompassed by one agency representative detached from files, records, equipment, and consultants. The outpost worker (even if assigned by specialized labor, health, employment, or counseling agencies) provides liaison and consultation service in the center and gives partial service to those who call personally but cannot render the complete service. Furthermore, even where it would be possible to render a complete service, agencies tend to prefer to have people come to their offices. Normal bureaucratic processes are here at work: a department is more visible with its own field offices, its own constituency, and the rest.

In actual practice, multi-service centers of this type usually also con-

286   STUDIES IN SOCIAL POLICY AND PLANNING

tain a general neighborhood information-advice-referral service, which refers to the agency staffs in or outside of the service center. Thus, *this type of multi-service center is actually a neighborhood information center, augmented by several "specialists" or liaison people* with particularly good access to certain specific services. However, in addition, such center usually attempts also to serve as general family case service offices. Experience has indicated that, whereas many counseling cases use brief and limited contacts, there is a gradual build up of very complex case situations needing the service of many agencies. The center then faces the dilemma of either cutting intake and discouraging requests, a negation of the original intent, or channeling cases to group action, which changes the center to the next type.[54]

Multi-service centers as combining information-referral-advice with advocacy and community organization. Some centers are multi-service in another sense. Theirs is a liaison role with other departments and agencies, a few of which may assign "outpost" staff to the office in the manner mentioned above, usually on a part-time basis. Generally, they concentrate on the information-advice-referral role, adding to it one or both of two additional functions in recent years: a measure of case or policy advocacy, on a staff level; or an investment in organization of clients or potential clients of a given service to press for general policy reform or for benefits affecting a considerable group. Welfare and housing programs have been the main objects of such organization.

As the community organization and social action component has grown, multi-service centers of this type have at times decided either to use the direct information-referral-advice staff to recruit for the social action or at least to sacrifice service to the individual so as to achieve broader policy objectives. They have often achieved useful reforms. When this occurs, however, one finds that the neighborhood still lacks an adequate, expert, broad information-advice-referral service and an accountable basic case service office for diagnostically-assigned cases.

Multi-service centers as the locus for case integration and accountability for multi-problem families. Some centers emphasize the initial function: concentrating on the most disorganized families they employ both "intensive" caseworkers and small caseloads, plus some outposts of specialized services, to assure a "concerting" of services to cope with the clients' needs, problems, and difficulties in attaining help. This emphasis has obvious usefulness, but successful discharge of this function does not relieve a

---

[54] *Ibid.*

community of the need to plan for some of the other functions relevant to a broader community.

A proposal: combining the information and case roles. None of the centers is a pure type. Several include elements of the neighborhood information center and the general practice case service center (personal or general social service center) as we have proposed it. It has, therefore, been suggested, particularly by those who would reform public welfare, that the core of a one-stop or multi-service center consist of

- ☐ a neighborhood information and advice service, as described earlier
- ☐ a quite independent general social service center for case services (to house the general practitioners, as described above)
- ☐ some social utilities which should be locally based, especially day care, short-term, drop-in child care, homemakers, etc.
- ☐ several locally-relevant specialist services (employment placement, a probation office, etc.).

In short, one location would include the personal or the general social service office, the information service, and specialist services. Available research and experience do not clarify whether or not the functions emphasized would be fully realized. Earlier experience would suggest the desirability of *physical proximity, but administrative separation* (rather than inclusion in one multi-service center), so as

- ☐ to permit an universalistic image of the *information-advice-referral service* (even for those who need no case services)
- ☐ to permit an universalistic image of all *social utilities*
- ☐ to permit maximum usage of and access to the *general case service* (any specialist services attached also affect public perception and attraction)
- ☐ to permit *specialist services* to locate in organizational bases, which maximize their effectiveness (an employment office, a court, a psychiatric clinic, etc.).

Similarly, organization for *policy advocacy* requires its own integrity, neither sacrificing nor sacrificed to case services to troubled people.

From this perspective, one may begin to think of local social service organization and a hierarchy of services, focusing on the needs of individuals and families, being realistic about the logic of organizations and bureaucratic dynamics, but not sacrificing the service need to such factors or to the valid, parallel concern for social action. The medical field provides the model: there are local health stations, nearby clinics and emergency rooms, small general hospitals at the next level, large hospitals with specialist facilities at the next level—and a few major centers for research and leadership.

OPTION 1

NEIGHBORHOOD INFORMATION CENTER
(Basic services as described in text)

Referrals to *social utilities* available by status, or to income security programs, or processing of forms for them. Many social utilities may have outposts in the very building or cluster of buildings which house the information center.

Referrals to local general (*personal*) social service office for case services, i.e., diagnostic service, basic counseling, case integration, continuity of care, and specialized referrals.

Referrals to *specialized diagnostically-based services,* most of which will be out of the neighborhood.

OPTION 2

"POLYVALENT" or GENERAL PRACTICE NEIGHBORHOOD SOCIAL WORKER
(Not office-based)
(Less than M.S.-level training)
(Basic services as described in text)

Referrals to *social utilities* available by status, or to income security programs, or processing of forms for them.

Referrals to local general (*personal*) social service for case services, i.e., diagnostic service, basic counseling, case integration, continuity of care, and specialized referrals.

Referrals to *specialized diagnostically-based services,* most of which will be out of the neighborhood.

OPTION 3

"POLYVALENT" or GENERAL PRACTICE NEIGHBORHOOD SOCIAL WORKER
(Not office-based)
(M.S. training)
Information-advice-referral services
Basic personal counseling
Case integration and accountability
Entry to some social utilities available by status and income
security programs

Referrals for access to certain other *social utilities.*

Referrals for *specialized case services,* most of which will be out of the neighborhood.

The options already proposed are outlined in the accompanying chart. The notion of a hierarchy may be communicated in the following listing:

First level of neighborhood social services
· information, advice, access, referral, advocacy
· personal-general case service center (local)
    (NOTE: Several information centers may feed into one case service center.)

Specialized services based in the neighborhood
· neighborhood health center
· neighborhood legal services (in areas where revelant)
· some social utilities
    drop-in community centers
    drop-in child care
    emergency homemakers, etc.
    child development programs

Specialized services serving several contiguous neighborhoods
· public library
· more specialized health clinics
· adult education
· recreation programs
· general hospital
· credit unions and more specialized consumer services
· mental health clinic

Specialized services on an area, borough, or county basis
· psychiatric hospital plus day or night hospital facilities
· specialized resources for some general hospitals (complex equipment)
· special classes for children with rather special needs.

Several of the component units might share space in multi-service centers or, probably more desirable, in a building cluster.

The list is illustrative, not definitive. As noted earlier, need density, availability of special staff and equipment, service characteristics requiring proximity to certain other resources would be determining. The concept of service hierarchies for ever-larger geographic units is the crucial idea. Experience is needed to fill out specifics. Local preferences, population density, stage of service development, and manpower factors will continue to dictate variations. There will have to be variations in the degree of centralization-decentralization of budgeting, planning, standard-setting, citizen participation in policy-making, and general administration to support the variations in degree of service decentralization. The premise is, however, that even where there is a policy of some neighborhood "community control," the higher governmental unit will set a framework of guaranteed provision. If the criterion is effectiveness of access and delivery patterns, it should become possible both to design an hierarchy relevant to a locality or a region and assuring local exercise of options, and to support such design by an appropriate, central structure for policy, technical services, and administration.

EMERGENCY SERVICES

Gerald Caplan and Erich Lindemann in psychiatry, David Kaplan, Howard Parad, Lydia Rapoport, and others in social work, and research workers from a number of other fields, have documented the unique nature of extreme personal stress, crisis, or emergency and of group disaster from the perspective of helping strategies.[55]

To Caplan, stress is "a situation in which one has an important problem which cannot be solved immediately by using one's old habits of dealing with problems."[56]

The variety of definitions and of crisis-oriented theories and their research status is not immediately relevant. What is important here are the insights that these theories and their derived experimental approaches offer with reference to interventive methods and the administrative structure of social services on the local level.

Building on the pioneering work of Erich Lindemann after Boston's Cocoanut Grove fire, a number of investigators have suggested the possibility that certain acute situational disorders should not be conceived as part of the same continuum as chronic problems. The stress or crisis has its own dynamics and symptomatology and its own way of being worked out—by the individual alone or, quite often, with help. Failure at successful management of the crisis, which may involve tragic loss of a loved one or other personal trauma, may be followed by the development of serious ongoing pathology. Successful coping is preventive of maladjustment and strengthening.

Waiting lists, complex application procedures, and restrictive eligibility approaches pose hazards for the person who has experienced acute stress of this kind. Traditional interventive approaches are often unsuited to the problem dynamics. A number of investigators have demonstrated effec-

---

[55] While the literature is considerable the following may serve as introduction and as a source of further references: Gerald Caplan, Editor, *Prevention of Mental Disorders in Children* (New York: Basic Books, 1961), especially Chaps. I, XIII, XIV. Howard Parad, Editor, *Crisis Intervention: Selected Readings* (New York: Family Service Association of America, 1965). Parad, "Time and Crisis."

[56] Caplan, *op. cit.*, 37.

tive and ingenious management of crises through interpersonal therapies and response to environmental realities.

There are other types of circumstances which also merit emergency service. While not necessarily in the wake of external disaster, the individual or family unit may experience a sense of extreme pressure or emergency which may be manifested in an urge to commit suicide, a decision to break up a marriage, an impulse to place a child in foster care, or a violent family conflict.

The need for immediate help to avoid imminent catastrophe if possible, to prevent a decision which will later be regretted, and to block the development of permanent personality pathology suggests that a variety of social institutions meeting individuals in crisis, ranging from police precinct stations to hospital emergency rooms and public welfare offices, should be prepared to cope with such situations. To date, the most extensive provision (although it is quite limited in coverage) is offered by a number of special suicide emergency programs (now being promoted and assisted by a center attached to the National Institute for Mental Health), a considerable expansion of emergency or crisis-oriented intake in psychiatry clinics, and a similar movement in some family service agencies.[57] Police departments and ambulance services encounter a large volume of cases and channel them into relevant systems.

Because the emergency, by its nature, cannot be system-specific, a general and well-known "doorway" to help should exist. It might very well consist of an SOS telephone number and a place to go.[58] Such telephone service should be manned 24 hours a day. It might be organized in conjunction with police or ambulance services or be independent. It might have ties to a widely-known neighborhood information center or, better, the general personal service center. The well-trained, sympathetic staff manning telephone or intake should be capable of coping with a person in extreme stress, exercising judgment as to the need for immediate police, general medical, or psychiatric home visit and able to arrange for a visit the next morning by the inquirer to

- a general health center, as the entry point to the medical system, including community psychiatric services
- the local general, personal social service office

---

[57] Parad, "Time and Crisis."

[58] The "SOS" service is organized in several places in Europe, the Samaritans in Great Britain, the suicide prevention services in the United States. All offer telephone contacts as a first source of help.

☐ the courts
☐ other systems.

While much that is relevant with reference to other systems is covered elsewhere in this volume, we might note here the implications for the general-personal social service unit. Obviously, waiting lists cannot be tolerated. Staff must be flexible and available. If special referrals are needed, accountability should be clearly assigned. Careful diagnostic arrangements are needed to assure effective evaluation and optimum help. The crisis case, above all, must not encounter impersonal routine and discontinuity.

SOCIAL SERVICES AS ANCILLARY OR AUTONOMOUS

One should note, if only in passing, that the discussion has focused on the autonomous social service system. We have dealt with the special helping services set up with a view to the needs of the total community and designed to assure maximum access to all. The bias is towards a universal system, designed not to lose those who find it difficult to know about and to use community resources.

There are, of course, also many social services which are ancillary. They are secondary activities of organizations and groups with other primary concerns: the social work service in the school, medical social service in the hospital, probation in the correctional system, day care or counseling attached to a factory, a rehabilitation program sponsored by a union—and so on. From some points of view, these other institutions are excellent as points for case finding, information, referral, direct service, help. From other perspectives, and in some instances, the more general and detached community services is to be preferred.

The balance between and relationships of these two systems, the ancillary and the autonomous, is a matter for study and planning not here attempted. Our focus has been only on the autonomous system and on its conversion into a coherent and effective network. There is no evidence at all that ancillary services, whatever their great values to the individuals and institutions served, offer any kind of substitute for this.

THE "COSTS" OF CHOICES

A case has been made for allowing and encouraging local options in the shaping of information services and general social service offices or multi-service centers so as to accommodate to local needs. Maximum decentralization, within a framework that protects the overall policy thrust, has been urged. Although already implied, it is also useful to add that choices involve some decisions about priorities and some hypotheses about consequences of different strategies. Each is presumed to have specific advantages but may also entail unique costs.[59]

While the local social service planner does not have access to research that enables him to predict the consequences of choices with certainty, some relevant experience has been assimilated.[60]

- □ General information and liaison services can be offered to all groups and classes without stigma if set up as separate entities and made universally available.
- □ Diagnostic components to such services close out certain populations at the entry point, but add to service sophistication.
- □ Specialized services, located in a multi-service center, affect the load and the effort to protect a "general practice" base, but may be urgent in specific neighborhoods.
- □ Emphasis on community action decreases individual services, unless separate auspices are provided.
- □ Information and liaison services generate a demand for more specialized social service than most communities can meet, but may rationalize allocation and generate action to expand provision.
- □ Some population groups are adequately served only by a basic general (personal) social service system with strong case advocacy components, whereas others are their own best advocates.
- □ Case advocacy plus client organization often generates policy and program advocacy that affects the cooperation of the specialized agencies on direct service to specific "cases." Here, too, priorities need to be assessed; nor is the pattern uniform.
- □ "Indigenous" personnel permit services to be expanded and enhance communication with deprived and deviant groups, but, unless roles are well defined and supporting services assured, services by indigenous personnel become "low quality" substitutes where intensive specialized help is needed.

None of these is an unchallengeable assertion. Exceptions may be identified. All are based on experience to date. Negative consequences as listed are often acceptable—given the local situation, priorities, and preferences.

Administrative structure may be approached from a comparable perspective. There are obvious advantages in accessibility and public knowledge to be gained by placing an information center and a general (per-

---

[59] For another approach to options, based on a different formulation of task, see Michael S. March, "The Neighborhood Center Concept," *Public Welfare*, XXVI, No. 2 (April, 1968), 97–111.

[60] Perlman and Jones, *op. cit.*; Kahn *et al.*, *Neighborhood Information Centers*; Carter, *op. cit.*

sonal) social service center together in a multi-service unit. However, if one combines the function of public welfare, family welfare, child welfare, services to the aged and to adolescents, and some aftercare components into one locally-based social service unit, it approaches a monolith —and a highly complex monolith at that. Therefore, to assure an independent source of feedback relative to needs and a possible way of generating pressure for constant reform, one might argue for a separately administered neighborhood information and advice center, controlled locally in the voluntary sector.

We have noted that coverage and service guarantees will probably require that the basic local social service network be public (probably an amalgam of what is now public child welfare, social services tied to public assistance, and anti-poverty centers). Careful analysis will be needed to determine in a given state the desirability of relating this comprehensive new entity to profit-making social service agencies or to nonprofit voluntary family and child welfare services through their incorporation into the public system or through contracts under which such agencies render the basic service in some localities or become specialized facilities accepting referrals.

The argument may also be made that, even if given a public "coverage" service of the sort projected, it would be desirable to maintain some general sectarian and nonsectarian family service programs, which overlap with the coverage program, so as to assure options for the individual, some yardstick operations, the values of competition, and a base for experiments.[61]

---

[61] "Services for People" argues for the advantages of market-type, competition in rendering social services.

SOCIAL PLANNING
HORIZONS

OBVIOUSLY planning is not always appropriate: tradition or preference, crisis, lack of capability, lack of decision flexibility, and overall social-political context often make it redundant or irrelevant. Even where called for, however, planning is often not possible: the lack of power or sanction, the absence of sufficient consensus, the poverty of resources for planning or for implementation, and the lack of adequate knowledge often make it ritual. Furthermore, given both appropriate context and feasibility, the planning that emerges will not necessarily be comprehensive. The issue is one of achieving planning sufficiently inclusive to meet both the questions posed and the opportunity for change. Finally, of course, planning is often unsuccessful: limited knowledge or poor judgment about substantive issues or inadequate provision for interrelationships among the stages or between any stage and the many instruments of implementation in the universe of politics, administration, and financing may undermine the complex series of mutually supportive steps upon which it depends.

Yet increased planning remains desirable and inevitable. The premise is that ". . . ideas are indispensable to the ordering of institutional energies." Organizational behavior is purposeful. Efficient action is not advanced by enshrining an ideology about the limitations of rationality.[1] The specialized, complex, fragmented worlds of institutions and programs cannot forgo the rational. Even those societies relatively affluent in money and manpower cannot ignore the need for deliberate choices among the ever-too-many demands upon their apparent abundance. The disjointed, the fragmented, the un-

---

[1] George Barnett and Jack Otis, *Corporate Society and Education* (Ann Arbor: The University of Michigan Press, 1967), 127; and Harold Wilensky, *Organizational Intelligence* (New York: Basic Books, 1967), xi.

coordinated, and the unconsidered waste scarce resources and keep a society off-target and away from its problems and challenges. Very modest planning, sub-optimization, efforts to deal with the most feasible among desirable but limited choices, approaches to major problems and issues one at a time all may pay off with progress on occasion. But such approaches, avoiding the reality of the interdependence of phenomena also may make things worse—or, at the least, are ineffective or wasteful. There is good cause to consider and often, where found appropriate, to strive for the increasingly comprehensive.

In the United States, at least, the distinction between the incremental and the comprehensive is quantitative, not qualitative. These are points on a continuum. Even the comprehensive or synoptic leaves some dimensions unaddressed and concentrates particularly on facets, levels, areas, or issues strategic in given context. For only one who believes in the highly centralized and master computer-managed worlds of some science fiction expects society to be planned fully on all its levels and coordinated in all its interrelationships.

In sum, if man would have his goals, his values, and his visions as touchstones, where so often only expediency and technology seem to guide, a social instrument for deliberate, reasoned choosing and designing must be shaped and strengthened. Thus, the case for enhanced planning despite all its complexity and limitations. Thus the explanation for increased planning. But, therefore, also, the commitment so to structure planning as to protect its democratic nature and to assure its support of the values and institutions held precious.

At the same time, efforts must continue to correct the primitive nature of the available planning frameworks, the lack of well-codified methodology, the uncertainty as to how social planners are to be trained. Furthermore, although a given planning organization and planner perforce must focus on the task at hand, the status of planning requires continued work in the field as a whole to accumulate practice-wisdom, to conduct research, and to evaluate effectiveness. Theory, practice, and training should be in focus.[2]

---

[2] Simultaneously, work should be encouraged to assemble (*a*) overall case studies in planning; (*b*) studies of planning subprocesses and components; (*c*) studies in social policy; (*d*) studies of planning effectiveness.

For example: Albert Waterston's *Development Planning* (Baltimore: The Johns Hopkins Press, 1965) was published for the International Bank for Reconstruction and Development. Waterston has published volumes in this series for the International Bank on Morocco, Yugoslavia, and Pakistan. The Syracuse National Planning Series, edited by Bertram M. Gross, includes, among others, volumes on Venezuela, Morocco, Tunisia,

As part of such endeavor, the political science challenges must be faced empirically, too. It should be possible to go beyond debate and to determine whether the synoptic effort is, in fact, always differentiable from the incremental in action or whether one can identify known points on a continuum. Is it realistic, too, so to analyze planning undertakings as to shed light on the question of the degree of comprehensiveness compatible with a given patterning of known variables? Fragmentary evidence and strong opinion, even when logically impressive, are no substitutes for a more organized approach to the already-considerable planning experience.

Given the present proliferation of efforts to develop and apply simulation, model construction, linear programming, operations research, and planning-programming-budgeting-systems (PPBS) linked to applications of the computer, careful case studies also may begin to clarify whether these are in fact programming tools and techniques or, rather, alternative planning systems. The entire development was too young and the returns too few, during the period of preparation of the present work, to permit firm generalization.

Within the parameters defined by limited knowledge and skill, on the one hand, and appropriateness or feasibility, on the other, a planner does find broad fields of possible intervention, in which planning appears both desirable and possible—often serving himself as advocate in making the case for planning and seeking to maximize consideration of its output. And because planning occurs in a diversity of contexts, he frequently is able to function in a situation in which his own preferences and goals are, in effect, his guiding lights; because they are also the preferences and goals of those who employ him and give his work sanction. Planning, to repeat, is a normative activity—not value-free social engineering.

This much said, one does not ignore institutional obstacles to social

Tanganyika, Israel, Mexico, Great Britain, Italy, and West Germany. Everett E. Hagen, *Planning Economic Development* (Homewood, Ill.: Richard D. Irwin, 1963), includes nine studies from the Center for International Studies, Massachusetts Institute of Technology. Also, United Nations, *Planning for Balanced Social and Economic Development: Six Country Case Studies* (New York: 1964, E/CN.5/346/Rev. 1). Other types of case studies are illustrated by: Peter Marris and Martin Rein, *Dilemmas of Social Reform* (New York: Atherton Press, 1967). Peter A. Rossi and Robert A. Dentler, *The Politics of Urban Renewal* (New York: The Free Press, 1961). Martin Meyerson and Edward C. Banfield, *Politics, Planning and the Public Interest* (Glencoe, Ill.: The Free Press, 1955). Aaron Wildavsky, *The Politics of the Budgetary Process* (Boston: Little, Brown and Company, 1964).

Further illustrations of relevant policy studies appear in the companion volume, Chapters VI and VII, especially the citations.

planning in the United States: the dispersion of authority among federal departments and the lack of a comprehensive national instrument for domestic-sector planning located in the executive branch of government; the need to redefine a federal-state-local pattern of relationships and fiscal sharing that is more attuned to present problems and needs; the difficulty of coping with the anti-planning bias in the ethic and its "conventional wisdom." To illustrate, there is ever-more "sectorial" or "facet" planning in the social realm, using the terms in the United Nations sense, with the basic problems of social policy and of the interrelations of sectors left unresolved. A high price is paid for this situation in many fields.

The champion of social planning soon learns that advocacy of more comprehensive, better-interrelated planning efforts forces upon him continued re-examination of the conception of "social," as the term is used in social planning, and of the continued separation of social from economic planning. One may define the universe of the social, in simple, pragmatic, operational terms, as all that is not pre-empted by or assigned to economic and physical policy-makers and not clearly in the domains of internal and external protection and defense. Or one may urge a definition that sees social welfare and, therefore, social planning, as encompassing a society's efforts to implement a guaranteed minimum of resources for individual and group development and living and to realize its goals and aspirations for its members—all this through mechanisms that assign consumption rights by nonmarket criteria. Either approach to definition, considered in overall context and in cross-national perspective, allows a prediction of expanded and enhanced social planning. The question of parameters is immediate and relevant.

Should more arenas be defined as within the scope of the social planner: transportation and tariff policy, for example? Should social planning develop more of its own structures and instrumentalities: social indicators and a Council of Social Advisors for the United States, for example? Or should the perspective be one of improved, integrated, general planning with a stronger social component?

Several of these questions are introduced in this final chapter, and possible responses are projected. Paradoxically, it is in the efforts—albeit frequently unsuccessful ones—to create planning systems in the less-developed countries of the world that an accumulation of experience and a formulation of issues that help focus the choices for the more industrialized lands as well are found. For this reason, and because the problems of underdeveloped countries are, per se, of great substantive importance and considerable interest, we shall turn to them now.

PLANNING FOR THE DEVELOPMENT OF POOR COUNTRIES

The affluent or "post-affluent" society, which has the industrial capacity for adequate production and thus might concentrate on issues of distribution of its product and of the self-realization of population members, comes to view economic growth alone as a limited human goal. Ways are sought to plan for an expanded and more effective social sector, while introducing what have been seen traditionally as social concerns into policies usually defined as economic, physical, and political. Social problems and crises continue as major points of departure, and there is still some preoccupation with economic growth; but there is also a degree of extrapolation in planning from fundamental human values. Plans are meant to implement aspirations, and not merely to solve problems.

The new nation, the poor land, or the "developing country," faces a somewhat different set of factors. Its levels of production and consumption are generally so submarginal that daily existence for the majority is a constant struggle. Skills, education, and technology are in desperately short supply. Only more money, more food, more production, it would appear, can make a significant difference. How are such countries to regard the role of social planning?

Many "developing" countries do attempt to plan. We note with Seymour Martin Lipset that new states, because they generally lack the means for spontaneous rapid economic growth, tend to introduce early some measure of large-scale governmental planning and direct state intervention into the economy. While the rationale is often "socialism," the more basic reality may be that new states must "demonstrate effectiveness to the various groups within the polity, and display national competence to the outside world."[3]

What is more, because only a "big push" that is coordinated can succeed, the planning in developing countries tends to be broad, addressing both social and economic concerns. Indeed, according to Gunnar Myrdal, a commitment to coordinated overall state intervention is more characteristic of such countries than of the developed ones.[4]

---

[3] Seymour Martin Lipset, *The First New Nation* (New York: Basic Books, 1963), 46.

[4] Gunnar Myrdal, *Asian Drama*, 3 volumes (New York: Twentieth Century Fund and Pantheon Books [paper edition], 1968). See especially, III, Appendix 2, "Elements in a Theory of Planning for Development," 1896–1923. Of course, Communist countries have also undertaken comprehensive efforts in all domains. Myrdal contrasts the poor follow-through of some "soft states" in Asia with the West and with the Communists, stressing the role of "social discipline." *Ibid.*, 895. Although developing countries are often "soft states," not successful in the planning process per se, the experience within

The subject has a long history, but most of the intensive work in present focus has emerged since World War II. The period began with a great thrust towards industrialization. The basic idea was that the underdeveloped and poorer countries would enter the economy of the twentieth century through large-scale capital investment and modernization, which would promote economic growth, and that improved social and political conditions would follow.[5] Initially, some of the undesirable consequences of the industrial and capital investment push were seen as inevitable ills. In this sense, they were viewed as societies had viewed them since the nineteenth century: one expects (and in a humane society, one tries to alleviate) unhealthy working conditions, low wages, child labor, disorganized family life, crowded housing, the evils of slums and delinquency.[6] This view was soon recognized to be inadequate, as economic development was blocked, hampered, or made inordinately costly as a result of social "obstacles," and as evidence accumulated that something could be done.

Obstacles

As reported in a United Nations analysis,[7] these roadblocks may be classified as:

Population factors. The evolving population structure (age distribution), density, geographic spread—in relation to what these are at the start of industrialization—may make population growth either asset or liability from the point of view of economic plans. Absolute population size may set a limit to the types of industrial development possible for a given country. Trends in economic growth may be wiped out by a rapid growth in population.

In the first responses to these insights, there was despair (death rates are cut far more easily and rapidly than birth rates), efforts at understanding (just what are the patterns), and then a taking into account of population factors in the planning (realistic projection). More recently,

---

such planning of conceptualizing the social and its role provides a valuable reference point for considering possible directions of development for social planning in America.

[5] For a more comprehensive statement, see: United Nations, *Report on the World Social Situation* (New York, 1961), especially Chap. II, "The Interrelation of Social and Economic Development and the Problem of Balance."

[6] *Ibid.*, 24.

[7] *Ibid.*, 25–30. For illustration, elaboration, and statistical detail, also see Robert L. Heilbroner, *The Great Ascent* (New York: Harper & Row, 1963, Torchbook paper edition), Chaps. II, III.

large-scale interventions have been launched (population control and planning).

Institutional factors. While population policy was a taboo subject in many countries and international bodies in the immediate postwar years —only to move to the center of the stage as its strategic nature was dramatized early in the nineteen-sixties—blockage in development because of "institutional factors" was recognized early, and many of the first social programs represented efforts to alleviate such factors.

Robert L. Heilbroner argues, in fact, that economic development is primarily a political and social process rather than an economic one. The kind of economic development currently sought is dependent upon the existence of a society in which wealth can be accumulated and incomes and employment progressively enlarged. Development occurs only if supported by social institutions and individual habits and skills. In this sense, much development is pre-economic and is largely concerned with shaping attitudes and creating needed institutional structures. Powerful social and political energies must be mobilized to sustain the change process, and these are often revolutionary in nature.[8]

Although rigorous proof is difficult, there is considerable agreement that successful industrialization also requires a significant increase in the components of rationalism and scientific thinking, cultural preparation for "routine" and "quality control," considerable social and geographic population mobility, the shift from what sociologists call status by ascription to status by achievement,[9] and from a status society generally to a contract society.[10] Economic change is truly a "great transformation" and "is not so much a reflection of nature as of human attitudes and institutions."[11]

In general, such transitions are facilitated by or are the causes of disappearance of

> larger institutions based on blood relationship or presumed blood relationship, such as class and tribal systems, with their multiple political, social and economic functions. . . . For . . . as a rule, at the higher levels of eco-

---

[8] Heilbroner, *op. cit.*, 1–20. Also see, José Medina Eschavarría, "Economic Development in Latin America: Sociological Considerations" (New York: United Nations Economic and Social Council, 1963, E/CN.12/646, mimeographed). Finally, for illustration and other sources, see Waterston, *Development Planning.*

[9] Irving Louis Horowitz, *Three Worlds of Development* (New York: Oxford University Press, 1966), is a critic of the view. See especially, 416. Also, Wilbert E. Moore, *Social Change* (Englewood Cliffs, N.J.: Prentice-Hall, 1963, paperback).

[10] *Report on the World Social Situation*, 1961.

[11] Heilbroner, *op. cit.*, 36.

nomic development the family tends to be smaller, more mobile, shorn of its economic production functions and of various functions assumed by educational, legal, police and welfare institutions of the state; but it remains a unit of consumption, and has even greater emphasis on psychological and emotional bonds and functions, as other bonds and functions diminish or disappear.[12]

The social strategies posited after World War II to cope with institutional factors blocking economic development were of two types. First, certain needed institutional changes were instigated or facilitated. Land-tenure reforms, collectivization of agriculture, legislation relating to the rights of women and educational facilities were introduced as strategic measures whose implementation had a ripple effect in bringing about institutional pre-conditions for the success of the new economic enterprises. Second, more careful study of the European and American experience in industrialization, and evaluation of "spontaneous" successes in some of the developing countries, led to questions about the oversimple formulas relating to institutional support for industrialization. Perhaps there were some options. Specifically, to illustrate, experimentation began with utilizing the extended family as a work group or as the basis for home industry. Group incentive seemed to work where individual initiative had not yet developed.[13]

Individual factors. There is an extensive if inconclusive literature about the relationship between the Protestant ethic (strains of which became important in all major western religions) and the rise of capitalism. Although the debate about the direction of causation has been unresolved, economic planners were quick to note, during the nineteen-fifties, the extent to which programs were handicapped by a labor force whose members lacked the "entrepreneurial" attitudes and motivations deemed essential to rapid economic growth.[14]

In many countries in desperate need of capital investment, initiative, risk, and new enterprise, the rich persisted in putting their funds into land or foreign investments. When the mercantile class invested at home, it was in real estate or commodity speculation or money-lending more often than in expensive equipment for long-term gains in manufacturing. The very poor appeared to have a limited time perspective, working to

---

[12] *Report on the World Social Situation,* 1961, 27.

[13] For example, Horowitz, *op. cit.,* 319.

[14] We do not discuss biophysiological hypotheses, migration theories, and a variety of genetic allegations. These are not part of the planning rationales here outlined. A major exception is the response of planners in many lands to the knowledge that problems of nutrition limit full participation in various instrumental roles.

meet immediate needs and not able to manage longer investment in skill development or the accumulation of a little surplus that would increase their options.

Although some efforts have been made to cope with problems deriving from counterdevelopment attitudes and motivational patterns, the major focus has been on deficits in skills and their correction. The assumption has been that the development of needed competence would create economic processes which, in themselves, would instigate necessary motivational systems and institutional supports in the context of the particular society. Thus provision for training and imparting of skill, in the broader sense, may be an effective social intervention measure.

Investment in human resources

For a long time almost everywhere, and in many places to the present, the social planning which was deemed necessary in conjunction with economic planning was justified with reference to the need to overcome obstacles or "bottlenecks" of the kinds mentioned as blocking economic growth. Few policy-makers or scholars dispute the usefulness of the formulation today, but there is some debate as to whether this is the major consideration or whether any society can afford to ignore other major considerations as well. For the conception of the role of social factors in development has continued to grow during the 'fifties and 'sixties.

The sad lessons of failures—the wastage of and poor returns from capital investment—led groups of experts in several countries to suggest that one must think not merely of overcoming obstacles to economic development by social measures. The alternative notion of "investment in human resources" was offered. As put by Gunnar Myrdal, ". . . The poor countries . . . are putting too little emphasis on the need for productive investments in human beings and directing too little attention to the need for raising labour efficiency." Simon Kuznets was clear on this point: ". . . The key is not in the physical stock of plant and equipment; it is in large part in the capital invested in human beings and in the whole economic and social structure that conditions the use of plant and equipment." And, quite specifically, in the terms of Charles P. Kindleberger, ". . . There is little doubt that investment in transport, communication and education have most to do with changing people—which is likely to be the critical ingredient in the growth process."[15]

---

[15] For all citations, *Report on the World Social Situation*, 1961, 31n. Also see, "Social Development Planning," United Nations, *Economic Bulletin for Asia and the Far East*, XIV, No. 2 (September, 1963), 3. Myrdal's later reservations about such perspective on developing countries are described in *Asian Drama*, I, 16–20.

The human investment perspective on the relation of social to economic elements in development has become a major one.[16] It is sometimes broadened to include all of social investment. The work, which has been done to demonstrate empirically that certain "intangible human factors are as important as tangible capital investment for economical growth and considerably more important than some kinds of capital investment . . . ," has had valuable effects. Most important, it helped to undermine a long-standing distinction between capital investment as promoting growth and social expenditures as "consumption," which diverts resources from growth.[17]

As noted in a variety of sources, and stressed in the United Nations' *Report on the World Social Situation* of 1961, which summed up thinking on this matter, recognition of the importance of human investment is not quite the same thing as having specific guidance on how to plan for it. The question must still be faced of which specific programs and facilities for which people, conveying what skills and attitudes, will successfully guarantee the attitudes, knowledge, and skill that meet the social requirements of a total development process.

Organizations, institutions, and ministries specifically charged with implementing human and social investment programs are, after all, committed to other goals as well. Some seek to satisfy the striving of individuals for self-expression, self-enhancement, and personal mobility. Others express deeply-rooted social commitment either to charity or social justice. All reflect the normal boundary maintenance and self-protective concerns of the professions and bureaucracies involved.

The response to the investment concept is further complicated by apparent and obvious problems of phasing and timing. It is quite clear to all concerned, to employ an oft-cited illustration, that a well-timed health program improves a needed labor supply, but may assure a labor surplus in a country with population pressure and slow economic growth. Poorly-timed investment in higher education has been known to create a well-educated and unusable labor force—which becomes a political liability.

Integrated, balanced development

When the inherent difficulty of the substantive issue—just what kind of resource investment, when, how, and in whom?—is joined with the or-

---

[16] A new *Journal of Human Resources* began publication at the University of Wisconsin in 1966, for example.

[17] *Report on the World Social Situation,* 1961, 31.

ganizational obstacles, the result is very far from the ideal situation projected in investment studies. Indeed, such studies are often much more clear cut as measures of payoff to individuals[18] of what investments have been made than as guides to the future for countries or population groups. The difficulty of specifying and handling the investment concept, the uncertainty of the results, and the ambivalence on the part of those who are somewhat more convinced of the meaning and results of investment in the more traditional economic sense have led to continued search for new formulations of the issue.

These considerations have induced additional patterns of thinking about the problem of social and economic development. One begins with the fact that economic activity and plans impose certain *requirements*: sanitation programs, worker training, housing, and so forth. However, no country is without its *norms* in these matters, norms going beyond the narrowly functional into realms defined as social justice. Certain social programs are highly valued on their own merits whether or not they represent immediately needed supports for economic development: efforts to improve life chances, enrich individual lives, ease pain. In the words of a recent analysis of Latin America: "No people is so poor that it will be prepared to do only the things it can afford according to a utilitarian scheme of priorities."[19]

In effect, some of the social justice ideals which developed in countries of the West that industrialized early have become internationalized; there is a "demonstration effect." Unlike North America and West Europe, which introduced legislation about working conditions, social security, and family welfare only after industrial development was more or less firmly established, developing countries adopt such measures early as matters of justice. They draw upon the experience of others in determining what *type* of housing to provide, how *well trained* workers are to be, what accident *rates* will be tolerated, and what health *levels* are desirable, for example.

The *Report on the World Social Situation*, of 1961, suggests the notion of "mutual requirements" to convey the conclusions that (*a*) "socially" motivated programs cannot be realized unless certain necessary conditions are present from the viewpoint of production and wealth; (*b*) a social

---

[18] See, for example, Gary S. Becker, *Human Capital* (New York: Columbia University Press, 1964).

[19] "Social Development and Social Planning: A Survey of Conceptual and Practical Problems in Latin America," United Nations, *Economic Bulletin for Latin America*, XI, No. 1 (April, 1966), 70.

sector "bottleneck," if ignored, may prove an unsurmountable obstacle to implementation of economic plans. In addition, (c) certain "consumption" motivated by social justice or political pressure, if not by rational analysis, actually may increase the capacity of the labor force to produce.[20] Development planning is preoccupied with the complementarities, with these mutual requirements from the economic and social side. In some ways, the process may be thought of as "balancing."[21] The General Assembly of the United Nations has repeatedly referred to a process of "balanced economic and social development," apparently in this sense, rather than in its strict economic meaning. The theme of balance pervaded most of the pronouncements and guides when the United Nations named the nineteen-sixties a "Development Decade." None of this, however, answers all questions or specifies all processes.

Examination of the experience in even the most planful of countries discloses that a *commitment* to balancing is certainly not enough.[22] Developing countries face dramatic and extreme problems: secondary school graduates may find themselves no better off than their fellows who avoided school, since economic growth has not been adequate to create more opportunities for the skilled; populations requiring more adequate food as they undertake more taxing physical work, in heavy industry perhaps, cannot be well fed—or at reasonable costs—because the agricultural sector has not kept pace.

The dilemma is essentially one of how to combine well-programmed and carefully-implemented balancing with the reality that some social programs will be launched whether or not they make sense economically and others will lag—because of politico-socio-cultural reasons—even if they do make sense. At the same time that the planner struggles with these forces from without, he must also allow for the limitations within. Projections are imperfect, cost-benefit data difficult to compute, assumptions about what people will do or how they will perform only approximate. Even where there is a free hand to attempt careful balancing, results are mere rough approximations of a rational model.

In effect, the problem of all social planning is here repeated: the component of rationality is under only partial control and, even when reason-

---

[20] Myrdal, *Asian Drama*, III, Appendix 2.

[21] "Social Development and Social Planning . . . ," 35.

[22] The concept of balancing has technical difficulties from the economist's perspective in the view of G. Myrdal, but they are not here relevant. Myrdal, *Asian Drama*, III, 1932–1937.

ably precise, does not account for all that occurs. The planner cannot expect to achieve a perfect score. He continues his work, however, if the results with his participation are better than they would be without it. He strives to do a better job technically while seeking the organizational sanctions and auspices that will place his work in appropriate context. He never forgets that, in overall development, it is national and international political considerations, in the widest sense, which provide his sanction and define the use to be made of his work. A plan eventually must become a political platform or program.

How may one integrate the several streams of conceptualization summarized briefly above, so as to achieve a useful framework for development planning? Clearly the *system* addressed must not be the social realm or economic development alone; all the records of wastage and failure are records of ignoring or underestimating one of the dimensions. The system for planning, then, is the society of the developing country. The target is not economic growth alone or social programs alone, but rather *development*. Development is usefully defined as "growth plus change"[23] or "growth and change of social and economic elements in the Society/Economy,"[24] and includes economic, political, and social dimensions.

In brief, committed to planning and to balance, the developing country seeks an integrated planning system. Unlike the advanced industrialized countries, there is no reason for a developing country to launch unrelated economic and social planning streams and face the task of their interrelations later. This does not mean, however, that in a planning process, which must include both economic and social dimensions, there need not be specialists concentrating on each field, led by a central planning staff. The experience is that social dimensions are underestimated or poorly handled if merely added to the concerns of economic planners.

The important point in defining the target as *development* (growth plus change) is the recognition that growth and change do require an intertwining of both economic and social dimensions, that economic growth alone is never an adequate formulation of the target, and that a society's assessment of its overall political and resource realities and its

---

[23] "Social Development and Social Planning."

[24] United Nations Research Institute for Social Development, *Social and Economic Factors in Development*, Report No. 3 (Geneva, 1966), 14. The original formulation is in United Nations, *The United Nations Development Decade, Proposals for Action* (New York, 1962).

preferences are very relevant to the specification of the development image which emerges.[25] The question becomes, "What kind of society do we think we can become and do we wish to become, given our resources, our potentialities, our political situation, our motivations?"[26]

SOCIAL FACETS AND SOCIAL CONCERNS

Thus, experience in development planning offers, not final answers, but strong evidence that one cannot forgo social planning and that its artificial separation from other planning is hardly to be recommended. A variety of implications have been noted. The industrialized, urbanized countries of the West, of which the United States is a prime example, also see the need to strengthen social planning; but the social sector is likely to be considered autonomous, or at least semi-autonomous, unless a very strong case can be made for an integrated approach, as the result of relevant experience. The integration of the economic-physical-social planning, if it occurs, will be more hesitant and less complete. Although in some ways strange, given the *a priori* commitment in the United States to rationality and modernization, the reluctance to create a unified planning system is not difficult to understand.

Basic industrialization in the United States took place at a pace too slow for today's developing nations, and at a social cost not tolerable to them,

---

[25] For a variety of country illustrations, see Hagen, *op. cit.*, or the University of Syracuse National Planning Series, edited by Bertram M. Gross.

[26] In view of the history of the subject, it is likely that planners so preoccupied will continue to find their specific cues for task definition on the social level with reference to three fundamental anchor points:

First, there is the issue of the *social minimum* currently demanded by the socio-political system and its values, a minimum to be sought whether or not there is an economic growth rationale. (Is primary education to be guaranteed to all, epidemic disease eradicated, sleeping in the streets ended?).

Second, there are the *social bottlenecks* to achieving the overall targets which have been projected—and which must be addressed at the very beginning. Stressing population control and education-training, this approach is illustrated by, Committee for Economic Development, *How Low-Income Countries Can Advance their Own Growth* (New York, 1966).

Third, there are the *social components of development targets*, which are not part of the minimum in the sense of being deemed essential to survival, nor solutions to bottlenecks to economic growth, but which are as integral a part of the development goal as growth in gross national product itself. For an earlier, pioneer United Nations formulation, see D. V. McGranahan, "Problems of Target-Setting in Planning for the Needs of Children," in Herman D. Stein, Editor, *Planning for the Needs of Children in Developing Countries* (New York: United Nations Children's Fund, 1965), 176–184; or United Nations Economic and Social Council, "Methods of Determining Social Allocations," (New York, 1965, E/CN.5/387, mimeographed).

in an era in which governmental intervention on today's scale was un-thinkable. We did not have the advantage of extensive social programs or of balanced growth. But we do now possess a great, modern industrial system, which plans somewhat for itself and in relation to government and which will plan more. There is also a considerable tradition of phys-ical planning and city planning, which is separate from the economic, and only recently concerned, in a complete sense, with becoming socially informed. Social sector programs expand, but the social planning appa-ratus remains modest and fragmentary. Some would limit it to responding to major social problems, others to coordinating the necessary measures. Many Americans fear that well-developed social planning will bring about a major qualitative change in the society.

The champions of improved social planning must take their place as relative newcomers and make their way in such context. Social problems create some sense of urgency about social planning, but the dynamic is not concern for economic development or political status—the catalysts in underdeveloped lands. Some American social planners are convinced of the need for a planning process that completely unifies the economic, the physical, and the social in the sense sought in developing countries on ideological or organizational grounds. Other planners are not sure that this is the way or are in opposition. Yet all of them seem to agree that substantial and simultaneous work is needed along several lines, eventually yielding the anchor points for an ultimate planning design:

☐ planning for social problem-solving, for recognized components of social welfare, and for coordination of social components
☐ planning for new program areas assigned to the "social" and for new social fields as they are developed
☐ adding, at an accelerated pace, social components or social concerns to economic and physical planning domains
☐ modest or major efforts to coordinate or join economic and social plan-ning in one of several ways.

Social sector planning

This is the most familiar and least controversial realm for social plan-ning. It is the domain envisaged by the majority of those who talk of social planning. It accounts for most of the content of the present work. Few people question the need to cope more effectively with social prob-lems (delinquency) or to utilize more efficiently resources allotted to specific intervention systems (social insurance, local social services, com-munity mental health programs, and so on). The primary planning issues, as we have seen, relate to definition of the task (particularly, resolution of value and priority issues), choice of system boundaries (both a technical and a preference issue), and certain critical decisions about policy options. Then the planner proceeds with all the essential components of effective programming and confronts all the organizational problems and related obstacles to coordination.

On the various governmental levels, and within the voluntary sector, as well as between levels and between the statutory and the voluntary, considerable intellectual and organizational progress is needed to assure adequate interrelationships among the many social components. We have documented this in some detail and suggested appropriate approaches.[27]

New "social" facets?

Clearly there is an arbitrariness born out of cultural context that decrees that health, education, and other systems such as those discussed in the present volume are considered to be in the "social" domain, while others are not. Cross-national comparisons, on the one hand, and examination of developments in the United States (particularly in the anti-poverty program and the Model Cities effort), on the other, hint that new assignments may well be made to the "social" domain over time.

We have already seen[28] the emergence of a new subsystem within the social sector concerned with aspects of housing policy and provision. Recreation and leisure time are domains long formally assigned to the "social," at least in their noncommercial aspects, but development and planning in these fields are as yet in their quite early phases. It is difficult to visualize what the other components will be in coming decades; but it is reasonable to predict new social inventions, some sufficiently extensive to develop into full service systems, seeking to further the humanization of the urban-industrial environment, the protection of primary-group values, and the response to developmental needs of people in a changing social scene. Already there are new channels for neighborhood participation (United States), communal eating (China), group child rearing (Israel), autonomous adolescent facilities (universal), which may be cited as harbingers—or, at least, as illustrations.

Social concerns in economic and physical realms

Transportation. It was only good observation in the course of the

---

[27] See the companion volume as well.

[28] Chapter V.

United States anti-poverty effort that led planners to decide that one of the most effective things they could do for a deprived area was to assure easy transportation for the unemployed to places where there were jobs. Once the step had been taken in several locations, utilizing anti-poverty funds to assure below-cost transportation for target areas, the idea seemed obvious and was much copied. Then it was noted, too, that many cities in the United States and elsewhere have, in fact, already subsidized transportation, sometimes as a clear and conscious aid and inducement to business and at others as a welfare measure to assist particular labor force groups. Indeed, one could argue that transportation might qualify as a social sector facet. However, since transportation obviously has components that clearly belong and are critical to the economic system, such assignment would be contested. Instead, transportation serves to introduce, as of expanding and already considerable significance, the inclusion of social (non-economic) concerns in fiscal, monetary, business, and commercial policy and programs. And the question then is raised: how, as overall planning increases, does a society assure that social aspects, consequences, and components of these broader realms are addressed adequately in a planning system?

First, let us illustrate further.

Taxation. We have already seen, in connection with the discussion of income security, that there are those who would seriously consider utilizing tax mechanisms to administer an income-transfer program motivated by social welfare concerns. Indeed, they even offer a tax rationale for this, noting that equity requires that there be governmental response to the negative side of a potential taxpayer's balance as there is now to the positive.[29] Similarly, it has long been established policy to allow industry tax abatement to provide economic incentive for actions consistent with public economic goals; more recently similar incentives have been employed to support social policy: housing construction, job creation, industrial training. All governmental subsidy, tax abatement, and exemptions may be regarded as expenditure with social impact and thus viewed in the same manner as is all social policy. Similarly, selective taxation (Poland's avoidance of sales tax on items consumed by children) is a way to advance social goals.

Many citizens react in horror to such notions on economic or "moral" grounds: tax policy, in their view, should concern itself with raising revenue to pay government's bills; the issues of income maintenance or help-

---

[29] Chapter IV, pages 135–143.

ing special groups should be coped with separately and on their own merits. If government fiscal policy goes beyond this, to cut inflation or encourage economic growth, this is interpreted as an essential *economic* measure. However, the issue is obviously more complex. If one enacts a new income-security measure, such as children's allowances, there is no avoiding, in the very context of planning the new program, the decision as to whether the new grant will be taxable. Indeed, as analysts discovered in the course of the income-maintenance debate of the late nineteen-sixties, one needs a quite different program if one assumes that given benefits will—or will not—be taxed. Nor can one ignore the exemption for dependents if one enacts a new form of income support; for example, one way to pay part of the cost of a children's allowance is to eliminate the exemption for children now allowable in the tax system.

But the intertwining of social decisions and tax policies is not limited to the arena of income maintenance. As has been noted by many students of the tax system, all major statutory and administrative policies in this realm have serious social consequences.[30]

The income tax system with its exemptions, graduation, deductions, income-splitting by spouses, special allowances for the aged, the handicapped, and the blind reflects very specific social policy. It is an instrument of monetary redistribution. It can complicate, facilitate, or perhaps encourage the entry or withdrawal of mothers from the labor market, adolescents' continuation in school, older workers' retirement or return to the labor force, consumption of specific types or savings, the setting up of their own households by adolescents, the separation of spouses.

The Chairman of the Joint Economic Committee noted, when the Congress, in 1968, enacted a tax surcharge dictated by major considerations of fiscal policy, that it might cost the country 3.5 million jobs. In fact, tax rules about deductible contributions are vital to the financing of voluntary social welfare organizations and foundations. The very rules for exemptions, deductions, reporting, and verification and the rigor of their enforcement do much, informally, to define moral codes!

Traditionally, tax laws have been written in an atmosphere of interest-

---

[30] For example, Harold M. Groves, *Federal Tax Treatment of the Family* (Washington, D.C.: The Brookings Institution, 1963), contains detailed references to the literature.

A major British source is Richard M. Titmuss, *Income Distribution and Social Change* (London: George Allen & Unwin, 1962). On redistributional effects, see Robert J. Lampman, "How Much Does the American System of Transfers Benefit the Poor?" in Leonard H. Goodman, Editor, *Economic Progress and Social Welfare* (New York: Columbia University Press, 1966), 125–157.

group bargaining, with most of the pressure relating to rates and sources of taxation. Modest attention, often as afterthought, has been directed to these social issues. Yet a society that increases social welfare measures generally will have to note the strategic leverage offered in tax legislation, too. Thus, the issue of a social component in tax planning will arise. Will it come, as it has in many countries, only through the activities of a "family lobby" and its equivalents, or should we seek the introduction of social concerns into the total process out of which the legislation emerges?

Tariff policy is a similar field with clear and considerable social ramifications. The rules drawn and the international agreements negotiated may strengthen or undermine a local economy. Given occupations may be encouraged or doomed. The population-holding power of regions or the out-migration of young workers may be affected. It is obviously appropriate to introduce social concerns into the decision-making process, as balancing is sought among foreign affairs strategy, economic interests, and labor union stakes. Similar considerations are also readily demonstrated in *natural resources* policy.

Highway construction. Sometimes the social component needed relates as much to monitoring for potential negative effects as to achievement of specific goals. The highway program may serve as illustration, because, again, it is a field in which the social aspects have been acknowledged relatively recently.

Only well into the 'sixties was it noted publicly that, because urban ghetto residents were politically weak, the routing of highways and throughways, which receive the bulk of their funds out of Washington, tended to ignore the interests of poor people.[31] Families were displaced from housing, often with inadequate provision for relocation. Coherent neighborhoods were destroyed: new ribbons of concrete separated children from schools, adults from community facilities. Citizens seeking to strengthen the local sense of "community" found the highway program a major obstacle—in the most literal sense.

Civil rights and anti-poverty pressure groups began to react to such a price for highway construction and often succeeded in re-routing roads or blocking them. These interest groups began to function where, in the past, only the automobile clubs, construction interests, and unions had been visible. Yet this is hardly adequate. Roads must and will be constructed. Long-range highway plans will be made. There can be no sat-

---

[31] Scott Greer, *Urban Renewal and American Cities* (Indianapolis: Bobbs-Merrill Company, 1965), 69.

isfactory solution in mere "watch-dogging." Again, we see an arena of planning in which many citizens, including those who would build highways, have a stake: the new task is one of introducing a social component into the ongoing planning.[32]

This field serves as well to introduce another aspect of social policy and the related planning challenge. Obviously, in highway as in housing construction, there is a major opportunity to train, and then to employ, potential members of the labor force currently closed out. Assurance of a social component in the staging of these programs allows coordination with general manpower policy and the development of training provisions. Careful scheduling of projects with such issues in mind can greatly improve the economy of a given area.

To those who would respond that only considerations of the market and public convenience should enter into road building (its already being clear that home construction must be more broadly conceived), one replies that government highway programs have always had many kinds of political and economic motivations and now constitute a direct subsidy to the automobile industry. It is neither less nor more justifiable, morally, to consider social consequences and opportunities as well. In fact, it is a characteristic of the "service" or "welfare state" that all so-called economic decisions are recognized as having broad social ramifications. The commitment is to discover and respond to these.

The economic and the social

We have made a case for the expansion of social sector programs and for their planning and coordination. We have documented the need for the introduction of social concerns and components into realms traditionally reserved to the economic and physical policy-maker and planner or to the politician alone. Is it assumed, therefore, that the entire argument in the first part of the present chapter has no validity? Is it not true, then, in a real sense, that *all* economic and physical programs are involved in the public interest and that many have critical impact on family life, individual development, community integration, and multifarious social goals? Is it misleading to suggest, for the United States, as has been proposed for non-industrialized countries, that planning must be balanced, unitary, consisting of economic, physical, and social *aspects*, but basically seen as one integrated process? Why stress social sector or social component planning alone?

---

[32] Thus, the 1968 federal highway legislation included major provisions for relocation of displaced people.

The answer requires a broad perspective and some repetition.

The basic argument for governmental planning *is* a call for integrated, balanced planning. Such planning will have economic, social, and physical aspects—perhaps even sub-units and sub-processes—whether in industrialized or underdeveloped lands. Included would be the planning for systems of service and intervention generally assigned to the social realm as well as provision for introducing social concerns and components into domains assigned by consensus or tradition to the economic and the physical sectors. Social planners, therefore, should be deployed in departments of planning in fields such as income maintenance or local social services, while also joining units concerned with broader economic and physical planning (general fiscal and monetary policy, for example). And, at each level of government, there is need to pull together these components and strands, sometimes in one overall unit and department and at other times in co-equal or at least organizationally parallel entities.[33] For only the integrated planning that is directly responsible to the chief executive at a given governmental level, and is through him organizationally related to the mechanisms for budgeting, legislative initiative, and administrative policy, can expect to be fully effective.

In short, such broad approaches do not preclude departmental planning in those governmental units concerned with particular problems or operations: correctional programs, mental health, education, the aged. There also is specialized planning within service systems in the voluntary sector. There is advocacy planning in special-interest groups, which bring pressure to bear upon specific social programs of government and the voluntary sector. Even if and when overall governmental efforts become extensive and integrated, thus blurring or erasing the traditional separation of the economic, the physical, and the social, one may therefore also expect continuation of specialized social planning.

In such perspective, one would favor the addition of social indicators to the general national economic indicators, or at least their parallel growth and increased correlation with the economic indicators.[34] One would prefer the Council of Economic Advisors to broaden its concerns (and name), rather than the setting up of a separate and new Council of Social

---

[33] See Chapter XI in the companion volume for discussion of organization and staffing for planning.

[34] In January, 1969, the Department of Health, Education, and Welfare published *Toward a Social Report* (Washington, D.C.: Government Printing Office, 1969). This represents an experimental step toward a separate social indicator series.

Advisors. However, should the development be parallel, not unified, there is urgent need for the councils' interrelation in the Office of the President.

To some, this general choice of direction appears undesirable; to others, it appears unrealistic.

There are those who accept the inevitability of more planning, but wish to see it somewhat less powerful; they are fearful of great centralization and skeptical about comprehensive planning, which seeks to account for or control much detail. Nor are they reassured by proposals to protect democratic goals and principles in such process.[35] In their view, just as there is need for emphasis on the planning prerogative of different governmental levels, protecting a "creative federalism," so it is desirable to keep power dispersed deliberately and to maintain the economic, social, and physical streams as separate. These proponents of controlled planning assume that economic, social, and physical developments will be integrated and balanced in the political and administrative process, involving executive and legislative branches, as well as departmental bureaucracies; they refuse to support the development of a single administrative body with sufficient power to shape the whole and to by-pass the interest-group pressures.

Among friends of the idea of balanced developmental planning who do not share such reservations, there are those observers who doubt that the economic sphere will sacrifice its head start to become a co-equal component of an overall process. With Gunnar Myrdal,[36] they note that economic planners in poor and unindustrialized countries have no choice: if they do not take account of the social sphere, they can expect only limited and quite costly progress. For them "take off" is unlikely. The industrialized West, in contrast, regards social planning with suspicion—as the relatively weak and late arrival that questions premises and practices long associated with economic growth. Can one expect full acceptance of a co-equal social component by those who shape economic developments?

This concern with the possible negative political consequence of well-integrated or centralized planning that assembles considerable power, and the general suspicion of the ideological roots of social planning and its potential effects on the economic system may very well combine for a significant period to keep the separate streams apart. In that case, one may encourage and even expect enhanced, separate planning in each of the

---

[35] See the companion volume, Chapters II, IV, and XII.

[36] Myrdal, *Asian Drama*, III, Appendix 2.

major spheres, economic, physical, and social, and increasing pressure over a longer period of time to establish provision for coordination and assuring mutual influence. Inevitably, we are convinced, such coordination, having dispelled myths and decreased fears, will offer the basis for eventual emergence of provision for seeing our domestic sector whole. Ways will be found, and many have been proposed, to take an integrated view of planning while protecting its democratic nature and avoiding overcentralized power. We shall discover that we do not need to protect our core values by truncating planning and artificially separating all that needs to be seen together. We shall recognize that gross national product and lower morbidity rates, educational levels and productivity increases, improved urban amenity and technological discovery are in effect aspects of that unity, and need to be planned for as such. The underdeveloped country cannot achieve economic growth without attending to these interconnections. An advanced country will not choose to do so.

Social planning, or socially-oriented general planning, has begun but much is yet to be done. Much is yet to be learned. The sum total of planning achievement is limited. Practitioners of such planning will continue to refine their methods, adapt organizational structures, and define the relevant training. Researchers and scholars are called upon to elaborate the theory, develop the needed knowledge. Practitioners and scholars together, joined by citizens at large, will seek to win sanction and opportunity to plan despite blockage and obstacles. For the solution of major social problems in America—or anywhere else in the world—and the achievement of a quality of life worthy of our capacities and our aspirations "is far more important than the preservation of any tradition, institution, procedure, alignment of professional responsibility, or set of theoretical assumptions."[37] On such premise much can be built.

---

[37] Joint Commission on Mental Illness and Health, *Action for Mental Health* (New York: Basic Books, 1961).

INDEX